Social Construction of
International Politics

Social Construction of International Politics

Identities & Foreign Policies, Moscow, 1955 and 1999

Ted Hopf

Cornell University Press

Ithaca and London

First published 2002 by Cornell University Press

First printing, Cornell Paperbacks, 2002

Library of Congress Cataloging-in-Publication Data

Hopf, Ted, 1959–
    Social construction of international politics : identities and foreign policies, Moscow, 1955 and 1999 / Ted Hopf.
        p. cm.
    Includes bibliographical references and index.

    ISBN 978-0-8014-8791-0 (pbk. : alk. paper)

    1. International relations—Social aspects. 2. Ethnicity. 3. Russians—Ethnic identity. 4. Soviet Union—Foreign relations—1953–1975. 5. Russia (Federation)—Foreign relations. I. Title.
    JZ1253 .H67 2000
    306.2'4—dc21

                                    2002004673

Cloth printing   10 9 8 7 6 5 4 3 2 1

Paperback printing   10 9 8 7 6 5 4 3 2

Contents

Preface

In February 1993 I received a phone call from the Grand Rapids World Affairs Council. They asked if I would give a talk on U.S. interests in central Asia. They must have figured that, as a Sovietologist, I knew something about that part of the former Soviet Union. They were wrong, but, being a political scientist, I did not let my lack of area expertise dissuade me from accepting their invitation.

A little research made it clear, to me at least, that the United States had precious few interests in central Asia. But, having written a book on deterrence theory and U.S. foreign policy in the Third World during the Cold War, I knew the lack of substantive interests had never been an obstacle to U.S. interventions around the world. My assumption thus was that, if Russia had interests in central Asia, then the United States would derive whatever interests it had there from the Russian presence, in tried and true Cold War fashion.

But I then had to ask why would Russia itself care about central Asia? It occurred to me that the Russian diaspora in these countries might provide such an interest, that there might be some kind of ethnonational bond between Russians in, say, Uzbekistan and Russians in Russia. I could see how certain political elites in Moscow could try to garner electoral support by offering to protect Russians in the near abroad from putative abuses by their new governments, but I wondered whether these Russians in central Asia even thought of themselves as Russians any more, rather than as merely Uzbek citizens.

At this point, my research stalled because I did not know how identities worked. I then fortuitously attended a talk by a visiting anthropologist, Dru Gladney, on Uighur identity in Sinkiang, China. I learned from that talk that what I should be doing was figuring out how Russians themselves were constructing their identities on an everyday basis in a variety of different social contexts in Uzbekistan.

I gave my talk in Grand Rapids in the Gerald Ford Presidential Library, but it was a talk that ended with question marks about how Russians abroad might in fact understand who they were.

Several different events came together to shape how I pursued my new interest in identity and foreign policy. I was already teaching a course on qualitative methods at the University of Michigan. I developed a course on the psychology and politics of identity with Gene Burnstein, a University of Michigan social psychologist. I played a minor role in the development of a collaborative research project headed by Michael Kennedy, a University of Michigan sociologist, on identity and social problems in the post-Soviet states of Estonia, Ukraine, and Uzbekistan. In addition to this being my first opportunity to work with researchers in these three countries, it gave me the opportunity to study and apply the methodology of focus groups to issues of identity. (It also caused me to abandon any delusions that I might do serious scholarship on Russian identity in Uzbekistan. On a preliminary trip to Tashkent and Bukhara with an anthropologist and a historian, it took me approximately two hours to realize there was absolutely no chance I could produce any creditable scholarship on Uzbek identity. I thank Teresa Truax and Marianne Kamp for letting me down so gently.)

There is no canonical treatment of identity in political science. This is quite unlike the subfield within which I had first specialized, international relations, in which Thucydides, Machiavelli, Rousseau, Kant, Carr, and Morgenthau immediately come to mind as constituting the fundamental starting point. The result is that my own understanding of identity is necessarily idiosyncratic and shaped by a great deal of happenstance, rather than the reading of a particular well-known consensually foundational literature.

Given my previous work on deterrence theory and Soviet lessons from its victories and defeats in the Cold War Third World, where I had used various models of decision making, I found that thinking of identity as a cognitive psychological phenomenon came quite easily. And these understandings were greatly enriched by teaching with Gene Bernstein, who introduced me to the works of Muzafer and Carolyn W. Sherif, Henri Tajfel, Jonathan H. Turner, and Marilynn B. Brewer.

But simultaneously with exploring the psychological side of identity construction, my own qualitative methods class seemed to inexorably move away from its original mainstream moorings of legitimizing comparative case studies for political science research. The episodic evolution can be documented in the syllabi themselves. From E. H. Carr, Giovanni Sartori, and Alexander George and Timothy McKeown to, first, Clifford Geertz, Paul Rabinow and William M. Sullivan, and Charles Taylor; then, Pierre Bourdieu, Anthony Giddens, and Hans-Georg Gadamer; then, Michel Foucault, Paul Ricoeur, and Margaret R. Somers; and, more recently, James Clifford and George E. Marcus, Harold Garfinkel, and Peter L. Berger and Thomas Luckmann. There is no particular logic at work here, but the stream of development does help illuminate the development of this book.

To be sure, my choice of authors depended greatly on the community of scholars with whom I developed relations at the University of Michigan, especially through the Colloquium for the Study of Social Transformation (CSST). It was through this group of mostly anthropologists, historians, and sociologists, all interested in critical social theory broadly defined, that I met several of the most important sources for my own thinking on identity. Jane Burbank, Fred Cooper, Ron Suny, Michael Kennedy, Peggy Somers, Muge Gocek, and Ann Stoler introduced me to an extraordinary range of theoretical trails to follow. Most of them, of course, I still have yet to explore, but some of them have ended up in this book.

I am strongly rooted in mainstream social science methods, doubtless to the annoyance of many who would prefer a wholesale abandonment of anything that smacks of positivism. I do not defend those roots at length here, but I have maintained this epistemological anchor as I have explored the works of scholars who weighed anchor long ago. My first move was toward interpretivism, toward an understanding that the only reality of interest is intersubjective, what humans construct themselves rather than the objective reality assumed, or assigned, by the putatively omniscient observer. The next accretion was an attention to structure, understood as a bounded intersubjective community of actions and meanings. I came to this concern by way of Geertz's web of meaning, Bourdieu's habitus, Giddens's structurationism, and Foucault's discursive formation. I also encountered narrativity as a way to understand how individuals understand themselves and others in the works of Somers and Ricoeur, the ethnographic works of Clifford and Marcus, and the phenomenological approaches of Alfred Schutz and Garfinkel.

I confess that I did not come to my own understanding of identity and international relations (IR) theory, initially at least, through reading those whose names we now associate with that issue: Alexander Wendt, Friedrich V. Kratochwil, John Ruggie, Nicolas Onuf, Robert B. J. Walker, David Dessler, and Richard Ashley. Indeed, I was deep into this project before the relevance of these critically important debates for a conceptualization of identity politics at the international level dawned on me. Still, my work on this book and the broader advance of constructivism as an alternative account of international politics came of age at more or less the same time. As a result, the book bears the marks of some of the criticisms leveled at constructivism. First, my efforts to provide in-depth, empirical case studies are partly a response to repeated calls for constructivists to cease and desist their discussion of theory, epistemology, and ontology and get on with demonstrating their comparative advantage in explaining real-world events. Second, and not unrelated, my attempts to marry the insights of "human science" to those of mainstream social science are reflected in the choice of research design. I am committed to deeply inductive interpretivist recovery of empirical evidence, while simultaneously using that evidence to test hypotheses deduced from a theory of how identity might affect foreign policy choice. Third, my explicit focus on the domestic origins of identity and interest is a response to a well-founded dissatisfaction with any theories of international politics that remain at a structural, or systemic, level of analysis.

As I began my research, I was extremely fortunate to join the Program on New Approaches to Russian Security (PONARS), the brainchild of Celeste Wallander and beneficiary of the Carnegie Endowment for International Peace. It is no exaggeration to say that this book would not have been possible without the years of conversation with the forty or so scholars who constitute this unique community of social scientists. Our semi-annual meetings, our continuous conversations online, and all the consequent relationships have combined to create an invaluable intellectual community. CSST at Michigan had pushed me in new theoretical directions, and PONARS has been crucial in ensuring that I did not allow theory to get ahead of my evidence.

In particular, I thank Matt Evangelista, Doug Blum, and Jim Richter, for their many detailed readings of drafts of this project over the years. I also benefited from the "collateral benefits" of innumerable conversations with Brian Taylor, Georgi Derluguian, Vadim Volkov, Oleg Kharkhordin, Eduard Ponarin, Steve Hanson, Yoi Herrera, Valerie Sperling, and Pauline Jones-Luong, all members of the PONARS community. Beyond PONARS, a very long list of people provided ideas and insights: Jacqueline Stevens, Doug Dion, Liz Wingrove, Pradeep Chhibber, Michael Ross, David Rousseau, and Bob Pahre, all colleagues at the University of Michigan. An extraordinary collection of graduate students provided a great deal of stimulation, in particular, Marek Steedman and Artyom Magun. More broadly, over the years I have learned from conversations with David Laitin, Alex Wendt, David Dessler, Iain Johnston, Hayward Alker, and Andrew Moravcsik.

As the book progressed, I presented its parts to very helpful audiences at the Watson Center at Brown University, thanks to Tom Biersteker; Cornell University's Department of Rural Sociology and Peace Studies Center, thanks to Lindy Williams and Judith Reppy; the Russian and East European Studies Center at the University of Chicago, thanks to Ron Suny and Sheila Fitzpatrick; the University of Virginia's Center for the Study of the Mind and Human Interaction and Russian studies program, thanks to Iurii Urbanovich and Allen Lynch; and the University of Chicago's Program on International Security, thanks to John Mearsheimer and Charlie Glaser.

For reading my very early drafts, I thank Alfred Meyer, Zvi Gitelman, David Hoffmann, Jack Snyder, Chaim Kaufmann, Mike Desch, David Dessler, Jonathan Mercer, David Meyer, Henrikki Heikka, and Mlada Bukovansky. These scholars deserve extra credit, and gratitude from my readers for reacting to the most primitive variations, steering me away from potential dead ends, and directing me in more productive directions.

I also thank my Finnish colleagues Tapani Vaahtoranta, Henrikki Heikka, Tuomas Forsberg, Christer Pursiainen, and Heikki Patomaki, all associated with the Finnish Institute of International Affairs. They not only reminded me that international relations is not a U.S. preserve, but also gave me a uniquely northern perspective on contemporary Russian realities. I include Iver Neumann in this group of provocateurs.

In similar fashion I single out Paul Kowert and Nicholas Onuf for inviting me to a conference on identity at Florida International University in February 1997. That meeting revealed for me the vast terrain of critical social theory that underlies the more conventional version of constructivism I offer in this book. Those two days of conversations made me realize just how difficult, but also just how necessary, it would be to produce a book that remained true both to the mission of mainstream social science to assess the merits of competing theoretical accounts of reality and to the epistemological demands of an interpretivist reconstruction of intersubjective reality.

I reserve a singular tribute to Mark Kramer, a PONARS member who, almost literally, led me by the hand through all the archives in which I worked while in Moscow researching Soviet foreign policy in 1955. Without his advice, his list of fax and telephone numbers, encyclopedic recall of all materials of possible interest, and his constant availability, I never would have made it to, let alone through, the many documents I came to enjoy. And because of Mark Kramer's help, I also am able to thank the archivists themselves. These include Kirill Anderson and Vera Levanovich of the Russian Center for the Preservation and Study of Documents of Russian History (RTsKhIDNI, now RGASPI, or the Russian State Archive of Sociopolitical History); Igor Boukharkine, Igor Lebedev, and Elena Belevicha of the Archive of the Foreign Policy of the Russian Federation (AVPRF); Sergei Mironenko of the State Archive of the Russian Federation (GARF); and Natalya Tomilina, Valentina Konstantinovna, Mikhail Kirillov, and Vitalii Afiani of the Center for the Preservation of Contemporary Documentation (TsKhSD, now RGANI, or the Russian State Archive of Recent History).

I also wish to thank Vladimir Magun for his many years of friendship and insights about Russian politics and society.

Closer to home I have learned much from conversations with Michael David-Fox, Peter Furia, and especially Dorothy Noyes, whose own work on Catalan nationalism remains, alas, only a tempting model of what I should do in the future. I thank Paul Beck for being all that a chair can be. For the final push to production, I am very grateful to Mark Sowerby and Brad Nelson.

Let me complete my acknowledgments with an expression of gratitude to five people who not only provided intellectual guidance along the way, but ensured the survival of the project itself. These are Ned Lebow, Patricia Weitsman, Ron Suny, Matt Evangelista, and Peter Katzenstein. Just a couple years into the project, my confidence about continuing in this direction was severely shaken. Had Evangelista, Katzenstein, and Suny not taken an interest in my work or, more precisely, positively valued it, I doubt I would have continued. Had Ned Lebow not arranged for my appointment as a Visiting

Assistant Professor of Peace Research at the Mershon Center at Ohio State University, I literally would have been out of the profession. Had Patricia Weitsman not convinced her colleagues at Ohio University to hire me for two quarters in 1999, I again would have had a hard time remaining in the profession. All this time, of course, I was slowly producing the manuscript that is now this book. All this time, all the people I have listed were providing the intellectual and professional support necessary for me to complete this work. It is impossible to thank each of them enough.

The first chapter provides a detailed theoretical account of the relation between identity and foreign policy I develop in this book and the methods and research design I employ. Here I foreshadow what is to come. The empirical focus is on Soviet foreign policy in 1955 and Russian foreign policy in 1999. The new interpretations of these two very important years in international politics are, I hope, of interest in themselves, but my primary purpose is more ambitious. I aim to show how a state's collection of identities, how it understands itself, can affect how that state, or more precisely its decision makers, understands other states in world affairs. Because of my focus in this book on articulating a constructivist account of identity and foreign policy, I do not pay attention to the extremely rich and valuable literature on Soviet and Russian foreign policy, per se. The omission is regrettable and belies the very impressive work that has been done on this topic over the last fifty years.

It is at the level of domestic society that I propose to find state identity and international political effects, not at the level of interaction among the states themselves. In doing this, I propose to domesticize the social constructivist approach to international politics, to bring society back into social constructivism—the society within states rather than the society between them.

To bring society back in, I have chosen an approach that is as inductivist as possible—all the while recognizing the impossibility of being fully inductive. I do not choose a priori theories, deduce hypotheses from them, and then gather data against which to test their competing implications. Instead, I try to find which collection of identities existed in Moscow in 1955 and 1999, develop an idea of the kinds of discourses that predominated there, and lay out the boundaries of these discourses for the society as a whole. Only after having created a picture of the identity terrain do I suggest how these identities of the Self might affect the identities of Others in international affairs. And only after taking these two steps do I then look at the dependent variable, if you will, of the understandings that the Soviet or Russian state had of other states in the world. And only in the concluding chapter of this book do I try to gauge how any alternative theories might have performed with regard to Moscow's foreign policy choices. In following this course, I have tried to remain true to the interpretivist method of aspiring to recreate the intersubjective reality of the subjects, deferring the treatment of the identities I find as evidence for as long as possible.

The year 1955 was after Stalin's death but not yet post-Stalinist. The Twentieth Party Congress did not occur until the next year. The overarching theme in Moscow's identity topography that year was difference versus deviance: Could difference, difference from the ideal model of the New Soviet Man, be permitted without the emergence of dangerous deviance, the bourgeois degeneration of the Soviet socialist project? This seemingly domestic issue was projected onto Soviet foreign policy toward Yugoslavia and the Third World. To those who understood difference at home as natural and nonthreatening, such as Nikita Khrushchev and Anastas Mikoyan, difference abroad, in the form of Tito's Yugoslavia and nonaligned states such as India and Egypt, was a possible opportunity, not a threat. To these Soviet leaders, toleration of difference at home, when read abroad, implied a multiplication of Soviet alliance opportunities in the world. In contrast, Vyacheslav Molotov, convinced that difference at home was dangerous deviance, argued against the rapprochement with Tito and was not supportive of expanding ties with India, Burma, Afghanistan, Egypt, and other decolonizing states. Their distance from socialism, to him, meant danger.

In 1999, four main identity discourses emerged. The first, which I call New Western Russian, involved an understanding of Russia as the West. Its polar opposite, New Soviet Russian, understood Russia through its Historical Other, the Soviet Union. The third discursive formation, Liberal Essentialist, understood Russia as meaningfully unique in a world of other unique states, each of which had an authentic, essential, irreducible Self. Finally, the fourth discourse, Liberal Relativist, treated each of the other discourses as ridiculous efforts to achieve some kind of illusory unity of Self when in fact Russia, and all the world, was just an ironic, incommensurable pastiche. The implications of these discourses for Russian foreign policy are perhaps best observed in the discursive treatment of NATO's bombing of Serbia in spring 1999. The New Soviet Russian discourse read this as an attack on Russia itself, through its ethnonational Serbian ally. The New Western Russian discourse was completely discredited by the West, the Other it wished Russia to become, because of that Other's indefensible barbaric behavior in contravention of international legal norms. The Liberal Essentialist discourse inferred a threat from NATO's actions, not because of any ethnonational concern with Serbian brothers but from the implications NATO's illegal act had for Russia's legal sovereign rights to pursue its own war against Chechen separatists. Meanwhile, the Liberal Relativist discourse never made it to foreign policy implications; with the exception of a few ironic parodies of the other discursive treatments of the war, it only appeared at the very margins of Russian foreign policy in 1999.

Only in the final chapter do I situate the empirical findings of the book vis-à-vis the international relations theory literature more generally, comparing and contrasting these findings with those of neorealism and normative and systemic constructivism.

I hope this book contributes to several discussions: international relations theory, methodology in the social sciences, Soviet and Russian foreign policy and domestic politics, and historical and cultural anthropology and ethnography of the Soviet Union and Russia. Most of all, I hope that it contributes to the broadening and deepening of how we go about making sense of world politics. If future IR scholars find themselves reading pulp fiction in order to understand a state's foreign policy, then I will consider this book a success.

TED HOPF

Columbus, Ohio, and St. Petersburg, Russia

Social Construction of
International Politics

1 /

Constructivism at Home
Theory and Method

A theory of society should provide conceptions of the nature of human social activity and of the human agent which can be placed in the service of empirical work.

ANTHONY GIDDENS, *The Constitution of Society*

In this book I develop a theory of social identity and foreign policy choice that can be applied in empirical work. Any social theory has to account for "the element of order in our social relationships."[1] After all, if all humans have their own personalities and at least some control over their surroundings, why do we see so much apparently patterned and ordered activity in social life? This question leads us to suspect the existence of social structures in any society.

A CONSTRUCTIVIST ACCOUNT OF IDENTITY

Every individual in society has many identities. Each identity has associated with it a collection of discursive practices, including a language with a vocabulary, written or verbal, and characteristic physical behaviors, such as gestures, dress, customs, and habits. Many of an individual's identities predominate in particular domains of social life. Some identities may appear in more than one discourse, and some, the most personal, appear in none. Every society is bounded by a social cognitive structure within which some discursive formations dominate and compete. An individual's identities contribute to the creation and recreation of discourse and social cognitive structure; at the same time, those identities are constrained, shaped, and empowered by the very social products they have a hand in creating.

[1] Talcott Parsons, *The Structure of Social Action* (New York, 1937), 102. See also Serge Moscovici, whose theory of social representation tries to dicsover how diverse individuals "in all their strangeness and unpredictability . . . can construct a stable and predictable world. . . ." "The Phenomenon of Social Representations," in *Social Representations*, ed. Robert M. Farr and Serge Moscovici (Cambridge, 1984), 44.

It might occur to the reader, as it certainly has occurred to me, that the field of psychology should have long ago produced robust and replicable theories of social identity that we can use. It turns out, however, that despite its name social psychology offers no theoretical account, social or otherwise, for the origins of an individual's identity or identities. Instead, the discipline's experimental work starts only after an identity has been established, either through priming in the laboratory or ascription prior to recruitment as a subject.[2] A primary aim of this book is to recover the social origins of identity.

I am not the first person interested in identity to point out this unfortunate irony. Peter Berger and Thomas Luckmann observe that "American social psychology was weakened" because it lacked "an understanding of social structure" within which psychological processes occur.[3] Richard Nisbett and Lee Ross lament the unintentionally ironic focus of social psychology on "individual differences in beliefs and theories," rather than on the social milieu.[4] Serge Moscovici goes so far as to call U.S. social psychologists "psychological experts who are sociological ignoramuses."[5]

The results of experimental psychology that are true to the identity concerns of this book are its experimental results about how identity works. Before turning to that discussion, I want to complement the indictment of social psychology for its important omission with notes about other theories of identity that make excessive commissions. I have in mind those accounts of identity that assume too much about the social world, making too many a priori foundational claims that both hinder the social context from speaking for itself and often put words in its mouth.

The most common form of this theoretical preloading is materialism, the argument that identities are merely the markers of distributions of material power. Pierre Bourdieu, for example, offers a general theory of social practice, but his master narrative holds that the propertied classes have created the institutions of an ordered society and that individual actions reproduce those power relations. I have no doubt that this is often true, but I prefer to

---

[2] So, for example, showing Jewish subjects Israeli flags, yamulkes, and menorahs is supposed to prime their Jewish identity, and African Americans, just by being African Americans, are supposed to have that identity in an experimental situation. See, for example, John D. Greenwood, "A Sense of Identity: Prolegomena to a Social Theory of Personal Identity," *Journal for the Theory of Social Behavior* 24, no. 1 (1994): 35–36.

[3] Peter L. Berger and Thomas Luckmann, *The Social Construction of Reality: A Treatise in the Sociology of Knowledge* (New York, 1966), 207 n. 32.

[4] Richard Nisbett and Lee Ross, *Human Inference: Strategies And Shortcomings of Social Judgment* (Englewood Cliffs, 1980), 30.

[5] Moscovici, "Phenomenon of Social Representations," 67–68. Kay Deaux compares social psychology to "Chapter 4 of an eight-chapter book. That chapter is very thorough; but how about paying a little attention to chapters 1 through 3." Kay Deaux, "Reconstructing Social Identity," *Personality and Social Psychology Bulletin* 19 (1993): 11.

treat it as a hypothesis to be empirically verified rather than as an untested assumption.[6]

I also reject as foundational the idea of deep-seated motives for group membership, because any theory based on this assumption implies a universal individual need for national, ethnic, or some other essential group identity. I believe needs have to be discovered empirically, not assumed a priori.[7] Another assumption concerns the relationship between the Self and the Other. This is discussed in detail later; suffice it to say here that theorizing in this vein assumes the Self requires an Other to generate its own identity, but often treats that Other as a threat to the Self. This assumption makes conflict and subordination inevitable in any identity relationship.[8] I acknowledge there is a necessary relationship between Self and Other, but assume neither the character of that relationship nor that it must necessarily be between the Self and another individual, as opposed to another idea or history or place.

I also reject the assumption that identities are intentionally or deliberately chosen, used, and/or strategically manipulated. Again, they might be, but we have no reason to make this an untested assumption. Instead of focusing on the "deliberate, reflexive, problem-solving, adaptive, evolutionary aspects of the Self," I wish to concentrate on the routine, repetitive, habitual, customary, and everyday.[9]

So what are we left with once we reject such assumptions as materialism, innate drives, dangerous Others, and strategic choice? The answer is a thin cognitive account of identity that is thickly inductive and empirical. Society is assumed to consist of a social cognitive structure within which operate many discursive formations. Identities constitute these formations. Individuals have many identities; they participate in a variety of discursive formations; and their daily social practices constitute both themselves and Others,

[6] See Alexander's efforts to rescue Bourdieu from a situation wherein identities are "simple epiphenomena of production and consumption relations in capitalist economies, a status that would leave them without empirical interest and without independent social effect." Jeffrey C. Alexander, *Fin de Siecle Social Theory* (London, 1995), 130–39, 159, 187. See also George E. Marcus, "Contemporary Problems of Ethnography in the Modern World System," in *Writing Culture. The Poetics and Politics of Ethnography*, ed. James Clifford and George E. Marcus (Berkeley, 1986), 173–86; Madan Sarup, *Identity, Culture, and the Postmodern World* (Athens, 1996), 55.

[7] On Emile Durkheim's specification of this need and its centrality to his and subsequent theories of social identity, see Jonathan H. Turner, *A Theory of Social Interaction* (Stanford, 1988), 126. See also Vivienne Jabri, *Discourses on Violence* (Manchester, 1996), 43.

[8] Anne Norton, *Reflections on Political Identity* (Baltimore, 1988).

[9] Sheldon Stryker and Anne Stratham, "Symbolic Interaction and Role Theory," in *Handbook of Social Psychology*, 3rd ed., ed. Gardner Lindzey and Elliott Aronson (New York, 1985), 311–28. My interest in avoiding intentionality in the first instance is also the reason I decline to use Erving Goffman's brilliant work on self-presentation theory. Erving Goffman, *The Presentation of Self in Everyday Life* (New York, 1959).

and the identities and discursive formations that constitute the social cognitive structure in which they live.

Nancy Fraser offers a feminist theory of identity that strikes the right balance between ontological openness and social structure: "People's social identities are complexes of meanings and networks of interpretation. To have a social identity . . . is just to live and to act under a set of descriptions. These descriptions . . . are drawn from the fund of interpretive possibilities available to agents in specific societies."[10] The theoretical account of identity I elaborate here provides for the empirical inductive recovery of those descriptions, their interpretation and aggregation into discursive formations, and their application to the understanding of how a state understands other states in international politics.

The Cognitive Dimension of Identity

Most theories of identity rely on a priori assumptions that imply more about how identity operates than I am willing to warrant. Unwilling to pretheorize in this fashion, I assume that the only motive for the ubiquitous presence and operation of identities is the human desire to understand the social world and the consequent cognitive need for order, predictability, and certainty.[11] Identities in my model operate like cognitive devices or heuristics. This move gets rid of much preloaded theoretical baggage and permits the use of the experimental literature to make sense of how identities work.[12]

According to this theoretical account of identity, an individual needs her own identity in order to make sense of herself and others and needs the

[10] Nancy Fraser, "The Uses and Abuses of French Discourse Theories for Feminist Politics," *Theory, Culture, and Society* 9 (1992): 52.

[11] Alexander, *Fin de Siecle Social Theory*, 116. This confidence in the reliability and predictability of Others, and an individual's effects on them, is sometimes referred to as "ontological security." See Turner, *Theory of Social Interaction*, 51, 164; Jabri, *Discourses on Violence*, 129. Symbolic interactionists also argue that people simplify complexity, seek to discover the identity of the Other and their own identity through him, and understand in order to predict "their own and others' later behavior." Stryker and Stratham, "Symbolic Interaction and Role Theory," 321–23. Consider Goffman's opening sentence: "When an individual enters the presence of others, they commonly seek to acquire information." *Presentation of Self in Everyday Life*, 1.

[12] Bruce Lincoln differentiates between those theorists, such as Pierre Bourdieu, who believe "taxonomic systems," of which identities are a primary component, "provide ideological mystification" for underlying power inequities and those, such as me, who see "taxonomy as primarily an epistemological instrument, i.e., a means of gathering, sorting, and processing knowledge about the external world: a science of the concrete in which the infinite data of experience are organized and given a form in which they become knowable and manipulable. . . . Categorizers come to be categorized according to their own categories. . . ." *Discourse and the Construction of Society: Comparative Studies of Myth, Ritual, and Classification* (New York, 1989), 136–37. See also Mary Glenn Wiley and C. Norman Alexander Jr., "From Situated Activity to Self Attribution: The Impact of Social Structural Schemata," in ed. Krysia Yardley and Terry Honess, *Self and Identity: Psychosocial Perspectives* (New York, 1987), 108.

identities of others to make sense of them and herself. The Self and the Other are mutually necessary and so are their identities. Human brains are limited in the volume of information they can process and so rely on cognitive economizing devices. This bounded rationality uses many cognitive shortcuts and heuristics, but the one that interests us here is identity.[13] Identities categorize people according to common features, making the other's actions intelligible and an individual's own actions vis-à-vis them intelligible to himself. This very simple logic of intelligibility goes a long way toward explaining why individuals routinely choose only a small fraction of the actions, verbal and otherwise, that are objectively available to them at any given time. Their choices are effectively bounded by the social cognitive structure, its discourses, and their identities.

An individual experiences this delimitation of choices as objective, but in fact it is the product of an intersubjective social structure. This is what Berger and Luckmann have referred to as the "social stock of knowledge,"[14] but it could be called, without great conceptual violence, Michel Foucault's discursive formation, Bourdieu's habitus, Clifford Geertz's web of meaning, or Edmund Husserl's life-world. Each of these, roughly speaking, is a particular sociohistorical temporal space within which particular intersubjective meanings predominate. If an individual wants to be understood by another, she must first identify who that other is, what he expects, and what he expects from her and then select how to act.[15] This is the cognitive side of the theory of symbolic interactionism. What George Herbert Mead calls communities of attitudes represent a cognitive framework that informs individuals how to respond to a situation. With time, situations acquire an intersubjectively understood collection of attitudes, orientations, actions, and perspectives.[16]

The experimental psychological literature shows that identities operate in ways reminiscent of other cognitive devices, such as scripts, schemas, and heuristics. What an individual understands himself to be, whether a man or a worker, helps determine what information he apprehends and how he uses it. In this view, an individual's identity acts like an axis of interpretation, implying that she will find in the external world what is relevant to that identity.[17] Serge Moscovici gives us an account of how identities operate cognitively. Identities, he writes, "conventionalize" the objects, people, and

---

[13] Herbert A. Simon, *Models of Bounded Rationality* (Cambridge, 1982); John Steinbruner, *The Cybernetic Theory of Decision* (Princeton, 1974); Daniel Kahneman, Paul Slovic, and Amos Tversky, eds., *Judgment under Uncertainty: Heuristics and Biases* (Cambridge, 1990).

[14] Berger and Luckmann, *Social Construction of Reality,* 40.

[15] Mary Douglas, *How Institutions Think* (Syracuse, 1986), 58.

[16] Turner, *Theory of Social Interaction,* 77.

[17] Hazel Markus, Jeanne Smith, and Richard L. Moreland, "Role of the Self-Concept in the Perception of Others," *Journal of Personality and Social Psychology* 49 (1985): 1494–512.

events we encounter. Identities simplify and homogenize by making the un-familiar familiar in terms of the identity of the Self. These objects, people, and events are "categorized" because individuals have a need to under-stand.[18] Once an individual assigns an identity to someone else, the other person becomes a member of a class assumed to have a particular set of as-sociated discursive practices. Otherwise incomprehensible or meaningless behavior becomes meaningful and the individual ascribes intentions and motives according to the identity classification scheme in use.[19] Moscovici goes further, boldly asserting that identities are the causes of choices and re-actions to others; motivations, aspirations, and cognitive principles are not "an actual cause."[20]

A social cognitive structure establishes the boundaries of discourse within a society, including how individuals commonly think about themselves and others. It establishes intersubjective reality, a more fundamental domain of social action than the objective world. Charles Taylor has argued that lan-guage itself accounts for "thinking in general terms"; language is a product of the human drive to create order in society. This notion is consistent with my own contention that people aim to understand and make predictable the wild variety that characterizes reality.[21] It prompts the necessary ontological observation that reality is not as it is represented but that "there is no knowl-edge of that [real] world outside of these categories."[22]

This discussion of identities as categorizers and simplifiers does not im-ply a lack of theoretical interest in personal, or idiosyncratic, identities.[23] But even the individual Self is read, and hence interpreted, through these simplified collective identities or categorizations. Moreover, as an infor-mation processor, a human cannot treat each and every person as a unique individual. Neither the memory space nor processing capacity exists in suf-ficient quantity. Berger and Luckmann even go so far as to argue that there is great ontological security in an individual's knowing that his own identity, even if unknown to the Self or unstable, is known to Others.[24] Individuals

---

[18] Moscovici, "Phenomenon of Social Representations," 7–8.

[19] Ibid., 31–37.

[20] Ibid., 61–65.

[21] Charles Taylor, *Human Agency and Language: Philosophical Papers*, vol. 1 (Cambridge, 1985), 224–26, 244–45.

[22] Margaret R. Somers, "Fear and Loathing of the Public Sphere and the Privatization of Citizenship: How to Deconstruct a Knowledge Culture," working paper no. 127, University of Michigan, Ann Arbor, Mich. 1997. Mitchell Dean, *Critical and Effective Histories: Foucault's Methods and Historical Sociology* (London, 1994), 65–66.

[23] In comments on this chapter Peter Sahlins correctly pointed out that my failure to start with the individual as idiosyncratic, rather than as part of a general if bounded field of iden-tity, discourse, and social cognitive structure, is not consistent with a truly open ontology. I recognize this as a cost of my pragmatic methodological choice.

[24] Berger and Luckmann, *Social Construction of Reality*, 100.

whose personal identities are problematic can still experience an order generated by society's capacity to categorize them. And every individual who wishes to be understood by Others must express herself in terms those Others can understand.

Logics of Others—Differences and Dangers

I use the logic of mutual constitution, the mutual need of Self and Other, to assess how identities operate as factors in the mutual social construction of Soviets and non-Soviets, Russians and non-Russians, both at home and abroad. A critical tension emerges in the logic of Self and Other: What is the Self to do with the difference he necessarily discovers in the Other? To critical social theorists this difference endangers the unity of the Self and so must be suppressed.[25] Cognitive theorists also expect the Self to assimilate the Other, but without an additional political explanation of why and how. Symbolic interactionists, on the other hand, understand Self and Other as being in a complementary, symbiotic, mutually constitutive relationship— issues of power and domination are again absent. I consider the Self's treatment of difference with the Other to be a critical empirical question, not an assumption. Identities are always relational, but only sometimes oppositional.

Otherwise discordant views do agree on one critical point: identities can only be understood relationally. We cannot know what an identity is without relating it to another. For example, being a great power is meaningless unless we can conceive of a nongreat power identity. How can an individual understand herself if there is nothing not herself? This assumption—to know A means we must know what is not A—drives a great deal of theorizing about the relationship between Self and Other.[26] It also has methodological implications. We cannot simply assign identities to people, events, and things as if they were objectively knowable. Instead, we have to reconstruct the phenomenological intersubjectivity that characterizes a collection of identities.

The interesting quality of an Other is most often associated with its difference, with its lack of similarity to the Self. Moscovici writes that difference is at once intriguing and alluring, frightening and alarming.[27] The response of the Self is to assimilate this difference, making it familiar and thus averting the danger of destabilizing what an individual knows about his own Self.

---

[25] A different explanation for the Self's inherent alienation from the external world in general is his failure to recognize that the objective reality out there is in fact his own creation. Nigel Pleasants, *Wittgenstein and the Idea of a Critical Social Theory* (London, 1999), 171–72.

[26] Taylor, *Human Agency and Language*, 230. Roy F. Baumeister, "The Self," in *Handbook of Social Psychology*, 4th ed., ed. Daniel T. Gilbert, Susan T. Fiske, and Gardner Lindzey (New York, 1998), 701–4.

[27] Moscovici, "Phenomenon of Social Representations," 27.

Berger and Luckmann describe another reason why difference often must be addressed through a range of "conceptual machineries." It is because it is a "constant threat to the taken for granted, matter of fact, sane reality of life in society."[28] What if the marginalia are really the core of reality and we are not? When Columbus came upon indigenous Americans in 1492, his own identity as one of God's chosen was fundamentally shaken. If these so different people were God's people too, how could he still be among the chosen? The differences seemed too great; they had to be suppressed, thus preserving Columbus's own preencounter identity by categorizing the other humans as pagans and subhumans.[29] This strategy, "nihilation," can involve the physical destruction of deviant Others or their public recantation and avowed integration into the normal world of the Self.[30] Another machinery of suppression is therapy, which aims at bringing the different Other "back into the universe of normalcy."[31]

Difference from the Other can result in the alteration of the Self's identity in the direction of that Other. Accommodation to the Other instills fear in the Self, which is always concerned with its loss.[32] Even so, this kind of resolution may be a strategic act of Self-preservation—a toleration of difference in order to save the Self.

The greatest threat to the Self is a comprehensive alternative identity, an Other that can plausibly be understood as a replacement. Recall Antonio Gramsci's theory of hegemony. What most threatens a bourgeois regime is not a coup or an armed rebellion but rather an alternative ideology that can credibly compete. Similarly, according to Berger and Luckmann, the single gravest threat to the Self comes when an individual meets an Other that can account for all of her, plus some additional content.[33]

Perhaps the most threatening Other is the closest Other, closest in the sense of being able to replace the Self more easily than any alternative. It is not nominal difference that threatens but intersubjectively relevant difference. This also suggests another category—irrelevant Others, Others so far out of the symbolic universe as to pose little or no threat to the Self. These Others are cognitively incommensurable with the Self. Berger and Luckmann offer the example of Jews and Muslims in medieval Christian Europe.

---

[28] Berger and Luckmann, *Social Construction of Reality*, 98.

[29] Tzvetan Todorov, *The Conquest of America: The Question of the Other* (New York, 1984).

[30] Berger and Luckmann, *Social Construction of Reality*, 115.

[31] Ibid., 113.

[32] Henrikki Heikka, "Beyond Neorealism and Constructivism: Desire, Identity, and Russian Foreign Policy," in *Understandings of Russian Foreign Policy*, ed. Ted Hopf (University Park, 1999), 57–108.

[33] Berger and Luckmann, *Social Construction of Reality*, 107. Antonio Gramsci, *Selections from the Prison Notebooks of Antonio Gramsci*, ed. and trans. Quintin Hoare and Geoffrey Nowell Smith (New York, 1971).

The trouble for Christian Selves began only when "the deviant universe appear[ed] as a possible habitat for one's own people," that threatening Other being Protestantism.[34]

One final relationship is a situation wherein the Self regards the Other as its negation, its opposite. This particular rendition of identity relations is associated with critical theorists, who argue that "dichotomies are exercises in power."[35] In this way of thinking, difference seamlessly slips into opposition. Anne Norton, for example, writes that "definition begins in negation . . . . Levi-Stauss's structures begin in litanies of opposition. The constitution of identity described by Freud and Lacan begins in . . . the opposition of Self and other. . . ."[36]

It turns out that the Soviet Self employed every one of these conceptual machineries in 1955 vis-à-vis other countries and with regard to its own domestic world. The sheer range of possible responses to a different Other should give anyone pause who wishes to theorize a single modal relationship between Self and Other, whether conflict, dominance, or accommodation.[37]

I conclude this section with another plea to avoid pretheorization. In general, the international relations literature investigates Self and Other as if the only Other for a state were another state. But there is no a priori theoretical or, indeed, empirical reason to believe so. Indeed, symbolic interactionism specifies a "generalized other,"[38] a significant other, or a reference group,[39] in a way that is intentionally vague. Some might be bold and say an individual's parents are his significant other, but just as many would reject the claim. After all, Mead and the Soviet literary theorist Mikhail Bakhtin both realized that the Self has not only multiple Others, but multiple kinds of Others, such as "real others with whom we are currently involved; imagined others, including characters from our own past as well as from cultural narratives; historical others; and the generalized other."[40]

[34] Berger and Luckmann, *Social Construction of Reality*, 122.

[35] Sarup, *Identity, Culture, and the Postmodern World*, 9. For an effort to get beyond the equation of differentiation with domination, at least in feminist theory, see Allison Weir, *Sacrificial Logics: Feminist Theory and the Critique of Identity* (New York, 1996), especially 150–85. There is evidence from experimental cross-cultural social psychology that Americans are more likely than Chinese to exhibit binarized ways of thinking. Alan Page Fiske, Shinobu Kitayama, Hazel Rose Markus, and Richard E. Nisbett, "The Cultural Matrix of Social Psychology," in *Handbook of Social Psychology*, 4th ed., ed. Daniel T. Gilbert, Susan T. Fiske, Gardner Lindzey (New York, 1998), 935.

[36] Norton, *Reflections on Political Identity*, 3.

[37] Lincoln, *Discourse and the Construction of Society*, 162–66. See also Iver B. Neumann, "Russia as Central Europe's Constituting Other," *East European Politics and Societies* 7 (1993): 350.

[38] Turner, *Theory of Social Interaction*, 32–33.

[39] Joel M. Charon, *Symbolic Interactionism* (Upper Saddle River, 1998), 73–78.

[40] Edward E. Sampson, *Celebrating the Other: A Dialogic Account of Human Nature* (Boulder,

Indeed, what constitutes an Other for any given Self is an empirical question of the first order. One of my main purposes in examining the topography of domestic identity is to explore how states understand themselves through domestic others, how state identities are constructed at home as well as through interstate interaction. Had I limited myself to other states as the only Others, the result would have been a most truncated theoretical exercise. As Deniz Kandiyoti has observed, "The question of what and who constitutes the West, or any other Other, often has less to do with the outside world than with the class, religious, or ethnic cleavages within the nation itself."[41] In their review of work on intergroup relations, Marilynn B. Brewer and Rupert J. Brown conclude that even in-group identities do not necessarily need specific out-groups.[42] In other words, even in the demanding case of in-group identification, identity can be maintained in the absence of identifying in opposition to another group.

Practical Habits and Normative Roles

Consistent with this cold, thin cognitive version of identity, I suggest that the most important mechanism for the reproduction of identity is not role and norm but rather habit and practice. I do not assume that individuals consciously understand their roles through social context and so deliberately abide by the appropriate norm (this is discussed in chap. 6). This conceptualization is too constraining theoretically; it narrows the social world of identity to a small number of positions and an even smaller number of expectable behaviors. Ontologically it is too crabbed; it assumes too few meaningful entities in its theoretical field.

Habit designates actions that are relatively unmotivated and the tendency to engage in a previously adopted or acquired form of action.[43] Max Weber suggests four categories of social action: rational, normative, emotional, and habitual; but he mostly ignored the last. Emile Durkheim also considers habit

1993), 106–7. Robert S. Perinbanayagam, *Signifying Acts: Structure and Meaning in Everyday Life* (Carbondale, 1985), 155, in which the author relates Martin Buber's contention that every individual has three defining relationships: with nature, with his fellow men, and with abstractions such as books and art. Sarup, *Identity, Culture, and the Postmodern World*, 41.

   [41] Deniz Kandiyoti, "Identity and Its Discontents: Women and the Nation," *Millennium* 20, no. 3 (1991): 439.

   [42] Marilynn B. Brewer and Rupert J. Brown, "Intergroup Relations," in *Handbook of Social Psychology*, 4th ed., ed. Gilbert, Fiske, and Lindzey (New York, 1998), 564.

   [43] This discussion of habit relies on Charles Camic, "The Matter of Habit," *American Journal of Sociology* 91, no. 5 (March 1986): 1039–87; Fritz Ringer, *Max Weber's Methodology: The Unification of the Cultural and Social Sciences* (Cambridge, Mass., 1997), 106; Geoffrey M. Hodgson, "The Ubiquity of Habits and Rules," *Cambridge Journal of Economics* 21, no. 4 (1997): 676–77; Mitchell Dean, *Critical and Effective Histories*, 67–68. The intellectual genealogy of habit can be traced to William James, *Principles of Psychology* (New York, 1890). Stryker and Stratham, "Symbolic Interaction and Role Theory," 316.

to be a primary cause of human action, claiming that it is not "ideas, sentiments or consciousness" that "most influence our conduct," but "habits—the real forces that govern us."[44]

It is the habitual form of action that accords most closely with my own social cognitive account of identity—the unthinking, unintentional, automatic, everyday reproduction of Self and Other through a collection of discursive practices that relies neither on the need for the denial and suppression of the Other nor on the conscious selection of behavior based on a particular norm. There is no effort to recover the intentions of actors because they are not considered to be evidence of how identities operate within a social cognitive structure.[45] This collection of discursive practices is most naturalized, is least likely to be consciously referred to by an individual, and so is most revelatory of identity in my account.[46]

What is wrong with norms and roles in a theoretical account of identity? The same thing that is wrong with other theoretical preloading. The assumption of materialism, of innate drives for group identity, and of danger from Others focuses attention too narrowly on what we have assumed instead of on the possible recovery of other things that matter. Similarly, the assumption that identities are reducible to roles and are governed by norms too narrowly conceptualizes the socially possible. A commitment to deep induction and empirical recovery is at cross-purposes with any theoretical

[44] Camic, as well, observes that a theorization of Weber's habit has been neglected, not least of all by Weber himself. Camic, "Matter of Habit," 1060. Nicholas Onuf has criticized my differentiation of these logics, essentially arguing that it is "norms all the way down," that habitual actions are themselves rooted in an already internalized normative order (personal communication, March 2001). Peter Katzenstein has similarly suggested that it is a distinction without a difference (personal communication, September 2001). I persist in drawing this distinction, primarily for methodological not ontological reasons. My narrow claim is that if we wish to understand the intersubjective world that constitutes an individual, we must not only concentrate on his or her explicit invocation of a norm to govern his or her conduct. Instead, or in addition, we must realize that evidence for the operation of a norm comes from what is unsaid, unthought, undeliberated, and uninvoked. I do not think of this as product differentiation but rather as an appeal to pay attention to sources of intersubjective evidence that have heretofore been mostly ignored by IR scholars.

[45] Ronald L. Jepperson, "Institutions, Institutional Effects, and Institutionalism," in *The New Institutionalism in Organizational Analysis*, ed. Walter W. Powell and Paul J. DiMaggio (Chicago, 1991), 147; Craig Calhoun, *Critical Social Theory. Culture, History, and the Challenge of Difference* (Oxford, 1995), 143; Sollace Mitchell, "Post-structuralism, Empiricism and Interpretation," in *The Need for Interpretation*, ed. Sollace Mitchell and Michael Rosen (London, 1983), 62; Pierre Bourdieu, *Logic of Practice*, (Cambridge, U.K., 1990) 13, 58; and Steven Lukes, "Conclusion," in ed. Michael Carrithers, Steven Collins, and Steven Lukes, *The Category of the Person: Anthropology, Philosophy, History* (Cambridge, U.K., 1985), 292.

[46] Berger and Luckmann, *Social Construction of Reality*, 14, 56. For Alfred Schutz's influence on ethnomethodology's focus on the taken for granted, see John Heritage, "Ethnomethodology," in *Social Theory Today*, ed. Anthony Giddens and Jonathan H. Turner (Stanford, 1987), 230.

conceptualization that short-circuits the process of discovery. If there are identities that are not roles and social practices not governed by norms, it is misguided to construct a theory that narrows a priori the initial vision. Indeed, both roles and norms are subsumable under a theory of identity that concentrates on practice and habit. The exclusive search for norms and rules necessarily precludes the recovery of everyday practice, but the search for everyday practice necessarily will recover the explicit invocation of norms.

I do not want to limit my search for identities to those that have positions, or whose practices are generated by a concern for norms, and to those situated in relationships regulated and defined by institutions. To put it more concretely, I explore in chapters 2 and 4 an identity I call center-periphery. What institutionalized norm could possibly govern all practices of the center vis-à-vis the periphery? Had I been looking for roles and norms, I would never have found this identity, its multifarious actors and practices, and its many consequences and relationships with other identities.

A significant methodological implication follows. If we believe in roles and norms, then empirical evidence should reveal actors self-consciously referring to both.[47] But in my empirical work, I have found individuals understanding others and themselves according to their identities and associated practices, not pointing out the whys and why nots, the dos and don'ts. Significant features distinguish habitual action from normative compliance. Generally, norms have the form "in circumstance X, you should do Y," whereas habits have a general form more like "in circumstance X, action Y follows." Obeying a norm is most likely to be conscious and deliberative, whereas habitual action is characteristically unexamined. Typically it is easier to violate a norm than to break a habit because our awareness of our own habits is often incomplete.[48]

Decision-Making Logics
Conventionally we understand that theories of international relations come in two main flavors: the rationalist, whose adherents assume decision makers calculate the instrumental values of their actions; and the institutionalist, whose adherents assume decision makers assess what they should do in any particular situation.[49] The former apply a logic of consequentiality, the latter a logic of appropriateness.

---

[47] Jack Bilmes, *Discourse and Behavior* (New York, 1986), 165–75.

[48] This is derived from Hodgson, "Ubiquity of Habits and Rules," 663–84. For experimental demonstrations that people act before they think, see John A. Bargh and Tanya L. Chartrand, "The Unbearable Automaticity of Being," *American Psychologist* 54 (1999): 462–79.

[49] March and Olsen, "The Institutional Dynamics of International Politics Orders," *International Organization* 52, no. 4 (1998): 949–54.

There are two problems with this formulation. First, the logic of appropriateness is not equipped to provide a nontautological account of norm selection. This lack opens the way for rational choice practitioners to offer their solution. As Lynne Zucker has observed, "normative frameworks . . . provide no criteria, . . . no independent measure of which norms are most important in a social system—it is only after the norm is internalized that it can be identified as institutionalized."[50] The logic of appropriateness is an inadequate account of norms because it does not offer any independent theory of what constitutes appropriateness in a given social context. My account of identity does just that by recovering the collection of identities that populate a social context. This collection, both as particular identities and as aggregated discursive formations, provides an independent (only in the methodological sense) theoretical source for an individual's receptivity to one norm over another, one set of discursive practices over another, and one identity over another. In sum, the problem of tautology raised by normative theories need not be solved by retreating to the exogenization of rational choice. It can be endogenized through a more comprehensive account of identity.

We could argue that the decision making involved in following a norm should not be visible to an observer at all because norms bind action via internal commitments that are not empirically available.[51] This is why evidence of a norm's being followed must be gleaned independently and indirectly. One possible way of doing this is offered here, through identities, whose daily practices are visible and whose relationship to individual decision making can be theoretically specified, and falsified.

But the second and main problem with this two-logic account is the absence of a third logic that accounts for a critical part of social life—the logic of the everyday.[52] This comes in several varieties. The logic of intelligibility refers to an individual's desire to be understood by those to whom she is communicating. The logic of thinkability refers to the probability of a particular interpretation of another person or event, given an individual's identities and social context. The logic of imaginability operates similarly, except that imagination has a far broader range of conceivability and is not bound by the possible; thinkability is a logic of practice, namely, memories of what

---

[50] Lynne G. Zucker, "The Role of Institutionalization in Cultural Persistence," in DiMaggio *The New Institutionalism in Organizational Analysis,* ed. Walter W. Powell and Paul J. DiMaggio (Chicago, 1991), 84.

[51] Alexander, *Fin de Siecle Social Theory,* 155.

[52] It could be argued that the logics of consequentiality and appropriateness are conceptually very close because of their shared disregard for habit. Camic, "Matter of Habit," 1076. Weber himself observes that norms in themselves make it easier to calculate the probable consequences of an individual's action, a key element of instrumental rational thought. Max Weber, *Economy and Society* (New York, 1968), 327.

has been done and of what has and has not worked before.[53] Summed up, these three elements of the logic of the everyday shape a large amount of an individual's interpretations and actions in the world. I believe we can observe this everyday logic in the collection of identities and associated discursive formations that can be found in a particular social context. These can be independently recovered and used as the basis for expectations about how individuals will interpret Others.

What kinds of social actions might individuals take? Weber offers three. The first, usage, convention, and fashion, involves the desire to gain social acceptance and is similar to complying with a norm. The second is instrumental rationality. The third is custom, which Weber insists is followed without fear of sanction, unlike a convention or instrumental rationality. Instead, "the actor conforms with them of his own free will, whether his motivation lies in the fact that he merely fails to think about it, that it is more comfortable to conform, or whatever else the reason may be." Conformity with a custom is not "demanded" by anybody. The example that Weber gives is eating breakfast: what, with whom, when, where, and duration, all depend on social practice.[54] The social power with which Weber endows habit and custom can be inferred from his comparison of them to law. He writes that "adherence to what has . . . become customary is such a strong component of all conduct and, consequently, of all social action, that legal coercion, where it transforms a custom into a legal obligation often adds practically nothing to its effectiveness, and, where it opposes custom, frequently fails to influence conduct."[55] If we believe Weber, it makes sense to develop a theory that empirically captures the daily practices of individuals, their customs and habits, rather than to list written laws or collect explicit normative obligations.

The logic of intelligibility assumes that individuals choose language and actions designed to effectively communicate with others, with the hope that they will be understood. This requires conformity with the social cognitive structure that governs the particular social context within which the actor is operating. His discursive practices are the recoverable empirical traces of his unthinking adherence to structural constraints. As Berger and Luckmann put it, "there is a bias toward tradition and stability. One does certain things not because they work [consequentiality], but because they are right—right in terms of ultimate definitions of reality."[56] People want to do the right

---

[53] Wittgenstein distinguished between knowledge gained practically, through action, and knowledge gained by the formal or conscious following of explicit rules. Alexander, *Fin de Siecle Social Theory*, 132.

[54] Weber, *Economy and Society*, 29, 319.

[55] Ibid., 320.

[56] Berger and Luckmann, *Social Construction of Reality*, 118. See also Joseph Rouse, "The Narrative Reconstruction of Science," *Inquiry* 33 (1990), 181–85.

thing, but not in the normative sense. They want to be accurately under-stood.[57] The operation of norms can be subsumed under a logic of intelli-gibility in that norms help give a social context its boundaries and limits.[58]

The second logic of the everyday is the logic of thinkability. Operating within a social cognitive structure implies a particular probability for various social practices. Whether it is the language that is chosen, the clothing that is worn, the food that is cooked, or the treatment of a neighbor's cat, any in-dividual has only a truncated set of possibilities available. Of course, indi-viduals do some things that are out of the ordinary. But we can have a fairly high level of confidence that an individual will construe a situation in this way not that way and be far more likely to construe it in one of these three ways than in that other way. Walter Powell, when discussing the new, new in-stitutionalism, observes that "institutional patterns shape behavior such that some courses of action are perceived as natural. . . ." Others are not per-ceived as natural or are not perceived at all.[59] Bourdieu puts it more strongly than I would: "certain beliefs become unthinkable. . . ."[60]

It is only a short theoretical step from the thinkable to the possible. Ob-viously, for a practice to be possible it has to be thinkable or imaginable. But many apparent possibilities go untried because they are unthinkable. Each one of us everyday could renounce the world and become an anchorite; many of us have a normative compulsion to empathize with the most needy. Why have we not pursued our normative impulse? Tautologically, and so triv-ially, speaking, it is not in our instrumental rational interest to do so. It is not normatively appropriate from the perspective of some norm that happens to be consistent with the outcome. But can we explain the tension and its apparent resolution in favor of inaction? How has the ascetic vocation be-come unthinkable? The reconstruction of the identity topography of a given individual can actually shed some light on a practice's relative thinkability and, hence, endogenize what would otherwise remain only trivially true.[61]

Despite my effort to focus on the various logics of everyday practice and to criticize the reliance on either consequentiality or appropriateness, they

[57] Zucker, "Role of Institutionalization," 83.

[58] Heritage, "Ethnomethodology," 245. See also Turner's discussion of the logic of intel-ligibility manifest in Husserl's life-world in *Theory of Social Interaction*, 105.

[59] Walter W. Powell, "Expanding the Scope of Institutional Analysis," in *The New Institu-tionalism in Organizational Analysis*, ed. Walter W. Powell and Paul J. DiMaggio (Chicago, 1991), 192. One of the central missions of ethnomethodology was to find, and transgress, this boundary between the unthought and the unthinkable.

[60] Pierre Bourdieu, *Outline of a Theory of Practice*, trans. R. Nice (Cambridge, U.K., 1977), 77. See also Moscovici, "Phenomenon of Social Representations," 12–30; Zucker, "Role of Institutionalization," 85–86; Berger and Luckmann, *Social Construction of Reality*, 92. For an empirical illustration, see Rogers Brubaker, *Nationalism Reframed: Nationhood and the National Question in the New Europe* (Cambridge, Mass., 1996), 24.

[61] For a discussion of these logics in sociology, see Bilmes, *Discourse and Behavior*, 185.

are all in fact present in every social context. I focus on the former for several reasons. First, they have been neglected. Second, they subsume norms. Third, they are more consistent with a theoretical account that stresses thick induction and empiricism. And fourth, they put the spotlight on the generally underreported power of the everyday, the taken for granted, the naturalized.

Identity and Interests

One of the most common criticisms of mainstream social science is its exogenous treatment of interests, as if the theorist could assign them with no ill effect on the utility of the resultant theory. A constructivist account of identity at the domestic level promises to endogenize the formation of interests by connecting them theoretically and empirically to identity and its associated discursive practices. Interests should be derivable from identity in the sense that an individual's identity implies his interests. This relationship should furnish a nontautological understanding of the origins of an interest that is endogenous to the more general theoretical account of identity and interest in another state. It is nontautological because evidence of the interest and its content is not the interest itself. It is endogenous because the origins of the interest and the identity of the individual are both located within the theoretical account of identity.

Let us define *interest* in terms of the dependent variable of this book. Interest in another state entails some positive value in having relations with that state. But why would a state have an interest in any other state? The two most common interests are strategic and economic. Strategic interests involve threats and opportunities. Threats involve danger to oneself; opportunities involve the possibility of averting danger through relations with others or collaborating for joint gains. But what constitutes a threat and what constitutes an opportunity? Why would one state be considered a threat and another an opportunity or ally? To get to a state's interest in either enemies or allies, we need a theory that can capture the meaning of those two types of states. That is what the social cognitive theory of identity provides here: an account of how a state's own domestic identities constitute a social cognitive structure that makes threats and opportunities, enemies and allies, intelligible, thinkable, and possible.

The second common interest is economic. One state has an economic interest in another state to the extent it profits from their trade and investment relations. Thus the United States has an obvious economic interest in low crude oil prices—or does it? The United States has an obvious economic interest in investing in Iranian natural gas reserves—or does it? The United States has an obvious economic interest in the most efficient transportation of natural gas from the Caspian Sea to western markets—or does it? The answers to these questions are well, no, sort of; it depends; and what do you mean? The complexity stems not from the idea that the United States has no unified interest but from the fact that there is no such thing as an unalloyed economic interest. Every single question demands an understanding of the identity politics underlying U.S. relations with the Middle East, Iran, and Russia.

The relationship between identity and interest implies that any individual, because of her understanding of herself through Others, necessarily has interests that are social cognitive products. She has, for instance, an interest in her mutual fund portfolio appreciating in value. That claim is not interesting at the proximate level, but from the point of view of identity it may be explained not by material acquisitiveness but by the identity of the mother, who happens to have two children approaching college age. Oddly, such an explanation has the advantage of parsimony because maternal identity can elucidate a broad range of social practices, whereas materialism will not speak to her interest in oboe lessons for one son, but in dancing lessons for the other and will make materialistic outcomes that are better understood as a social identity in practice, such as insisting her sons get summer jobs. This maternal identity has been accumulated through years of daily practice, in interaction with multiple defining Others such as parents, siblings, friends, heroines in novels and on stage, historical events, and idealized conceptualizations of mothers. It is evoked when Others treat her as a mother, as well as when the social context itself reminds her that she is a mother.

The theoretical cost of the failure to regard individuals as social selves is manifest in the highly regarded effort of Dennis Chong to bring norms and values under the sway of rational choice theory. He begins by defining instrumentally rational actions as those that secure "private ends."[62] How can we speak of private ends if the Self cannot even know its own identity without an Other?[63] If the mother understands herself through her sons, how is her concern for her sons' well-being to be explained through instrumental rationality combined with private ends? One of the terms has to give—either she is instrumentally rational in pursuing social ends or she pursues her private ends through value-rational action.

[62] Dennis Chong, *Rational Lives: Norms and Values in Politics and Society* (Chicago, 2000), 3. Chong apparently fails to find Weber's fourfold distinction among actions—instrumental-rational, value-rational, affectual, and habitual—very illuminating. Indeed, when Chong summarizes the findings from his main case study (the public resistance to siting an Apple Computer facility in Williamson County, Texas, because of Apple's domestic partner provisions), he separates the instrumental reasoning from the emotional and affective—the habitual is missing. Chong, *Rational Lives*, 182. Camic, "Matter of Habit," 1060.

[63] Chong's view of the individual permits him to assert that "rational individuals" prefer benefits for themselves, rather than for society at large. Chong, *Rational Lives*, 5. This is an extraordinary universalist claim—the last twenty years of cross-cultural psychology have shown that only the United States and northern Europe have the kinds of Selves that would warrant confidence in Chong's assertion.

Chong stipulates that individuals choose more attractive alternatives "instead of being driven by internal values, identities, and dispositions."[64] But this only begs the question of how a person knows relative attractiveness. How can we understand the mother's belief that Yale is more attractive than Stanford unless we know that she understands herself as an Ivy Leaguer? Chong displays a common misconception of the relationship between identity and interest, asserting that the best evidence against his view is individuals who operate contrary to their self-interest. According to the account of identity I offer here, however, individuals always operate according to their interests—but those interests do not always correspond to the ones assigned by the omniscient objective observer. As Bourdieu wrote, all interests are particular historical constructions, but interested action is a universal.[65]

Chong's efforts to make norms part of the rational choice story are imaginative, but take no account of noninstrumental logics. He bring norms within the rational choice framework by claiming that norms are chosen for instrumental reasons of self-interest. This claim is consistent with the logics of consequentiality and appropriateness, but ignores the logics of daily practice. In fact, norms need not be chosen to be applied. Norms need not even exist for individuals to persist in patterns of behavior that look as if they were norm-, rule-, and law-governed. Everyday logic has little to do with interests, conventionally construed. It is the cognitive need for order and predictability, or the individual's interest in that order, that produces the outcome of order that we too glibly assert is the product of proximate interest in a particular norm or rule.

Chong's model of interest has a hard time explaining why so many actions are never chosen or even considered.[66] Unless it considers instrumental means-end calculations or social pressure, Chong's model presumably misses almost all of the taken-for-granted background that accounts for most of daily life. Jane Cowan describes the kind of absent interest that positive models can never capture. Cowan's fieldwork was conducted in a Greek village where the practice of drinking coffee is a gendered affair. Older married women "genuinely hav[e] no desire to go to the kafeteria. . . . But the formation of this desire, or its absence, must be examined in the context of the married woman's interests. . . . For a married woman it is against her interests, as a wife, mother, and lady of the community, a kyria, to assert her interests as a woman or an autonomous person." In fact, to go to this kind of cafe would identify her as sexually dissolute and flirtatious. Her absence of interest, or absent preference, is a form of "anticipatory surrender."[67] The private Self ac-

[64] Ibid., 178.

[65] Loic Wacquant, "Toward a Reflexive Sociology: A Workshop with Pierre Bourdieu," Sociological Theory 7 (1989): 41–42. Calhoun, Critical Social Theory, 142.

[66] Chong, Rational Lives, 13.

[67] Jane K. Cowan, "Going Out for Coffee? Contesting the Grounds of Gendered Pleasures

tually may have an interest in going to the kafeteria, but the social self, the one implicated in those multiple identities, the one whose existence lies outside rational choice theory, has no such preference. And this absent preference would go untheorized were it not for the logic of the unthinkable.

Which is more interesting—knowing that older married Greek women have no interest in going to the kafeteria or knowing that this interest is absent because of a particular social cognitive structure; discourse on sexuality, family, and hierarchy; and gendered identity? The latter can involve an entire collection of present and absent interests for the entire population of the village. Such is the possible explanatory power of being able to recover endogenous identity, discourse, and social cognitive structure instead of exogenously assigning interests through a priori theorizing or cursory empirical observation.

I end with an example from Rogers Brubaker's history of French and German citizenship policy. It captures the kind of empirical story I recount in chapters 2 and 4, as well as a similar understanding of how identity and interest relate to one another in theory and in practice. Brubaker argues that the "interest of the French state" in a broad definition of citizenship was not the result of demographic or military imperatives. Rather, this "interest was constituted by a certain way of thinking and talking about the French nation-state." The French self-understanding as state-centered and assimilationist "engendered an interest in the civic incorporation of second-generation immigrants," whereas German self-understanding implied their civic exclusion. Brubaker shows how "cultural idioms framed and shaped judgments of what was politically imperative, and what was in the interest of the state. . . ." Cultural idioms "constitute interests, as much as express them." He quotes Gareth Stedman Jones: "We can decode political language to reach an . . . expression of interest since it is the discursive structure of political language which conceives and defines interest in the first place. What we must therefore do is study the production of interest and identity within the political languages themselves."[68]

In this book, I find the interests of the Soviet Union and Russia within popular identities. I use these identities to hypothesize about the interests of the state vis-à-vis other states if a particular identity or collection of identities within a discursive formation were to constitute the state. The practices that make the world intelligible and the interests that are thinkable and

---

in Everyday Sociability," in *Contested Identities. Gender and Kinship in Modern Greece,* ed. Peter Loizos and Evthymios Papataxiarchis (Princeton, 1991), 180–202. On the absence of interest where there is no choice, see also Stryker and Stratham, "Symbolic Interaction and Role Theory," 336.

[68] Rogers Brubaker, *Citizenship and Nationhood in France and Germany* (Cambridge, Mass., 1992), 15–17, 91, 16. The only difference is that the language I use to derive the cultural idiom is far broader.

imaginable given the available identities are both used to specify the relationship between identity and interest.

Identity, Discourse, and Social Cognitive Structure

I put together a theoretical account of identity in three steps. The first is the inductive empirical reconstruction of the identity topography of Moscow in 1955 and 1999. The second is the synthetic creation of discursive formations that bring various identities together in a more coherent structure than pure induction can supply. The third is positing that any Soviet or Russian foreign policy decision maker is part of a social cognitive structure that comprises the identities and discourses and that these constitute any Soviet decision maker's understanding of himself. His (in this case, it is always "his") understandings of other states, therefore, must necessarily involve the interaction between this complicated social Self and those external Others. The relationships among identity, discourse, structure, decision maker, and other states is diagrammed in figure 1.

The meanings of the identities I find in Soviet and Russian texts are established both contextually and intertextually—contextually within the texts in which they are found and intertextually with respect to other texts. I make no effort to discern the intended meaning of the authors because authors do not control the meaning of their own words once they are uttered in public.[69] So I first attribute meaning contextually, by looking at the text itself. For example, identities found at the Second Writers' Congress are related to other speeches given at the writers' congress, identities in a high school history textbook are made meaningful by the other identities found in that book, and so on. But this is only a first cut. This contextualized meaning must then be related to meanings that have emerged in all the other textual sites: daily newspaper articles, scholarly journals, popular novels, film reviews, and so on. An identity at this level receives a more gestalt reading of its intertextual meaning. Bourdieu warns us that those who "take a shortcut, who dispense with the complete [which is impossible in any case] system of signifiers within which the relational value of each of them is defined, are inevitably limited to an approximate discourse which, at best, only stumbles onto the most apparent significations by . . . picking out decontextualized themes."[70] Let me say immediately that I am certain I stumble a lot in the chapters to come.

---

[69] As Saussure put it, language speaks to us; it is through language that we come to know who we are. Sarup, *Identity, Culture, and the Postmodern World*, 46. Norton, *Reflections on Political Identity*, 46; Paul Ricoeur, "The Model of the Text: Meaningful Action Considered as Text," *Social Research* 38, no. 4 (1971): 534; Taylor, *Human Agency and Language*, 231. Remember the married women in Cowan's Greek village—no matter what they intend their visit to a kafeteria to mean, the meaning that is inferred is quite different. Cowan, "Going Out for Coffee?"

[70] Bourdieu, *Logic of Practice*, 4. Intertextualism is a form of structuralism, a recognition that meanings of discrete identities involve relationships to others.

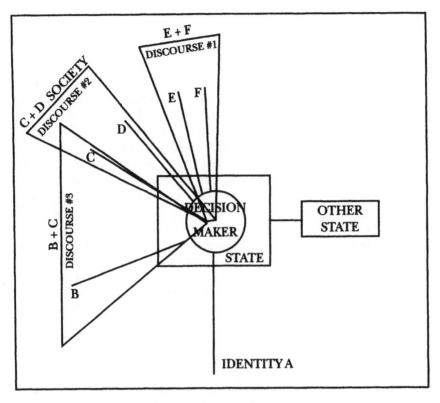

Figure I   Social Cognitive Structure

The power that a social cognitive structure exerts can best be illustrated in terms of language. "Language involves both habits and rules; it is a social institution par excellence. It disciplines our behavior and provides us with a very limited choice of meaningful utterances from the vast array of sounds that could conceivably be vocalized."[71] We are all boundedly rational in our calculations of reality. So a social cognitive structure, with its constituent discursive formations and identities, provides a social account of the origins of our "meaningful utterances," actions, and interests. What I mean by such a social cognitive structure is akin to Geertz's web of meaning, viz. a sociotemporal historical site within which there is a collection of intersubjective meanings to the discursive practices of its members. Within this space there are logics of intelligibility, thinkability, and imaginability that operate like (linguistic) structures—they push and pull people to conceptualize,

---

[71] Hodgson, "Ubiquity of Habits and Rules," 677. Moscovici, "Phenomenon of Social Representations," 8, 23–26.

and so discursively to act, in a finite set of ways.[72] Every society is a social cognitive structure, every society comprises particular discursive formations that constitute that structure, and every individual has a multitude of identities that may or may not be part of a discursive formation.

Figure 1 shows us a decision maker who has six identities (A–F). Five of these identities (B–F) constitute three discursive formations. The sixth identity (A) is not implicated in any discourse. These discursive formations together constitute the social cognitive structure within which the decision maker is situated when she tries to understand another state. She reads the other state through her understanding of her own state and that understanding is itself related to the discourses and identities that constitute her.

For example, the mother of a friend of mine, who lives in San Francisco, was visiting from New Jersey. She had been a prison guard all her adult life. They were sitting in a restaurant when two men in uniform entered; they were dressed in leather jackets and trousers, had handcuffs on their belts, wore caps with an insignia, and had moustaches and aviator sunglasses. They were tall and fit. This woman turned to her son and wondered aloud what branch of law enforcement they were with. Her life experience made the two men instantly familiar, she *knew* they had to be cops of some kind, whereas her son *knew* they were part of San Francisco's gay culture.

Edward E. Evans-Pritchard describes how this web of meaning operates in his study of the Azande: "In this web of belief every strand depends on every other [contextuality/intertextuality], and a Zande cannot get out of its meshes. . . . The web is not an external structure in which he is enclosed. It is the texture of his thoughts and he cannot think that his thought is wrong."[73] Berger and Luckmann call language itself a "constraining structure," one that "creates zones of meaning."[74] One of the most important cognitive heuristics identified by Daniel Kahenman and Amos Tversky is the availability heuristic, which they experimentally demonstrate to have a significant effect on a person's capacity to interpret the outside world.[75] But, like their colleagues, they exogenize or stipulate what is available. By contrast, this book, through the recovery of identity, aims to furnish an account of availability independent of the manipulations of the researcher.

---

[72] Anyone can think outside the box, so to speak, but it is not usual to do so, and we need not pay attention to all the deviations in order to gain an understanding of what is actually happening within the structure.

[73] Edward E. Evans-Pritchard, *Witchcraft, Oracles and Magic among the Azande* (New York, 1937), 194. See also Steven Collins, "Categories, Concepts, or Predicaments? Remarks on Mauss's use of Philosophical Terminology," in *The Category of the Person*, 46–47, 51–52, 58, 70–72.

[74] Berger and Luckmann, *Social Construction of Reality*, 38.

[75] Kahneman, Slovic, and Tversky, eds. *Judgment under Uncertainty*, 163–210.

The presence of this social cognitive structure can account for the relatively high level of order and patterning we observe in social life—its practices and identities and its capacity to render a range of actions either meaningful or meaningless. In the absence of such a structure, individuals would be forever renegotiating meaning.[76] Every situation, every action, every conversation is objectively unique; so, in principle, "the social world consists of an indefinitely large number of differentiable situations of action."[77] Yet, we still observe a remarkably high level of predictability, order, and consistency. How else can we account for this than with the presence of an overarching social cognitive structure within any society, as well as with more discrete discursive formations with their own unique collections of practices and a still larger collection of identities that make sense of local reality?

Bourdieu calls this result a "gnoseological order," a homogenous conception of time, space, number, and cause, which makes understanding possible between intelligent beings. We end up with "consensus on the significance of the social world which makes a fundamental contribution to the reproduction of social order."[78] Let me reiterate that empirically locating identities is the first step in specifying the discursive formations that in turn constitute the social cognitive structure prevailing at any particular time and place.

A METHOD FOR FINDING, UNDERSTANDING, AND APPLYING IDENTITY

My aim is to recover the identities and discursive formations that constitute the social cognitive structures of Moscow in 1955 and 1999. The backbone of an interpretivist epistemology is phenomenology and induction. Phenomenology implies letting the subjects speak, in this case through their texts. Induction involves the recording of these identities as atheoretically as possible. With the exception of the Russian nation, for example, I did not look for any particular Soviet or Russian identities; they emerged from the

---

[76] Stryker and Stratham, "Symbolic Interaction and Role Theory," 322. An individual in a modern western society who refuses to be bound by these patterns of meaning is often adjudged clinically insane by the other members of society who do conform to the "normal" distribution. We need not be devotees of Foucault to see the disciplining effects that social cognitive structures have on society's members. Ivana Markova, "Knowledge of the Self through Interaction," in *Self and Identity: Psychosocial Processes,* ed. Krysia Yardley and Terry Honess (New York, 1987), 66.

[77] Heritage, "Ethnomethodology," 242.

[78] Pierre Bourdieu, "Symbolic Power," trans. Colin Wringe, in *Identity and Structure: Issues in the Sociology of Education,* ed. Denis Gleeson (Driffield, U.K., 1977), 112 and 119. Bourdieu credits Berger and Luckmann and Schutz as his inspirations for these ideas.

texts themselves. The trick is to remain ontologically open for as long as possible before imposing an analytical theoretical order, or closure, on the numerous ambiguities and differences in the texts.

My first rule for choosing texts is to select those that were most widely read. For 1955, I looked at a sample from the daily Soviet press, as well as from popular novels, high school textbooks, the proceedings of the Second Congress of Soviet Writers, and specialized academic journals. For 1999, I sampled the daily Russian press and read textbooks, but I also surveyed booksellers on the Moscow streets and in the metro stations to select the most popular novels of the year. I collected no material on Soviet or Russian foreign policy until I had already collected, analyzed, and written up the results of the domestic identity reconstruction based on these primary texts. For 1955, I reconstructed how Soviets understood foreign policy exclusively from archival materials; for 1999, I relied on a sample of open sources, none of which I read until I had completed work on the domestic side.[79]

Reconstructing domestic identity involved both contextualizing the meanings of identities within the texts and relating them intertextually to the vast variety of other texts for that year. There is an increasing level of theorization, and hence room for interpretive slippage, with each move, from the collection of raw identities to their contextualization to their intertextualization. But the next step, resituating these identities into discursive formations, is the most challenging and the most open to multiple reinterpretation. The move from identity to discourse was not so problematic for 1955, when an official discourse was ubiquitous. But 1999 proved to have four discrete discursive formations, each one inferred from a collection of different identities. This move involves implicit judgments about the connections of identities that can be challenged both directly, by offering alternative discursive analyses, or indirectly, through a critique of the resulting interpretation of foreign policy.

Finally, interpretivist epistemology recognizes the limits of its own methods by asserting only the most modest of truth claims. My work produces what I call a relative, working truth, that is, claims to validity that I expect to be true only in relation to other interpretive claims, not to some objective reality.[80] The claims to validity are "working" because they operate only in

---

[79] For practical reasons, and especially for 1999, texts sometimes discussed both domestic identity and foreign policy. I put aside those texts until I had finished all the purely domestic texts and then came back to them to read for the domestic identity terrain. There was undoubtedly some leaching of the foreign policy–dependent variable into the domestic, but it was both guarded against as much as possible and read only against an already comprehensively specified domestic identity topography. I thank Ned Lebow for stressing the importance of this caveat.

[80] See Friedrich Kratochwil, "Evidence, Inference, and Truth as Problems of Theory Building in the Social Sciences," in *Theory and Evidence. Evidence and Theory*, ed. Richard Ned Lebow

comparison to other claims; they are not the truth, but merely the most plausible account yet offered.

Inductive Recovery of Identity

Theorizing is a form of interpretation, and it destroys meaning. As soon as we begin to impose categories on evidence, that evidence stops meaning what it meant in its earlier context. For a work on identity, it is absolutely imperative that meanings remain what they mean and do not become what the researcher needs to test a hypothesis. Categorization, the assigning of labels to pieces of textual evidence that are assumed to "mean the same thing," is to be avoided even though it is irresistible. Bourdieu writes that premature evidentiary closure "was very hard for him to escape from." The difficulty resulted from a combination of the "structuralist vulgate" and "social demands," presumably from his fellow sociologists. The situation is made all the worse "by the fact that interpretation cannot put forward any other proof of its truth than its capacity to account for the totality of facts in a completely coherent way." He concludes, "this explains why it was so hard to accept and really take into account in my analysis the objective ambiguity of a whole set of symbols and practices [and] to classify them as unclassifiable."[81]

The interpretivist ideal is to report as evidence all that does not fit into the theorized categories. This ideal is not attainable in practice, of course, but the researcher still must try to resist the categorization of meaning for as long as is practicable. And I mean practicable; no law governs this situation. For example, I began my research by reading Vera Panova's novel *Span of The Year*. My aim was to record all the identities that appeared in that text. In notes, I elaborated possible meanings that these identities appeared to have within the context of the novel. Only with time, and hundreds of texts later, did the identities found in *Span of the Year* settle into a particular set of meanings. The possible meanings of an identity narrowed into a very few that dominated, both quantitatively and across the textual terrain, all other competitors.

One pitfall that we can avoid is the problem of anomalies. Anomalies exist only if we have already created a theoretical framework. If we instead try to postpone the creation of that theoretical commitment, anomalies become additional possible categories for later interpretation. The inductive recovery of identity allows the texts themselves to establish the so-called disruptions of the field. Harold Garfinkel's studies in ethnomethodology deliberately manipulated conventional conversation to find out the bound-

---

and Mark Lichbach, manuscript. Karl Popper has called this kind of working truth "situational certainty." Karl Popper, *Objective Knowledge* (Oxford, 1972), 178–79. See also Charles Taylor, *Sources of the Self: The Making of the Modern Identity* (Cambridge, Mass., 1989), 72.

[81] Bourdieu, *Logic of Practice*, 10–11.

aries of normalcy. Textual analysis can replicate this technique. The writers of novels and newspaper articles and writers speaking at professional meetings provide evidence. Whether implicitly or explicitly, these individuals point out how identities relate to one another, how Selves relate to Others, how difference relates to deviance, which understandings are thinkable, which formulations are intelligible, and which realities imaginable. As Moscovici advises, "the study of social representations requires that we revert [*sic*] to methods of observation. . . . The value of experimental methods is indisputable when studying simple phenomena that can be taken out of context. But this is not the case for social representations which are stored in our language and which were created in a complex human milieu. . . ."[82]

What I do with texts resembles narrative analysis, understood as a "means of illuminating structures." It does not grasp social cognitive structures directly but rather reconstructs them indirectly by "making narratives thick enough to deal not only with the sequence of events and the conscious intentions of actors in these events, but also with structures—institutions, modes of thought, and so on. . . ."[83] The thick narrative analysis of a text involves discerning the meaning of identities for the actors in the text, whether a fictional character in a novel, an example in a textbook, a rendition of life in Uzbekistan, or a speaker at the Second Congress of Soviet Writers. This thick contextualization is then followed by thick intertextualization. There is no strict temporal sequence. As texts accumulate, so too does my own vague outline as to how they are aggregating at the discursive level. But I wish to ensure that those emergent categorizations affect the inductive reconstruction of identities as little as possible.

In sum, induction promises the capacity to conduct research while we are "out of our minds," that is, without our feeling compelled to test theories in the first instance or to theorize reality according to some well-known templates.

Intertextualization, or the Boundaries of Meaning

Having gathered a group of contextualized identities, what do we do with them? The answer involves both the broader contextualization of these identities in relation to other texts and the move from these broader identities to discursive formations that include more than one identity. It also entails the move from a domain where reliability (my confidence that another scholar reading the same materials will end up with the same understandings) is substantially reduced. Recovering identities is largely an inductive

---

[82] Moscovici, "Phenomenon of Social Representations," 67. See also Taylor, *Sources of the Self*, 58.

[83] Peter Burke, "History of Events and the Revival of Narrative," in *New Perspectives on Historical Writing*, ed. Peter Burke (University Park, 1998), 240–44.

process of reading and relating texts; establishing these identities' intertextual meanings and, still more, their aggregation into discursive formations is a more theory-driven exercise.[84] Again, no laws mandate that particular identities should hang together in a synthetic coherence established by the researcher. Any other researcher could come along and say that my particular arrangement of identities into a particular discursive formation is in fact poorly conceived. But fortunately the proof, at least as far as this book is concerned, is in the ability to predict the dependent variable—understanding other states. My interpretivist understandings are falsifiable. In fact, we could argue that interpretivism is uniquely endowed with falsifiable links. Not only can its implications falsify its claims, but its aggregation of identities into discursive formations and its assignment of contextual and intertextual meanings may all be challenged.

The meaning of an identity is initially given by its context within its particular source. But its meanings soon are elaborated by the accumulation of texts in which the identity appears. These additional contextualizations may merely reinforce a prior understanding of that identity, they may offer different meanings entirely, or they may show that certain circumstances yield different meanings. This process is the beginning of the intertextualization of the meanings of an identity. There is a multistage process of interpretation for any identity appearing in a text. At first, the identity is understood according to its apparent meaning. Then it is reunderstood according to its relationship with other texts. Finally, its meaning is integrated into the operation of a discursive formation that includes many other identities.[85]

Let us take an example. A 1955 journal article presents gender relations in central Asia as primitive. It is possible, on this contextual basis alone, to infer a continuum of modernity to premodernity for gender relations in the Soviet Union. But the place of gender in the Soviet project more generally (i.e., in the identity of the New Soviet Man) can only be inferred after we have examined many texts in which gender is modernized across different contexts. Only then can we read back the more general gender identity onto that original ethnographic article. Gender in one place turns out to be part of an effort to reconstruct the meaning of gender more generally, and that more general understanding informs the more isolated instance. Finally, this example might end up in a discourse on Soviet modernity that not only articulates gender relations, but also the relations between Russians and non-Russians, center and periphery, difference and deviance, and Soviet foreign policy itself. Although not the most visible identity in that discourse,

---

[84] This is akin to the move from Paul Ricoeur's hermeneutics of trust to the hermeneutics of suspicion, that is, from the phenomenological faith in the subjects' renditions of reality to a presumed capacity to discover a deeper social structure of which they are not aware.

[85] Jabri, *Discourses on Violence*, 90–94.

the way it has appeared in various texts contributes to the reproduction of its own particular gender identity and to the operation of the discourse as a whole.

At this last step we must recall Hayden White's warning: "that the shape of the relationships which will appear to be inherent in the objects inhabiting the field will in reality have been imposed on the field by the investigator in the very act of identifying and describing the objects that he finds there. Historians in effect constitute their subjects as objects of narrative representation by the very language they use to describe them."[86] White's charges are pertinent as I move from the contextual to the intertextual, but they are even more so as I move to the discursive. As the empirical chapters make clear, some identities remain as they appear in the texts; some get relabeled to make them meaningful within my emergent theory; and others, as they become part of a discursive formation, are relabeled, resignified, and retheorized, so that they would be unrecognizable in their original text. But there are two justifications for this strategy. The first is the claim that social (cognitive) structures often are not apparent to their members; the second is that I have an independent test waiting for my retheorizations—hypotheses derived from domestic identities and their discourses are evaluated against the empirical record of Soviet and Russian understandings of external Others. When my renderings of the discourse are wrong, we see it in the empirical record.

Perhaps contextualization at a higher level of social and textual aggregation involves the employment of a kind of qualitative factor analysis. After the identities are gathered, named, and categorized, it appears as if some of them cluster together and others never associate. If this appearance survives our going back through all the raw identity material, we can make an aggregative claim that these clusters constitute analytically separable discourses. Separability generally implies meaningful difference, although discourses need not be at odds on everything.

Finally, discourses are arranged or positioned with respect to one another. In the realm of discursive politics, we can assess discursive formations as if they were in "active or potential competition."[87] This observation has less import for 1955, when there was a single dominant discourse. In 1999, it is useful to understand the four discourses as if they were positioning themselves to capture adherents. As events unfold, both domestically and abroad, the adherents of each discourse offer understandings of those events from within their own collection of identities. Are the understandings convincing? Discursive formations gain and lose power as a consequence. We commonly talk of parties, interest groups, bureaucratic organizations, and

---

[86] Hayden White, *Tropics of Discourse: Essays in Cultural Criticism* (Baltimore, 1978), 95.

[87] Lincoln, *Discourse and the Construction of Society,* 7.

classes engaging in politics; it might make sense to add discursive formations to that ontology.

Interpretivist Claims

A constructivist account of identity based on an interpretivist epistemology can offer robust claims to reliability, narrow claims to generalizability and predictability, and tentative claims to validity. Interpretivists expect other researchers using the same theoretical apparatus and collection of texts to reproduce their results, at least in principle.[88] They are empowered by their evidentiary findings to make general statements about the nature of identities and how they work, both within the particular case itself and also in some other temporal or spatial domains. Interpretivism is committed to the principle that additional evidence is always available and that its presence can affect the meaning of whatever has already been assembled. As a result, we can never assert confident claims to validity, except within the narrow confines of the evidence we have already assessed. As for theoretical generalizability, predictability, and validity, however, we may reasonably expect the theoretical account of identity employed here to work elsewhere—if it proves its capacity to capture the connection between domestic identity and foreign policy in the Soviet and Russian cases.

As an interpretivist, I should have no greater or lesser confidence in the reliability of my findings than any social scientist using mainstream methods. If I give my list of texts to another scholar, I expect that she will find the same identities with the same meanings that I did, with three stipulations. First, reliability should be very high in contextualizing identities within their sources, less high when it comes to intertextualizing them, and still less high (and perhaps quite low) when aggregating identities into discursive formations. The problem is caused by the increasing level of theoretical priors and idiosyncratic personal expertise involved in synthesizing discourse from identities. The ultimate arbiter of this exercise is the reader, who offers alternative readings and so questions the very validity of my own.

Second, reliability depends a great deal on the instructions I give to my independent colleague. The most common procedure is to supply a selection of texts and the coding rules used, in this case perhaps a list of identities, and what constitutes evidence for their presence. This procedure should produce the highest level of intercoder reliability. But I could just give a sample of texts without any instructions other than "please find the identities here." The result would no doubt be fewer similar identities being

---

[88] As we take seriously the interactive effect of researcher and subject, our confidence in reliability dissipates.

recovered and also a collection of different identities. I raise these issues not to reduce confidence in the interpretivist method's reliability but rather to point out how extremely difficult it is to achieve.

Third, interpretivist epistemology, strictly speaking, expects no reliability at all, except under the easiest possible conditions of instructing my colleague about coding rules. Interpretivists expect each observer to produce her own unique effect on the evidence, textual or otherwise. This goes double during the move from identity to discourse.

Interpretivism is not commonly associated with the business of generalization and prediction, but it can be. Interpretivist epistemology eschews any pretensions to these ends because of its commitment to the proposition that every social reality is an open system, subject to hitherto undetected variables from within and outside. Every effort to generalize is therefore foolish because the social conditions that give rise to confidence in the understanding of the moment may disappear over time and certainly from place to place. Interpretivism assumes that social phenomena cannot be presumed to be identical across contexts; it holds that all phenomena are meaningfully different until demonstrated to be otherwise.[89]

Interpretivism is on the horns of a dilemma. It believes that somehow the interpretivist exercise of reconstructing a local web of meaning can obviate the problem of incommensurability, at least within a particular case. But why does this logic not also apply beyond the case? An open system has no boundaries, and yet interpretivists close boundaries, in effect, whenever they make validity claims within a case. Either they can make no such claims even within a case (but they do) or they must acknowledge the criteria for establishing boundaries within which meaningful similarity prevails across cases. I argue, cautiously, that the latter move is defensible. I further suggest that the ideal form of interpretivist epistemology is violated in the practice of executing its research. This thus makes interpretivism more of a generalizing and predictive method than intended.

Interpretivists themselves generalize. Clifford Geertz, for example, in his interpretation of the Balinese cock fight, attributes meaning to the actions of some and subsequently assigns the same meaning to others performing what he identifies as the "same" actions.[90] Other discursive analysts also generalize. Michel Foucault argues that his "archaeology provides the principle

---

[89] Charles Taylor, "Interpretation and the Sciences of Man," in *Interpretive Social Science: A Second Look* ed. Paul Rabinow and William M. Sullivan (Berkeley, 1987), 79. Ira J. Cohen, "Structuration Theory and Social *Praxis*," in *Social Theory Today*, ed. Anthony Giddens and Jonathan H. Turner (Stanford, 1987), especially 280–302.

[90] Clifford Geertz, "Deep Play: Notes on the Balinese Cockfight," in *Interpretive Social Science: A Second Look* ed. Paul Rabinow and William M. Sullivan (Berkeley, 1987), 195–240. On Geertz's use of generalization, see Alexander, *Fin de Siecle Social Theory*, 99–119.

of the discourse's articulation over a chain of successive events."[91] Bourdieu asserts that the habitus "produces practices which tend to reproduce regularities."[92]

So, what kind of generalizations can we safely make from interpretivist evidence? Those that can be justified using the theory and empirical evidence of the case. In this book, for example, I must first establish that the identities I have empirically recovered mean what I say they mean, aggregate into the discursive formations I say they do, and then become part of the social cognitive structure that characterized Moscow in 1955 and 1999. All this must be done before I demonstrate their effects on Soviet and Russian understandings of other states in those two years. Having done this, I can generalize from those findings only if I can justify the assertion that the theoretically meaningful parts of my account of identity are likely to be operative in the future and in other places. The defensibility of this claim will vary according to the substantive issue area.

Our confidence that a particular understanding of another state generalizes beyond the particular instance should increase the more deeply embedded it is in some discourse of the Self; the more it may be validated according to other, independently established, historical regularities; and the more alternative theoretical accounts reinforce its applicability to other times and sites. But, regardless of the level of confidence, it must be tentative and circumspect, modest and measured. The capacity to predict should be treated as a variable that never approaches unity, that may be zero, and that should always be regarded skeptically.[93]

Empirical generalizations must be quite limited and cautious, but this is not true of theoretical generalizations.[94] If my theoretical account of identity, discursive formations, and social cognitive structure turns out to account for Soviet and Russian understandings of other states, then the theory should be considered to be applicable to other domains, even though the empirical evidence itself is necessarily uniquely bound to its historical context.

Interpretivist practice demonstrates a greater potential for generalization and prediction than its epistemology, but the same claim is not true of the validity of its findings. Shared interpreted reality, or intersubjectivity, makes interpretivism go. Recovering this kind of reality requires an open ontology,

---

[91] Michel Foucault, *The Archaelogy of Knowledge* (New York, 1972), 167.

[92] Bourdieu, *Outline of a Theory of Practice*, 78.

[93] Jonathan H. Turner, for example, urges that we not confuse law with empirical generalization, in "Analytical Reasoning," in *Social Theory Today*, ed. Anthony Giddens and Jonathan H. Turner (Stanford, 1987), 160. The task here includes distinguishing between natural and social kinds.

[94] Stryker and Stratham, "Symbolic Interaction and Role Theory," 315.

one that admits that additional texts and meanings and identities are always present and unaccounted for. In this sense, all validity claims are only tentative. Interpretivists try to bound their theorized domain while recognizing its ultimate openness.[95] As Hans-Georg Gadamer observes about hermeneutics, its first principle "is to admit the endlessness of the task."[96] There is no place to stop, no place we can claim that we have accounted for all that we must account for. Instead, we must rely on conventions, mainstream neopositivist conventions, to ground any claims to validity. The most important is comparison to alternative understandings of the same phenomena. Relative working truth is the best we can hope for.

One possible demonstration of the validity of my theoretical findings would be that elements of the social cognitive structure that operated effectively to illuminate Soviet reality in 1955 were still operative in 1999. This finding would show that the method used here successfully captured identities that had become so embedded in social discourses as to be understood as structures.[97] A further demonstration of the validity of the theoretical account offered in this book would be its capacity to make Soviet and Russian understandings of other states intelligible.

Some conventions may increase confidence in the validity of the account I offer. My own interpretations should be compared to existing accounts. This includes not only my reading of Soviet and Russian identities, but also of the domestic context more comprehensively and the understandings of other states. If my rendition of the domestic scene is consistent with other independent accounts, the reader may be more confident in my account. If alternative theories of international politics, such as neorealism, liberalism, and systemic or normative constructivism, cannot satisfactorily capture the outcomes for which my own theoretical account offers a compelling understanding, the reader should have heightened confidence in its validity.

Confidence in an account and its predictions also stems from the nature of the cases selected. Hypotheses that pass a test in two identical or very similar cases should have less presumptive validity than hypotheses that prove compelling in different contexts. Clearly the communist state of the post-Stalinist Soviet Union of 1955 and the postcommunist, post-Soviet, democratizing, and liberalizing state of 1999 Russia were significantly different. Moreover, our confidence in a theory's validity is still more enhanced if a crucially hard case is selected. My theoretical account of identity assumes that even a semitotalitarian, authoritarian elite is in the area of foreign policy (presumably the most statist of all governmental outputs) subject to the

[95] Paul Rabinow and William M. Sullivan, "The Interpretive Turn," in *Interpretive Social Science: A Second Look*, ed. Paul Rabinow and William M. Sullivan (Berkeley, 1987), 14.

[96] Hans-Georg Gadamer, foreword, *Truth and Method* 2nd German ed. (New York, 1997), 340.

[97] Jürgen Habermas, *On the Logic of the Social Sciences* (Cambridge, Mass., 1994), 78–86.

influence of identities that operate in a presumably subordinated, repressed society. If this theory works under those conditions, then certainly we can expect it to be valid in less demanding, liberal democratic circumstances.

The presumptive validity of an account is increased if it offers an impressive empirical record in its support. I discuss my sampling principles in greater detail next, but it is important here to note that I used a broad range, large number, and wide variety of sources to compile the historical record on which the identities are not only gathered but tested.

Sampling Identity

The first question that most readers are likely to ask is, "Where did those identities come from?" This question demands a clear justification. In my choice of texts I sought both variety and representativeness. I outline the sample in table 1.

Nothing published in the Soviet Union in 1955 went uncensored. One objective, therefore, was to find texts less subject to intense scrutiny, such as the specialized journal *Sovetskaya Etnografiya*,[98] which was designed to help recover Russian and non-Russian ethnonational identities. Among the newspapers, *Literaturnaya Gazeta* is the least official, even under the editorship of Boris Riurikov. *Pravda*, the official publication of the Communist Party of the Soviet Union (CPSU), was chosen to represent the dominant party discourse. *Krasnaya Zvezda*, the official daily of the Main Political Administration of the Soviet armed forces was chosen to capture a military point of view. The proceedings of the Second Congress of Soviet Writers, convened in December 1954 but discussed throughout the subsequent year, were collected as a verbatim transcript and included a wide-ranging debate between the predominant discourse and the first emergent signs of difference. The Russian-language textbook for non-Russian speakers authored by Fedor Sovetkin was chosen especially for its elucidation of the relationship between Russian and non-Russian identities. The archives provided insights into elite understandings of domestic identities that I had recovered from public textual sources. The memoirs of Fedor Burlatsky, an aide to Nikita Khrushchev, and Alexei Adzhubei, his son-in-law, provided information about Khrushchev and his colleagues on the Presidium.

Finally, I included four novels that were very popular at the time: Vera Panova's *Span of the Year*, Aleksandr Korneichuk's *Wings*, Leonid Leonov's *The Russian Forest*, and Ilya Ehrenburg's *The Thaw*. The last gave its name to an entire period, but the other three are not well known outside the Soviet Union and Russia. However, contemporary accounts tell us that they

---

[98] Unless otherwise noted, all titles of Russian-language books, newspapers, and journals have been transliterated, and all titles of Russian-language articles have been translated into English by the author. In addition, all translations of Russian-language texts are by the author.

Table 1
Textual Sources of Identity

Moscow 1955			
Journals	Newspapers	Conferences	Writers
Kommunist	*Literaturnaia Gazeta*	Second Congress of	Ehrenburg
New Times	*Krasnaia Zvezda*	Soviet Writers	Korneichuk
Sovetskaia Etnografiia	*Pravda*		Leonov
			Panova

Memoirs	Archives		Textbooks
Adzhubei	AVPRF, Archives of the Foreign		Sovetkin
Burlatsky	Policy of the Russian Federation,		
Khrushchev	Ministry of Foreign Affairs		
	GARF, State Archive of		
	the Russian Federation,		
	Presidium special files		
	RTsKhIDNI, Russian Center		
	for the Preservation and		
	Documentation of Latest History		
	(formerly Institute of Marxism-		
	Leninism)		
	TsKhSD, Center for the Preservation of		
	Contemporary Documents (formerly		
	CPSU, Central Committee)		

Moscow 1999			
Journals	Newspapers	Serious Nonfiction	Novelists
Iskusstvo Kino	*Izvestiia*	Chubais	Koretskii
Kommersant Vlast	*Kommersant*	Magun	Leonov
	Komsomolskaia	Papernyi	Marinina
	Pravda	Vishnevskii	Pelevin
	Krasnaia Zvezda		
	Literaturnaia Gazeta		
	Moskovskie Novosti		
	Moskovskie Vesti		
	Moskovskii Komsomolets		
	Nezavisimaia Gazeta		
	Pravda		
	Segodnia		
	Sovetskaia Rossiia		
	Trud		
	Vecherniaia Moskva		
	Vremia		

(*continued*)

Table 1 (*continued*)
Textual Sources of Identity

Moscow 1999

Memoirs	Textbooks
Barkhatov	Bogoliubov
Falin	Danilov
Korzhakov	Dmitrenko
	Gadzhiev
	Ostrovskii
	Petrov
	Volchok
	Zuev

sparked a fair amount of controversy, and in the judgments of western scholars they all were significant, written by well-known and quite popular authors. Novels are an especially important textual source of evidence for my theoretical account of identity. Novels describe background daily practices, the commonplace habits of interpersonal relations, and the boundaries of normalcy. In them, examples of the unintended adherence to a discursive practice are likely to arise and incidental asides about identity are likely to be made.

Theorists of discourse and identity understand that popular fictional works are an especially important source of identity and its discursive practices.[99] Soviet novelists in 1955 were in the business of being as realistic as possible and so frequently reproduced the mundane background so critical to the theoretical account of identity offered here. It would not be inaccurate to suggest that novels provide, if only partially, hints at the "private transcripts" of Soviet daily reality,[100] the kinds of semipublic texts that allow deviance from the dominant discourse to penetrate into public consciousness. Because I could not conduct ethnographic research, I believe it is critical to try to retrieve from novels what conversation was like, casual conversation between average and not-so-average Soviets.[101] Novelists routinely recreate settings and situations for action, again providing an indirect textual representation of daily life. Finally, especially in the case of the Soviet Union, novels are perhaps the least official of any public text available. Berger and Luckmann explicitly recommend against becoming enthralled with theories, ideas, and

[99] Lincoln, *Discourse and the Construction of Society*, 7; Burke, "History of Events," 240–44; Moscovici, "Phenomenon of Social Representations," 52.

[100] Scott, *Domination and the Arts of Resistance* (New Haven, 1990), 26–28.

[101] Berger and Luckmann, *Social Construction of Reality*, 152–53.

worldviews in a society at the expense of attention paid to "commonsense ideas that must be the central focus" of anyone trying to recover the topography of identity.[102]

The sample for 1999 is similar to that for 1955, with important exceptions. First, there was at this time broad diversity in the daily press and so no need to ferret out hidden transcripts in obscure scholarly journals. I chose *Iskusstvo Kino*, however, because of its analysis of Russian film. Because I did not include Russian cinema in my sample of texts, I wanted to catch at least a glimpse of the medium through this critically acclaimed journal. I chose *Kommersant Vlast* simply because it is a high-quality weekly newsmagazine situated somewhere between *Time* and *Newsweek*, on the one hand, and *The Economist*, on the other. I sampled many more newspapers in 1999 than in 1955 simply because 1955 showed little variance from one paper to another, whereas in 1999, I could read the entire spectrum of Russian identity in the newspapers, from postmodern ironic treatments of daily life to premodern antisemitic and racist tracts. I stayed somewhere between those two extremes, choosing to sample fifteen papers once a month for the entire year. This yielded a total sample of some nine hundred articles to treat as texts, compared to the daily review of *Pravda* and *Literaturnaya Gazeta* in 1955 that presented some 2,100 articles for review.

The selections of serious nonfiction were made from conversations with Russian intellectuals who insisted that I must read these books. I selected novels through an informal survey of dozens of booksellers on Moscow's streets and metro landings, as well as cashiers in several *Dom Knigi* (House of Books). When I asked what books were selling best in late 1998 and early to mid-1999, four novelists came out on top (I chose for purely personal reasons not to read books on the occult). The three memoirs were by political elites and appeared in or around 1999. The textbooks were selected following the recommendations of sellers in pedagogical bookstores in Moscow. Again, no selections were made that were not mentioned by multiple sources. All the text books are recommended by the Russian Ministry of Higher Education for use in Russian high schools; many are in their second and third editions.

I used these sources to reconstruct Soviet and Russian identity in Moscow in 1955 and 1999. They are incomplete: there is no poetry, no cinema, no songs, and no television shows. But I believe the list is sufficiently representative, both broadly and deeply, to satisfy a test for surface validity.[103] Other scholars may argue that had I included a particular newspaper or novelist, my results would have been different. And that is how it should be—it is why interpretivists have such modest epistemological claims.

---

[102] Ibid., 13–14.
[103] Moscow itself was chosen because this is where foreign policy elites live and work.

For the dependent variable, Moscow's understandings of other states, I collected data for the two years in different ways. In the case of 1955, my sources were the archival records of the Central Committee (CC), Ministry of Foreign Affairs (MFA), the Soviet government, and the Presidium of the Communist Party. Foreign policy materials collected along with the domestic texts were read only after the domestic identities and discursive formations had been elaborated and hypotheses deduced from them about Soviet foreign policy choices. For 1999, there were no archival materials. I derived Russian elite understandings of other states from the open texts listed in table 1. Again, the two operations—recovering domestic identities and gathering evidence about Russian foreign policy choices—were done in that order.

Constructing Foreign Policy at Home

Every foreign policy decision maker is as much a member of the social cognitive structure that characterizes her society as any average citizen. Charged with the daily responsibility of understanding other states in world politics, she is most unlikely to be able to escape from this structure. Her understandings of these other states rely on her understandings of her own state's Self. In large part, understandings of Self are constructed domestically out of the many identities that constitute the discursive formations that, in turn, make up the social cognitive structure of that society.

It makes good sense to start a study of a state's understanding of other states at home, by reconstructing the topography of domestic identities in that state, working from there up and out to the decision maker herself. If we find that a domestic identity does indeed end up accounting for the understanding of another state, then we can have confidence that this way of understanding identity, in fact, works. If, however, we find that a state is understood differently from our hypothesized expectations, there are three possible explanations. First, we have failed to recover that identity from the domestic terrain, but with further research it may be accessible. Second, the decision maker herself has personal views that are unique and so have no trace in a discursive record. Third, the source of that particular identity is not within the state itself but rather is the product of interaction with other actors in world politics. These last two explanations are not part of the account of identity offered here.

In addition to these two omitted possibilities, I have consciously made other omissions. As already noted, I perform a textual recovery of identity in this book, not a practical or ethnographic one. This is a merely pragmatic choice in this instance. Further, I make no effort to perform a sociolinguistic analysis of Soviet and Russian identity. Neither semiotic nor speech act theory is applied, although, again, their use would doubtless be rewarding.

What follows is an assessment of whether the particular account of identity offered in this chapter can provide a convincing account for a state's understanding of other states in the world. In the next chapter, I reconstruct the domestic identity terrain of Moscow in 1955 and generate hypotheses about how Soviet leaders should have understood a variety of other states if in fact these identities were relevant to the construction of the Other. In chapter 3, using archival sources, I test whether the identities recovered in chapter 2 imply the understandings that appear in the analyses of Soviet elites of other states, in particular Yugoslavia, India, Egypt, China, and the West more generally. In chapter 4, I present the identity terrain of Moscow in 1999, including four discursive formations that I suggest these identities constitute, and I deduce hypotheses for Russian understandings of other states based on each of these four discourses. In chapter 5, I test these hypotheses against Russian understandings of other states, in particular Yugoslavia, China, the United States, and Europe. Finally, in chapter 6, I summarize the results of the empirical chapters and compare the performance of my second-image constructivist account with those of neorealism and of normative and systemic constructivism.

The Russian Nation, New Soviet Man, Class, and Modernity
Identity Relations in 1955

In this chapter, I elaborate the four most prevalent identities that constitute the predominant discursive formation and its sites of contestation in Moscow in 1955. I raise the possibility of connecting these identities, practices, and intersubjective understandings to Soviet understandings of Others abroad and I hypothesize that Soviet elites, understanding who the Soviet Union is in particular ways, understand Others in the world through these identities.[1]

SETTING THE SOVIET DOMESTIC STAGE IN MOSCOW 1955

At Joseph Stalin's death, the main contenders for leadership were Lavrentiia Beria, Vyacheslav Molotov, Giorgii Malenkov, and Nikita Khrushchev.[2] Of the party leadership, the Old Bolsheviks were Molotov, Lazar Kaganovich, Anastas Mikoyan, and Kliment Voroshilov. The influence of the secret police was seriously diminished after Stalin's death. Lavrentii Beria's execution in October 1953 left no representative of the police on either the Presidium or the CC Secretariat.[3] In February 1954, the Soviet leadership decided to cultivate virgin lands to increase agricultural output. By autumn 1955, an additional 32 million acres had been tilled in Kazakhstan and southern Siberia. Although 1954 was a big success, 1955 was a dismal failure; the harvest was saved only by bumper crops in Ukraine.

Khrushchev's January 1955 CC plenum speech was strongly in favor of heavy industry and other Stalinist totems. The next month the Supreme Soviet increased spending, compared to 1954 levels, on heavy industry by 27

[1] For a not unrelated strategy for reconstructing a topography of social identity, see Stephen Kotkin, *Magnetic Mountain: Stalinism as a Civilization* (Berkeley, 1995), especially chap. 5.

[2] Roger Pethybridge, *A Key to Soviet Politics: The Crisis of the Anti-Party Group* (New York, 1962), 47. See also George W. Breslauer, *Khrushchev and Brezhev as Leaders: Building Authority in Soviet Politics* (London, 1982); James G. Richter, *Khrushchev's Double Bind: International Pressures and Domestic Coalition Politics* (Baltimore, 1994).

[3] Pethybridge, *Key to Soviet Politics*, 17–41.

percent and reduced it on light industry by 23 percent. The production of producer goods rose by 16 percent in 1955, compared to 9 percent for consumer goods. The previous year had seen equal growth rates for both sectors.[4] Defense spending was increased by 12 percent in 1955, having been reduced by 10 percent the previous year.[5] Representatives of the military voted against Malenkov at the January 1955 plenum, the first time a plenum had been used in this way since 1934.[6] In January 1955, Khrushchev convinced the Presidium to oust Malenkov from his post as prime minister, charging him with excessive bias against heavy industry and too much favoritism toward the state over the party apparatus. Nikolai Bulganin succeeded him as chairman of the council of ministers.

At the July 1955 CC plenum, Khrushchev's suggestion to create a commission to investigate and report on Stalin's repressive past was supported only by Bulganin, Aleksandr Saburov, Mikhail Pervukhin, Aleksandr Kirichenko, and Suslov. Molotov, Voroshilov, and Lazar Kaganovich objected, and Mikoyan withheld judgment.[7] The resulting report, although exonerating Stalin of any malfeasance in suppressing the Left and Right oppositions on his road to power and in pursuing collectivization, excoriated him for the indiscriminate and politically motivated murders of thousands of party members, military officers, and intelligentsia.[8] By June 1955, several hundred thousand of Stalin's prisoners had been released, including those who had been imprisoned upon their return from German prisoner of war camps.[9]

Official de-Stalinization had barely begun in 1955 Moscow, and Khrushchev clearly had not yet emerged as the signature leader of the Soviet communist party and state. The Thaw had only just begun and there was plenty of political maneuvering under way around the most fundamental problems: food, individual freedom from the party and the state, and trade-offs between consumer welfare and military-industrial investment.

MOSCOW IDENTITIES IN 1955

The texts of Moscow 1955 reveal many more identities than can be discussed here.[10] The identities I have chosen are those that were distributed most

---

[4] Sidney Ploss, *Conflict and Decision-Making in Soviet Russia: A Case Study of Agricultural Policy, 1953–1963* (Princeton, 1965), 98.

[5] George D. Embree, *The Soviet Union between the 19th and 20th Party Congresses, 1952–1956* (The Hague, 1959), 277.

[6] Raymond L. Garthoff, *Soviet Strategy in the Nuclear Age* (New York, 1958), 24.

[7] Iurii V. Aksiutin, *Nikita Sergeevich Khrushchev: Materialy k Biografii* (Moscow, 1989), 32–33.

[8] Roy A. Medvedev and Zhores A. Medvedev, *Khrushchev: The Years in Power* (New York, 1978), 67–68.

[9] Ibid., 19–21; Embree, *Soviet Union*, 289.

[10] A partial list of identities that appear in texts (but in far fewer numbers than those that

broadly and deeply across and within the most texts. Not only did they appear in scholarly journals or popular novels, but they were also evident in elite discourse and official publications and pronouncements. There were four main identities at work. Although each had boundaries, each also related to the others, providing meaning for the others in an intertextual way. These four primary identities are class, modernity, nation, and the New Soviet Man (NSM).

In the following, I sketch out the bold lineaments of each identity by contextualizing it within its own textual sites. I then relate it to other identities, elaborating the apparent predominant discourse and where contestations occurred. I conclude with hypotheses about each identity's possible consequences for Soviet foreign policy choices in 1955.

Class

It is not surprising to find class analysis in Moscow in 1955; the Soviet Union was a Marxist-Leninist state. Class operated both substantively and syntactically. It provided substantive identity to individuals and groups based on their positions in the production process. The working class, peasantry, bourgeoisie, and intelligentsia were identities with substantive meaning. But class also operated syntactically, demanding that individuals and groups be related to one another in a hierarchical and binary fashion. Class identities were hierarchical in that the working class was at the apex of revolutionary potential, followed by its ally, the peasantry, and then, not so closely, by the working intelligentsia and petit bourgeoisie. At the bottom were the big bourgeoisie, the capitalists, and the imperialists—at the other end of the spectrum because they were the antithesis of revolutionary potential. They were the opposite, the Other. The hierarchical relationship is evident by reading class from top to bottom, following the arrow, in figure 2. Along with these ordered relations among class identities came their binary oppositions. The working class was not simply different from the bourgeoisie; they were diametric opposites. One cancelled out the other; an individual could not be both or a little of each. Either an individual was a worker or he was not. Either an individual was a bourgeois or she was something else. An individual could not be a bourgeois worker. Ambiguity, uncertainty, temporization, or just plain irrelevance was not allowed for anyone subjected to class analysis. The two factors together produced an identity, both binarized and hierarchical, arrayed along a metric of progressive and regressive, good and bad, friendly and hostile and permitting no escape from a fixed classification.

All identities are necessarily, at least partially, destructive of others, but

---

were chosen) includes citizen, family, language, party member, worker, Marxist, intelligentsia, patriot, veteran, and individual.

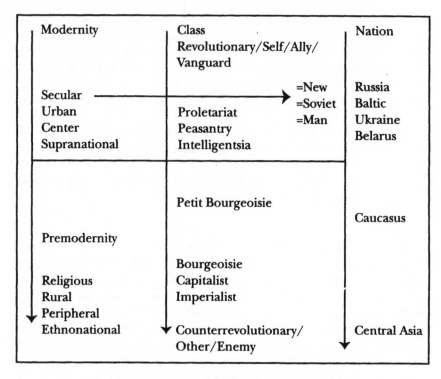

Figure 2 Topography of Identities, Moscow 1955

Soviet class identity, with its totalizing binarization, erased more Others than most. Because of its binary syntax and its understanding of this group membership as the single defining and essential feature of a person, class was privileged over national, ethnic, and individual identities.

At the Second Congress of the All-Union Soviet of Writers held in December 1954, Natan Rybak, a Ukrainian author, advanced the official view that Bogdan Khmelnitsky had led a liberation struggle to reunify Ukrainians with the "great, fraternal Russian people." But from whom had the Ukrainians liberated themselves? Rybak described a struggle against the Polish gentry, explicitly excluding "the Polish people in general."[11] This class-based analysis could not apprehend the struggle as either interethnic or international; instead, it could be construed only as a battle between antagonistic classes, the Polish landowners and the Ukrainian peasantry. In the dominant and official Soviet discourse of the time, class trumped nation. If a national identity still existed, it was the working class that maintained the

[11] *Vtoroi Vsesoiuznyi Syezd Sovetskikh Pisatelei: 15–26 Dekabrya 1954 Goda, Stenograficheskii Otchet* (Moscow, 1956), 227.

nation's "best traditions."[12] Nations in socialist societies were different from bourgeois nations because the latter still suffered from "antagonistic-class contradictions."[13] Class analysis erased any important national and ethnic identities and resulting differences in the Soviet Union. Industrialization begat a working class whose consciousness transcended nation.[14]

Class origins could also determine individual identity. In Vera Panova's novel *Span of the Year*, Gennady's father wonders how his son could have been such a miscreant: "If we had been former landowners or capitalists, you could understand it. But I have worked on the railroads since I was 14 and his mother was a cleaning woman. . . ."[15] In another popular novel of the time, Leonid Leonov's *The Russian Forest*, Polya imagines an encounter with her father, Vikhrov, whom she has never met, but whom she knows has been rumored to be of questionable class identity. She expects to confront him in a "sumptuous suite of carpeted rooms, with housemaids in starched caps, with plush curtains reeking of expensive cigars, capped off by a bronze bust of a double-headed eagle."[16] At the same time, being a member of the working class was desirable. Sergei, Vikhrov's adopted son, cannot escape the identity of being a professor's son, no matter how much zeal he puts into his job at the train station and even though "he looked more grimy-faced than anyone else," he never "belonged."[17] To some degree, a person's character was read through class. Bad conduct was explained by bourgeois practices, whereas those with working class backgrounds were expected to act like the new Soviet men and women they were.

It seems that Khrushchev understood society in class terms. He developed affirmative action programs for young people who worked after their tenth year of school. They were given advantages in admission to higher schools.[18] These "production candidates" had gotten their hands dirty with manual labor. Khrushchev disliked *beloruchky* (those with white hands), who only got academic and political medals from school.[19] Khrushchev's op-

---

[12] I. Grozdova, "Criticism and Bibliography," *Sovetskaia Etnografiia* (SE) 2 (1955), 177.

[13] "Editorial: The Great Power of Leninist Ideas of Internationalism," *Kommunist* 1 (1955): 6.

[14] B. Gafurov, "Friendship of Peoples—Source of Power for the Soviet State," *Pravda*, 15 August 1955, p. 3. Gafurov was the first secretary of the Tadzhik Communist Party at the time.

[15] Vera Panova, *Span of the Year* (Westport, 1977), 172.

[16] Leonid Leonov, *The Russian Forest* (Moscow, 1966), 33. She is surprised to find her expectations misplaced. Only near the end of the novel does she find such an office, but it belongs to her father's antagonist, Gratsiansky (694). Note the connection between class and imperial Russia.

[17] Ibid., 447.

[18] Mervyn Matthews, *Class and Society in Soviet Russia* (New York, 1972), 293.

[19] Mervyn Matthews, *Narodnoe Obrazovanie in the Soviet Union: Policies and Institutions since Stalin*, (London, 1982), 136. Fedor Burlatskii has observed that Khrushchev had a "black-white" view of the world. *Russkie Gosudari: Epokha Reformatsii, Nikita Smelyi, Mikhail Blazhennyi, Boris Krutoi* (Moscow, 1996).

position to Malenkov's support for a diversion of investment to consumer goods from heavy industry was rooted perhaps in Khrushchev's understanding of class and was not merely an effort to outmaneuver Malenkov politically. If Sidney Ploss is right and the beneficiaries of the increased production of consumer goods would have been primarily urban bureaucrats and the most highly paid workers, Khrushchev was the champion of the interests of the peasantry and broad working class.[20] Fedor Burlatskii has observed that even when he was in high positions, Khrushchev "psychologically did not desert his original profession of metalworker."[21]

But class identity need not be so total and destructive. At least in popular literary works, class identities transcend the simple binarizations of official discourse.[22] Understanding others according to their class origins was a complicated and contentious dimension of identity. Although apprehending someone as a member of a particular class may have had straightforward implications, understanding someone as having originated from a particular class was not so simple. After all, what if yesterday's peasant is today's proletarian? Or, and this almost nullified the universalizing effects of class, what if someone is a member of a class, but not at all of that class?

For example, in *The Russian Forest*, Lena is introduced as an abandoned waif who comes to rest within a landlord's family before the Bolshevik Revolution. She is horrified that her turn will come to be "sued for the past, even for things of which she knew nothing."[23] Lena demonstrates, through her "everyday practice" as a nurse in the village, that the dominance of a formal class identity over all other aspects of understanding is misguided.[24] As the novel develops, Lena repeatedly transcends her accidental class origins, becoming a local deputy, although her husband, Vikhrov, is attacked on the basis of his selection of her as his wife. But the effort to undermine Vikhrov through his wife's unfortunate association with the Sapegin family is depicted as illegitimate and unavailing.[25] Class identity had lost its power to fix

[20] Ploss, *Conflict and Decision-Making in Soviet Russia*, 93. Ploss makes this argument only in passing, but offers evidence consistent with this interpretation.

[21] Burlatskii, *Russkie Gosudari*, 24.

[22] The Russian semotician and folklorist Iurii Lotman writes that Russia is historically predisposed to think in binary terms. Iurii M. Lotman and Boris A. Uspenskii, "Binary Models in the Dynamics of Russian Culture to the End of the Eighteenth Century," in *The Semiotics of Russian Cultural History*, ed. Alexander D. Nakhimovsky and Alice Stone Nakhimovsky (Ithaca, 1985), especially 32–33. Vladimir Paperny traces a large collection of binaries in the Soviet Union from the early postrevolutionary years to Stalin's death in *Kultura Dva* (Moscow, 1996), which is a kind of linguistic architectural history of the Soviet Union. See also Sergei Medvedev, "Power, Space, and Russian Foreign Policy," in *Understandings of Russian Foreign Policy*, ed. Ted Hopf (University Park, 1999), 15–56.

[23] Leonov, *Russian Forest*, 371.

[24] Ibid., 390.

[25] Ibid., 421.

hierarchies and binary oppositions. Other identities, such as that of nurse, developed through daily practice, could trump class, if the person did not behave like the despised bourgeois Other.

Class analysis related directly to the understanding of other states. A proletariat who ignored the need to include the peasantry in a revolutionary coalition could not prevail, according to the dominant Soviet discourse. Some Soviets could countenance alliances with the working intelligentsia and even the petit bourgeoisie, but these alliances assumed that the proletariat would be in the vanguard and that the revolutionary process itself would transform the less reliable classes into groups with more advanced revolutionary consciousness. If Soviet leaders understood the external world through the dominant discourse on class identities, we expect that they would welcome as allies only those they could identify as classmates, thereby binarizing the world into two irreconcilable camps. If, however, the Soviet understanding of its own class identity was characterized by a relaxation of hierarchy and binarization, then we expect a more catholic alliance policy in foreign affairs. Alliance choice in the domain of class should come down to whether Others were indeed binarized Others or just different from the Soviet Self.

Modernity

The Soviet project was one of the three most modern endeavors of the twentieth century, along with fascism and liberalism. Rational, secular, industrial, material, supranational, and ahistorical, the construction of socialism in the Soviet Union was supposed to confer a modern identity on all Soviets.[26] Modernity, like class, offered a hierarchical ordering principle— from primitive to modern. The hierarchy from modernity to premodernity, and its constitutive elements, is presented in figure 2, reading from top to bottom, following the arrow. But unlike class, there was no binary opposition between the two. Instead, individuals, nations, and countries were understood to be somewhere on the path to modernity, with the Soviet Union and the capitalist West being furthest along the road.[27] The discourse of modernity comprised three identities: religion, the relationship between town and country, and the relationship between the Moscow center and the Soviet periphery. Being modern could not be separated from an individual's class identity. The closer an individual came to proletarian status, the more modern he was.

[26] Max Horkheimer and Theodor W. Adorno, *Dialectic of Enlightenment* (New York, 1993). See also Kotkin, *Magnetic Mountain;* Susan Buck-Morss, *Dreamworld and Catastrophe: The Passing of Mass Utopia in East and West* (Cambridge, Mass., 2000), especially chap. 1.

[27] On the exercise of power entailed by denying an Other a modern identity, see Edward E. Sampson, *Celebrating the Other: A Dialogic Account of Human Nature* (Boulder, 1993), 157.

It is important to not read our ideas of modern into Soviet conceptions of modern in 1955. Being modern was not embracing technology, progressive politics, sexual emancipation, or convenient and abundant consumption. Instead, being modern was being on the road to communism, dealing with problems rationally and quantitatively, eschewing religious beliefs, extolling the construction of dams, factories, and hydroelectric projects, measuring progress by material indicators, leaving ethnic and national identities behind, and treating history as just an interesting story.[28] After all, modern Soviets were building a future not tied to the past. Socialism was strong through "its faith in the victory of the new over the obsolete."[29] The ideal Soviet worker was modern in all these ways; it was hoped the peasant and the intelligentsia would be someday. There was no hope for the bourgeois.

The discourse of modernity manifested itself in many ways. A. K. Pisarchik described the emergence of modernity in a Tajik village, reporting what was new there: "new production relations, a new consciousness, a new position for women, radios, schools, new holidays (in particular, May 1 and November 7 are the 'most happy and joyous celebrations,' instead of Ramadan or the rites of spring), industrially-produced clothing and food." The only thing holding back these "mountain Tajiks" was, according to their ethnographer, "some old customs and superstitions."[30]

The official discourse of modernity, although predominant, was riddled with ambiguity and tension. In June 1954, the Institute of World Literature and the Institute of Eastern Studies sponsored a conference in Moscow on how to study the epics of the Soviet peoples. Its proceedings reveal an intense debate between those scholars who wished to appropriate these epics in order to offer modern ahistorical Soviet interpretations of the past and those who demanded local, historicized understandings. The latter felt that having "epic heroes mouth revolutionary speeches" should be impermissible.[31] T. M. Akimova, in particular, objected to authors writing about Rus-

---

[28] In 1955, the editors of *Pravda* selected 369 photographs for its front page. Of these, fully one-third, or 123, were of physical, material Soviet modernity: industrial plants, dams, steam shovels, locomotives, turbines, hydroelectric stations, cargo ships, coal mines, a nuclear research reactor, lathes, blast furnaces, and so on. There were 56 photos of the Soviet countryside, but most of these featured tractors, mechanized milking equipment, and other features of material modernity, not bucolic bliss. In comparison, there were only 21 photos of Soviets enjoying themselves (less than 4 percent) at the beach, in parks, at health sanatoria, and the like.

[29] "Noble Task of Soviet Literature," *Pravda*, 18 September 1955, p. 1.

[30] A. K. Pisarchik, "Garm Ethnographic Expecition 1954," *SE* 4 (1955): 134. See also "Holiday of Culture for the Turkmen People," *Pravda*, 14 October 1955, p. 2.

[31] U. B. Dalgat-Chavtaraeva, "Meeting on Questions for Studying the Epics of the Peoples of the USSR," *SE* 1 (1955): 178–80. See also T. M. Akimova, "Peoples of the USSR," *SE* 1 (1955): 195.

sian fairy tales of the seventeenth century as if they were derivatives of Soviet songs sung in the twentieth.[32]

There were also occasions on which it was acknowledged that premodernity had something to offer contemporaneous socialist forms. A. D. Bekhman observed that by studying the history of housing, the new manufactured housing for collective farmers could take into account "local construction traditions and the experience of folk architecture."[33] One rare occasion on which premodernity struck back was a letter to the editor of *Pravda* in which a corresponding member of the Academy of Medical Sciences of the USSR lambasted a dissertation on Kirghiz folk medicine.[34] The expected treatment of this theme within the dominant discourse would have been to treat Kirghiz folk remedies with ridicule, and this was precisely what the dissertation writer did. But the writer of the letter accused the graduate student of abject ignorance for not appreciating the possible contributions of Kirghiz folk medicine to modern Soviet medical practice.

Some numbers: Moscow had disproportionately few of the country's churches. Of the 13,400 churches that existed in 1958 only 212 of them were in Moscow, compared to, for example, 2,100 in Lviv *oblast* in western Ukraine, 600 in Kiev, and 300 in Kursk. In 1955, one-half of all children born in Moscow were still baptized. And, reflecting deep differences in generational and gender identity, 83 percent of public churchgoers were women and 90 percent were over 50 years of age.[35]

Religious identities were one of the most salient markers of premodernity within the predominant discourse. Modernity's eventual triumph over religious identity was to occur through the inexorable work of class and generational identity. Proletarian consciousness would crowd out the need for religious identity, and the replacement of the old by the young would naturally eliminate the carriers of obsolete religious ideas. Soviet officials were

[32] Akimova, "Peoples of the USSR," 193–94.

[33] A. D. Bekhman, "Features of the New in the Architecture of Russian Peasant Housing," *SE* 3 (1955): 55.

[34] I. Akhunbaev, "About One Illiterate Dissertation," *Pravda*, 12 November 1955, p. 2.

[35] Nathaniel Davis, *A Long Walk to Church: A Contemporary History of Russian Orthodoxy* (Boulder, 1995), 33, 198–210. In a report to the CC, the Council of the Orthodox Church communicated that on the January 19 holiday of the Epiphany there were long lines at Moscow churches, sometimes up to eight hundred people, mostly old women. Center for the Preservation of Contemporary Documentation, fond 5, opis 30, delo 93, stranitsa 9. [henceforth TsKhSD, f., op., d., p.)

scrupulous in reporting the age and sex of religious observers in their reports on gatherings of believers to the CC.[36]

But it was also realized, as a practical matter, that eliminating the social practices that constituted these identities at an acclerated pace was an "error."[37] Nevertheless, the tension between a semitolerant state and the perpetuation of these unwanted religious ideas was palpable. The readers of *Sovetskaya Etnografiya* were warned against mistaking religious practices for mere traditional customs. The editors identified baptism, circumcision, communion, miracle-working, and holy shrines as the kinds of social practices that had deep religious content.[38] This set of guidelines about understanding religious practice was spurred by the November 1954 CC decree "On Errors in Scientific-Atheistic Propaganda among the People," which was supposed to reduce excessive harrassment of churchgoers in the Soviet Union. The language of this official understanding of religious practice was so vague that in February 1955 the State Committee on the Affairs of the Russian Orthodox Church reported to the CC instances of *oblast* committee (*obkom*) party secretaries misleading people by interpreting the CC decision as if it "meant that all were free to worship with no interference from anyone."[39] Even the stoning of a village soviet (*selsoviet*) chairman was blamed on the chairman, not the enraged believers. The story that was reported to the CC was that a sacred well that had been filled in under Stalin had been restored in June 1955 by the Orthodox community in Orlovskii *oblast* to celebrate a holy day. The *selsoviet* chairman, Kireev, kept filling it in and posted guards to keep people away. Despite the fact that the villagers eventually stoned the chairman and his security detail, State Committe Chairman Karpov reported to the CC that this was a case of "unadvisable administrative" methods for dealing with believers.[40]

Meanwhile, there was a series of public official acts that appeared to mark heightened official value for religion in the Soviet Union. Two Catholic bishops were consecrated in Lithuania in accordance with the instructions of the Vatican. During the summer, church leaders began to appear at official receptions for foreign dignitaries. The Pandida Kambo Lama, spiritual leader of Soviet Buddhists, was brought to Moscow to meet U Nu of Burma. In addition, some limited church rebuilding was begun and the first new edition

---

[36] See, for example, G. G. Karpov, July 30 report to the CC, *TSKhSD*, f. 5, op. 30, d. 93, pp. 22–25.

[37] From the CPSU CC plenum of November 1954, in "Tasks of Soviet Ethnography in Conducting Scientific-Atheistic Propaganda," *SE* 1 (1955): 3. Davis argues that this resolution was signed by Khrushchev in order to end a vigorous antireligious campaign that had gone on the previous five years. Davis, *Long Walk to Church*, 30.

[38] "Tasks," 5.

[39] TsKhSD, f. 5, op. 30, d. 93, p. 10.

[40] Ibid., 25.

of the Orthodox Bible since 1917 was published.[41] Both Metropolitan Krutitskii and Kolomenskoi Nikolai were awarded Orders of the Red Banner in the Kremlin by Voroshilov, chairman of the Presidium of the Supreme Soviet. True, in his congratulatory remarks Voroshilov never mentioned religion, but the metropolitan did note his "church duties," even if couched in terms of "civic feelings and love for the Rodina [Motherland]."[42] The next day Mufti Ishan Babakhan ibn Abdulmadzhikhan, chairman of the spiritual council of central Asian and Kazakh Muslims, was awarded the Order of the Working Red Banner. Religion was not mentioned at the ceremony.[43]

At the prosaic level, popular writers spoke of religion in their novels in passing, without comment, as if such practices were a natural part of daily life. In so doing, these authors did much more to reproduce the normalcy of religious practice than had they written treatises defending it. Panova in *Span of The Year* describes Dorofea making the sign of the cross over her future husband, shot and lying on a train, "the only symbol of blessing and safeguard she knew." A man apologizes for not drinking on a woman's saint's day. Other men discuss whether it is possible to believe in God, with no conclusion. In this way, the popular novel reproduced a religious identity for its reader through inadvertence; religious practice was presented as background. In *The Russian Forest,* "because she had nothing else to give her at parting," an old woman makes the sign of the cross over Polya as she is about to resume her espionage behind German lines in December 1941.[44] A Russian who helps save Polya's life makes the sign of the cross before the Germans hang him.[45]

The practice of Islam, primarily in central Asia, received a far less tolerant understanding in the predominant discourse than did Orthodox practice by Russians, perhaps because religious practice in central Asia was understood in Moscow as constitutive of national identities. No similar concern appeared to have existed of Orthodox practices reproducing the Russian nation. Traditional wedding ceremonies, bride prices, and marriages between minors were seen as evidence of the need to increase atheistic agitational-propaganda (agitprop) in central Asia.[46] In *Pravda* a man with five wives was condemned for his "amoral" behavior. The lesson was that the *obkom* secretary should "struggle against people who manifest feudal-bai attitudes toward women." The *oblast* procurator was to investigate the matter

[41] Embree, *Soviet Union,* 286–87.

[42] *Pravda,* 17 August 1955, p. 1.

[43] *Pravda,* 18 August 1955, p. 2. But the mufti received his award from Uzbekistan CC member Sharof Rashidov in Tashkent, not from CPSU Presidium member Voroshilov in Moscow.

[44] Leonov, *Russian Forest,* 606–7.

[45] Ibid., 612.

[46] "Sessions Devoted to the Results of Expeditionary Work in 1954," *SE* 3 (1955): 158.

and make the polygamist answerable for his actions.[47] Here the connection between religion and class backwardness was manifest.

Religious identity was officially premodern in 1955 Moscow, but was increasingly tolerated as a widespread social practice among millions of believers. Although it was not understood as making any kind of contribution to the modern Soviet project, unlike traditional medicine, aesthetic vernacular, or historical authenticity, it was understood as a part of Soviet identity, if even undesirable.

One of the more prominent identity narratives embedded within the discourse on modernity was the understanding that the norms and practices of urban life would eventually replace those characteristic of the countryside.[48] In trying to make the countryside modern, official Soviet representations often tried to blur any differences between country and city life. In Fedor Sovetkin's Russian-language textbook, he has pictures of a worker's home and a collective farmer's home on facing pages. They are indistinguishable.[49] In a review of two ethnographies of Tajik and Uzbek peasantry, I. Gurvich criticizes the authors for paying too much attention to "the old forms of daily life," such as illustrations of "poverty-stricken homes and primitive tools," instead of new homes.[50] In the Yakut Museum, there was a modern home of a local coalminer, distinguished by "contemporary urban furniture, carpets, lace curtains, a bookstand with books, and a telephone." The coalminer, the worker, was represented as more developed than the local *kolkhoznik* (collective farmer). In his log home there was "electricity, a radio, and store-bought furniture," all symbols of rural modernity. Only his carved cupboard with "national ornamentation, the details of his clothing, and the fur shoes speak of national traditions." Note how national identity was related to the official discourse on premodernity.[51]

---

[47] *Pravda*, 5 January 1955, p. 2. See also M. Chunakov, "We Are Going to Moscow . . . before the Dekada of Turkmen Literature and Art," *Pravda*, 4 October 1955, p. 2. The *dekada* was a celebration held both in Moscow and in the home republic aimed at commemorating that people's Soviet culture. Each republic's *dekada* would be invited to Moscow to present its culture to an official audience in the center.

[48] Closely related to this were official Soviet attitudes toward typical daily life (*byt*) after the revolution. It was seen as reactionary, less-developed, and potentially counterrevolutionary. Only Stalin's rise to power in the early 1930s brought a halt to the attacks on this *poshylyi* way of life. See Svetlana Boym, *Common Places: Mythologies of Everyday Life in Russia* (Cambridge, Mass., 1994), especially 29–48; Vera S. Dunham, *In Stalin's Time: Middleclass Values in Soviet Fiction* (Durham, 1990).

[49] Fedor F. Sovetkin, *Uchebnik Russkogo Yazyka dlya Molodezhi, ne Vladeiushchei Russkim Yazykom* (Moscow, 1954), 22–23.

[50] O. A. Sukhareva, "Ethnographic Study of the Kolkhoz Peasantry of Central Asia," *SE* 3 (1955): 37.

[51] I. Gurvich, "Ethnographic Materials in the Yakut Local Museum," *SE* 2 (1955): 135.

Significantly, aspects of Russian national premodernity were criticized more for their bad taste than as signs of a premodern national identity. L. N. Chizhikova and M. N. Shmeleva endorse Tambov villagers' use of oil paintings, plaster, and "urban furniture of factory production," but decry the "influence of urban lower middle class tastes" of the early twentieth century. "Many of the rooms are tastelessly decorated with postcards, photographs, posters, pages from magazines, paper flowers, and repulsively blotched rugs of which too many are sold in the Sosnovka bazaar."[52] But unlike Gurvich, who scornfully describes Yakut national customs as backward, local "traditional forms of Russian folk architecture" are discussed as "valuable progressive achievements of preceding periods . . . which are acquiring new features appropriate for socialist daily life."[53] The predominant discourse of modernity had different positions for Russian and non-Russian primitiveness.

In *Span of the Year,* characters brag to their country cousins about the comforts of life in the town, even while living miserably.[54] In *The Russian Forest,* a Muscovite tells Polya, "'You are that girl from the provinces—sorry, the periphery,' she corrected herself after the fashion of the age, which strove to level all citizens so that none felt offended."[55] Varya ridicules her father for preferring a crude painting of a gypsy on his office wall to a rendition of the Magnitogorsk power station complex.[56] Polya herself, after six weeks in Moscow, "was glad that the silly shine of provincial newness was rubbed off her at last."[57] The subordinate position of the country to the city is reflected in an exchange between Gratsiansky and Vikhrov, antagonists in *The Russian Forest.* Gratsiansky asks Vikhrov perfunctorily how things are going and then doesn't wait to hear Vikhrov's "provincially conscientious report."[58] The slow-witted, although honest, rubes from the sticks (or the depths, *glubinka,* in Russian) just could not ever keep up with the urbane sophisticates from Petersburg.

Khrushchev's recollections combine issues of class, modernity, and urban-rural difference. Not only does he refer to a hierarchy between urban and rural, and worker and peasant, but even among the workers he differentiates between those who are more and less modern. He writes that construction work and masonry were for those from the countryside who had less class self-consciousness than metalworkers. Khrushchev offers the following anecdote: "One builder is laying bricks handed to him by another. The one

[52] L. N. Chizhikova and M. N. Shmeleva, "Contemporary Russian Peasant Housing," *SE* 1 (1955): 70.

[53] Ibid., 71. See also Bekhman, "Features," 55.

[54] Panova, *Span of the Year,* 58.

[55] Leonov, *Russian Forest,* 12.

[56] Ibid., 25.

[57] Ibid., 196.

[58] Ibid., 639.

above yells, Vanka, give me more stuff. What stuff? A pail of water. There is none; a cow came and drank it."[59]

Khrushchev's sixtieth birthday party at his Moscow *dacha* showed his relationship to the countryside and how this positioned him with respect to his more modern colleagues. Molotov, Malenkov, Voroshilov, Mikoyan, and Bulganin helped him celebrate in 1954. Aleksei Adhzubei, Khrushchev's son-in-law, describes the scene as if the country bumpkin had wandered into an urban salon: "Khrushchev, with a chapped, sun-burned face, with a halo of gray hair around a mighty skull, was like an arriving relative who was violating the decorous order of the feast. That evening he was in his best form, spouting proverbs, sayings, puns, and Ukrainian stories." Khrushchev was conscious of the difference his own actions were creating with his guests, feeling that his "simple-mindedness would grate on some of his guests, but this did not at all bother him. . . . Without a jacket, in a Ukrainian shirt . . . Khrushchev invited his guests to take off their jackets, but nobody wanted to."[60] As Adzhubei tells it, Khrushchev was the very embodiment of the backward Soviet countryside, whereas his colleagues understood themselves as the inevitable modern future.[61]

Although the predominant discourse was certainly about the superiority of the modern urban future over the primitive country past, there were popular accounts of the countryside that celebrated its stability, simplicity, security, and small scale over the stormy, complicated, demanding, and impersonal qualities of life in the urban Soviet Union.[62] The periphery, closer to the people, was understood as being superior to the center, where "all those armchair agronomists . . . help our leaders plough and sow on paper. Do they give any thought to this in Moscow?"[63] This observation occurs in *Wings*, the Aleksandr Korneichuk play to which, at its opening performance in Moscow, Khrushchev gave a standing ovation.

In sum, the Soviet discourse on modernity privileged the urban over the

---

[59] Nikita Khrushchev, *Vospominaniia. Izbrannye Fragmenty* (Moscow, 1997), 139.

[60] Aleksei Adzhubei, *Te Desiat Let* (Moscow, 1989), 97–98. Khrushchev's earthier bearing was strikingly apparent in a comparison of his speeches in India to those of his traveling companion, Bulganin, to whom he refers as "my friend." The familiarity was not reciprocated. *New Times*, no. 52 (December 22, 1955).

[61] However, Khrushchev did not appear to wish a rural future for his son, Sergei. He called the potato harvest the "greatest stupidity" because "yesterday I found out that my Sergei is leaving for a week to Volokolomaskii region to pick potatoes. Calculate what these potatoes are worth to us. This value is not taken into account, but he will tear up his shoes, he does not have the right clothes, and all these he will tear up. This is not taken into account at all." TsKhSD, f. 5, op. 30, d. 107, p. 181.

[62] Leonov, *Russian Forest*, 684.

[63] Aleksandr Korneichuk, *Wings*, trans. John Gibbons, (Moscow, 1957), 49. These are the words of Varvara Dolina, a very productive *kolkhoz* worker to Pyotr Romodan, a new *obkom* first secretary.

rural, most especially at the material level of understanding. Phones, machines, radios, electricity, industrially produced goods, proper decorative accoutrement, and sophisticated habits of speech and dress were all signs of superior modernity. The only way in which the rural was valued was for its homespun and sincere character, often embodied by Khrushchev himself.

Modernity, projected into religion and the urban-rural divide, was embedded as well in discussions of the center and the periphery, or regional identities. There was a hierarchy among Soviet places.

Aleksei Surkov differentiated literatures according to "maturity," establishing a hierarchy among non-Russian literatures. He identified Ukrainian and Latvian as the most mature, followed by Georgian, Armenian, and Azeri in the next tier.[64] This hierarchy of identity—Russia, Slavic Ukraine and Belarus, Baltic republics, Caucasus, and then central Asia—was reproduced in many places, including Soviet civil defense plans in case of atomic war with the United States. In a letter attached to a February 10 memorandum from the minister of internal affairs, Sergei Kruglov; minister of defense, General Georgy Zhukov; and minister of medium machine building (the atomic weapons labs), Boris Vannikov, the coauthors rank Soviet cities according to political, economic, and strategic significance. They identify three groups. But even before specifying them, they identify the center— Moscow and Leningrad are above categorization. What did it mean to be in one group rather than another? Seventy percent of the populations of Moscow and Leningrad were slated for civil defense protection in the event of an atomic attack, but only 40 percent of the populations of group 1 cities, 30 percent of group 2, and 20 percent of group 3. The hierarchy of importance clearly was reflected in more than just literary discussions.[65]

Konstantin Simonov, successor to Aleksandr Tvardovsky as editor of *Novyi Mir,* the most widely read literary journal at the time, told the writers' congress who lived in the periphery and who in the center. He called Moscow and Leningrad the "customary literary centers," whereas Kursk, Rostov, Voronezh, Krasnoyarsk, Khabarovsk, Simferopol, Novosibirsk, and Omsk were parts of the "periphery."[66] The authors from that periphery replied with sarcasm. Georgii Markov, hailing from Irkutsk, noted that "we, Siberian writers, rarely, extremely rarely, see among us writers from Moscow and Leningrad. Come, comrades, see what is happening with us."[67] Galina Nikolaeva

---

[64] *Vtoroi Vsesoiuznyi Syezd Sovetskikh Pisatelei,* 13. Surkov was the first secretary of the writers' union.

[65] State Archives of the Russian Federation [hereafter GARF], Khrushchev special file, t. II, op. 3, d. 464, p. 366.

[66] *Vtoroi Vsesoiuznyi Syezd Sovetskikh Pisatelei,* 84.

[67] Ibid., 122. Other Russians also complained that Russian Soviet literature written not in Moscow and Leningrad had been ignored at the congress, for example, 290–91.

defended the center, commenting that, although she agreed with Valentin Ovechkin and Mikhail Sholokhov that writers should spend time outside of Moscow, "this suggestion is hard to fulfill, because a certain asceticism would be necessary, a renunciation of all the conveniences of the capital, to which we have become so accustomed."[68] Her sentiments were supported by Aleksandr Fadeev, who advised Ovechkin not "to flaunt his knowledge of life in comparision with his other colleagues."[69] The implication was that real life was in the periphery, not in the urban confines of Moscow. This was met by applause.

The main delegate from Udmurtiia invited his colleagues to "liberate themselves from the extraordinary attractive power of the Crimea and the Caucasus" and come to his republic, where "they should not be surprised to find that they are no longer felling trees by hand . . . , but in fact use the same modern technology as elsewhere in the Soviet Union."[70] Being in Moscow or Leningrad was being more modern and hence more developed along the (r)evolutionary road to socialism.

A Soviet understanding of itself as modern had implications for how it apprehended other states in the world. We expect that Soviets would understand other countries using the same array of practices that they believed constitute modernity at home. The first consequence would be an effort to find out just how modern other states might be compared to the Soviet Union. We can, for example, imagine Pisarchik conducting his ethnographic work not in Tajikistan but in countries such as Germany, China, Yugoslavia, or Egypt. Because industrial production was the single most important material indicator of modernity, it would not be hard to predict which country ended up where in the Soviet hierarchy. Given the Soviet appreciation that parts of the Soviet Union, in particular central Asia, were moving from premodernity to modernity, we expect the Soviets to have appreciated that many parts of the world, especially the decolonizing and recently liberated parts, were in a modernizing position as well.

Soviet modern identity got more complicated when its religious component was introduced. Officially, at least, virtually every country in the world was far less secular than the modern Soviet Union. On the other hand, Soviet tolerance of religious identity in 1955 was growing, but perhaps only of the kind of belief that did not threaten to reproduce minority national identities that were, in turn, obstacles to the establishment of more progressive class consciousness, or socialism. It is possible that Soviet analyses of religious identities in other countries did not always see them as significant hin-

---

[68] Ibid., 386.
[69] Ibid., 507.
[70] Ibid., 492.

drances to modernity and socialism. It could also be expected that some religions, such as Islam, excited more Soviet anxiety because the social practices that constituted them were understood as obstacles to the development of class consciousness and a more modern identity. We also expect Soviets to have equated modernity with more urbanized countries, apprehending rural agricultural states as backward and premodern. The official Soviet appreciation of the rural in other countries was most likely to have come from Khrushchev himself, if anyone.

Nation

It has been argued by many historians of nationalism that every nation needs a usable past.[71] But what could be a usable Soviet past? Because of its identity as a modern supranational phenomenon, it could not look back to any particular native territory or primordial creation myth.[72] The Soviet Union was the product of a revolutionary ideology, a vanguard party, and a victorious alliance of peasantry and proletariat. There was no usable past prior to the Great October Socialist Revolution of 1917—at least officially. But in fact, the usable past that was continually invoked in 1955 to situate the Soviet Union was the Russian past. This social practice of reproducing a Russian historical identity as more central to the triumph of the present system than any non-Russian contribution manifested itself in many ways.

The single most significant and pervasive aspect of Russian national identity was its relationship to non-Russian identities in the Soviet Union. And the most common relationship between Russian and non-Russian was the hierarchical subordination of all non-Russian nations to their Russian vanguard, their older brother, as it was so often put. This understanding was consonant with the pre-modern identity ascribed to non-Russians living in the periphery by Russians living in the center. The hierarchical relationship between Russia at the top and Central Asia at the bottom can be read in figure 2. Only much more rarely was it acknowledged that Russian national identity was being affected positively by its interactions with non-Russians, although at least the possibility was acknowledged. But non-Russian national identities were not simply acted on by Russian national discourse. In part because of the Soviet affirmative action policy in non-Russian areas of the Soviet Union, non-Russian national identities were being reproduced on a

---

[71] For example, Anthony Smith, *The Ethnic Origins of Nations* (London, 1987); Benedict Anderson, *Imagined Communities: Reflections on the Origin and Spread of Nationalism* (London, 1991).

[72] Indeed, the very modernity of the Soviet project denied it the most powerful social practices: tradition, habit, and custom. These exert their constitutive power when they are "understood simply as how things were, are, and should be done." Anthony Giddens, *Central Problems in Social Theory* (Berkeley, 1979), 200. I thank David Hoffmann for stressing this point to me.

daily basis, within the hierarchical structure already described. And the Russian identity would have been impossible without its myriad peripheral nations to serve as significant Others.

Soviet national identity was Russian. Russian national identity was the modern vanguard for non-Russians in the periphery. Russia was at the top, with all others aspiring to erase the difference between them and the Russian center as quickly as possible. But non-Russian national identities were also being reproduced through daily practice, even within this hierarchical identity topography. Although the Stalinist slogan of national in form, socialist in content[73] was the official structure within which national identities had to operate, in fact the actual structured relationships were far more complicated and might be characterized as hierarchical in form, with Soviet national content.

Two kinds of social practices characterize the reproduction of the identity arrangments. The first are simply explicit declarations of difference and subordination. The second are inadvertent daily practices, the processes that naturalize and normalize the more open assertions. An example of the first was Stalin declaring that the essence of the national question in the Soviet Union was to "destroy the economic, political, and cultural backwardness of certain nations . . . in order to give them the opportunity to catch up with central Russia. . . ."[74] An example of the second, naturalizing practice was the omission of any mention of the Russian people in the eighty-nine May Day Theses.[75] The absence of any national identity in this most official of declarations reminded readers that the modern ideal of a supranational Soviet Union was still alive.

The Soviet Union appropriated the Russian national story as if it were the natural progenitor of the Bolshevik Revolution. In Sovetkin's Russian-language textbook for non-Russians, the student is presented with many patriotic themes about the Motherland, but they are all essentially Russian. The military history is a series of heroic Russian exploits. Stalin's November 1941 speech during the military parade on Red Square is quoted, calling on all to remember a pleiad of Russian military greats. It is followed by stories about Aleksandr Nevskii, Dmitrii Donskoi, Aleksandr Suvorov, Mikhail Kutuzov, Kliment Voroshilov, and Semen Budyennyi.[76] Sovetkin's text appeals

---

[73] Stalin unveiled this formulation at the sixteenth Party Congress in 1930. See Robert Conquest, *Soviet Nationalities Policy in Practice* (New York, 1967), 63.

[74] Quoted in Tashmukhamed N. Kary-Niiazov, *Ocherki Istorii Kultury Sovetskogo Uzbekstana* (Moscow, 1955), 122.

[75] Reproduced in *Pravda*, 25 October 1955, p. 1. In the competition for a new Soviet anthem, there were eighty submissions. None of the ten finalists mentioned Russia in any way in their texts. The texts are available in Russian Center for the Preservation and Study of Documents of Russian History [hereafter RTsKhIDNI], f. 82, op. 2, d. 279, pp. 185–97.

[76] Sovetkin, *Uchebnik Russkogo Yazyka dlya Molodezhi*, 102–14.

to young people to remember Suvorov's efforts to "nurture his soldiers in respect for everything Russian." The textbook closes with the "Hymn of the Soviet Union," whose first line privileges both Russians as the vanguard of Soviet socialist construction and Russian history as the one common to all Soviets. "The indestructible union of free republics which Great Rus has united forever. . . ."[77]

Some numbers: Of the 168 million works of literature published in Russian in 1955, 71 percent were books by Soviet writers and the rest were Russian classics.[78]

The fact that Russian was the language of the center, and of peripheral elites in communication with Moscow and among themselves, made Russian appear to be the natural choice. At a 1954 conference on ethnography, there was a consensus that more epics should be published in native, or as V. M. Sidelnikov called them, "national languages."[79] But if non-Russian languages were national languages, what was Russian? The answer is transnational or universal, the language of the Soviet Union. The logic of this dilemma spawned the official conclusion that "to deprive any student the right to learn Russian would be . . . national discrimination."[80]

The Soviet past was constructed from Russian history, language, and literature. The growing local (northern peoples') dissatisfaction with "traditional forms" of literature was applauded and attributed to "the direct influence of Russian literature," which permited local authors to write "innovative works on contemporary themes."[81] In referring here not only to Soviet Russian writers, but to classical Russian works as well, M. A. Sergeev turns Russian literary history into the past common to all Soviets.[82] Not only were Russians in a privileged position vis-à-vis all non-Russian nations con-

---

[77] Ibid., 188. See the remarks of the Mordvinian author at the Second Writers' Congress in *Vtoroi Vsesoiuznyi Syezd Sovetskikh Pisatelei*, 231–32.

[78] Vitalii S. Samuilov, ed. *Pechat SSSR v 1955 godu: Statisticheskie Materialy* (Moscow, 1956), 125.

[79] Dalgat-Chavtaraeva, "Meeting," 180.

[80] I. A. Kairov, ed. *Narodnoe Obrazovanie v SSSR* (Moscow, 1957), 266. Similarly, whites historically have tended to imagine themselves to be racially invisible, a neutral universal category, hence nonracial and superior to racialized Others. Annalee Newitz, "White Savagery and Humiliation, or a New Racial Consciousness in the Media," in *White Trash: Race and Class in America*, ed. Matt Wray and Annalee Newitz (New York, 1997), 132. Perhaps a more benign form of this logic of Otherization is the common tendency to believe one's own speech is unaccented, while all Others have accents.

[81] M. A. Sergeev, "Literary Works of the Peoples of the North," *SE*, 3 (1955): 186.

[82] Aleksei Surkov also lauded those non-Russian literatures that "master the experience and tradition of Russian classic and Soviet literature" in his opening speech at the writers'

stituting the Soviet Union, but they were also the forebears of contemporary ideal Soviet culture. According to this stream of thought, Soviet identity's heart and soul were both Russian.

The Soviets had to differentiate their Russian national identity from the imperialist side of the czarist one. Aleksei Surkov opened the second day of the writers' congress with a condemnation of the czarist policy of using the Russian language as an "instrument of forceful Russification, as a means of assimilation and elimination of the uniqueness of the national cultures of oppressed peoples."[83] So, then, how did Russian become the Soviet lingua franca? Surkov suggested that millions of non-Russians had volunteered to study Russian and the "honored role of being the means of [communication] . . . *fell to* the Russian language."[84] In other words, the Russian language was the natural choice of all Soviets. Daily life itself, the economic and cultural needs of non-Russians, accounted for the demand for Russian language instruction "from below."[85] At the congress, Nairi Zaryan differentiated between czarist times, when no non-Russian writers ever had their works translated into Russian, and then when a Moscow schoolgirl listed not only Mikhail Lermontov and Aleksandr Pushkin, but Ovanes Tumanian as her favorite poets.[86]

There was nothing about Russian national identity that required that its relationship to others be one of superiority, rather than of mere difference, inferiority, or simple irrelevance. But once the Russian national identity was contextualized within a topography of identity including modernity and class, Russian identity became the subject of the same syntactic arrangement. The relationship that was predominant in 1955 Moscow was Russia as the modern vanguard of all non-Russians of the periphery.

In the official Soviet history of central Asia, whose new edition appeared in 1955, there was a big change in Soviet understanding of Russian imperial history. Czarist Russia went from being seen as the crudest of imperialist exploiters to a producer of progressive effects, consistent with the view of

---

congress in December 1954, in *Vtoroi Vsesoiuznyi Syezd Sovetskikh Pisatelei*, 13. See also V. Bertse, "On the Vivid Truth of Characters," *Pravda*, 28 September 1955, p. 3.

[83] *Vtoroi Vsesoiuznyi Syezd Sovetskikh Pisatelei*, 12. This formulation was repeated in the official history, Kairov, *Narodnoe Obrazovanie v SSSR*, 265.

[84] *Vtoroi Vsesoiuznyi Syezd Sovetskikh Pisatelei*, 13. Emphasis added.

[85] Kairov, *Narodnoe Obrazovanie v SSSR*, 266.

[86] *Vtoroi Vsesoiuznyi Syezd Sovetskikh Pisatelei*, 234. What went unreported was the fact that when "the writers of the small nations of the Soviet Union spoke" at the congress, the "buffets and corridors filled up" with delegates leaving the hall. This was reported by a Yugoslav delegate to the congress, Marina Francichevich. Her reports were translated from the Yugoslav press and sent to Zimianin, head of the Fourth European Department, Ministry of Foreign Affairs. *Archive of the Foreign Policy of the Russian Federation* [hereafter AVPRF], f. 144, op. 16, d. 740, p. 14.

Russia as vanguard of the revolution. In February 1954 in Tashkent, a conference on the history of prerevolutionary central Asia and Kazakhstan discussed and endorsed this new history of the Uzbeks.[87] In the previous 1947 edition, czarist expansion in central Asia was imperialist, any economic or cultural advances were for Russians only, and all revolts against Moscow were progressive. The new edition credited Russia with spurring capitalist development and so "undermining backward medieval forms of economy."[88]

The non-Russian's place on the (r)evolutionary ladder is captured by a typical title, "The Young Art of the Turkmen People," as if all pre-Soviet Turkmen cultural achievements did not qualify as art[89] and only after exposure to Russian Soviet art could Turkmen art develop toward modernity, toward socialism. In a review of an Azerbaijani opera, *Seville*, K. Karaev writes that Azerbaijani music "still hasn't achieved the broad use of the developed musical ensemble, which in Russian classical opera has such great significance." A "first step" had been made in *Seville*. The critic concludes that Azerbaijani opera was "developing under the benevolent influence of Russian classic opera."[90] After extolling the Russian contributions to the All-Union Agriculture Exhibition's series of performing arts, V. Olivkova criticizes other "national" ensembles for being excessively narrow. As a positive example, she cites the Bashkir folk dance troupe, which performed Russian, Tatar, Chuvash, and Bashkir dances. In other words, non-Russian groups should include Russian works in their repertoire, but Russian groups need not go beyond the Soviet play list.[91]

One of the great achievements of the ethnography faculty at Moscow State University was its study of the influence of Russian culture on other, non-Russian peoples.[92] Vilis Latsis, at the writers' congress, declared the "great literature of the Russian people" to be the "spiritual mother" of Latvian literature. He went on to describe Jan Rainis, "our national pride" as a product of the "mighty influence of Pushkin, Lermontov, and Nekrasov. . . ."[93] M. Ibragimov, a writer from Azerbaijan, after extolling the influ-

[87] This was Kary-Niiazov, *Ocherki Istorii Kultury Sovetskogo Uzbekstana.*

[88] Ibid., 49. For an insightful interpretation of the significance of Kary-Niiazov's book, see Lowell Tillett, *The Great Friendship: Soviet Historians on the Non-Russian Nationalities* (Chapel Hill, 1969), 192–96.

[89] M. Kedrov, "People's Artist of the USSR" *Pravda*, 21 October 1955, p. 2. See also Dalgat-Chavtaraeva, "Meeting," 180.

[90] K. Karaev, "Seville," *Pravda*, 2 September 1955, p. 2.

[91] V. Olivkova, "Concerts at the All-Union Agricultural Exhibition," *Pravda*, 25 September 1955, p. 2. According to S. Ignatiev, a Bashkir *obkom* secretary, Russian culture influenced Bashkir culture to be national in form and socialist in content. See his May 31 memorandum to Khrushchev on the occasion of Bashkiria's *dekada* in Moscow in TsKhSD, f. 5, op. 30, d. 103, 44.

[92] K. I. Kozlova and N. N. Cheboksarov, "Ethnography in Moscow University," *SE* 2 (1955): 111.

[93] *Vtoroi Vsesoiuznyi Syezd Sovetskikh Pisatelei*, 110. For a similar expression of Ukrainian ap-

ence of Russian Soviet literature on his republic's work, enumerated how the Russian language itself had improved the "musicality, tone, and form" of Azeri literature.[94] Tashmukhamed Kary-Niiazov expresses similar sentiments about the Uzbek language, recalling that Marx was 50 when he began to study Russian; Engels recommended its study; and the "great Russian scholar Lomonosov said that in Russian we find 'the splendor of Spanish, the vitality of French, the power of German, the delicacy of Italian, and above all else, the richness of Greek and the succinctness of Latin.'"[95]

Some numbers: Russian literature was published in sixty-nine other languages, and Ukrainian literature in thirty-five; the next most published literature in a different language was Latvian, in thirteen.[96]

Russians were understood as the privileged carriers of the modern Soviet future to the less developed non-Russians. Among the indices of modernity brought to the Yakuts by the great Russian people were "permanent settlements, forts, cabins, and . . . prisons."[97] This view of Russia's place vis-à-vis non-Russian Others was so authoritative that it appeared in the lead *Pravda* editorial devoted to the elaboration of the Revolution Day slogan on the "multinational socialist state." The exact message was that "with the fraternal support of the great Russian people, all Soviet nationalities received the opportunity to build socialism. . . ."[98]

Russian subordination of non-Russians was not only public talk. It appeared as well in asides, omissions, word choice, inclusions, and allusions.

---

preciation, see Mikola Bazhan's address (125). For Byelorussian sentiments, see Petrus Brovka's comments (176). For Turkemenistan, see K. Kurbansakhatov (286–87); S. Babaev, "Holiday of Culture for the Turkmen People," *Pravda*, 14 October 1955, p. 2. (Babaev was the secretary of the Turkmenistan party.)

[94] *Vtoroi Vsesoiuznyi Syezd Sovetskikh Pisatelei*, 296. The mass readership of *Pravda* was also exposed to this view of the Russian senior partner bringing enlightenment to more backward peoples. See, for example, B. Pokrovskii, review of the Bashkirian opera, "Salavat Iulaev," *Pravda*, 2 June 1955, p. 2. On the necessarily subordinate position of Armenian literature to its Russian teacher, see Akop Salakhian, marking the one-hundred-fiftieth birthday of Khachatur Abovian in *Pravda*, 8 October 1955, p. 2. (Salakhian was the secretary of the Armenian section of the Union of Soviet Writers.) See also Sergeev, "Literary Works," 187.

[95] Kary-Niiazov, *Ocherki Istorii Kultury Sovetskogo Uzbekstana*, 269–70. Although in no way apparent in the last quotation, Soviets did sometimes find their own paeans to the Russian nation fulsome and cloying. Giorgii Malenkov deleted the following passage in a speech he was to give to the Moscow party *aktiv* in July 1955: "So the people, at the initiative of the Russian people and its genius representative, creator of Soviet nationality policy, V. I. Lenin. . . ." RTsKhIDNI, f. 83, op. 1, d. 12, p. 36. He had used the phrase at a meeting of the party organization of the Ministry of Electric Power Stations two weeks before (137).

[96] Samuilov, *Pechat SSSR v 1955 Godu*, 126.

[97] Gurvich, "Ethnographic Materials," 133.

[98] "Under the Banner of Friendship of Peoples," *Pravda*, 2 November 1955, p. 1.

The scholars who celebrated the bicentennial of Moscow State University by writing a history of ethnographic studies there, by mentioning only Russian scholars and by referring only to Russian contributions, effectively reproduced the centrality of Russia.[99] The report to CC Secretary Petr Pospelov on the "State of Ethnographic Science in the Soviet Union,"which begins, "It is sufficient to name the greatest scholars who glorified Russian science in all the world,"[100] treated Russia as if it were the natural starting point for any discussion of Soviet ethnography. An article on Leninism in *Kommunist,* the official theoretical journal of the party, is entitled "Leninism—The Greatest Achievement of Russian and World Culture."[101] The omission of all other Soviet national cultures was as meaningful as Russia's presence.

Nikolai Bulganin, chair of the Council of Ministers, in his February 1955 speech before the Supreme Soviet, measured Soviet grain output in Russian poods.[102] Official state architecture in 1955 in Moscow was based on eighteenth-century Russian artistic style. Workers' clubs were designed like the palaces of noblemen or Russian imperial offices.[103] Alone among republic Supreme Soviet proceedings, the Russian legislature's activities received daily front-page treatment in the nationwide party daily, *Pravda.*[104] The parliamentary sessions themselves convened in the Kremlin, in the same facilities used by the All-Union Supreme Soviet. Ukraine's Supreme Soviet proceedings, on the other hand, despite being the second most covered, appeared greatly abridged on page 2 of *Pravda.*[105] The physical arrangement of Supreme Soviet meetings portrayed Russia as the chosen nation, the center, with non-Russians at the edges. At the December meeting, for instance, Moscow, Leningrad, and Belarus were seated front and center. At the back and on the sides of the Hall of Congresses at that December session of the Council of the Union were the delegations from Northern Ossetia, Georgia, Tajikistan, Mordovina, Chuvashia, Udmurtia, and Buryat Mongolia. Seated front and center during the proceedings of the Union of Nationalities were Russia and Ukraine. In the back rows were "national okrugy" and Southern Ossetia.[106]

On July 12, 1955, the Soviet government celebrated the one-hundredth birthday of the "outstanding Russian naval commander," Pavel Stepano-

---

[99] Kozlova and Cheboksarov, "Ethnography in Moscow State University," 100–111.

[100] TsKhSD, f. 5, op. 17, d. 518, p. 26.

[101] M. Iovchuk, "Leninism—The Greatest Achievement of Russian and World Culture," *Kommunist* 1 (1955): 23.

[102] Speech reproduced in *New Times,* no. 7 (February 12, 1955).

[103] Frederick C. Barghoorn, *Soviet Russian Nationalism* (New York, 1956), 154.

[104] *Pravda,* 23–28 March 1955, p. 1.

[105] See *Pravda,* 1 April 1955, p. 2.

[106] Each of the republics had twenty-five delegates, so it was not the size of the Russian delegation that entitled it to the honored positions in the hall. For the seating arrangements, see TsKhSD, f. 5, op. 30, d. 97, pp. 58–59.

vich Nakhimov.[107] When the Soviet state celebrated its navy, it found a Russian past. Admiral Sergei Gorshkov, in his *Pravda* paean to the Soviet navy, hailed Russian seafarers who had explored the Pacific, Arctic, and Antarctic oceans; Russian naval warriors such as Peter the First, Spiridov, Ushakov, Seniavin, Lazarev, Nakhimov, and Makarov, who gained "glorious victories over our [whose?] enemies"; and revolutionary Russian seamen who led uprisings in 1905, 1907, and 1917.[108]

Russian identity was also reproduced in contemporary literature. Leonov's *The Russian Forest,* a dense, lush, eternal stand of trees, is a metaphor for Russia itself. The forest is depicted as natural and pure, as opposed to the Soviet reality of corruption and modernity. Mother Russia is "a symbol of permanence in an impermanent world."[109] One character, Yegor Sevastyanich, when asked by a procurator whether he is a party member, replies, "No, but I am a Russian," as if that is sufficient to satisfy the inquiry about his devotion to duty.[110] The narrator observes that all Russians, not Soviets, answer the call to defend their country.[111]

Sometimes Russian identity was produced merely by its presence in a description of Soviet reality. In a review of Egorov's film *Icy Sea,* L. Kudrevatykh continually refers to it as a Russian film about Russians. He begins with "the centuries-long history of Russia is rich with inspiring feats" and ends by stating that the film "shows the force of character, generosity, and courage of a simple Russian man." The film is about the adventure of five men on a remote island in the White Sea struggling to survive, not seemingly a theme demanding an ethnonational treatment. So, "calm, business-like, and laconic, Aleksei Khimkov's portrayal of N. Kriuchkov is a forefather of contemporary Russian captains who storm the ice of the Arctic Ocean, sail the Antarctic, and conquer undiscovered ocean waters." What is more, "Russian candor, poetic lyricism, devoted fidelity to duty and honor—these are the main things in the character of Stepan Sharapov. . . ."[112] We come away from this review thinking the Soviet Union was Russia.

Only rarely in the predominant discourse was it acknowledged that there could be a less hierarchical relationship between Russians and their peripheral comrades. Abdulla Kakhkhar, an Uzbek author, observed at the writers' congress that Russian literature not only influenced non-Russian

[107] See *Pravda,* 12 July 1955, p. 3.

[108] Sergei Gorshkov, "Reliable Defense of Ocean Frontiers," *Pravda,* 24 July 1955, p. 3.

[109] Edward J. Brown, *Russian Literature since the Revolution* (Cambridge, Mass., 1982), 101. See also George Gibian, *Interval of Freedom: Soviet Literature during the Thaw, 1954–1957* (Minneapolis, 1960), 44.

[110] Leonov, *Russian Forest,* 383.

[111] Ibid., 616.

[112] L. Kudrevatykh, "A Film about the Feat of Courageous People," *Pravda,* 23 March 1955, p. 3. See also N. Abalkin and Iury Lukin, "On the Theatrical Playbill," *Pravda,* 4 September 1955, p. 2.

artists, but that it, "at the same time, absorbs the diversity of artistic forms of these [non-Russian] literatures, expanding its themes, and enriching its artistic palate."[113] A lead editorial in *Pravda* was as generous as any in 1955 Moscow, stating that "the greatest values of Russian culture are endlessly dear to the working people of all nationalities of the USSR; the Russian people in its turn relate with deep respect to the cultural values of every socialist nation."[114] This careful wording does not at all equate the importance of Russian and non-Russian culture, but at least admits that Russians can appreciate, if not benefit, from Others.

Only rarely did the periphery strike back. At the Second Writers' Congress, a Ukrainian writer, Oles Gonchar, assailed the publication of a three-volume work on Soviet literature that included only Russian authors and called on Russians to translate more works from Ukrainian.[115] Andrei Lupan, a Moldovan author, expressed surprise at the congress that Soviet literature could be discussed all day without any mention of a Moldovan contribution. He suggested that the large number of Moldovan books he had sent to be displayed in the exhibition hall "must have got lost" because they were not there.[116] A writer from Yakutiia observed that even during czarist times, Russian writers would come and visit, including such luminaries as Ivan Goncharov and Mikhail Lomonosov. The question was, why did no one visit now? "It is a lot closer now with modern air travel, with all the conveniences. Goncharov had to travel by horse-drawn sleigh. But now, our favorite Russian, Soviet writers would be met by a wonderful automobile, a Zis-110, if only they would come visit us."[117] M. P. Petrov, a writer from Udmurtiia, revealed that the editors of *Literaturnaya Gazeta*, after thirty-eight years, still did not know how to spell Udmurts in an issue published right before the congress.[118]

As others have observed,[119] Soviet nationality policy created and sustained non-Russian nations. To the extent that non-Russians, especially those living

---

[113] *Vtoroi Vsesoiuznyi Syezd Sovetskikh Pisatelei*, 272. Boris Polevoi also spoke of the "mutual enrichment" enjoyed by Russian and non-Russian writers of children's literature (41). Polevoi was a member of the union's governing secretariat. Kairov's official history of Soviet education also makes the observation that national cultures and languages have contributed much that is new to Russian culture and language. Kairov, *Narodnoe Obrazovanie v SSSR*, 266.

[114] "Under the Banner of the Friendship of Peoples," *Pravda*, 2 November 1955, p. 1.

[115] *Vtoroi Vsesoiuznyi Syezd Sovetskikh Pisatelei*, 151.

[116] Ibid., 172. Kakhkhar voiced similar complaints about national literatures in general being slighted at the congress (273), as did G. Mustafin, a Kazakh writer, about the rare appearances of any Kazakh literature in either *Literaturnaia Gazeta* or *Uchitelskaya Gazeta* (330). The latter was the official newspaper of the teachers' union. The Estonian writer Lembit Remmelgas thought it "strange" that the *Great Soviet Encyclopedia* did not have a single Estonian writer listed (342).

[117] Ibid., 485. Protodiakonov's comments were repeatedly interrupted with applause.

[118] Ibid., 491. Applause followed.

[119] Ronald Grigor Suny, *The Revenge of the Past: Nationalism, Revolution, and the Collapse of the Soviet Union* (Stanford, 1993); Yuri Slezkine, "The USSR as a Communal Apartment, or

in central Asia, the Far East and North, and the Caucasus, were regarded as less far along on the socialist path than their Slavic and Baltic brothers and sisters, it was expected that the development of a national consciousness would have to precede the emergence of a proletarian one. Refuge was sought in the belief that a national consciousness would not degenerate into bourgeois nationalism because of the help of the Russian vanguard in the center. And a degenerate bourgeois national identity was not one a Soviet citizen would want attributed to her. The February 21, 1948, law that resulted in the imprisonment of many nationalist deviants put them in the same company as "spies, saboteurs, terrorists, Rightists, Mensheviks, Socialist Revolutionaries, anarchists, white emigres and participants in other anti-Soviet organizations, groups and people who represent a danger through their anti-Soviet ties and hostile activities."[120] On this contradictory basis, non-Russian national identities were both cultivated and controlled. As early as the Tenth Party Congress in 1921, Soviet party leaders enunciated the need for socialism with local characteristics, while at the same time privileging Russians. This included "developing the Soviet state in forms corresponding to the national-daily life conditions of the non-great Russian peoples"; having courts, economic and political organs, and administration operate in the native language and be composed of local people knowing the "life and psychology" of the local people; developing cultural-educational institutions in the native language; and developing schools in the native language.[121]

Some numbers: Of the 987 million books published in the Soviet Union in 1955, 84 percent of them were in Russian, and another 6 percent were in Ukrainian.[122] Of the books translated from one language to another, fully 93 percent of them were translations from Russian into some local language.[123]

In Ukrainian cities in 1958 21 percent of the children attended Ukrainian schools, as opposed to 79 percent in 1927. But of the 1,200 newspapers published in Ukraine, 1,000 were in Ukrainian; however, 89 percent of the journals were in Russian.[124]

How a Socialist State Promoted Ethnic Particularism," *Slavic Review* 53, no. 2 (summer 1994): 414–52.

[120] GARF, Khrushchev special file, t. II, op. 3, d. 464, p. 45.

[121] Quoted in Kary-Niiazov, *Ocherki Istorii Kultury Sovetskogo Uzbekstana,* 124 (from the Tenth Party Congress's resolutions).

[122] Samuilov, *Pechat SSSR v 1955 Godu,* 47.

[123] Ibid., 50–51.

[124] Ivan Dzyuba, *Internationalism or Russification? A Study in the Soviet Nationalities Problem* (London, 1968), 117–57.

Non-Russian nations were especially salient in 1955. This visibility was because the Presidium agreed to release hundreds of thousands of prisoners from camps that year, many of whom were incarcerated according to national origins. According to an April 4 Ministry of Internal Affairs (MVD) report to the CC, 873,000 "special settlers" had been removed from the MVD rolls.[125] Although released, these people were almost never permitted to return to the place from where they had been forcibly expelled.[126] Although the MVD reported an extraordinarily high level of gratitude from the newly freed prisoners, complaints were voiced, often revolving around a protest against essentializing their ethnic identity at the expense of the rest of their identity. So, for example, a German woman declared that her "German nationality cannot be the basis for limiting her rights," and indeed her factory, Komsomol, and party organizations supported her appeal to be removed from the list of "special settlers."[127] Although they had been released from prison, they still had to register once a year, as if on probation for crimes the state was now tacitly admitting they had never committed.

Khrushchev writes about the dilemma national identity provided for the Kremlin leadership. He claims that the CC decided that the position of regional first secretary should be occupied by a local person and "not some Russian sent from Moscow." But this compromise did not suit Beria, who argued, before his arrest, that Russians exercised a preponderance of power in the republics and must be reined in. In a June 1953 letter to the CC Presidium, Beria outlined in detail the overwhelming preponderance of Russians in the Byelorussian state, party, economic, and police apparat, recommending a wholesale appointment of Byelorussian cadres immediately. According to Khrushchev, this stirred up a lot of trouble in the republics because local party organizations began to "fulminate not only against Russians, but also against those national cadres who didn't struggle with Russian 'domination'."[128] According to Khrushchev, he accused Beria at the Presidium meeting at which he was arrested of wanting to "unify nationals and unite them against the Russians. All enemies of the Communist party have always counted on inter-national struggle, and Beria also began with this."[129] What Khrushchev does not confide to his readers is that he voted for Beria's proposals on the national question in western Ukraine, Byelorussia, and Lithuania at the June 1953 plenum. Moreover, Khrushchev prepared his

---

[125] This was out of a total population of special settlers in January 1, 1955, of 1.7 million, including 730,000 Germans, 195,000 Chechens, 118,000 Crimean Tatars, 137,000 Ukrainians, and 106,000 Balts. From an April 4, 1955, MVD report to the CC, in GARF, Khrushchev special file, t. II, op. 3, d. 464, pp. 51–55.

[126] GARF, t. II, op. 3, d. 464, pp. 39–30.

[127] GARF, Khrushchev special file, t. II op. 3, d. 463, p. 32.

[128] Nikita S. Khrushchev, *Vospominaniia: Izbrannye Fragmenty* (Moscow, 1997), 274.

[129] Ibid., 280.

own memorandum on nationality policy in Latvia, closely following Beria's outline. Khrushchev was not at all unaware of problems between Russians and locals. At the July 1955 CC Plenum, he called for the creation of more republican ministries in the economic area "in order to strengthen the friendship among our peoples."[130] And in his draft speech for the Twentieth Party Congress, Khrushchev claimed that the party policy of delegating more authority from the center through the creation of republic ministries was evidence of concern for non-Russian sensibilities.[131]

It does not appear that the June 1953 CC compromise was fully implemented. In 1955, Ukraine, Byelorussia, Karelia, Kazakhstan, Turkmenistan, Tajikistan, and Kyrgystan each had two Russians or Ukrainians as the top two party leaders in their republics. Estonia, Latvia, Lithuania, Moldavia, Armenia, and Georgia had two leaders from the titular nationality. Azerbaijan and Uzbekistan had split leaderships.[132] Five republics had no titular representation, four of them in central Asia.

At times it had to be admitted, even at the highest levels, that national form was violated during the quest for socialist content. Aleksei Surkov, in his opening address to the writers' congress, acknowledged that many translations into Russian were "scandalously distorted, their content mangled and watered down."[133] A minimalist version of national form was that non-Russians should at least use their own languages to reproduce socialist content.[134]

Some Soviets were aware that the daily practices of non-Russians were producing national identities and not modern Soviet ones. The authors of a monograph on Tajik peasantry were criticized for showing Tajiks in their indigenous clothing rather than in "modern Soviet dress . . . which is very typical for contemporary villages."[135] O. A. Sukhareva, discussing the development of central Asian culture, lauds a "general Soviet culture" characterized by "urban dress, an urban style of housing, polyphonic music, easel paintings and sculptures." She points out that this universal Soviet cultural identity was expressed with local color and in indigenous languages.[136] The Stalinist expression given to this compromise was apt—national in form, so-

---

[130] CC Plenum, July 12, 1955, 42. At this meeting he called himself a "Russian man." The CC Plenum transcripts are available at the TsKhSD, but I received my copies from Mark Kramer, for which I am most grateful.

[131] TsKhSd, f. 1, op. 2, d. 3, p. 146.

[132] Embree, *Soviet Union*, 334–335.

[133] *Vtoroi Vsesoiuznyi Syezd Sovetskikh Pisatelei*, 14. Kedrov made the same observation about Turkmeni theater—it neglected its own national culture (2).

[134] This was the position taken in the official 750-page commemoration of the fiftieth anniversary of Soviet education in 1957, published by the Academy of Pedagogical Science. Kairov, *Narodnoe Obrazovanie v SSSR*, 257.

[135] Sukhareva, "Ethnographic Study," 37.

[136] Ibid., 39. Chunakov reports that Turkmenistan surprises "foreign visitors [by] playing symphonic music," another step on the road to modernity. *Pravda*, 4 October 1955, 2. A Turkmeni composition singled out for praise was "Cantata for the Communist Party." M. Sabin-

cialist in content. In other words, Soviet nationalities would continue to reproduce their particular ethnic identities for the foreseeable future, but these identities would not violate a higher, Soviet socialist identity, the one to which all aspired and would inevitably develop.

Other institutional practices reproduced non-Russian identities. The Soviet legislature, the Supreme Soviet, was divided into a Council of the Soviet Union and a Council of Nationalities. The latter was deliberately designed to represent non-Russian identities at the highest level, although its seating arrangements reproduced the superior position of Russia and the subordination of the periphery. On April 23, M. I. Aliev, the Azerbaijani minister of foreign affairs, testified in Moscow before the Supreme Soviet committee on international affairs, attesting to Baku's assent to the new borders created by the recently signed agreement between the Soviet Union and Iran. In his testimony, Aliev pointed out that Azerbaijan was willing to sacrifice the land for the sake of the union.[137] As has been noted by many scholars of nationalism, administrative boundaries, in this case among the republics, are a daily and hence powerful institutional buttress of identities.[138]

There were many ways in which non-Russian identities became Soviet or Soviet Russian identities.[139] It was a matter of finding national figures who could be turned into Soviet heroes, rather than national ones. So, for example, a ballet premiered in Moscow with Maya Plisetskaya in the lead role. But it was not a purely artistic event—its composer, a Tatar, had died in the Great Patriotic War. In Byelorussia, a monument was unveiled to a local Byelorussian for defending the Soviet Union as a partisan in Byelorussia. An analagous commemoration occurred in Lithuania. In Bashkiria, a monument was unveiled to a comrade-in-arms of the leader of the peasant rebellion, Emelian Pugachev. These events have in common that they were official Soviet constructions of local indigenous identity in a way that thwarted the reproduction of non-Russian national identities. A second

---

ina, "The Music of Soviet Turkmenia," *Pravda*, 23 October 1955, p. 4. Perhaps the importance of this song can be inferred from the fact that it was the highlight of the gala finale to the Turkmeni exhibition in Moscow. Among those attending were most of the Presidium and Burma's U Nu, who was visiting Moscow at the time. *Pravda*, 25 October 1955, p. 2.

[137] *Pravda*, 24 April 1955, 2.

[138] Peter Sahlins, *Boundaries: The Making of France and Spain in the Pyrenees* (Berkeley, 1989), 103–32.

[139] Rita Smith Kipp describes a similar process in the case of Indonesia. The Djakarta government, through the creation of an ethnic theme park outside of the capital, Taman Mini Indo-Indah (Beautiful Indonesia in Miniature), has tried to read Indonesia's many ethnic minorities through the homogenizing needs of the central state. Rita Smith Kipp, *Dissociated Identities: Ethnicity, Religion, and Class in an Indonesian Society* (Ann Arbor, 1993), especially 110–12. Comparisons to Stalin's and Khrushchev's Exhibition of the Achievements of the Economy (VDNKh), which had national pavilions read through the center, are appropriate. Jamey Gambrell, "The Wonder of the Soviet World," *New York Review of Books*, 22 December 1994, pp. 30–35.

track was to use non-Russian social practices to reproduce Russian identities. For instance, the complete works of Pushkin were translated into Armenian for the first time and the House of Folk Art in Kiev opened an exhibition devoted to the Russian revolution of 1905.[140]

On January 6, Chuvashia's *obkom* secretary asked Petr Pospelov, CC secretary, to allow Cheboksary, the Chuvash capital, to celebrate its four-hundredth anniversary in June 1955. The Scientific and Cultural Secretariat of the CC asked the Academy of Science's Institute of History to research the age of the city. The Institute reported that what little evidence there was supported the four-hundredth anniversary. On January 27, Aleksei Rumiantsev, the head of the Scientific and Cultural department of the CC, sent a memorandum to the CC in support of the *obkom* secretary's, Isliukov's, proposal. Rumiantsev advised that the Division of Historical Sciences of the Academy of Sciences prepare materials on the history of Cheboksary and the Chuvash people, in collaboration with the Chuvash division of the Academy of Sciences, concentrating on the Soviet period.[141] Through these highly institutionalized procedures, Moscow ensured that local national history was publicly commemmorated as Soviet.

Soviet national identity in 1955 was fundamentally Russian. Bereft of an origination myth and nation of its own, the modern class-based Soviet project appropriated Russian history, culture, and language. In so doing, a relationship with non-Russian identities was unavoidable. While any type of relationship would have been possible, the hierarchical one that developed was consistent with the broader identity topography of center and periphery, urban and rural, and more and less desirable class identities. The modern Russian center was understood, and understood itself, as the vanguard of the Soviet project for all premodern, modernizing, peripheral non-Russians. But non-Russian identities were not to go away any time soon, if only surviving in national forms. Both institutional and social practice reproduced these peripheral identities on a daily basis. Although these national identities might become urbanized, modernized, and even socialized, they would remain national Others to the Russian center.

The Soviet understanding of itself as the Russian nation had foreign policy implications. Being Russian should result in quite different understandings of other states in the world. Being Slavic should mean one set of

---

[140] These events are from the chronicle of cultural life in the Soviet Union, Institute of History, Academy of Sciences of the USSR, *Kulturnaya Zhizn v SSSR: 1951–1965—Khronika* (Moscow, 1979), 175–209. See also Ali Mazrui, *Cultural Engineering and Nation-Building in East Africa* (Evanston, 1972), 3–37.

[141] TsKhSD, f. 5, op. 17, d. 518, pp. 1–4. For the CC treatment of a new history of northern Ossetia and Astrakhan's four-hundredth anniversary celebration request, which was denied, see 54–56, 75.

understandings for Yugoslavia, Bulgaria, Poland, and Czechoslovakia and another for equally socialist non-Slavic allies in Hungary and Rumania. The Slavic identity should result in Soviet appreciations of similarities that would not be present in other non-Slavic states, just as at home Ukraine and Bye-lorussia were understood differently than non-Slavic Estonia and Georgia. Soviet Russian identity included the appropriation of Russian history, and this too should produce differential effects on the understandings of oth-ers. States with whom Russia had a history, such as Germany, China, and Yu-goslavia, should be understood in that historical context, whereas states such as India, Vietnam, and the United States should not be situated in that way.

The hierarchical relationship between the Russian vanguard and the So-viet periphery should also be replicated in the international context. Just as Russia was the modernizing and socializing vanguard for central Asia, the Soviet Union would be expected to understand itself as the vanguard for the decolonizing world. Understanding itself as the vanguard implies not only that the Soviet Union could help countries become more modern and pro-gressive, and hence erase differences between them, but also that the Soviet Union was the center, the older brother, the state that had already built so-cialism. In other words, the Russian national identity should imply Soviet presuppositions of a superior position vis-à-vis the decolonizing world, just as Russia assumes vis-à-vis the Soviet periphery. Just as the Russian national identity received no value from its relationship with non-Russians at home, the Soviet Union should expect no influence on itself from its relationship with other states. Just as Russia was the template against which the Soviet pe-riphery was measured, we should expect the Soviet model to be applied to evaluate other states in the world. Finally, just as the Soviets recognize the inherent tension between their Russian national identity and the existence of non-Russian identities, we should expect Soviets to realize that the na-tional identities of inferior states should be handled with great care, espe-cially given the Russian historical legacy with some of them.

The New Soviet Man

Within the predominant discourse resided the ideal Soviet identity: the New Soviet Man (NSM). He was the Soviet citizen without undesirable iden-tities: nation, religion, provinciality, traditions, or inferior class origins. He transcended national and ethnic identities, was an avowed atheist, and had a working-class consciousness. He was most modern, a product of the most modern project, and a distilled product, an ideal from which all impurities had been painstakingly removed.[142] The collection of identities that con-

---

[142] Dina Spechler offers an analogous ideal type, the Zhdanovite article or book, in Dina R. Spechler, *Permitted Dissent in the USSR: "Novy Mir" and the Soviet Regime* (New York, 1982), 2. For a treatment of the pre-Soviet origins of "Russian new person," see Boym, *Common Places*, 88–95.

stitute the New Soviet Man are in the top half of Class and Modernity in figure 2.

The NSM was an ideal type. He could not be found on the streets of Moscow or in any other town or village in the Soviet Union. The NSM was not even evident on the most official of documents, the Soviet passport, which included a line for the most unmodern of identities, nationality.[143] It is precisely because the NSM did not and could not exist that this identity furnished the opportunity for the most open and vigorous contestation of identity in 1955 Moscow. Soviets themselves could not agree on what a realistic ideal type could be; many others thought the idea ridiculous and instead celebrated difference. The main axis of the debate was just how closely Soviet renderings and understandings of one another, especially in literature, art, media, and film, should be hewed to this ideal type. The identity stakes were very high because the more idealized the type authorized by Soviet officials, the more Others became dangerous deviants, not just different Soviets. On the other hand, if the NSM was allowed to be many things, not just one, differences were authorized and deviants became harder to find. This type of simultaneous recognition and tolerance of difference resulted in the Tashkent party *obkom* secretary, A. Alimov, recommending someone to the CC in Moscow based on the fact that "He is bespartinnyi [not in the party], but he is a real Soviet man."[144] Although his colleague may not be ideal (he was not in the Communist Party), he had the attributes needed to build socialism in Uzbekistan.

There were a number of important distinguishing characteristics of the NSM. It often subsumed or enveloped all the previously discussed identities of modernity, class, and nation. The critical boundary marked by the NSM was between deviance and difference, and the discussions of 1955 were about these boundaries. What constituted a meaningful deviation from the Soviet identity, such that a person could be deemed not Soviet, was the central theme of discussion. Those who understood deviance to be dangerous desired portrayals of typical average Soviets in all media. Those who understood deviance to be difference wished to have more ambiguous and relaxed boundaries between the ideal Self and the Other. The NSM also implied the absence of a private sphere, whereas those who entertained difference appreciated the possibility of the personal, a private domain separated from social meaning and purpose.

---

[143] Mervyn Matthews, *The Passport Society: Controlling Movement in Russia and the USSR* (Boulder, 1993), 27–31. When the MVD reported its crime statistics to the CC, it also included age, sex, nationality (if not Russian), employment status, and party affiliation or group membership. GARF, Khrushchev special file, t. IV, d. 466.

[144] In a letter to the CC, TsKhSD, f. 5, op. 31, d. 28, p. 115. This formulation is not unlike the one found in Leonov, *Russian Forest*, about the person who is not a communist, but is at least a Russian.

Boris Polevoi, in his address on children's literature at the writers' congress, identified the ideal Soviet heroes: Chapaev, freedom fighter; Pavel, young communist and diligent worker; Tanya, fearless popular avenger; Liza Chaikina, glorious partisan of the Kalinin woods; and Aleksandr Matrosov, soldier who "gives up the life he loves when the honor and independence of the Motherland call. . . ."[145] Those who wished to find the NSM in Soviet texts in 1955 wanted their protagonists to be unambiguous models.[146]

Even Dorofeya, a good communist mother saddled with a miscreant son Gennady in Panova's *Span of the Year* was criticized at the writers' congress by Konstantin Simonov for not "offer[ing] a decisive condemnation" of Gennady. Panova should have portrayed Dorofeya's tragedy as a product of her own making, her failure to control her son, rather than depicting her as a "victim of circumstances." Panova, according to Simonov, wrongly wrote a book that shows how a mother's love for her own son can blind her to the societal duty that she has to bring him up in the manner required by Soviet morality, by Soviet ideas of the family, not traditional ones.[147] V. V. Ermilov accused Panova of creating a complacent heroine in Dorofeya and of failing to make any moral judgments even in the subtext of the novel. Concluding, Ermilov observed that "after all, heroes of Russian literature were always merciless in their moral condemnations of their own actions and errors."[148]

The most common tension immanent in those Soviets who understood the NSM to be the ideal citizen of the future Soviet Union was between the recognition of its simultaneous desirability and impossibility. Several factors made it impossible. If socialist (un)realism were to triumph in its pure form, the resulting version of Soviet society would be both ridiculous and untrue to a class analysis of the society. Polevoi, who had earlier in his address saluted the heroes in children's books, still acknowledged that heroes should have a "full range of human feelings, who can commit follies out of joy, and who can falter in desperation." He criticized those who in the months leading up to the congress had been demanding ideal heroes in literature and the arts. He compared them to people who would "advocate making men's suits only with broad shoulders and big chests, since that is what Soviet men should be." The audience erupted in laughter. Polevoi closed his remarks by citing the ludicrous example of Lev Kassil, an author who was so frightened by critics who demanded idealized heroes that he had his young couple in his last book kiss through a handkerchief (again, laughter at the congress).[149]

---

[145] *Vtoroi Vsesoiuznyi Syezd Sovetskikh Pisatelei*, 43.

[146] This may be the totalitarian problem with abstract art. Hitler's "degenerate" and Stalin's "formalistic" art shared one dangerous characteristic—they permitted multiple interpretations.

[147] *Vtoroi Vsesoiuznyi Syezd Sovetskikh Pisatelei*, 92.

[148] Ibid., 470–71.

[149] Ibid., 54–55.

As long as class identities existed in the Soviet Union, albeit nonantagonistic ones, there would be conflict. And indeed that conflict could be explained through the existence of these class identities. The problem with the
NSM was that he was already there, living as a communist in a class-free won-
derland. The CC itself, in its message to the writer's congress at its opening,
warned against the "tendency to embellish reality, to ignore the difficulties
of development. . . ."[150] The "'vestiges of capitalism' that still plague popular consciousness . . . "[151] were being missed. The common label affixed to
these stalwart defenders of the ideal was "theorists of no conflict."[152] The
most authoritative summary of the writers' congress appeared in *Kommunist*.
Its editors warned against ignoring conflicts, singling out the depiction of
life in the countryside as depicted in the theater and on the big screen,
where *kolkhoz* life was "varnished and prettified." To engage in this whitewash
is to "demobilize the Soviet people. One must not underestimate the danger of the vestiges of the past. . . ."[153] Rumiantsev, CC secretary for Culture
and History, and his deputies P. Tarasov and A. Sazonov authored a CC di-
rective against the release of a number of films in 1955 because their "appearance on the screen could only discredit Soviet cinematography." How?
Women in these films were shown doing nothing but wanting a new dress,
flirting, and seeking an eligible bachelor. The impression was created that
kolkhozniki "never work, and that their lives are happy go lucky and carefree,
proceeding in utter happiness. . . ." Young people in films are depicted "like
all sugar and honey and sickeningly sweet. . . ."[154]

Recognizing the impossibility of the ideal, official Soviets suggested that
writers should aim at depicting the "typical" Soviet person, hoping thereby
to avoid the inclusion of either the ideal or miscreant extremes. Fyodor
Gladkov, the chair of the Union of Soviet Writers, denied that socialist realism, "idealizes reality," calling it instead "concentrated emphasis on the typical features of living characters. . . ."[155] Dmitrii Shepilov, the editor of
Pravda, observed that "the ideological maturity of a writer, the power of his
talent, manifests itself more clearly than anywhere in the *art of generalization*,
in the capacity to pick out from all the *diversity of reality* the most decisive for
characterizing the leading tendencies." When such talent is absent, creativ-
ity becomes "uninspired and *empirical*, it gets turned into naturalistic writings of everyday life which does not reveal the sense of the great deeds being

---

[150] Ibid., 9.

[151] Ibid.

[152] See R. Kurbansakhatov's remarks for a critique of this school, in Ibid., 288.

[153] "Toward a New Raising of the Ideological-Artistic Level of Soviet Literature," *Kommunist* 1 (1955): 19.

[154] The films being panned are A. Frolov's *Good Morning* and B. Barnet's *Liana*. TsKhSd,
f. 5, op. 17, d. 548, p. 37; and *Attesta Zrelosti* and *Strekova*, (53–54).

[155] *Vtoroi Vsesoiuznyi Syezd Sovetskikh Pisatelei*, 216.

accomplished by the Soviet people."[156] A more cogent statement of socialist realism could not be made. Nor could there be a more impossible task: depicting typical reality. The discussion comes back to the meaning of deviance, the boundary between difference and deviance, and the movement from Us to Them to Other.

The way that any individual Soviet understood deviance appears to have depended on how she understood class and modernity. If she adhered to a binarized and hierarchical version of class analysis, she was also likely to be most worried about straying from the NSM. If, however, a more relaxed view of class was acceptable, and if premodernity was not considered to be an evil or a danger, then deviance was treated as natural and unthreatening. In short, those worried about class identity were concerned that the exposure of less reliable class elements to deviations from the ideal in the mass media or literature might pull them farther into the bourgeois abyss.[157] Deviation was condemned because its manifestations—"the sickening morals of bourgeois society, drunkenness, boorish attitudes toward women and the family, and hooliganism" were all indicators that the Soviet project was still vulnerable to bourgeois degeneration.[158]

Although communist morality dominated Soviet society, it could not be forgotten that

> in the consciousness of some Soviets still live vestiges of capitalism, remnants of old bourgeois ideology. . . . People who are entangled in the snares of private property psychology—self-seekers, money-grubbers, idlers, plunderers of public property, careerists, and shams are not yet extinct. Such people are in a race for profits, for personal well-being, at the expense of the interests of society. . . . The presence of these vestiges is explained . . . by the fact that the old concepts, ideas, and customs that were the product of the exploitative system still litter the consciousness of some workers, peasants, and intelligentsia.[159]

Different appreciations of threat to the NSM turned on understandings of just how vulnerable the Soviet project was to unstable class identities. The

[156] Ibid., 547. Emphases added.

[157] Jim Richter has suggested another way in which modernity and the NSM were connected: the predominant discourse of the idealized public figure transforming nature versus the insurgent discourse of a flawed person with personal space aspiring to deal with the empirical reality that exists. Personal communication, March 2001.

[158] "The Moral Cast of the Soviet Man," *Pravda*, 4 April 1955, p. 1. Rumiantsev urged the dismissal of Boris Riurikov as editor of *Literaturnaya Gazeta* over an article by E. Vorobyev, "The Hero and His Enemy," which Rumiantsev claimed allowed the "enemy a microphone." TsKhSD, f. 5, op. 17, d. 356, pp. 15–16.

[159] M. Zhuravkov, "On Communist Morality," *Pravda*, 10 April 1955, p. 2.

resulting sentiments represented an official Soviet concern that exposure to deviations from the typical might start a course of societal degeneration. Others, however, suggested that the Soviet system at home was so strong that deviation was innocuous, and that, indeed, if Soviets were to know their problems and enemies, they had to be publicly discussed. This discussion took various forms. One reached right to the top—the argument between revealing deviation in order to vanquish it or trying to erase it in order to reduce its corrupting effects to a minimum occurred in the MVD. In July, S. Perevertkin, deputy minister of the MVD and the head of the Political Department of the Border Forces, appealed to the CC to open the border-guard museum to the public. Until then, only party and soviet *aktiv;* soldiers and workers at the defense, internal affairs, and state security ministries; and foreign communist border guards could go see exhibitions on fighting the Basmachi, white Finns, hostile capitalist states, and other threats to the Soviet Union.[160]

Tolerating deviance or promoting exposure to it so as to innoculate Soviet citizens was one thing, but it was another to argue that deviance was a positive good, that difference actually strengthened Soviet identity. The latter was expressed in popular novels of the time.

In *The Russian Forest*, Vikhrov's old schoolmate, Cheredilov, advises the iconoclastic forester that he should stop trying to preserve Russian woodlands, he should "step aside. The engine will crush you. . . . Let others live, and you will live to 121 yourself." Cheredilov advises expedience in the face of the collective juggernaut. But the author, in the voice of the narrator, mocks Cheredilov's "wooden, edifying tone, like a radio." Vikhrov, meanwhile, cannot believe that this man is the same one who had "sung songs at student parties, and in a way that had brought tears to one's eyes."[161] In this version of events, the NSM is depicted as less than human, more of a cog in a machine mouthing the appropriate slogans. Korneichuk's hero in *Wings*, Pyotr Romodan, is the new *obkom* secretary in an agricultural region of Ukraine. In a meeting with Gordei Dremlyuga, the chairman of the *oblast*'s soviet, about preparations for the upcoming conference of leading agricultural workers in the *oblast*, Romodan expresses surprise at the fact that many of the speeches, written by Dremlyuga's aide, Kirill Vernigora, are alike. Romodan asks whether Vernigora "really believes that all the speakers think in exactly the same way?" It turns out that the speakers had sent in drafts of

---

[160] GARF, Khrushchev special file, t. III, d. 465, pp. 257–58. Consistent with this relaxed concern with exposure to deviance, Sergei Kruglov recommended to the CC that people crossing into the Soviet Union from capitalist countries should no longer be prosecuted for border violations, usually meaning a sentence of one to three years in the camps, if they were seeking a better life in the Soviet Union. Instead, suggested Kruglov, they should be resettled to Kazakhstan (t. V, d. 467, p. 84).

[161] Leonov, *Russian Forest*, 416–17.

their remarks, only to have them purged of any criticism of Dremlyuga and his incompetence. To Romodan's decision that the critics be allowed to speak, Dremlyuga replies that the "prestige of the raikom secretary and the leadership of the party itself will be undermined." But Romodan, instead of acknowledging the costs of allowing deviation from the script, contends that allowing Garbuz, the drunkard *kolkhoz* chairman, the *raikom* secretary accused of insisting on his appointment over the objections of the *kolkhozniki* themselves, and Dremlyuga all speak will ensure a fair debate.[162] The tension between the search for uniformity and confidence in difference is played out in this meeting and in the subsequent scenes of the play. Tereshchenko, a horticulturist, expresses his confusion at the prospect of having the *obkom* secretary and *oblast* soviet chairman disagree on some issue. He asks, "what line am I to take; whom shall I support?"[163] One subsequent scene, a political lecture to *kolkhozniki*, gives rise to the character "Comrade Nudnik," a dull mouther of Marxist-Leninist slogans.[164]

The NSM had no private identity.[165] His ideas, interests, and actions were all calculated according to how he could serve the construction of socialism in the Soviet Union. There was no room in his life for private pursuits, unless they were instrumental to the achievement of public aims. "The public activities of a Soviet man and his daily life are inseparable. . . . V. Maiakovskii justly wrote: Communism is not only of the land, or in the sweat of the factory. It is at home at the table, in relations with the family and in daily life." This understanding of the NSM evinced a very deep appreciation for the power of social practice. After all, it was precisely the nonpublic social actions of millions that had reproduced religious and national identities. The official view admitted to no separation, so private indiscretions "inevitably lead to de-ideologization, to the loss of political vigilance; a man stops being a real communist."[166] Projecting this account onto the country revealed the true fear: backsliding away from the Soviet project, much the same as tolerating deviance more generally.

As in most discussions of identity, there was an acknowledgement that a purely public NSM was impossible, perhaps even undesirable. But the question remained of how to demarcate the boundaries between the public and

[162] Korneichuk, *Wings*, 72–77.

[163] Ibid., 122.

[164] Petr Kapitsa, dean of Soviet nuclear physics, sent a letter to Khrushchev complaining that "dogmatists of the Nudnik type" predominated at Academy of Science meetings. These, Kapitsa wrote, do not differ much from the meetings of *kolkhozniki* in Korneichuk's play. Petr L. Kapitsa, *Pisma na Nauke, 1930–1980* (Moscow, 1989), 316. The letter is dated December 15, 1955.

[165] On conceptions of public and private in prerevolutionary Russian and early Soviet times, see Boym, *Common Places*, especially 73–88.

[166] "The Moral Cast," *Pravda*, 4 April 1955, 1. See also Zhuravkov, "On Communist Morality," 3.

private. Simonov spoke of this problem at the writers' congress. He observed that although public interests have primacy over personal ones "the word primat means primacy, not extirpation." He lamented that in Soviet literature there were many examples of authors eliminating the private, so that "raikom secretaries have been deprived of the right to dream, eat, get medical attention when sick. Not to mention love and personal happiness."[167] The struggle between the official effort to make the private public and the popular effort to keep the private personal can be understood as a Soviet effort to glorify and mythologize the mundane, to heroicize daily practice, whereas average Soviets just wanted a normal conventional daily life, one without any public meaning. But Soviet officials sensed that permitting personal practice would only reproduce identities at variance with the public project—constructing socialism. To Soviet officials, there was no such thing as a private practice that did not have implications for the state's project. Social practices in private that might be constituting unwanted premodern identities could have their meanings transformed through connection to a public identity.

The meaning of the NSM and his many connections to the modern, class, and national identities may be summarized in the discussions of the writers' congress, in particular the discussion that surrounded Ilya Ehrenburg's *The Thaw*.[168] Khrushchev later commented on Ehrenburg, the Thaw, and *The Thaw*, capturing the tension between difference and unity nicely: "In choosing on the coming of the thaw, the leadership of the USSR, including myself, simultaneously were rather afraid of it." What was there to fear? A flood that would "emasculate us. . . . We feared losing previous possibilities of running the country, restraining the growth of feelings inconvenient for the leadership. . . . We feared that the leadership would not be able to direct the process of changes . . . such that it would remain *Soviet*."[169] The issue, then, was nothing less than Soviet identity itself.

Both the writers' congress and the discussion around Ehrenburg's slim 1954 volume reflected the complicated ambiguity that attended the effort to demarcate the acceptable boundaries of deviance. Marina Franichevich, the head of the Yugoslav delegation attending the congress, reported that Soviet writers, faced with the official demands of socialist realism, were all "trying to find a way out through compromise."[170] At the congress, *The Thaw* became the subject of discussion precisely because its heroes were not ideal. At a time when the average Soviet novel was produced in an edition of 30,000, Ehrenburg's book was a kind of sensation. It was sold on the black

[167] *Vtoroi Vsesoiuznyi Syezd Sovetskikh Pisatelei*, 102.
[168] Ilya Ehrenburg, *The Thaw* (London, 1955).
[169] Khurshchev, *Vospominaniia*, 506–7. Emphasis added.
[170] AVPRF, f. 144, op. 16, d. 740, p. 10.

market for exorbitant sums and was circulated in typewritten copies as well.[171] Anatolii S. Cherniaev, in his memoirs, reports that *The Thaw* was "bought up, read, and heatedly discussed in editorials, at different plena, in kitchens and living rooms, in student corridors and at village youth meetings [*posidelki*], in both drunken and sober company, and in the metro and on streetcars."[172]

Konstantin Simonov, the last speaker of the second day of the congress, and the successor to Tvardovsky at *Novyi Mir*, began by saluting Ehrenburg for dealing with the "rough edges in life," and for showing that a "good Soviet man" need not come in a perfect package. But, ultimately, Simonov could not tolerate the ambiguity, and said so, complaining about the "contradictory feelings" caused by the novel. These contradictory sentiments were evoked because Ehrenburg's heroes do not have enough good qualities, according to Simonov. They see too much bad in their lives.[173] The first secretary of the Komsomol, A. A. Rapokhin, criticized Ehrenburg for forcing his readers to meet "unhinged people, traumatized people, spiritually disturbed people, careerists, and ass-kissers."[174] Galina Nikolaeva accused Ehrenburg of not knowing how to use "our fundamental weapon of typification. Ehrenburg populated his *Thaw* entirely with petty, passive atypical people and created in it a strange atmosphere of inertia for us."[175] M. P. Petrov found Ehrenburg's characters so odd that he felt as if the action in the novel were taking place in "some remote town in pre-revolutionary Russia."[176] The intolerable deviation here was ambiguity, atypicality, and premodernity.

In fact, this debate appears in the novel itself. Savchenko, an unsuccessful artist, complains that Koroteyev, an engineer, wrongly attacked a romantic novel at a public meeting at the library. Savchenko claims that Koroteyev only gave the party line against flawed characters and pointless romance. Volodya, Pukhov's cynical son, defends Koroteyev, arguing Koroteyev was right not to say what he thought; it is always better to be strategic. Volodya's father upbraids his son for this attitude. Savchenko continues that the public is really thirsting for books like this. Then Pukhov's daughter Sonya a true believer, speaks up. Her words hint at the interesting alliance against the deviant of cynics and true believers. She says Koroteyev

---

[171] Maurice Friedberg, *A Deacade of Euphoria: Western Literature in Post-Stalin Russia, 1954–64* (Bloomington, Ind., 1977), 155. *The Thaw* was reissued in 1955 in an edition of 45,000 copies. Edward Crankshaw, *Russia without Stalin: The Emerging Pattern* (New York, 1956), 136.

[172] Anatolii S. Cherniaev, *Moia Zhizn i Moe Vremia* (Moscow, 1995), 219. He also identifies the works of Panova as "a subject of spontaneous mass discussions" in the mid-1950s, 217.

[173] *Vtoroi Vsesoiuznyi Syezd Sovetskikh Pisatelei*, 91. See also 295.

[174] Ibid., 243.

[175] Ibid., 386.

[176] Ibid., 491.

was right; "a novel has to educate, not confuse the reader. . . ." Cynics see deviants as naive; true believers see them as dangerous. Savchenko concludes, "you cannot put everything so neatly into pigeonholes."[177]

Z. Kedrina offers a balanced perspective of *The Thaw.* She argues it is not the fact that bad leaders are shown in the book that "distresses us," because they should be in our literature. No, what "annoys us is that Ehrenburg did not show the struggle itself." He shows "Zhuravlev, along with the barracks that were unfit for housing, being swept away by a hurricane, and not by the efforts of positive figures, who remain inactive." The truth of a communist future should not have been revealed by a strong wind, but by "the struggle of people for communism, criticism, the battle between new and old."[178] In sum, Ehrenburg lost a golden opportunity to educate society about how deviance was disciplined and extirpated by the deliberate efforts of Soviet society, not by acts of God.

Ehrenburg's response to his critics, including to those had who published attacks in the media prior to and during the congress, came one day after Simonov's address.[179] He began by condemning those who lived in a world of simplicity, of binarization, of

> black and white. Such authors embellish the outsides of their heroes, but impoverish them spiritually; they do not want for gold in depicting communal apartments; workshops in their writings look like laboratories, kolkhoz clubs like boyars' mansions; but this treacly phoney world is populated by primitive creatures, wax goody-goodies who have nothing in common with Soviet people, with their complicated, deep internal lives.[180]

Ehrenburg then asked his audience ironically, "Isn't it time to open a section in the Union of Writers for adult literature?" This slap was met with applause. To justify his appeal for a more candid treatment of problems in the Soviet Union, Ehrenburg argued that the time of danger was past, that now "a generation has grown up for which our society is the only rational

---

[177] Ehrenburg, *The Thaw,* 32–33.

[178] Z. Kedrina, "Literature Intrudes into Life," *Literaturnaya Gazeta* (LG), 22 March 1955, p. 3. M. Kuznetsov made precisely the same criticism of Ehrenburg at a three-day conference at the Gorky Institute of World Literature devoted to Russian Soviet literature of 1954, reprinted in LG, 2 April 1955, p. 3.

[179] *Vtoroi Vsesoiuznyi Syezd Sovetskikh Pisatelei,* 142–44. It is of note that Ehrenburg's short talk was met by prolonged applause both at his introduction and at the talk's end. Alone among all the speakers, some two hundred of them, Ehrenburg was ironic and playful in his remarks.

[180] *Vtoroi Vsesoiuznyi Syezd Sovetskikh Pisatelei,* 143. Note Ehrenburg's clever appropriation of modernity for the realist position, declaiming those who support the Soviet ideal as "primitives."

one."[181] In other words, Soviet identity had already been secured; alternatives were unthinkable. To the extent that Soviet rule was consolidated, the coast should be clear for deviance.

How far the Thaw had gone in 1955 and how serious a danger it was regarded by the guardians of orthodoxy can be gauged from a report by Rumiantsev to the CC on what he considered to be a dangerous deviation: a *Literaturnaya Gazeta* party where they made fun of socialist realism. To paraphrase Rumiantsev's report, on April 16 *Literaturnaya Gazeta* put on a program at the House of Film, including "Bonfire in LitGaz," "In the International Life Section," "Discussions on the Question of O-Opera," "From Memoirs on the 2d Congress," and "Examination in the Literature Institute." In Rumiantsev's opinion, "The contents, in particular the monologue 'From the 2d Congress' and 'Examination' promote philistine views of serious and important questions of literary life." In other words, they laughed at the debate over difference. Rumiantsev quotes an offensive passage from the "From Memoirs on the 2d Congress": "All the reports at the congress were read and discussed for a long time, re-read, re-discussed, verified, edited, verified, anew rewritten, discussed, etc. etc. So that each of the speakers could say about his report the famous words of Tolstoy—'In three waters it has been drowned, in three bloods it has swum, in three salt baths it has been cooked. We are purer than pure.'" In "Examination," they wanted to prove the congress had no results, so a student, asked to characterize the results of the congress, at first hopelessly wrung his hands, then was silent for a long time, and finally asked for the next question. Finally, Rumiantsev points out that the more liberal partygoers, such as Konstantin Simonov and Boris Riurikov, received only "friendly jests," whereas the upholders of orthodoxy, such as Surkov, were "skewered."[182] To the extent that the identity of the NSM and his guardians were ridiculed and satirized, the boundaries of difference were expanded as at no time since the 1920s.

The connection between the identity of the NSM and Soviet foreign policy revolved around the issue of deviance. Just as this level of tolerance for ambiguity and difference varied at home, it should vary abroad as well. Soviet understandings of other states should in part be situated in their tolerance for difference, difference from themselves, from their understandings of Self. For example, understandings of China and people's democracies would be refracted through the Soviet understanding of socialism at home. Chinese, German, or Yugoslav deviations from this Soviet identity would be treated differently, depending on how deviation was regarded at home. Similarly, countries such as India and Egypt, and the decolonizing world in general,

---

[181] Ibid.
[182] TsKhSD, f. 5, op. 17, d. 536, pp. 42–43.

would be understood through the model of the Soviet domestic periphery. Soviet tolerance for deviation abroad is expected to rest on tolerance for deviation at home. If Soviets understood the Soviet project to be secure at home, and hence free for difference, they would understand the same abroad. In terms of alliances, there should be a positive correlation between an understanding of a secure self and potential alliance opportunities.

These inferences and consequent hypotheses do not just follow from the NSM; they were explicitly offered by the Soviets themselves. First of all, the Soviets had reason to be anxious about conflict at home in 1955. The weekly MVD reports distributed to the Presidium catalog hundreds of labor camp insurrections, prison riots, acts of violent crime, strikes at labor camps, and violations of the border in both directions.[183] Closer to home, Sergei Kruglov, MVD chief, reported to the CC that 8,000 young people committed crimes in Moscow in 1954, over 10 percent of whom were members of the Komsomol.[184] Soviets arguing about whether or not deviations from an ideal Soviet person should be treated as healthy or dangerous found themselves referring to the external Other, the West, as the primary interested party in Soviet domestic order. So, for example, Boris Riurikov, editor of *Literaturnaya Gazeta,* tried to show the congress audience that revealing conflicts in literary works was good because it facilitates their resolution and eases their disappearance. He tried to reassure them by reminding them that "in our country there are no antagonistic classes, but there are vestiges of the old and the capitalist camp."[185] Riurikov argued that the kinds of deviance seen at home not only did not make the Soviet Union vulnerable to the West, but in fact facilitated the amelioration of these deviations.

Most important, whatever his ambivalence, Khrushchev appeared to have shared the understandings expressed by Riurikov, Ehrenburg, Leonov, Panova, and many others that difference was tolerable, if not positively desirable, at home. Others feared the appearance of disunity before the masses, who presumably expected unanimity and decisiveness. Khrushchev explained to the July plenum why he rejected Voroshilov's concerns about bringing Molotov's mistakes before the full plenum. Khrushhev said that Voroshilov had argued that "there was no reason to put this question before the plenum since people will think that we have a fight and this will play into the hands of our enemies. But I did not think there was a fight—we will . . . put him in his place, so that he won't violate the principles of collective leadership."[186] In other words, difference can have an educative effect.

---

[183] GARF, Khrushchev special file, t. III, d. 465.

[184] GARF, Khrushchev special file, t. I op. 2, d. 463, p. 31.

[185] *Vtoroi Vsesoiuznyi Syezd Sovetskikh Pisatelei,* 314. See also M. G. Papava's speech in which arguments are equated to oxygen (567).

[186] CC Plenum, July 12, 1955, 33.

Moreover, Khrushchev appeared to have accepted the idea of personal space and did so in an international context. In response to a reporter's question in India, he notes that in a nation of 200 million only 8 million were in the Communist Party and 18.5 million in the Komsomol and concludes that "the question of ideas, of convictions, is a personal question for each man. In the USSR, communists and non-party members, atheists and believers work side by side for the good of the people."[187] Here is the litmus test for Soviet identity. If an individual is a productive member of society contributing to the construction of socialism, she is a good Soviet citizen. This interpretation of Khrushchev fits perfectly with his attitude toward the working class and peasantry and his barely veiled disdain for city-slicker bureaucrats. As he told an audience of Indian boy scouts, "Only labor ennobles the spirit of man and gives him all the resources for life."[188]

HYPOTHESIZING ABOUT THE CONSTRUCTION
OF SOVIET FOREIGN POLICY AT HOME

Class, modernity, nation, and the NSM—these are the four primary identities that dominated Soviet conversation in Moscow 1955. Each anchored Soviet understandings of Others in world politics in particular ways. But, just as important, each also related to identities at home, reinforcing some defining elements, complicating others. The idea of the Soviet vanguard, the Soviet Union as leader, was central to the class, modern, and national identities. These three combined together into a powerful self-identification for the Soviet Union as the superior member of any alliance, group, or partnership; they reified the hierarchical syntax characteristic of their identities. Class identity and the NSM were closely linked in their binarization of the world. Either an individual was a worker or he was not; either an individual was an example of the Soviet model or she was not. Both class and the NSM push the transformation of differences into danger, both at home and abroad.

Our hypotheses about the effects of these identities on foreign policy are:

- The more strictly class analysis was pursued, the more likely the Soviet Union understood its allies in a more constrained and binarized manner. Potential allies should have to pass a class identity litmus test. The more loosely class analysis was applied, the more likely the Soviet Union understood its allies in a more accommodative manner that did not turn difference into danger. Potential allies should be allowed to perform poorly on any class identity test.

[187] Speech before the Indian parliament, *Pravda*, 22 November 1955, p. 2.
[188] *Pravda*, 22 November 1955, p. 3.

- The Soviet modern identity should lead to potential allies being understood through Soviet understandings of its own modernization. More precisely, the Soviet periphery should be the Self through which the decolonizing world was understood. In the modernization process, the Soviet Union should understand itself as the vanguard for others.
- Modernity should also stimulate Soviet understandings of itself as a great power in an international hierarchy characterized by material power.
- The Russian national identity, being part of Soviet self-understanding, articulated itself in relation to others. Russian historical relations with others became the relevant Soviet past with them; Russian cultural and linguistic relations with others became the Soviet version of the same. The result should be Soviet differentiation among states according to its reading of Russia in those contexts.
- The more strictly construed the NSM was, the more binarized and dangerous differences with other states should be instantiated. The more deviance allowed from the model, the more differences should be permitted with potential Soviet allies. There should be a positive correlation between a sense of security at home and the number of potential allies abroad.

3/

Identities as Social Structures
Enabling and Constraining
Soviet Alliance Choices in 1955

Soviet leaders made many foreign policy choices in 1955. They withdrew from Austria; created the Warsaw Pact; recognized West Germany; visited India, Burma, and Afghanistan; rebuilt relations with Tito's Yugoslavia; attended the Four Power summit in Geneva; and continued deepening commitments to China. With one exception, I account for these choices based on the domestic identities and discourses of Moscow. The identities of class, modernity, nation, and the New Soviet Man (NSM) explain much about the origins of Soviet interests in these foreign policy choices. But an additional identity, that of a great power, emerged from Soviet discourse on foreign policy itself, not obviously connected to any domestic identity formations or discourses.

This is an important finding in several ways. First, it shows that systemic constructivists are right to think that at least part of a state's identity is produced through interaction with other states and not with its own society. Second, it shows that neorealists are partially right because there is in fact a great power identity for the Soviet Union. Third, it shows that the theoretical account used here is falsifiable, that is, the methodology can alert us to instances when domestic identities and discourses in themselves are insufficient to provide an account of a state's identity and interests. Finally, it offers the possibility of elaborating an account of how the international discourse of great power politics could fit with the domestic discourse of class, modernity, nation, and the NSM.[1]

IDENTITIES AND FOREIGN POLICY

Class Divisions

There were three categories of states for which class analysis had consequences for the Soviet Union's understandings of its identities: bourgeois

---

[1] I wish to thank Nicholas Onuf for compelling me to rethink just what a great power identity entailed.

capitalist states, especially in the West; socialist allies in eastern Europe and China; and decolonizing states. The common effects of class analysis include the binarization of identities between proletariat and bourgeoisie; the construction of a hierarchy of development and progress; and the siting of the working class at the center, with the Soviet Union, and its Communist Party, as the vanguard of that center.

At the official level, the working class in Europe, North America, and Asia was the natural ally of the Soviet Union, with the Soviet Union being the vanguard of that class.[2] What made them such reliable allies was the fact that their material conditions objectively gave them the same interests vis-à-vis capitalism and imperialism. This analysis clarified why the countries of people's democracy in eastern Europe and the socialist countries of China and North Korea were placed above all others in the hierarchy of Soviet allies. Because socialism had triumphed in these countries, the working classes were in control and thus, the natural allies of the Soviet Union. Expanding on this theme, official Soviet understandings of the class nature of friend and foe derived from class relations at home. Having established socialism, there were no antagonistic contradictions in Soviet society and thus no class conflict to be projected onto foreign affairs. Matters were precisely the opposite in the capitalist world, where inevitable class conflict between the proletariat and the bourgeoisie drove the latter to seek superprofits abroad to buy off the workers' aristocracy. Crises of overproduction, combined with niggardly wages and chronic unemployment, led to underconsumption, all to be resolved through the search for new markets. The result was inherent expansionism, efforts to restore capitalism in countries that had become socialist, and efforts to dominate those that had freed themselves from imperialism and colonialism. So, by their class nature, capitalist countries were essentially bellicose.[3] War itself, therefore, as the product of private property relations, would disappear only when socialism had triumphed everywhere.[4]

[2] This paragraph relies on "Editorial: The Great Power of Leninist Ideas of Internationalism," *Kommunist* 1 (1955): 3–4. The importance of class identity as a custodian of hierarchical order can be inferred from the following event. Pospelov sent a draft of a letter to *Kommunist* to Suslov for his review and approval. What could have necessitated such a course of action? In a previous article in the party's main theoretical journal, the Soviet Union had been described as having not yet completed the construction of socialism. Such a self-understanding meant that the Soviet Union was no longer the undisputed vanguard of socialism in the world. After all, China and peoples' democracies were already building socialism, too. Center for the Preservation of Contemporary Documentation, fond 5, opis 30, delo 90, stranitsa 104 [hereafter TsKhSd, f., op., d. p.].

[3] This is a distillation of various official renditions of world politics, but it relies most heavily on Lenin's theory of imperialism. See also I. Sotnikov, "Stephanopoulos vs. Marxism," *New Times* no. 8 (February 19, 1955): 16.

[4] V. Zagladin and L. Sedin, "Lenin and the Struggle for Peace," *New Times* no. 16 (April 16, 1955): 7.

The very concept of peaceful coexistence was expressed in terms of class identity. Just who were the actors Soviets thought could exist peacefully with one another? They were not different nations, different religions, different ethnic groups, different regions, or even simply different states. They were "countries with different social systems." The axis of difference was a class-based one. Other states were simply, and often identified as, capitalist.[5] The class identity of the Soviet Union as socialist vanguard was in inherent opposition to capitalism. The Soviet Union could not understand who it was without evaluating itself in relation to the capitalist, imperialist Other.

Soviet understandings of class also accounted for the Soviet expectation that its alliances were natural communities of identical interests borne of common class identity. Soviets frequently foresaw and called for unity among decolonized states against imperialism, expecting that the anticolonial or antiimperialist identities of these countries could overcome national, interstate, or ethnic differences; among workers and progressive publics against bourgeois governments; and among peasants, workers, and intelligentsia in allied states in opposition to reactionary forces. Unity was always preferred over difference and was expected along natural lines of class identity.

A class understanding of socialist allies implied a strict scrutiny of their adherence to the standards of the Soviet model and criticism of any deviation from the same. The logic of the closest Other implied a heightened concern for the Other that was most constitutive of the Self. The Ministry of Foreign Affairs (MFA) briefing books provided by Zimianin to CPSU Presidium member Lazar Kaganovich prior to his official visit to Czechoslovakia in May 1955 were largely a comparison of Czech reality to the Soviet model. The materials included notes on the theses of the Czech Communist Party; Soviet ambassador Firiubin's report on his trip to Slovakia in April 1955; and the biographies of leading Czech cadres. The last were similar to biographies of Soviet party cadres, containing date of birth, education, party membership, employment history, war record, and class origin. The report to Kaganovich found fault with the Czech party's theses as if they were the product of a local Soviet *obkom* mistake, rather than of another state. Reflective of an appreciation of the dangers of difference, it was recommended that more party vigilance be directed at "the activities of the other parties entering the National Front," because "imperialists aspire to use reactionary elements that have entrenched themselves in these parties for subversion." Such activity was carried on by bourgeois parties from Nazi times, Slovak nationalists, and anti-Stalinist youth movements. The threat of national identity was supplemented and often reinforced by the power of religious

---

[5] As in a Ministry of Foreign Affairs (MFA) memorandum on NATO circulated to the Presidium in March 1955. Archive of the Foreign Policy of the Russian Federation [hereafter AVPRF], f. 06, op. 14, d. 115, p. 4.

identity in the countryside, especially where "the Catholic clergy enjoy great authority among the people."[6] This analysis was comparable to the Soviet understanding of any more backward area of the Soviet Union—threats from nationalist, religious, and bourgeois identities.[7]

Perhaps nothing was more important for Soviet understanding of the decolonizing world than its class analysis of its own periphery in central Asia. According to conventional Marxism, the liberation of the colonial world was most likely to come through revolutions in the metropole rather than through the efforts of the colonized. This was so because no working class, or its vanguard, the Communist Party, existed in the periphery. But the Soviet understanding of its own revolution gave rise to a new Leninist corollary: the noncapitalist path of development. Colonial peoples did need not wait for revolution in Europe or for a working class to develop at home; through national liberation, they could come to power and embark on the noncapitalist path to socialism, just as had been accomplished in central Asia with the aid of a surrogate vanguard in Russia.[8]

With this understanding of their own periphery, Soviets came to understand how socialism could happen in a preproletarian, premodern, precapitalist decolonizing world. Without this Soviet Leninist understanding of socialist development in its own domestic periphery, the Soviet encounter with the decolonizing world in 1955 would have been much different and Soviet interests there would have been much less important.

If class identity alone dominated the Soviet understanding of other states, the West would be a most dangerous Other, allies would be expected to adhere strictly to the Soviet model, and the decolonizing world would have only the most long-term socialist prospects and only if it accepted the Soviet Union as its vanguard. Differences with allies would be neither welcomed nor tolerated, differences with the capitalists would be expected and defended against, and differences with the decolonizing world would be both expected and expected to disappear over time.

The Modern Metric

The Soviet apprehension of its own modernity implied hierarchical understandings of the rest of the world. Soviet modernity was read through its

---

[6] Report to Lazar Kaganovich, in Russian Center for the Preservation and Study of Documents of Russian History [hereafter RTsKhIDNI], f. 81, op. 3, d. 88, pp. 59–95.

[7] For another comprehensive analysis of a socialist ally, in this case North Korea, that was distilled through the Soviet account of itself, see the memorandum prepared by Suslov and Molotov for the CC Presidium dated January 17, in TsKhSD, f. 5, op. 30, d. 120, pp. 1–2. In his speech in East Berlin on the sixth anniversary of the German Democratic Republic, Suslov explicitly identified the East German "working class as its [the Soviet Union's] reliable faithful ally," not mentioning the East German state. *Pravda*, 7 October 1955, pp. 3–4.

[8] For an official rendition of this idea, see M. Kammari, "Lenin and the Creative Role of Popular Masses," *Pravda*, 21 January 1955, p. 3.

own premodern periphery in central Asia, the experience by which the modern Soviet Self and the many degrees of premodernity evident in foreign contexts were grasped. The Soviet vanguard at home was an identity through which Soviets could comprehend the USSR's relationship to less developed, premodern allies in the rest of the world. We were like you once— this could have been the title of many Soviet speeches and analyses of the entire non-Soviet world, but especially of countries such as India, Burma, Afghanistan, and China. In a preponderance of speeches and articles, the Soviet Union was the exemplar that had already traversed the path to modernity that others were just beginning. Soviet assessments of others abroad are almost identical to the Soviet Union's assessments of itself. The identities and practices were transferred from the domestic to the foreign, as if this were not a meaningful boundary at all.

Soviets differentiated between an exoticized premodern periphery in the decolonizing world and the modern core of the Soviet Union and Europe. They contrasted those "swarming, dark-eyed, merry, lively"[9] people of Asia and Africa with those living in Europe, Japan, or North America, let alone in Russia, to which such descriptions were never applied. Reporting on the conference for peace held in Moscow in May, V. Iordansky described the "Uzbeks and Tajiks in their multi-colored robes" and delegates from "sunny Georgia."[10] Within the boundaries of this exoticization were parts of the Soviet periphery.

Soviet modernity, as mediated by gender, family, and religion in central Asia, was applied to Moslem countries in the Middle East. "A resolution on social questions [in the Arab East] demands equality for women. . . ."[11] The Soviet understanding of how the Soviet state had modernized central Asia included a prominent place for the emancipation of women from their veils, houses, and husbands.[12]

Yuri Zavadsky, a "People's Artist of the USSR," took a trip to India along with Aleksei Surkov, the chair of the Soviet Writers' Union. On their way, they stopped in Karachi, where "the modern, substantially built European quarter" was juxtaposed with "appalling poverty."[13] In his trip to Vietnam, A. Kozhin saw "narrow streets full of people . . . like bubbling rivulets." The

[9] For example, N. Sergeyeva's report on the Bandung conference in *New Times*, no. 17 (April 23, 1955): 22.

[10] V. Iordansky, "Mandate for Peace," *New Times*, no. 20 (May 14, 1955): 12–13. Recall as well Sovetkin's "swarthy" Kazakh in his Russian language textbook. F. F. Sovetkin, *Uchebnik Russkogo Yazyka dlya Molodezhi, ne Vladeiushchei Russkim Yazykom* (Moscow, 1954), 132.

[11] The texts of the resolutions of the Asian Conference for Detente, which met in Delhi just two weeks before the Bandung conference appear as a special supplement to *New Times*, no. 16 (April 16, 1955).

[12] See, for example, T. N. Kary-Niiazov, *Ocherki Istorii Kultury Sovetskogo Uzbekstana* (Moscow, 1955), 541–44.

[13] Yuri Zavadsky, "Thirty-Five Days in India," *New Times*, no. 18 (May 1, 1955): 28.

"sun shines merrily."[14] N. Sergeyeva, in Vietnam, comments on a "round, chocolate-brown face with a friendly smile and black eyes shining. . . ."[15] At the world youth festival held in Warsaw in August, A. Letnev, a Soviet reporter, describes "the delegates from five continents": Ho Thi Giang, a Vietnamese woman, had "lively brown eyes and a charming smile"; Walter Kaufmann, "a well-known writer" from Australia, as the European model, warranted no further physical description; Robert McInnes was a "short, stocky, light-haired fellow" from Scotland; Georges Randrianaly from Madagascar was a "stocky fellow with raven-black hair and shining black eyes"; and, within Europe, the "small wiry effusive fellow," Yves Soustelle, from France, met up with the Soviet representative Anatoli Kulik, a "calm light-haired lad of athletic build."[16]

The premodern connection between the Soviet and global periphery was officially institutionalized as well. Soviet President Kliment Voroshilov sent greetings to the Bandung conference, but so too did the chairs of the presidia of the five central Asian republics. And the leaders of the decolonized world reciprocated such Soviet understandings. The Indonesian ambassador to Moscow, Subandrio, told first deputy foreign minister Kuznetsov that the next Bandung conference could be attended by the Soviet Union, or more precisely "its Asian republics."[17] The preparatory committee for participation in the Delhi conference on detente was heavily weighted toward central Asia, reflecting the official Soviet understanding of its own periphery and its relation to Asia and the Third World.[18] When the Soviet ambassador to Egypt, Danyl Solod, proposed to Moscow the way to set up a permanent cultural exhibition in Cairo, he asked for materials on desert reclamation in central Asia.[19]

The metric of modernity was applied to the more modern as well as to the premodern. For example, Lodz was described as a "new socialist city" because it had new squares; new tram services to distant suburbs; new nurseries and kindergartens created from the "sumptuous mansions of the manufacturers"; new hospitals and institutions of higher education, "there being none before Liberation," including a university, "half of whose students are the children of workers and peasants"; and new theaters, including an opera house.[20] Modernity was arranged hierarchically, from premodern to mod-

[14] A. Kozhin, "Dong Quan," *New Times*, no. 21 (May 21, 1955): 28.

[15] N. Sergeyeva, "Liberated Vietnam," *New Times*, no. 27 (July 1, 1955): 21.

[16] A. Letnev, "The World Youth Festival," *New Times*, no. 33 (August 11, 1955): 12–22.

[17] AVPRF, f. 100, op. 48, d. 6, p. 29.

[18] In *Pravda*, 16 February 1955, p. 4.

[19] TsKhSD, f. 5, op. 30, d. 123, p. 162.

[20] Letnev, "World Youth Festival," 27. See also Bronislaw Wiernik, "New Horizons," *New Times*, no. 44 (October 27, 1955): 20–22. On Bulgaria, see Olga Shulenina, "The Plovdiv Fair," *New Times*, no. 40 (September 29, 1955): 28–29.

ern. The Soviet Union was an advanced industrial power, but its eastern European allies were only "advanced industrial-agrarian states,"[21] which was better than being merely agrarian. This arrangement was tied to the class identity of Soviet allies in the world—the more agrarian an ally, the smaller its proletariat, the bigger its peasantry, and, therefore, the less reliable its socialist transformation and its alliance with Moscow.

Becoming modern in Poland, and in people's democracies in general, meant becoming Soviet, just as becoming modern in the Soviet Union meant becoming a Russian in Moscow. The new modern identity was associated with new interests and social practices. The parable of Soviet modernity was externalized in the story of two Polish brothers, Michal and Marin, in which many elements of the Soviet narrative are present. The two men are peasants in Jankowice, where "the new and the old were still in conflict" and where peasants are still "gripped by superstitions." Whereas Michal becomes the chair of the new cooperative farm, his brother Marin, influenced by his wife Anna, who has been scared by the village priest, declines to join at first. Only when his own crops fail and he lusts after the Ursus tractor being used on the collective, does Marin come around. The moral of the story was that modernity and progress were inevitable, held back only by religion, superstition, and irrational fear.[22]

Soviet understandings of itself as the ultimate modern project placed other countries on a hierarchical continuum. Other countries were identified, situated, judged, ranked, and apprehended according to how Soviets related them to their own domestic modern identity. Soviet policy toward the decolonizing world in 1955, in particular, is not comprehensible without an appreciation of how the Soviet modern identity informed its own apprehension of Self.

National Expectations

National identity in the Soviet Union articulated itself in foreign policy in three ways. The first was the way the Russian national identity substituted for a Soviet national past. The second was the way the multinational identity of the Soviet Union implied understandings of nationalism and multinationality abroad. The last was the way the national identities of other states were appreciated by Soviets.

It was customary for Soviets to refer to the "long historical ties" that bound the Soviet Union to another country. But the absence of a Soviet history meant that Russian ties were actually invoked. Sometimes the connection between Russian and Soviet identities was seamless, as in this declaration in

---

[21] I. Laponogov, "International Role of the European People's Democracies," *New Times*, no. 46 (November 10, 1955): 13.

[22] A. Letnev, "New Life in an Old City," *New Times*, no. 40 (September 29, 1955): 22–24.

Burma by Khrushchev: "Russia has never gone to war against England, but England has attacked our country both in the past, and in our Soviet times."[23] In trying to make the point that Soviet culture was superior to the past, he listed Russian art, Russian ballet, and Russian culture as the values that some of the Russian intelligentsia feared the Soviets would destroy rather than transcend.[24]

Touring Bulgaria, Boris Chirkov, a Soviet author, notes that in a Sofia museum tenth-century weaponry used by Russia and Bulgaria in alliance against Byzantine invaders could be found. Other exhibits were devoted to the efforts of Russia and Bulgaria to deliver the latter from the "Turkish yoke" in the Russo-Turkish war of 1877–78. Monuments to the "liberators" numbered in the hundreds and fresh flowers graced all of them. "The Bulgarian lovingly and respectfully calls his Russian friend Uncle Ivan." The Soviet commentator then takes the short step of remarking on the many newer monuments to the second Russian liberation of Bulgaria, the 1944 version.[25] Khrushchev reproduced this special shared Slavic identity, referring to "centuries-old bonds of friendship" with Bulgarians.[26] When Molotov had a dinner for UN delegations in New York, the attendees were Yugoslavia, Poland, and Czechoslovakia, or the Slavic collection.[27]

But nothing is more eloquent than silence. The day after his trip to Bulgaria, stopping in Rumania, Khrushchev gave the same kind of speech, summarizing the trip to Yugoslavia, but he did not identify any ancient ties with the non-Slavic Rumanians.[28] In some cases, Soviet actions reminded an ally of the Russian essence of the Soviet Union. On March 18, TASS reported that in Port Said, Egypt, a monument had been unveiled in memory of the Russian sailors of the World War I cruiser *Peresvet*, who died there in January 1917. The ship was sunk by a German submarine on its way to the "Rodina." It was peculiar because the czarist navy was being commemorated, the monument was erected by the Soviet defense ministry, and it was unveiled by the Soviet military attaché in Egypt. Understanding

---

[23] Nikita Khrushchev, speech reprinted in *New Times*, no. 52 (December 22, 1955): 4–8, quotation on 4.

[24] Ibid., 8.

[25] Boris Chirkov, "Autumn in Bulgaria," *New Times*, no. 46 (November 10, 1955): 22–23.

[26] *Pravda*, 4 June 1955, p. 1. Said during the visit to Sofia of the Soviet delegation that had just left Yugoslavia. See also the report of S. Krushinsky, a "special *Pravda* correspondent," to Dmitrii Shepilov on July 8. TsKhSD, f. 5, op. 30, d. 121, p. 49. See also N. I. Beliaev, "The Indestructible Friendship of the Bulgarian and Soviet Peoples," *Pravda*, 21 November 1955, p. 3. For an elaboration on the theme of historic national ties, see also his November 19 report to Voroshilov, in TsKhSD, f. 5, op. 30, d. 117, pp. 199–207.

[27] *Pravda*, 27 September 1955, p. 4.

[28] *Pravda*, 5 June 1955, p. 1. Nor did A. I. Kirichenko, Presidium member and first secretary of the Ukrainian Communist Party, during his speech at the congress of the Russian Communist Party. *Pravda*, 25 December 1955, p. 2.

itself as nationally Russian, the Soviet Union presented itself as if it were Russia.

Multinational Others evoked the multinational Soviet identity. Bulganin, welcoming the U Nu delegation from Burma, spoke for the "entire multinational Soviet people," not the Soviet identity that appeared when speaking to European audiences.[29] The Soviet understanding of itself as multinational affected the composition of official Soviet delegations. On May 10, a Soviet delegation set out for Warsaw to create the eponymous pact. Among the expected figures of Prime Minister Bulganin, Foreign Minister Molotov, Defense Minister Marshal Georgii Zhukov, and Marshal Ivan Konev were also the chairmen of the councils of ministers of Russia, Ukraine, Byelorussia, Latvia, Lithuania, and Estonia. The implication here was that the nations who had suffered Nazi occupation during World War II defined who the Soviet Union was in this instance.

Soviet nationality policy at home was reflected in Soviet understandings of national identities abroad. It was straightforward to support working class or peasant movements led by communist parties wherever they existed in the decolonizing world. The outcome in China was attractive. But the stubborn fact was that successful communist movements in the periphery were rare. Instead, whatever antiimperialist thrust there was came in the form of nationalist rebellions against colonial and imperial rule. How the Soviets understood these movements in 1955 can be better apprehended by grasping how nations were understood at home. National diversity was acceptable as long as socialist content remained. Jawaharlal Nehru's India and Gamal Abdel Nasser's Egypt were acceptable as long as the content of their actions could be construed as aiming toward a socialist future. In both arenas, foreign and domestic, national identity was regarded as both a natural feature of development and as a feature that must disappear in time.

Cognizant of its own multinational Self and the problem of international relations at home, Soviets understood national identities abroad as potential obstacles to the development of amicable relations between states. And the expected solution could be the same: "through joint struggle for the great cause of socialism, in joint labor in the construction of a new life," national differences would be eroded. As a factory worker wrote in his comments on Soviet-Chinese relations, "Workers of different nationalities, if they stand at the same lathe, rapidly find a common language."[30] The lesson was that national difference could be erased at home through development and ideological education; relations between states were not understood any differently.

Relations with other nation-states were affected both by the fact that the

[29] *Pravda*, 4 November 1955, p. 2.
[30] *Pravda*, 14 February 1955, p. 3.

Soviet Union understood itself as Russian and by the fact that international relations already existed at home. Relations between Russians and non-Russians tracked closely with the hierarchy associated with class and modernity. The Soviet Union as vanguard, the Soviet Union as senior partner, the Soviet Union as model—each flowed naturally from the Soviet national, class, and modern identities.

Deviance and Difference, Danger and Opportunity

If the official Soviet discourse could acknowledge that deviations from the NSM could still be good citizens of the Soviet Union, the possibility arose that noncommunist states and movements in the world could be good allies in a common struggle against imperialism. The binarization of the world into socialist and imperialist camps reduced the number of potential allies for the Soviet Union. Acknowledging difference at home made the acceptance of differences abroad less threatening. By making class only one of many possible identities for another state, the Soviet Union multiplied its possible relationships in the world. The "zone of peace," formally introduced at the Twentieth Party Congress in February 1956,[31] declared more than half of mankind available as alliance partners for the socialist community. It is impossible to overstate the importance of this particular Soviet self-understanding because it transformed, and greatly expanded, Soviet conceptualizations of its own interests abroad.

The NSM was an idealization. The politics of this identity concerned how far an individual or state could deviate from this model and still be regarded as a participant in the construction of socialism. The levels of tolerable deviance, difference, and ambiguity were closely related to the observer's confidence in the domestic security of socialism. The more an observer feared for its stability and vulnerability to bourgeois degeneration, the less she could tolerate any manifestations of difference and ambiguity. Tolerance of these manifestations multiplied Soviet opportunities for allies because many more could qualify. Intolerance, on the other hand, not only foreclosed opportunities, but also fixed the practices that could imaginably constitute a current ally.

The implications of this identity were manifest in Soviet understandings of other socialist countries, of prospective allies in the decolonizing world, and of the level of threat represented by the capitalist West. The Soviet fear of difference in its own allies was evident in the MFA briefing books prepared for Kaganovich prior to his trip to Czechoslovakia. Strong class identity implied a low tolerance for deviation from the ideal, but Soviet tolerance of differ-

---

[31] It was under discussion for many months prior to that. See Molotov's copy of a December 1955 draft of Khrushchev's speech, in TsKhSD, f. 1, op. 2, d. 3, p. 44.

ence is present in Khrushchev's treatment of deviance in the German Democratic Republic (GDR). In a speech before his East German guests, Khrushchev declared that "we understand how hard it is to achieve cooperation . . . among parties on all questions." On such occasions "political wisdom" is needed and "mutual concessions must be made." Khrushchev acknowledged that "the fact that our Soviet forces remain on your territory may provoke certain grievances, but we are confident that the necessity of this measure will be correctly understood."[32] Significantly, Khrushchev did not impute any sinister motives to those Germans who might be aggrieved; they were not allies of imperialism or bad Germans. This view of tolerable and explicable German difference was consistent with Khruschev's attitude toward the Thaw at home. For Khrushchev, an alliance with a similar Other should not be sacrificed for the sake of ensuring adherence to the ideal on all points.

How could Khrushchev have thought he could loosen political control over Soviet allies in eastern Europe and not suffer some kind of backlash, as occurred in Hungary in 1956? Zbigniew Brzezinski's answer resonates with the themes of this book. He argues that Khrushchev's ultimately misplaced confidence rested on the conviction that, as long as eastern Europeans were ideologically united with the Soviet Union on questions of economic construction and as long as they enjoyed strong ties between their ruling parties, variety in domestic political arrangements would not threaten the alliance.[33] There is a strong parallel here with official Soviet ideas on how non-Russian nations' adherence to socialist practices could permit the continuation of national identities. Khrushchev understood eastern Europe in the same way that he understood the non-Russian parts of the Soviet Union.[34]

Khrushchev's confidence in the benign potentialities of difference were evident in one of his draft foreign policy sections for his Twentieth Party Congress address. Therein he argued that the presence of so much difference in the world was evidence of the strength of socialism. He declared that the "socialist idea is so attractive that many understand socialism in their own way, but oppose imperialism."[35] Difference equaled strength.

Peaceful coexistence with the capitalist Others, or detente, as it came to be known, cannot be understood apart from the official domestic Soviet rela-

---

[32] Nikita Khrushchev, speech reprinted in *Pravda*, 20 September 1955, 4.

[33] Zbigniew K. Brzezinski, *The Soviet Bloc: Unity and Conflict* (Cambridge, Mass., 1967), 168–76.

[34] For Soviet confidence in eastern European stability based on a similarity to the ideal Soviet Self, see Alexander Chakovsky, "The Message of Soviet Culture, *New Times*, no. 2 (January 8, 1955): 22; O. Kozlova, "Notes of a Belgian Visit," *New Times*, no. 25 (June 18, 1955): 26; I. Elvin, "Rumania Completes Her Five-Year Plan," *New Times*, no. 35 (August 25, 1955): 26–27.

[35] TsKhSD, f. 1, op. 2, d. 3, p. 59.

tion to difference. Allowing for peaceful relations with the Other, the capitalist imperialist West, was akin to living at home with all those who did not measure up to the NSM. Khrushchev made this explicit when explaining the Soviet policy of peaceful coexistence to the Indian parliament in November. He pointed out that "after all, there are people in our country who do not belong to the Communist Party. . . . In the USSR Communists and non-Communists, atheists and believers work jointly and harmoniously for the good of the people. . . ."[36] In a subsequent speech in Punjab, Khrushchev observed that in the pursuit of peace "we are seeking friends . . . regardless of their political views, race or religious beliefs. What is important is that there be a common desire to promote peace." And then, just as if he were speaking about religion or ethnicity at home, he told his Bombay audience that he "dislikes capitalism very much. I speak of coexistence not because I want capitalism to exist, but because I cannot help recognizing that this system does exist."[37] Still later, in Bangalore, Khrushchev expressed the wish to compete peacefully with capitalism to demonstrate the superiority of socialism.[38] This understanding of the relationship between Self and Other abroad paralleled that of the deviant and the ideal at home. It was often suggested that Soviets who believed in God, who practiced folkways, and who had petite bourgeois attitudes would naturally evolve toward the ideal, under the influence of that ideal. In a retrospective survey of 1955, it was said that "the desire to find *what unites countries, not disunites them,* became a universally accepted slogan."[39]

In Bombay, Khrushchev laid out his views about the kinds of relations states could have with one another, introducing degrees of permissible difference among states. "Friendship has different meanings. There is the friendship when people live in harmony [*dusha v dushu*], but there is also such a *friendship* when people live as neighbors, but don't call on each other as guests. (Laughter and applause) So it is with states. Between some of them there is no real friendship, but they live on the same planet, and somehow must get along." Khrushchev called this kind of relationship coexistence.[40]

There was ample evidence of difference among imperialist powers in 1955. First Deputy Foreign Minister V. Kuznetsov noted in a report to the MFA Collegium that at the UN, the United States and France were at odds over Algeria, and the United States and Britain could not agree on new

[36] Nikita Khrushchev, speech reproduced in *New Times*, no. 50 (December 8, 1955): 4.
[37] Ibid., 5.
[38] Ibid., 7.
[39] "The Passing Year," *New Times*, no. 52 (December 22, 1955): 2. Emphasis added. Khrushchev made precisely this point at the CC Plenum, July 1955, while discussing relations with Yugoslavia, saying "we should pay most attention to what unites us, and not to what still divides us" (15).
[40] Nikita Khrushchev, in *Pravda*, 26 November 1955, 1. Emphasis in original.

members for the UN.[41] Ivan Kurdiukov, MFA Far East Section head, and Mikhail Kapitsa, a special MFA adviser on the Far East and China, described and explained British differences with the United States over China and Taiwan.[42] Konrad Adenauer's visit to Moscow in September was understood as demonstrating the possibility of autonomous West German action vis-à-vis the US.[43]

Toleration of difference at home and within the socialist family was also related to the acknowledgement, appreciation, and expectation of differences among imperialist, capitalist, bourgeois states and within the ruling elites of those states. This made the relationship between Moscow and the West one of contingency and reciprocal causation rather than predetermined conflict. It restored agency to Soviet action. Instead of being faced by a united front of inexorably hostile imperialist states bent on the destruction of socialism, Soviets recognized differences among those states and among the elites ruling those states on relations with the socialist world. Soviet policy could respond to these differences, but could also make them emerge. And it was important, that gone were the days of understanding the West as a single homogenous entity with a single overriding interest; of understanding the United States, Germany, France, and Britain as imperialist distillates; and of treating capitalist encirclement as a permanent feature of international life.

The consequences of this emergent differentiation of understanding can be seen in a memorandum sent to Boris Ponomarev, at the Central Committee International Department (CCID), entitled "Changes in the Arrangement and Correlation of Forces in Bourgeois Circles in the Main Capitalist Countries on Questions of War and Peace."[44] As the title intimates, the author, I. Bakulin, was communicating the various positions occupied by different groups within western countries on foreign policy questions of interest to Moscow. The "new Soviet foreign policy since 1953" was credited with causing a growth in power in the West for a softer line with respect to the Soviet Union and its allies.[45] This new policy included the Austrian treaty; rapprochement with Yugoslavia; trips to Afghanistan, Burma, and India; and the evacuation of bases in Finland. The recognition of neutrality in the developing world had increased the relative power of socialism. By recognizing difference, the Soviet Union had multiplied the number of its potential allies.

---

[41] AVPRF, f. 100, op. 48, d. 55, p. 57.

[42] AVPRF, f. 100, op. 48, d. 128, p. 61.

[43] This was gleaned from canvassing Moscow's foreign diplomatic community during and after the visit. TsKhSD, f. 5, op. 30, d. 116, pp. 156–57.

[44] TsKhSD, f. 5, op. 28, d. 285, pp. 5–14 (December 7, 1955), with an additional twenty-three classified pages.

[45] Ibid., 5.

This recognition of difference among the imperialists permitted Soviets to understand the West as less threatening than would have been the case had the homogenized, completely class-driven view remained in place. For example, in a memorandum from the MFA Information Department to Ponomarev, it was recognized that English and French participation in "aggressive blocs" led by the United States was not completely explained by anti-Soviet motives in London and Paris. Instead, the author, N. Solodovnik, suggested that these countries "had their own special aims within the capitalist world." England, for example, was trying to "overshadow Germany in Europe" and was enjoying "great power" status as a result of membership in NATO, the Southeast Asia Treaty Organization (SEATO), and the Central Treaty Organization (CENTO).[46]

The Soviet Union had more reason to concern itself with how it would look to the international community in 1955 than perhaps in any other year. This is because Khrushchev and his colleagues dramatically increased the access of foreign visitors to the Soviet Union. In fact, the inflow of visitors became so great that Interior Minister Kruglov, KGB Chairman Ivan Serov, and Deputy Foreign Minister Valerian Zorin developed new simplified procedures for the registration of foreign tourists and business persons.[47]

> *Some numbers:* In 1950, 156 foreign delegations visited the Soviet Union; in 1955 739 did. The All-Union Agricultural Exhibition, which opened in Moscow in June, later to become the All-Union Exhibition of Economic Achievements (VDNKh), recorded over 5 million visitors by September, including 700 delegations from 67 foreign countries.[48]

Regardless of the external audience, the Soviet Union found itself frequently presenting the Soviet Self. In doing so, it had to confront the same issue that bedeviled the writers' congress, the tension between idealized socialist realism and daily socialist reality. In response to the expectations of other states about the Soviet Union, the Soviets stressed aspects of the Self that were at dramatic variance with the ideal of the NSM. This was especially the case when it came to religious and national identities. In a *New Times*

[46] TsKhSD, f. 5, op. 28, d. 255, pp. 4–5. This document is a seventy-page memorandum dated December 12, 1955, of which only twelve pages are declassified.

[47] State Archive of the Russian Federation [hereafter GARF], Khrushchev special file, tom. I, d. 465, pp. 224–25. This opening up to the outside was consistent with measures taken to open up to the inside. For example, the Kremlin was opened to visitors in January.

[48] See "Three Months of Work of the All-Union Agricultural Exhibition," *Pravda*, 5 September 1955, p. 1.

blurb on a visit to the Soviet Union by a Syrian delegation, it was mentioned that the Syrians had visited mosques.[49] Only an understanding of Syria as a Moslem country would cause an official Soviet to reunderstand Soviet mosques as a sign of commonality or identity with another state. Reporting to the CC, Council of Ministers, and MFA on the hadj of twenty Soviet Muslims to Mecca and Cairo, I. Poliansky of the Council on the Affairs of Religious Cults pointed out that this trip did much to "counter Western lies about the death of religion in the Soviet Union."[50] As proof that no iron curtain existed, it was reported that a Belgian parliamentary delegation in its visit to Latvia could go anywhere it wished, including to mass at one of Riga's churches.[51] The western understanding of religious freedom as constitutive of legitimate governance introduced an additional way to think about this issue in the Soviet Union, one that challenged the official discourse on modernity. We might say that this interaction with the Other provoked official Soviet reconsideration of the advisability of pursuing that ideal in earnest.

Interaction with the external world implied a more complicated Soviet view of religious and national identities in the Soviet Union, but it did not affect the modern industrial developmental part of that model. The travels of a U.S. lawyer in the Soviet Union, collected in *The Red Carpet,* were used to demonstrate that U.S. expectations of a backward Soviet Union were wrong. The American was forced to acknowledge, for example, that "there was an improvement in the quality of clothes they were wearing . . . and a comparative multitude of goods in shop windows . . . ; rent is negligible, income taxes are low, medical care is free, and pensions are automatic; machinery and equipment appear equal to those of the US; their weaponry should be among the best in the world; and we must not underestimate Russian potentialities."[52]

In negotiating the Austrian State Treaty, the Soviets found themselves asking that the Austrian government adopt a number of constraints on its domestic conduct. Article 6 of the treaty concerned human rights, guaranteeing civil rights, as well as forbiddng any discrimination on the basis of race, sex, language, or religion.[53] Although there is no evidence that the Soviet Union lobbied for or against these provisions, it did implicitly accept their legitimacy by agreeing with the other great powers that they were to be binding on another sovereign government.

[49] "U.S.I.S. Forgery," *New Times,* no. 6 (February 5, 1955): 18.

[50] TsKhSD, f. 5, op. 30, d. 93, p. 31.

[51] "The New York Times," *New Times,* no. 39 (September 22, 1955): 20.

[52] O. Yaroslavtsev, "An American Lawyer Looks at the Soviet Union," *New Times,* no. 12 (March 19, 1955): 31–32.

[53] The text of the treaty is reprinted in *New Times,* no. 22 (May 28, 1955): 8–23. Article 6 appears on 9.

These examples are revealing fragments, but it is equally informative to look at a single instance when a Soviet official was worrying about how to present the entire Soviet identity to a particular audience. In this case, the Soviet ambassador to Egypt, Danyl Solod, in a July 28 memorandum to Dmitrii Shepilov, recommended the following actions be undertaken in the next seven years to "strengthen our ties and influence in Egypt": (1) open an industrial exhibition in Cairo (modernity), (2) increase exchanges on May Day and Great October celebrations (class), (3) undertake a media campaign about those subjects most distorted by the western media and of most interest to Egyptians—family, marriage, childrearing, religion, living conditions, military life, and personal property and its inheritance (class and modernity), (4) send the ballet (modernity), and (5) ask to send the fleet to Alexandria in 1956 (great power).[54] In these recommendations, we find the Soviet commitment to modernity, a dollop of class, and the effects of interaction with the western Other on issues of religion and modernity.

Just as the NSM kept bumping up against difference at home, the Soviet model came across the same kinds of challenges to universalism and homogeneity abroad. Although the official Soviet view expected other socialist countries to follow in the footsteps of the vanguard in Moscow, deviations from this path were not equated with a country's losing its identity as a socialist ally of the Soviet Union. Deviation, although hardly desirable, was understood as unavoidable and remediable. And under the guidance and assistance of the vanguard in Moscow, these deviations would become less serious. Just as an ally could deviate from the socialist model and still be understood to be a socialist ally, a bourgeois capitalist country could behave in ways that seemingly violated class solidarity with the capitalist vanguard, the United States. From the official class point of view, these differences were neither expected nor understood to be particularly promising for the Soviet Union. On the other hand, those who appreciated difference at home and in the socialist camp were also more inclined to understand deviance within the West as both increasingly expected and as a real opportunity for Soviet relations with the capitalist world. No less than the disappearance of capitalist encirclement hung on the resolution of these two understandings of difference. Finally, the meanings of the NSM were not isolated from the interactions Soviets had with foreigners, both at home and abroad. The national, religious, and modern elements of the Soviet ideal were continuously challenged by the necessary exchange of practices with those who held different understandings of them. Difference existed both at home and abroad and presented dangers and opportunities in both places.

[54] TsKhSD, f. 5, op. 30, d. 123, p. 166.

Great Power Identity: Modernity and International Practice

Soviet understandings of itself as a great power endowed with sovereign rights in a world where material power mattered and other states possessed equal rights to normative protection constituted the Soviet great power identity. This identity rested on a number of social practices. The understanding of the importance of material industrial, military, and strategic power was closely associated with the Soviet discourse on modernity. Soviet modernity's fixation on material indices of progress and power—industrialization, mechanization, hydroelectric stations, dams, natural resources, and other quantifiable measures of movement toward the future—fit easily with what constituted great power status internationally in 1955. This material aspect of modernity implied a Soviet appreciation of the material sources of great power identity in international politics. The international norm of sovereignty, however, did not appear to have had a broader social origin than the MFA.[55] Although both the modern and sovereign aspects of this identity were continuously reproduced within the MFA, modernity was also a daily practice within society at large.

The most common theme in Soviet foreign policy discourse in 1955 was that geographical location mattered in understanding the interests of a state, including the Soviet Union. The Soviet Union's geographic location, bordering on Japan, North Korea, China, Afghanistan, Iran, Turkey, and Europe, meant that Soviet interests were affected directly by what went on in these countries. The MFA statement on the Middle East, for example, said that Soviet security was directly affected by the creation of the Baghdad Pact and that the Soviet attitude "should be even more understandable" because the USSR was close to these countries. And because the United States was far away, its presence in these areas should be less "understandable."[56]

The second component of material power was an appreciation of resources, such as population, minerals, and land, as constitutive of a country's value. China was deemed a great power not least of all because of its population. The 600 million Chinese were continually invoked as evidence of the power of the socialist camp. Khrushchev calculated Indian power in the same way, opining that because India had 370 million people, it was "one of the most powerful states on the globe."[57] The importance of the Middle East was defined in terms of its oil and its location at the crossroads of transportation routes from Asia to Europe.[58] When Molotov defined a great

---

[55] It could be argued that the sovereign identity of all states in international politics has the domestic function of authorizing unrivaled sovereignty at home. I present no evidence for this hypothesis here.

[56] "Statement on the Middle East," *Pravda*, 3 March 1955, p. 6.

[57] *Pravda*, 14 December 1955, p. 2.

[58] A. Miller, "Friends and Foes of the Arab Nations," *New Times*, no. 19 (May 7, 1955): 16.

power in his UN General Assembly address, he identified a country that "disposes of the most powerful military and economic resources and which bears special responsibility for the fate of the world." He then named the Soviet Union, the United States, Britain, and France.[59]

Although clearly recognizing that being a great power conferred a certain status in world affairs, the Soviet Union was also a bit defensive about having such an identity itself. On the one hand, Khrushchev declared India a great power, telling his Indian hosts that the only reason India was not "officially considered to be a great power of the world" was "apparently because colonizers want to humiliate your state and your people. . . ."[60] On the other hand, Soviet leaders did not as commonly refer to their own state as a great power. Indeed, Soviet officials spent a fair amount of time thinking about how their country could remain a great power without having others understand them as one. Reporting on the UN General Assembly meeting, for example, First Deputy Foreign Minister V. Kuznetsov wrote that one positive outcome of the session was that the Soviet Union came off looking like a "peaceloving power."[61] In a March 29 memorandum to Deputy Foreign Minister V. A. Zorin, in which the reactions of the CCs of the fraternal communist parties to the draft Warsaw Pact treaty were reported and assessed, the Romanian suggestion that countries be listed in alphabetical order was endorsed, "because it is conventional and shows equality." The author of the memorandum, G. Tunkin, also recommended the adoption of the Romanian proposal to produce the treaty in all eight languages, despite the fact that NATO used only English and French, "because we stand for the equality of languages and such a change would be perceived positively by the participants of the treaty."[62]

The Soviet Union seemed to feel the need to reassure others, such as UN and Warsaw Pact members, that it was not a traditional great power. Deputy Minister of Foreign Affairs V. Semenov told the Egyptian ambassador in Moscow, after the latter expressed concern about the "dangers" for Egypt of having good relations with Moscow, that "Egypt can be certain that the Soviet Union isn't a crocodile which can suddenly unleash its jaws and gobble up Egypt."[63] Sharing a great power identity with others, in this case the United States, Britain, and France, was a mixed blessing because it was im-

---

[59] Vyacheslav Molotov, speech reprinted in *Pravda*, 24 September 1955, p. 3.

[60] *Pravda*, 14 December 1955, p. 2.

[61] AVPRF, f. 100, op. 48, d. 55, p. 57.

[62] AVPRF, f. 82, op. 14, d. 54, pp. 27–37. An April 1 memorandum reduced the number of languages to four: Russian, Polish, German, and Czech.

[63] TsKhSD, f. 5, op. 30,d. 123, pp. 46–47. This meeting occurred on August 27 and was reported to Khrushchev and Shepilov. During the course of the conversation, Ambassador El Kun intimated that Egypt might have to request Soviet aid if Israel were to get western support. Semenov replied that the Soviet government would examine such a request "attentively" at that time.

possible to share such an identity without being identified by others as being like the company the Soviet Union was keeping.

The last element of material power in the Soviet great power identity concerned its appreciation of relative power balances in world politics. Khrushchev expressed a geopolitical grasp of the Baghdad Pact in a speech in Kashmir, observing that the alliance was obviously aimed against the Soviet Union, and so it was "our task to weaken that alliance and we want India to grow in strength."[64] The Soviet creation of the Warsaw Pact also was based on a geopolitical calculation to respond to the rearmament of Germany and its entry into NATO. This account was offered hundreds of times over the course of the year.[65] The text of the May 14 treaty referred in its preamble explicitly to the formation of NATO, the remilitarization of Germany, and the consequent military threat from the West as the causes of the pact.[66] Finally, diplomacy was also regarded as a way of affecting the balance of power. Khrushchev, for example, justified recognizing the Federal Republic of Germany (FRG) by arguing it might reduce German dependence on the United States and "give support to those forces that advocate a more independent foreign policy."[67] Khrushchev told FRG Chancellor Konrad Adenauer to his face, in private, that because NATO is "aimed at us, we do all we can to weaken it. This is a legitimate desire. . . . I am certain that if the FRG were in the same situation it would act as we, and it would be right, deriving from its interests, from the interests of its people."[68]

The Soviet great power identity also included a regard for the power of norms in international affairs, in particular, respect for sovereignty and independence. This view presumed the existence of sovereign independent states whose sovereignty and independence must not be violated. If not honored, these norms would lead to conflict and war among states. World War II was cited as an example of what could happen in world affairs if such norms were not respected.[69]

---

[64] Nikita Khrushchev, speech reprinted in *New Times*, no. 52 (December 22, 1955): 27.

[65] As, for example, in a letter from Bulganin to Dwight Eisenhower, in which the prime minister concludes that the existence of all those U.S. alliances and the deployment of U.S. troops abroad compelled the Soviet Union to "unite with a number of allied states in a military sense." *Pravda*, 25 September 1955, p. 1. See also his draft speech for the meeting of the states that created the Warsaw Pact on May 14, in TsKhSD, f. 5, op. 30, d. 126, p. 74.

[66] The treaty is reprinted in Jan F. Triska and David D. Finley, *Soviet Foreign Policy* (New York, 1968), 487–91.

[67] Draft telegram to the Soviet Embassy in East Berlin in early July 1955, in AVPRF, f. 6, op. 14, d. 184, p. 48. This speaks also to Khrushchev's appreciation for difference.

[68] AVPRF, f. 6, op. 14, d. 206, p. 33. This statement was made during the September 1955 visit of Adenauer to Moscow.

[69] See, for example, O. Bogdanov, "Peaceful Coexistence and International Law," *New Times*, no. 33 (August 11, 1955): 6–9.

As noted in the section on class divisions, peaceful coexistence was partly understood through class analysis, the units of analysis being socialist and capitalist countries representing the working and bourgeois classes, respectively. But the Soviet understanding of peaceful coexistence was based on more than class; it had an international normative foundation, too. Let us look, for example, at how Soviets appreciated the version of peaceful coexistence (*dasa shila*) that emerged from India, China, Indonesia, and Burma during the Bandung conference of 1955. *Dasa shila*, in its demand that states respect one another's sovereignty, equality, and territorial integrity, resolve all differences peacefully, and develop mutually rewarding economic and cultural exchange, offered a set of normative constraints on the conduct of interstate relations.

In the context of Soviet relations with the decolonizing world, *dasa shila* provided a way of reconciling Soviet great power status with amicable relations with weaker and smaller states. In the joint statement marking the end of Nehru's visit to the Soviet Union, both sides agreed that "smaller and weaker states have a vague and possibly unreasoning fear of bigger Powers."[70] Recognizing this natural security dilemma, both sides declared that adhering to the five principles enunciated in Bandung was the best remedy for these irrational concerns. Soviets understood the five principles of *dasa shila* as normatively regulating great power politics. Through the support of and adherence to these normative international practices, the Soviet Union could soften its image as a traditional great power.

The MFA was the institutional site for the (re)production of a geopolitical understanding of others in world politics. But any Soviet understanding of Others was still a discursive product, not just the provenance of a single institutional site, no matter how continuously constituted by international practices. The cases of Soviet relations with Yugoslavia, China, India, and Austria demonstrate the complexity of the outcomes.

In order to illuminate the effects of institutional reproduction, let us look at Foreign Minister Molotov. Molotov understood other states through class analysis at some points, especially when interacting within the CC, but offered an understanding of the same states geopolitically when working within his ministry and when interacting with foreign officials.[71]

When the second secretary of the Fourth European Department of the MFA, D. Sevian, produced a summary of Soviet-Yugoslav relations since the June 1955 Soviet visit there, he enumerated three categories, none of which

---

[70] As expressed by the Egyptian ambassador; the joint statement is reprinted in *New Times*, no. 27 (July 8, 1955): 2.

[71] There is an interesting possibility here, unrealized by me, of distinguishing between the logic of appropriateness (Molotov is fulfilling his institutional role) and the logics of the everyday (Molotov's interactions with his colleagues in the ministry and with foreign leaders constitute a discursive formation of its own).

had any class content: number of political delegations exchanged, volume of economic intercourse, and number of cultural exchanges.[72] When presented with a draft MFA statement on the Middle East, Molotov inserted the word "national" before the "interests of Middle Eastern countries" and the word "state" before the struggle for "independence of Yemen, Syria, and Lebanon."[73] Molotov's blue penciling reflected an understanding of what the international relations discourse understood or demanded. On a subsequent draft, Molotov added language to show that the Soviet Union supported "the state sovereignty" of Afghanistan.[74] In an analysis of a possible normalization of Soviet-FRG relations sent on August 23 from A. Orlov, the Soviet chargé in East Berlin, to S. G. Lapin, head of the Third European Section Head, for ultimate distribution to Molotov, there was not a hint of class-based analysis. Instead, the report read like a political analysis in the *Wall Street Journal*.[75]

Seemingly, an issue most ripe for a class-based vanguardist understanding would be a national liberation movement against an imperialist power. But the Soviet understanding of the uprising in Algeria, at least when situated in the MFA, was anything but revolutionary. V. Kuznetsov, when explaining why the Soviet Union supported putting Algeria on the UN agenda, resorted to a purely legalistic interpretation of Soviet obligations, not an outline of the class obligations of the socialist vanguard. He claimed that "within Algeria there exists a danger to the cause of peace in the region and it cannot be seen as the internal affair of one state."[76] A similar clear choice was presented to Bulganin by the Cameroon Students' Association, whose chairman had asked the Soviet Union to place the Cameroon independence question before the UN Security Council. A. Aritiunian, head of the MFA First European Department (the fact that such a question ended up in a European section, rather than an African, colonial, or decolonizing de-

[72] AVPRF, f. 144, op. 16, d. 722. See also Gromyko, "Questions of State Relations with Yugoslavia," in TsKhSD, f. 5, op. 30, d. 121, pp. 3–8. This was a May 12, 1955 memorandum to Pospelov containing a list of issues that Andrei Gromyko, representing the MFA, thought should be pursued in Yugoslavia during the upcoming Khrushchev visit. The MFA did respond to demands, however. When the CCID requested a memorandum from the MFA Information Department on the FRG's domestic economic conditions, Boris N. Ponomarev received a document based on class analysis. TsKhSD, f. 4, op. 28, d. 284.

[73] AVPRF, f. 6, op. 14, d. 100, pp. 17–18.

[74] Ibid., 51.

[75] AVPRF, f. 82, op. 43, d. 14, pp. 20–80. The same could be said of an October 19 memorandum from Lapin to Khrushchev and the rest of the Presidium devoted to "The Plans of Western Powers with Respect to the Creation of Zones of Reduced Tension in Europe." There were no class identities in evidence. The words "capitalist" and "imperialist" did not even appear in the text. Western proposals were treated as natural efforts to reduce the probability of war in Europe. Although they were in the interests of the West, they were worthy of "significant attention." TsKhSD, f. 5, op. 28, d. 283, pp. 1–15.

[76] AVPRF, f. 100, op. 48, d. 55, p. 74. This was a report to the MFA Collegium assessing Soviet performance at that fall's General Assembly session.

partment, says much about how the issue was preunderstood), sent a memorandum to Bulganin saying the Soviet government should refuse because it would "provoke a negative reaction from the French government" and because "at the present time it would be inexpedient of us to involve ourselves in the affairs of French colonies." Aritiunian recognized the tension in the Soviet identities of sovereign great power and leader of the world revolutionary movement. The latter identity did not prevail, in part because the Soviet Union recognized the French position as a UN trustee for Cameroon and the Soviet position in the UN could not abide ignoring its rules. This shows the normative power of international practice.[77]

That the axis of tension here was between the identities great power and class vanguard was revealed in Khrushchev's very unusual front-page response to a single question from a *Pravda* correspondent.

> Correspondent: "In light of the appearance in several French newspapers of various reports about your comments on Northern Africa in conversation with the French parliamentary delegation, couldn't you summarize the content of the given question?"
>
> Khrushchev: "I had in mind and have in mind first of all that the USSR does not interfere in the internal affairs of other states and that the correct resolution of this question can be found taking into account, of course, the legal rights and national interests of the peoples of the French Union."

In other words the Soviet state was bound by its normative understanding of international relations to stay out of the business of arming the National Liberation Front, while it simultaneously defended the right, on the very same grounds, of Egypt to acquire arms from wherever it wanted because it was a sovereign state with equal rights. But then Khrushchev addressed the other end of the axis.

> Khrushchev: "The position of the Soviet people is the position of moral support and sympathy for the national-liberation aspirations of peoples, and has been well known for a long time and, as it seems to me, requires no special clarification."[78]

The implication here was that the Soviet understanding of France and Algeria was simultaneously geopolitical and vanguardist, with Khrushchev resolving the contradiction by invoking both state interests and public sentiments.

---

[77] GARF, Bulganin special file, rolik. 5446, op. 84, d. 24, p. 74.

[78] *Pravda*, 4 October 1955, p. 1.

In a very profound way, the international normative discourse served as a powerful constraint against the Soviet formulation of interests purely according to its class vanguard identity. To the extent that others in world politics behaved in ways consistent with normative practice, the Soviet Union itself was involved in political interaction with other states, and these relations were institutionally reproduced in the MFA, understandings of the external world that included respect for sovereign rights were more likely.

Summary

Before turning to the case studies themselves, let me summarize the identities and their effects on foreign policy.

- *Class* identified the Soviet Union as the vanguard of both the socialist alliance and the decolonizing world. A natural unity was expected among its allies. Decolonizing states were expected to be able to skip capitalism, given Soviet help, just as the central Asian republics had done. Peaceful coexistence assumed binarized class relations were mitigable.
- *Modernity* placed the Soviet Union at the top of the evolutionary ladder, just as Russia was the vanguard for backward areas of the Soviet Union at home. Both the decolonizing world and the socialist community were understood as lower on the evolutionary ladder, but moving toward the Soviet present.
- *Nation* meant the Russian nation as the default identity for the history-less Soviet Union. Whenever an historical legacy was evoked, most especially with the Slavic countries to the West or countries with which imperial Russia had had relations, the Soviet understanding of Russian national identity affected the construction of that relationship. Soviet understandings of multinationaliy at home also infused Soviet relations with nationalisms abroad.
- *Difference* (or NSM) accompanied all Soviet understandings of Others abroad and was most closely correlated with how strongly class identity affected the overall construction of another state. Class crushed difference, demanding homogeneity and adherence to the Soviet ideal. Toleration for difference, on the other hand, created new alliance opportunities and reduced the threat from the West.
- *Great power* reinforced the modern appreciation for material power in world politics while reproducing the recognition of international norms of sovereignty.

These five identities constituted the discursive formation within which Soviet decision makers operated when thinking about which kinds of international relations were possible or imaginable.

SOVIET RELATIONS WITH OTHER STATES IN 1955

Although the Soviet understanding of another state was a blend of all five identities, some identities predominated in particular contexts. So, Yugoslavia was understood primarily as difference from the Soviet ideal and in relationship to the Russian nation, China's identity was a combination of class, nation, and great power relations, India was the Russian periphery in the discourse on modernity, and Austria was understood largely geopolitically, in relationship to Germany.

Yugoslavia, an Acceptably Deviant Little Brother

Yugoslavia was understood simultaneously as a deviant from the ideal Soviet socialist model, a little brother of the Russian nation, and an actor of geopolitical importance against the West. Those Soviets who understood difference at home as tolerable were also most eager to reestablish an alliance with Yugoslavia. Those Soviets most worried about class degeneration at home were opposed to an alliance, fearing it would legitimize dangerous deviance at home and within the socialist community. Many Soviets understood Yugoslavia as a little Slavic brother to great Russia, reproducing a hierarchical relationship with the prospective ally. Finally, Yugoslavia's restoration to allied status was understood as a geopolitical move against the West and as a restoration of Yugoslavia's sovereign rights, which had been violated by Stalin.

Chronology:

December 1954, trade resumed with Yugoslavia

January 7, 1955 when the Yugoslav trade delegation left for home, it was seen off by a Ministry of Foreign Trade representative from the Section on Western Countries.

January 10, China and Yugoslavia resumed diplomatic relations.

May 14, on the same day as the Austrian State Treaty and the formation of the Warsaw Pact, the Soviet leadership announced its trip to Belgrade.

May 26, the Soviet delegation left for Belgrade. Among its principals were Khrushchev, Bulganin, Anastas Mikoyan, Shepilov, and Andrei Gromyko. Molotov stayed home. Tito granted a rapprochement only at the state, not party, level.

June 2, in a joint communique, the Soviet delegation conceded that Yugoslavia was building socialism and that there were different forms of socialist development.

June 28, Tito accepted a Soviet invitation to visit.

July 9–13, the CC plenum met to discuss relations with Yugoslavia.

August 6, at a reception for the parliamentary delegation, the head of the Fourth European Department of the MFA was present, as were

Russian Orthodox Metropolitan Krutitsky; a representative of the Kolomensky Monastery; the business manager of the Moscow Patriarchate; and Archimandrite Maksim, the abbot of the Antioch Church in Moscow.

November 6, U.S. Secretary of State John Foster Dulles and Tito met on Brioni Island.

Soviet relations with Yugoslavia in 1955 were made thinkable by the Thaw at home. The previous policy of treating as potentially dangerous whoever was not the Self was abandoned in favor of the opposite: whoever was not definitely the Other might be regarded as at least partly the Self. As Khrushchev told his CC plenum audience after his trip to Yugoslavia, Tito had told him that "Yugoslavs now have 'strong differences with the Westerners', and are on the path of independent development."[79] Returning from Yugoslavia, L. Slapov and V. Platkovsky, two Soviet journalists, wrote that "the main thing is that Yugoslavia has put an end to capitalist oppression and has pursued deep democratic reforms."[80] In other words, the important Yugoslav identity was that it was not the Other; it no longer had to pass the harder test of similarity with the Soviet model. Yugoslavia's differences from the Soviet model were acknowledged, but were not understood as changing that country's identity from socialist ally to bourgeois enemy. Nikolai Pervukhin, a candidate Presidium member, criticized those who drew the boundary lines too finely. Quoting from Lenin's essay on Leftist excess, he pointed out that "'people who still do not know that all boundaries, even in nature and society, are mobile and to a significant degree conditional, nothing will help except long training and education, political and life experience.'"[81]

Anastas Mikoyan reminded his colleagues that if they continued to adhere to the old formula of measuring an ally by how much it was like the Soviet Union, they should accept that China had more differences with the Soviet Union than Yugoslavia did. Suggesting that Soviet reality was the ideal, Mikoyan also established that difference from the Soviet Union need not mean departure from the socialist path. "We consider Chinese leaders to be real Marxist-Leninists . . . because they use in the interests of communism not only peitit bourgeois, but bourgeois elements. . . ."[82] Mikoyan suggested that holding Yugoslavia to Soviet standards was unfair. He asked the plenum, for example, why Yugoslavia should have *kolkhozy;* the Soviet Union had not had them until ten years after its revolution. Khrushchev then in-

---

[79] CC Plenum, July 9, 1955, morning session, 11.

[80] L. Slepov and V. Platkovsky, "Under the Sign of Friendship: Travelogue on Yugoslavia," *Pravda,* 14 October 1955, p. 3.

[81] CC Plenum, July 11, 1955, evening session, 19.

[82] CC Plenum, July 11, 1955, morning session, 7.

terrupted, "How many kolkhozy are there in Poland?" Bulganin said 6 percent. Khrushchev said, "And yet we don't accuse our friends, the Poles." Mikoyan then offered what kind of Soviet identity this double standard produced: "It is one of the worst manifestations of great power chauvinism. Everything is excused and allowed for us, but nothing is permitted others." Mikoyan praised Yugoslavia for protecting its economy from foreign competition and capital, observing that no U.S. firms operated there.[83]

Khrushchev and Mikoyan willingly recognized difference. Why were others not so inclined? The chief opponent of recognizing Yugoslavia's socialist identity was Molotov, and his opposition was predictably borne of a strict adherence to a class analysis of this potential ally. Fiodor Burlatskii has written that Khrushchev's original understanding of Yugoslavia was a Stalinist one based on class analysis: it was no longer a socialist country because it was subordinate to foreign capital and permitted private property. But Khrushchev ordered the creation of a commission to produce a new political and socioeconomic analysis of Yugoslavia and to determine whether it was socialist or capitalist. Once the Shepilov Commission had decided that Yugoslavia was socialist, and only then, were contacts initiated with Belgrade.[84]

Molotov, according to Andrei Alesandrov-Agentov, never abandoned class analysis and opposed any rapprochement with Tito because of his "unbending class" position. This understanding meant that Molotov "saw relations with states with different social systems as a struggle in which softness was unforgivable and concessions inadmissible. Therefore, the extreme inflexibility . . . in his approach. . . ."[85] Apparently, the Shepilov Commission's

---

[83] Ibid., 8.

[84] Fedor Burlatsky, *Russkie Gosudari* (Moscow, 1996), 51–52.

[85] Andrei M. Aleksandrov-Agentov, *Ot Kollontai do Gorbacheva* (Moscow, 1994), 53–54. Aleksandrov-Agentov worked in the MFA's European Department in the mid-1950s. There is evidence that popular understandings of Yugoslavia were similar to Molotov's. In a May 25 memorandum on which a summary is presented of the discussions at meetings of the Moscow party *aktiv*, Yekaterina Furtseva, secretary of the Mosgorkom, reports that there was some question of whether the Soviet government was manifesting weakness by going to Belgrade. TsKhSD, f. 5, op. 30, d. 90, p. 52. In letters to the editor of *Krasnaia Zvezda*, Major General V. Moskovsky, sent to Pospelov on July 7, just days before the CC plenum was to deal with this issue, readers asked for a class analysis of Yugoslavia; they wanted to know to which camp Yugoslavia belonged, whether it was on the road to socialism, what kinds of differences existed between the socialism there and in the Soviet Union, and other information that would allow readers to understand Yugoslavia on the basis of class identity (67–71). These manifestations of confusion and the desire for clarification occurred among socialist allies at the same time. The Soviet ambassador to Poland, Panteleimon Ponamarenko, in a letter to Khrushchev in June, reports that at party meetings in Poland they asked about Yugoslavia's socialist credentials, whether the rapprochement was not just expedience, and so forth. TsKhSD, f. 5, op. 30, d. 121, pp. 86–87. The Soviet ambassador to China, Iudin, reported the same concerns at party meetings and in letters to editors there. TsKhSD, f. 5, op. 30, d. 116, p. 172.

findings remained unconvincing to Molotov. At the July plenum, Molotov cited Yugoslavia's position that societies could evolve peacefully toward socialism as evidence that they "ignore class and the class struggle." Given the absence of this class basis for forging relations with Yugoslavia, Molotov suggested that better relations between the two countries were still possible, but based on the examples of Finland or India, "who don't belong to the socialist camp."[86] Believing that Yugoslavia lacked the practices that constituted being socialist, Molotov consigned it to membership in another group of states. Molotov's position might be evaluated as true to Lenin's admonition, "better fewer, but better," that it is more rewarding to have fewer allies if the allies you have can pass the class examination. Molotov did acknowledge that Yugoslavia was a somewhat better site for Soviet investment because there were still "the revolutionary traditions of the partisan struggle, sympathy for the Soviet Union, and nationalized industry." But the bad news was that Yugoslavia, during its departure from the ranks of people's democracy (1948–55), "took steps backwards" by reducing planning and collectivization.[87] By deviating from the Soviet class ideal Yugoslavia had disqualified itself from alliance membership.[88] In these debates Molotov represented the recent Stalinist past.

Neither Khrushchev nor Mikoyan claimed that Molotov should not assess Yugoslavia's fitness as an ally based on its class identity; they merely applied different standards. Unlike Molotov, they believed Yugoslavia passed the class identity test, if only because the questions they used were not true or false.

Khrushchev delivered the first report about the recent talks in Yugoslavia at the July plenum. He began by asking his audience a rhetorical question: "How normal is a situation when the Soviet Union, a *country of socialism,* is essentially in a hostile relationship with Yugoslavia, with which in the past it was closely bound by ties of ardent friendship and whose leaders declare their resolve to build a *socialist* society in their country?" If Yugoslavia was socialist, bad relations with Moscow were not intelligible. Khrushchev reminded his colleagues that relations with Yugoslavia used to be "fraternal," that is, as between members of the socialist community.[89] Khrushchev told the plenum that the leadership had "better familiarized themselves with the situation in the country" during their trip to Belgrade. What mattered to

---

[86] CC Plenum, July 9, 1955, evening session, 7.

[87] Ibid., 8.

[88] Yugoslavia was referred to as a capitalist country in MFA documents at least once, in a memorandum on NATO written by V. Semenov, head of the ministry's Third European Department, and N. Solodovnik, head of the ministry's Information Department, and distributed to the Presidium. AVPRF, f. o6, op. 14, d. 115, p. 4.

[89] CC Plenum, July 9, 1955, morning session, 1. Emphases in original.

them there? Khrushchev reported that the commanding heights of the economy were owned by the state; "denationalization" (i.e., bourgeois backsliding) had not occurred; and foreign property had not been returned to its original owners. But the situation was more "complicated" in the countryside. Although *kulaks* were limited by ceilings on landholding, petty commodity trading still prevailed. In other words, there was a class basis for concern; or as Khrushchev so blatantly put it, "the question of 'kto-kogo' is still far from being resolved in Yugoslavia." The more the Yugoslav economy became integrated with the capitalist West, the more the danger of class degeneration at home.[90] The conclusion was that only an alliance with the Soviet vanguard in Moscow could save Yugoslavia from going capitalist.

Although Yugoslavia was not a bourgeois state because state power was in the hands of the proletariat and working peasantry, "during the years of close economic ties with the West conditions were created for the growth of petit bourgeois and private property elements . . . ", but the bourgeoisie had not been strengthened.[91] In defending his delegation's decision to renounce all economic claims against Belgrade, Khrushchev reminded the plenum that "now a struggle for Yugoslavia is going on" between the United States and the Soviet Union, between U.S. economic aid and Soviet.[92]

Mikoyan also defended Yugoslavia's class identity, rejecting Molotov's identification of Yugoslavia with Finland and India. He demanded a Leninist "approach to the definition of the character of a state. . . . First, one must examine who owns the means of production, i.e., class relations; second, the general domestic politics of the state and in whose hands rests power; and third, its foreign policy." Mikoyan pointed out that Yugoslavia was not like India or Finland. "How can Yugoslavia be called a bourgeois state when all the main means of production . . . are public . . . the class of landlords and capitalists has been completely liquidated . . . land ownership is limited to 15 hectares, and one cannot hire more than 5 people?"[93] In order to establish whether "we are dealing with communists or not," Mikoyan proposed the verification of the Yugoslav party's "social composition, its leadership, its policies, its ideology, and its past and present." Mikoyan was impressed that the Yugoslav party had been born underground and had "never participated in bourgeois parliamentary politics." Moreover, the party members were mostly workers and peasants, and 58 percent had little education.[94] Mikoyan read short biographies of the Yugoslav party leadership, giving particular attention to their class origins, and revolutionary or partisan activities: "Vukmanovich—he came from the intelligentsia, was an illegal

[90] Ibid., 9. *Kto-kogo* here means "Who will get whom?"
[91] Ibid., 10.
[92] Ibid., 12.
[93] CC Plenum, July 11, 1955, morning session, 6.
[94] Ibid., 13.

[meaning he engaged in illegal work against the regime], and was a leader of the partisans. . . . Kocha Popovich is from a bourgeois family. . . . What is bad, even though he has bourgeois origins, if a man goes to war and washes away the stigma of his origins? He didn't choose his parents. . . ."[95]

But Khrushchev's and Mikoyan's defense of Yugoslavia's differences from the Soviet ideal did not distract them from that prospective ally's deviations. A deviant at home could act in ways that disqualified him not only from being an ideal Soviet man, but even from being a Soviet citizen. A country such as Yugoslavia could also deviate so much as to become "anti-Soviet." Khrushchev identified a number of aspects of Yugoslav reality that violated Soviet conceptions of authentic socialism. At the plenum, he pointed out that the Yugoslav Communist Party did not subscribe to the "Marxist-Leninist position on the leading role of the party," treating it as just one among many social organizations responsible for cultural and educational matters. Yugoslav communists also rejected the idea of two world camps.[96] These deviations were relevant to the kind of ally that Yugoslavia could be. In Khrushchev's speech at the Belgrade airport, he observed that the strongest alliances are those between countries led by Marxist-Leninist parties with common positions on ideological matters.[97] According to Khrushchev, he told Tito that on ideological questions the CPSU could not compromise, "considering it to be its sacred duty to defend the purity of Marxist theory" and, he could have added, Soviet socialist identity.[98]

Other aspects of Yugoslav reality raised concerns among Soviet foreign policy makers. Yugoslav claims that a country could evolve toward socialism

[95] Ibid., 14. This is exactly the position assumed by the narrator in Leonid Leonov, *The Russian Forest* (Moscow, 1966), with respect to Polya, who is brought up in the house of the local bourgeois. Shepilov also defended Yugoslavia's class identity at the plenum. CC Plenum, July 11, 1955, evening session, 24. For a class-based justification of the upcoming summit, see "For the Further Improvement of Soviet-Yugoslav Relations and for the Strengthening of Peace," *Pravda*, 18 May 1955, p. 1.

[96] CC Plenum, July 9, 1955, morning session, 12. In a draft of a speech that Malenkov delivered on the very same day before the party organization at the Ministry of Electric Power Stations (whose head he had become as a consequence of his removal as chair of the Council of Ministers in January), there was similar concern for Yugoslav comrades' incorrect understanding of the role of the party and the class struggle during the period of socialist construction. RTsKhIDNI, f. 83, op. 1, d. 12, p. 125.

[97] *Pravda*, 27 May 1955, p. 1.

[98] CC Plenum, July 9, 1955, morning session, 13. Shepilov identified three ideological questions on which Yugoslav and Soviet communists could not agree in their July 7 exchange of letters. Although the CPSU could accept many roads to socialism, the dictatorship of the proletariat must not be challenged; the leading role of the Communist Party in the "world liberation movement" must be recognized, and communist parties must be differentiated from social-democratic ones; and proletarian internationalism must be recognized as a constitutent part of Marxism-Leninism. CC Plenum, July 11, 1955, evening session, 25.

implied that western European social democracies might be on the same path as the Soviet Union. This would excessively expand the boundaries of an authentic socialist identity. Soviet claims to be the true interpreter of Marx and Lenin were questioned by Yugoslav claims that its system of worker management in factories would lead to the disappearance of the state. The Soviet Union had no such councils, had a not inconsiderable state apparatus, and had finessed the issue by claiming the state was in the hands of the working class. The implication here was that an inferior had found a better way of realizing Marxism in practice. This was not a welcome deviation.[99] This particular deviation not only violated the class identity of the Soviet Union, but also challenged its vanguard identity in the socialist movement, as if some subordinate could come up with an alternative formulation of truth. Although Khrushchev was willing to acknowledge, just as Russians did at home, that Moscow could learn from non-Soviets and non-Russians, Yugoslavs, according to some Soviet observers, were going to the opposite extreme of claiming a "monopoly position for their own experience." The deepest Soviet fear was the social effects of this alternative socialist identity. Yugoslav claims to a different socialist reality implied the "danger that the bacilli of decomposition will begin to spread. . . . These germs are concealed within Yugoslav pretensions." In conclusion, Yugoslavia's entry into the socialist camp, Soviet recognition of its socialist identity, "will only harm the common cause, introduce discord and ideological dissonance. Many Yugoslav innovations, leaking out and spreading, can turn out to be contagious. . . ."[100]

Soviets not only pointed out the consequences of Yugoslav deviations for the kind of ally Yugoslavia could be and the implications for the Soviet vanguard position among socialist countries, but also expressed fears that these deviations could lead to class degeneration in Yugoslavia itself. Soviet reporters writing from Yugoslavia found that "self-management" in Yugoslav industry sometimes caused serious problems that were recognized in Yugoslav media. These ills included "localism," or excessive regard for an individual's own plant over the country as a whole, and "chauvinism," or the

---

[99] Soviet concern was expressed by Zimianin's blue penciling in the margins of the text of the speech given by Edvard Kardelj, a Yugoslav party leader, to the Norwegian Workers' Party in Oslo. A copy was sent to Zimianin, the head of the MFA First European Department by the Soviet Ambassador to Yugoslavia, Valkov, on January 25, 1955. AVPRF, f. 144, op. 16, d. 740, 8, 16. See also an August 15 report to Shepilov from V. V. Platkovsky, *Pravda* correspondent, in TsKhSD, f. 5, op. 30, d. 121, pp. 62–83.

[100] S. Krushinsky's July 8 report to Shepilov in which his discussion of this matter appears under the telling heading, "The Danger of Yugoslav Vanguardism," in TsKhSD, f. 5, op. 30, d. 121, pp. 50–60. Indeed the Soviet ambassador Ponomarenko to Poland at the time reported to Khrushchev in a June 18 letter that Polish students had asked at a party meeting whether Yugoslavia had not already established a path to socialism different from the Soviet one (87).

defense of a particular region's interests elevated above the social good.[101] Yugoslav deviance in agriculture was also interpreted as dangerous to socialism. Slepov and Platkovsky reported from Ljubliana, the Slovenian capital, that there was a danger of "exploitative tendencies" getting stronger in the countryside because "small commodity production" predominated there. The "economically strong peasantry are using a July 1954 law to buy and sell land and hire wage labor," resulting in the "kulak, like an eel, slipping out of government limitations and using all kinds of loopholes."[102]

Class analysis implied a fixing of Yugoslavia in the hierarchy of socialist development. In the slogans for the thirty-eighth anniversary of the Bolshevik Revolution, reflecting official Soviet concern for Yugoslavia's imperfect identity, Yugoslavia was notable by its absence from the ranks of countries of popular democracy,[103] being placed between the socialist allies of the Soviet Union and its new friends in the decolonizing world, such as India and Indonesia, and neutral countries such as Finland and Austria. On this dimension, Yugoslav socalism was understood as being at a lower level of development, fraught with economic difficulties that "we well understand since we in the Soviet Union *had* many formidable difficulties . . . in the *early stages of our economic development.*"[104]

Toleration of difference made the contemplation of an alliance with Yugoslavia possible, and understanding Yugoslavia through the Russian national identity made the remaining differences less threatening. A common Slavic identity made the two countries more similar. Soviets credited the Soviet-Yugoslav friendship with "firm roots in the past," the "Russians having helped the Yugoslavs against foreign invaders. . . . This is well known and remembered in Yugoslavia." A Montenegrin peasant was reported to have said, "we have always loved the Russians [and so] the Soviet Union is our kin brother."[105] The lead editorial that introduced and justified the upcoming Belgrade summit to the Soviet public mentioned the need to strengthen the "age-old friendship of the peoples of our country with the fraternal peoples of Yugoslavia."[106] This common Slavic past was expected to yield a promising relationship between the two countries.

[101] L. Slepov and V. Platkovsky, "On Yugoslavia: Travelogue," *Pravda,* 21 October 1955, p. 3.

[102] L. Slepov and V. Platkovsky, "On Yugoslavia: Travelogue," *Pravda,* 13 November 1955, p. 3.

[103] *Pravda,* 25 October 1955, p. 1.

[104] B. Burkov, "Three Weeks in Yugoslavia," *New Times,* no. 45 (November 3, 1955): 27–28. Emphases added.

[105] Ibid., 26. Yugoslavs who attended the performance of the Beriozka folk troupe also reported "old friendships" with Russians. V. Platkovsky, "The Yugoslav Public on the Performances of the Beriozka Ensemble," *Pravda,* 5 August 1955, p. 5. See also Slepov and Platkovsky, "On Yugoslavia," 21 October 1955, 3.

[106] "For the Further Improvement," 1. These mentions of age-old ties were references to

Kaganovich explained to the July plenum why Yugoslavs would not accept U.S. influence by citing the fact that the Yugoslav people are "connected to the peoples of the Soviet Union by centuries of strong ties of brotherhood."[107] He went on to differentiate Yugoslavia from India or Finland based on the fact that "Yugoslavia is a special state, close, and related [*rodstvennoe*] to us. . . ."[108] Khrushchev, in a speech before a congress of industrial workers in the Kremlin, cited the "age-old traditions of friendship" and the fact that "more than once we have fought together against common enemies."[109] Shepilov lamented the "loss of the second biggest Slavic country after Poland"[110] and Aleksei Kirichenko mentioned that "many centuries of fraternal friendship and joint struggle against common enemies unites us with the people of Yugoslavia."[111]

Marina Franichevich, a Yugoslav delegate to the Writers' Congress reported that in meetings with Soviet writers, the latter very often stressed *slavianstvo* (Slavicness). Soviet hosts at the congress even held a dinner for Slavic delegations, "where again there were many speeches and toasts about Slavicness and Slavic friendship." Franichevich noted how this particular Soviet/Russian understanding of Yugoslavia had the undesirable and unmerited effect of reducing the differences between the two countries to a "quarrel between brothers,"[112] as opposed to what it really was, a deep substantive dispute. This use of the idea of common interests borne of common ethnohistorical roots exemplifies how understood similarity may spawn expectations of cooperation or ameliorated conflict in world politics.

The objections of Franichevich notwithstanding, Yugoslavs themselves reproduced the Russian national identity of the Soviet Union through their own array of social practices. For example, very often Soviet delegates would

---

common Slavic roots. That the roots were Slavic, and not just Serbian or Russian, is established by the fact that Khrushchev referred to the same "centuries-old bonds of friendship" with the Bulgarians. *Pravda*, 4 June 1955, p. 1. See also Krushinsky's report to Shepilov, in TsKhSD, f. 5, op. 30, d. 121, p. 49.

[107] Speech at CC Plenum, July 11, 1955, evening session, 9.

[108] Ibid., 13.

[109] *Pravda*, 19 May 1955, p. 2. He repeated this formulation in his Belgrade airport speech, *Pravda*, 27 May 1955, p. 1.

[110] CC Plenum, July 11, 1955, evening session, 22.

[111] CC Plenum, July 12, 1955, morning session, 4.

[112] AVPRF, f. 144, op. 16, d. 740, p. 21. There was even a Slavic Committee of the USSR, chaired by A. S. Gundorov, about whose functions I have learned little. It is referred to in TsKhSD, f. 5, op. 30, d. 93, p. 15, in materials on religious practices in the Soviet Union. Mikoyan expressed the minority Soviet viewpoint in the July plenum, arguing that it was wrong to explain the rapprochement by "Slavic commonality." CC Plenum, July 11, 1955, morning session, 16. There were also no references to Slavic fraternity in the official joint communique of June 2 or in the July 16 editorial in *Pravda* that summarized the plenum meeting.

be asked to sing traditional Russian folk songs.[113] And the leader of the first Yugoslav cultural delegation to the Soviet Union remarked that as soon as people heard us "speaking a Slavic language" they would "come up to us and shake our hands."[114] In this way, despite the official Soviet commitment to developing a Soviet identity that transcended nation, external Others such as Yugoslavia brought the privileged Russian nation to the discursive foreground.

In his opening speech to the July plenum, Khrushchev lectured his colleagues about the importance of never losing sight of the national identities of otherwise socialist countries. He introduced this section of his report with the preface: "Comrades! Speaking of the lessons of the history of Soviet-Yugoslav relations, we should especially dwell on the questions which have enormous significance for the future fate of the entire socialist camp . . . relations among nations . . . and the struggle against both great power chauvinism and bourgeois nationalism." Recognizing the strength of national identities, Khrushchev cited Lenin's admonition to approach the "national question with maximum flexibility, delicacy, and tact." As far as petit bourgeois prejudices went, nationalism was the "most stable and alive," he explained. He ascribed these national identities to underdeveloped class relations, in countries with "small farm production and patriarchy." Even when acknowledging Yugoslav national identity, Khrushchev located that country within a developmental process that both showed Yugoslavia on a lower rung of the ladder and indicated this troubling feature would disappear with time. The salience of national identity was related as well to "the feeling of distrust toward nations who in the past oppressed other nations." This was a reference to Yugoslav suspicions of the Soviet Union based on Belgrade's understanding of Moscow as Russia. Khrushchev cited Lenin to the effect that concessions were necessary to nationalist sentiments if this nationalist distrust were to dissipate more rapidly. Khrushchev then turned to a domestic analogue to Yugoslavia, citing Russian relations with Ukraine as a good example of the Leninist approach to nationalism in practice.[115]

The intimate connection between understandings of nations at home and abroad was reflected in the fact that Khrushchev shifted seamlessly into a discussion of the "inadequacies of Leninist national policy in our own country." He criticized excessive centralization of decision making in Moscow bureaucracies and called for the development of national culture,

---

[113] For example, V. Babkin, "A Soviet Student in Norway," *New Times*, no. 24 (June 11, 1955): 26.

[114] Interview with Miroslav Cangalovic, *New Times*, no. 27 (July 1, 1955): 7. Tito, in his speech on liberation day, referred to the Soviets repeatedly as Russians. *Pravda*, 30 July 1955, p. 3.

[115] CC Plenum, July 9, 1955, morning session, 18.

"national in form, and socialist in content."[116] As important as the content of Khrushchev's speech was the fact that he and his audience saw nothing unusual about discussing the nationalism of Yugoslavia and other socialist allies as if they were discussing nationality policy at home. Soviet understandings of relations with other states depended on how relations among the nations within the Soviet Union were construed. They depended on how the Soviet discourse on the nation captured these relationships.

Khrushchev's most significant conclusion from comparing Soviet relations with Yugoslavia to Russia's relations with non-Russians within the Soviet Union was that the mistakes and inadequacies that marked Soviet nationality policy at home also had damaged relations with Yugoslavia. Khrushchev confessed that "insufficient tact and flexibility" had been shown Yugoslavia, and this "embittered the national feelings of the Yugoslavs and naturally did not lead to the disappearance, but to the redoubling of their nationalistic errors."[117] Khrushchev did not limit his inferences to the relationship with Yugoslavia but applied these lessons to all alliances within the socialist camp. He declared on the last day of the plenum, in his concluding speech summing up its proceedings, that "the expansion of fraternal relations among our union and autonomous republics and among the countries of the socialist camp are questions of nationality policy."[118] Khrushchev declared that the greatest harm would be done if we "manifested conceit, arrogance, and disrespect for our foreign friends, and an unwillingness to deal with their national peculiarities."[119]

Mikoyan defended Yugoslav nationalism by reminding his colleagues that other socialist allies were as nationalistic. He recalled that there was plenty of nationalism among the Poles and among other communist parties. And yet "we didn't break off our relations with them, but instead helped them grow out of their nationalism." Mikoyan's defense of national difference

---

[116] Ibid., 19. In his speech to the Moscow party *aktiv* two weeks after the plenum, Malenkov also connected the "lessons of Yugoslavia" to the nationalities policy at home and relations with all countries with popular democracies. He even told his comrades that determining Soviet policy toward Yugoslavia "is unthinkable without examining this line from positions and principles of the policy of the communist party on the national question." RTsKhIDNI, f. 83, op. 1, d. 12, p. 27.

[117] CC Plenum, July 9, 1955, morning session, 19. Malenkov told his Moscow party *aktiv* audience that relations "between big and small nations" should be understood from Leninist positions, just as "relations between soiuz and republic organizations, between soiuz and autonomous republics and oblasts" should be understood. RTsKhIDNI, f. 83, op. 1, d. 12, p. 29.

[118] CC Plenum, July 12, 1955, 42. The linkage between questions of domestic and international nationality policy was clear in the distilled and somewhat sanitized summary of plenum results published as "For the Development of Friendly Relations between the Soviet Union and Yugoslavia," *Pravda*, 16 July 1955, p. 1.

[119] CC Plenum, July 9, 1955, morning session, 20.

preserved a vanguard role for Moscow in overcoming this undesirable feature of underdevelopment. In response to Molotov's concern that Yugoslav nationalism might infect other socialist allies, Mikoyan declared that the communist parties in the Countries of Popular Democracy (CPDs) were so strong, having been "brought up under our leadership," that no one should expect the influence of "Yugoslav nationalistic ideas" to have any effect. This argument had its domestic analogue—socialism was so secure here that a little nationalist devation was no mortal threat. Mikoyan then referred explicitly to Soviet experiences in Kazakhstan and Uzbekistan, as if their relationship to Soviet socialism was the same as that of the CPDs.[120] Mikoyan pointed out that Ryskulov, a bourgeois nationalist, used to head Kazakhstan. At that time there were few communists or workers in Kazakhstan and many peasants. In other words, its class identity was weak. "But Ryskulov was useful to us because he was connected to the Kazakh people." And, Mikoyan continued, Faizul Khodzhaev was a bourgeois nationalist leader of Uzbekistan. "What did our support lead to? Didn't wonderful communist parties grow up in Kazakhstan and Uzbekistan?"[121]

Just as Russian identity within the Soviet Union situated all non-Russians in a subordinate position in the predominant discourse, so was Yugoslavia placed in that hierarchy. As a Slavic brother, Yugoslavia was far more like Ukraine than Uzbekistan, but it still was not an equal to Russia. Yugoslavia's fraternal characteristics were always compared to the Russian center, never the reverse. V. Maevsky, one of the first Soviet journalists to report from Yugoslavia in 1955, linguistically connected Serbs and Russians, describing how "words related to Russian were easily picked up in Serb speech."[122] S. Krushinsky reported that "they write, as we do, in cyrillic." Moreover, "the development of social thought here was influenced beneficially by the great Russian revolutionary democrats—Vissarion Belinsky, Nikolai Dobroliubov, and Nikolai Chernyshevsky." This was precisely the relationship of subordination often drawn between Russian and non-Russian peoples in the Soviet Union. It continued with Krushinsky's observation that Lev Tolstoi, Anton Chekhov, and Maksim Gorky were "favorite writers" in Yugoslavia. Events from the past, such as "local sailors serving Peter I and achieving honor and glory in the Russian navy" were interpreted as bonds relevant to the alliance being forged today. This journalist also discovered that many Yugoslavs had named their daughters Tanya, "in honor of the heroic daughter of the Soviet people Zoya Kosmodemian-

---

[120] Voroshilov also referred to the Soviet experience with its republics as a vague model for how relations between the Soviet Union and CPDs should develop. CC Plenum, July 12, 1955, evening session, 21.

[121] CC Plenum, July 11, 1955, morning session, 4.

[122] V. Maevsky, "Belgrade Today," *Pravda*, 24 May 1955, p. 4.

skaia."[123] The Russian relationship to its little Slavic brother was replicated in Soviet views of the relationship between the Soviet Communist Party and its junior partner in Belgrade. Dmitry Shepilov told his colleagues at the July plenum, that we "need to patiently correct the serious ideological errors of our young cadres of Yugoslav communists."[124]

Whereas Khrushchev and Mikoyan comprehended Yugoslav nationalism in terms of non-Russian republics at home, Molotov understood Yugoslavia's national identity as a class deviation, not merely a national difference. The consequence of class turned Yugoslavia from a potential ally into a potential adversary; understanding difference as danger made Yugoslavia an unavailable ally. At the end of Khrushchev's introductory speech, the plenum took a break. It resumed that evening with Molotov at the rostrum. Khrushchev's words had accommodated difference, national and otherwise, at home and abroad, but Molotov's speech called for continued unity in the face of danger. Molotov identified Yugoslav nationalism as the principal cause of the rift between Moscow and Belgrade. He cited the fact that in May 1945, in a speech in Ljubljana, Tito had criticized the Soviet Union for not supporting Yugoslavia's claims on Trieste. Additional nationalist excesses included threats against Albania and the desire to create a Balkan federation headquartered in Belgrade. Molotov repeatedly identified the dangers of nationalism in Yugoslavia as being its *otryv* (break) from the Soviet Union and the socialist community. He warned that national patriotism must never become a source of hostility toward the Soviet Union. Molotov feared falling ideological dominoes. Defending the swift and decisive action against Tito, Molotov warned that a failure to act could have done "great harm to the ideological growth of the communist parties and the cause of communism." For example, what would have happened had Poland become infected, a country with "one and one-half times the population of Yugoslavia. One must also remember other countries."[125]

Molotov's last sentiment opened the last broad theme in the Soviet discussion of the meaning of an alliance with Yugoslavia. Molotov argued that Yugoslavia's nationalist identity was a dangerous class deviation because it threatened the Soviet alliance with other socialist countries in eastern Europe. Several interlocking discussions constituted this articulation of Soviet great power identity. The first concerned the allocation of culpability for the rift in relations. To the extent that the Soviets blamed themselves, it was an indictment of its failure to adhere sufficiently strictly to its ideal nationality

---

[123] S. Krushinsky, "On Yugoslavia: In Dubrovnik," *Pravda*, 18 July 1955, p. 4.

[124] CC Plenum, July 11, 1955, evening session, 21.

[125] CC Plenum, July 9, 1955, evening session, 1–3, quotation on 3.

policy at home. It was also an indication that being a great power required a great deal more sensitivity to the international norm of sovereignty, especially when dealing with smaller, weaker states. The second concerned the kind of ally Yugoslavia could be for the Soviet Union. The positions revolved around the class–great power axis. Khrushchev and Mikoyan gave Yugoslavia a passing grade in its class exam, but Molotov failed it. In so doing, Molotov concluded that Yugoslavia could be an ally in the geopolitical sense, but could not be a member of the socialist fraternity.[126] Meanwhile, those who argued for Yugoslavia's inclusion in the alliance on class grounds reinforced their point by citing national ties and geopolitical gains.

Soviet great power identity expressed itself partially as a modern concern with geography, material resources, and the balance of power. Each of these elements contributed to the Soviet understanding of Yugoslavia as a potential ally. Bulganin explained the need to effect a rapprochement with Yugoslavia, noting "its important strategic position in southeastern Europe, with a population of 16 million."[127] Bulganin rhetorically asked, "what have we lost in Yugoslavia?" He answered by listing its economic potential, right down to industrial sites, mineral resources, and ship tonnage. He went on to call Yugoslavia the "strongest country in Europe . . . with an army of 42 divisions. . . . It occupies a very vulnerable and important place for the Soviet Union. . . . Yugoslavia juts far to the east. If we imagine future military events, let's say we have to move our armed forces to the West. We would then have on our left flank 40–50 divisions of the Yugoslav army." Khrushchev interjected, "Plus Americans." Bulganin observed the Soviets would have to leave 70–80 divisions there to cover the area.[128]

Yugoslavia was understood in balance of power terms, in relationship to the United States and NATO. As Khrushchev outlined in his opening speech at the plenum, the danger of hostile relations with Tito was partly due to the possibility that the United States would succeed in "restoring capitalism in Yugoslavia and achieve its complete withdrawal from the socialist camp."[129] He pointed out that the United States hoped to use Tito as an exemplar, expecting other nationalist communists to be attracted by his example.[130] Other Soviet leaders defended the rapprochement with Tito and criticized Molotov's resistance on the grounds that the loss of Yugoslavia would harm

---

[126] At a March meeting of the CC Presidium, Molotov opposed establishing party ties with Yugoslavia, but acquiesced to state relations. Seweryn Bialer, "Soviet Contention over Yugoslavia," in *The Development of the Communist Bloc*, ed. Roger Pethybridge (Boston, 1965), 132.

[127] CC Plenum, July 9, 1955, evening session, 11.

[128] Ibid., 12.

[129] CC Plenum, July 9, 1955, morning session, 1.

[130] Ibid., 2. Molotov later warned of dominoes falling in eastern Europe if the USSR allied with Tito. Note 125.

the strategic position of the Soviet Union and socialism. Mikhail Suslov declared that "the struggle for multiplying our allies occupies one of the most important places in the struggle between the two camps." Soviet aims should be to "use in this struggle all and any possible allies, even if only temporary . . . and break off and distance from the imperialist camp the less stable or wavering forces and at least neutralize those of them that we cannot attract to our side." The United States, meanwhile, was trying to get Yugoslavia, India, Burma, and Indonesia into alliances with it. Kirichenko declared that "we cannot but be interested in the strategic situation of Yugoslavia and also, in the event of anything unexpected, the location of Yugoslav armed forces, and . . . who will enjoy the resources of Yugoslavia. Even if Yugoslavia were to become neutral, this would be good. But we hope for more."[131]

Commitment to class identity explains the gulf separating Molotov from his critics. Whereas Molotov's critics saw the loss of Yugoslavia as being harmful to the socialist camp, Molotov saw its retention as harmful. The difference was between the geopolitical appreciation of Yugoslavia's strategic potential and Molotov's class-based view of the need for ideological homogeneity within the bloc.

What was at stake here was nothing less than the criteria by which the Soviet Union could pursue allies in the world. It might not appear at first glance to matter much whether Yugoslav-Soviet relations improved at the state or at the party level. But, in fact, it meant so much that three days of discussions at the plenum were devoted to the issue of whether it was correct to pursue better relations at the party level. It mattered this much because the two ideas meant two very different relationships. Yugoslavia as a state may have been understood as a sovereign entity, but Yugoslavia as a member of the socialist fraternity meant both its hierarchical subordination to Moscow as the vanguard of the world socialist movement, and its adherence to a long list of domestic desiderata.[132]

What was at stake here was the very identity of the Soviet Union as a socialist power. That was why Molotov categorized Yugoslavia with Finland and India, effectively turning the relationship into one that would have no implications for the meaning of socialism or for Soviet leadership of the socialist community. This vast difference in understanding at the two levels was

---

[131] CC Plenum, July 12, 1955, morning session, 4. See also Malenkov's speech, CC Plenum, July 11, 1955, evening session, 119; Malenkov's speech to the Moscow party *aktiv* two weeks later, in RTsKhIDNI, f. 83, op. 1, d. 12, pp. 22–24.

[132] Kaganovich, for example, described rapprochement along party lines as meaning membership in the socialist camp for Yugoslavia. CC Plenum, July 11, 1955, evening session, 12. At his meeting with the Moscow party *aktiv*, Malenkov said that Molotov's position amounted to "renouncing the struggle for the complete return of Yugoslavia to the socialist camp, . . . the return of Yugoslavia to the family of fraternal peoples, to our common communist family." RTsKhIDNI, f. 83, op. 1, d. 12, p. 26.

also why Suslov could say that there was no reason for a complete break in party relations with Belgrade and "even less so" at the state level. Suslov further elaborated this differentiation, calling Soviet espionage on Yugoslav territory not only a violation of the "principles of equal rights in relations between sovereign countries [a normative reading], but even more so in relations between communist parties."[133] Efforts to reestablish party ties represented the Soviet urge to restore homogeneity to the socialist community. As Suslov put it, it was the Soviet Union's "class internationalist duty" to bring the Yugoslav communists back to Marxism-Leninism and to "return" Yugoslavia to the socialist camp. This was the language of salvation for the deviant, a redemption that could be offered only by the authentic center.[134]

Suslov alluded to the fact that the Soviet Union had violated international normative standards governing relations among all states, let alone among socialist ones. This theme provided Soviets with an understanding of why relations with Yugoslavia had become so troubled. The Soviet Union had, according to Khrushchev, committed actions that had wounded Yugoslav national pride, such as using Soviet intelligence agents to recruit Yugoslav citizens and officials as sources of secrets.[135] Khrushchev termed such actions the "grossest violation of norms in relations among fraternal parties and states." What was worse, it could have led to conflict. He also expressed regret at the Soviet creation of joint stock companies in Yugoslavia and elsewhere in the socialist world. Not everyone liked the fact that Yugoslavs objected to these companies and accused them of nationalism. "I ask you, what kind of nationalism is there here?"[136] The national sensibilities of others were understood through domestic Soviet nationality policy and international norms of the sovereign rights of others.

The Soviet acknowledgement of their violations of the norms of sovereignty and national sentiments in the case of Yugoslavia led to a consideration of the less desirable meanings of being a great power. Mikoyan raised the issue of what kind of Soviet Union could so have abused Yugoslavia. His answer was that it had made "mistakes of great power character." For example, in 1948, Stalin and Molotov had sent Tito a letter reproaching his party for not having held a congress. But the CPSU had not convened a congress and would not until 1952. "Isn't this really a great power approach to a small nation?" Mikoyan asked the plenum.

Or, take this example. The Cominform decided that Yugoslav communists faithful to Moscow should rise up against their leadership. The leadership suppressed them and several died, and others ended

---

[133] CC Plenum, July 11, 1955, evening session, 29. See also Shepilov, CC Ibid., 156.
[134] Ibid., 30.
[135] Ibid., 4.
[136] Ibid., 5.

up in prison. We demanded that the Yugoslav commission investigate this with the participation of Soviet representatives. On what basis? Our state demanded the right to participate in the investigation of the affairs of Yugoslav citizens. This is great power chauvinism! . . . And, if we accept the position offered by Molotov, that all foreign communists must love the Soviet Union more than their own countries, then this won't be "conventional great power chauvinism," but a chauvinism at a higher stage of development, so to speak, not great Russian, but great Soviet chauvinism (laughter and stirring in the hall), that, as Lenin said, can mean only one thing—the betrayal of communism.

Yugoslav nationalism, was no more dangerous than "this great power chauvinism."[137]

Finally, there was a clear and consequential connection between thinking of Yugoslavia geopolitically and a toleration for difference. Unlike Molotov, whose understanding of class identity limited his apprehension of Yugoslavia to a site of potentially disruptive deviance, Khrushchev and other members of the Soviet foreign policy elite understood Yugoslavia both as geopolitically valuable and as not the West. As Khrushchev put it, "as communists . . . we must think not only of organizing forces which *firmly stand on our socialist positions*, but . . . also those forces *which cannot go with us to the end and can disagree with us on ideological questions*. We need to make sure that such forces do not end up opposed to the socialist camp."[138] Khrushchev and Mikoyan accused Molotov of writing off a potential ally. Mikoyan asked whether Yugoslavia was really closer to the imperialist camp, as Molotov had said. Yugoslavia had refused to join NATO; it had prohibited any U.S. military bases there, or economic or military advisers; and it supported Chinese entry into the UN and the return of Taiwan.[139] Kaganovich, by accusing Molotov of "sectarianism," of being excessively fearful that dealing with Tito risked "the loss of the boundary between communists and noncommunists," identified the cost of treating difference as deviance.[140] Toleration of difference at home made Soviet geopolitical interests in Yugoslavia thinkable.

The Soviet experience with Yugoslavia demonstrates that to know how a state understands another state it is worthwhile to begin by finding out how a state

[137] Ibid., 15–18. Mikoyan's irony was based on Lenin's famous essay, "Imperialism—Highest Stage of Capitalism." In *The Lenin Anthology*, ed. Robert C. Tucker (New York, 1995), 204–74.

[138] CC Plenum, July 9, 1955, morning session, 2. Emphasis added.

[139] CC Plenum, July 11, 1955, morning session, 12.

[140] CC Plenum, July 11, 1955, evening session, 23.

understands itself. There was a close and clear connection between Soviet domestic identities and the predominant discourse of Soviet policy toward Yugoslavia. The understanding of the Soviet Union as a privileged bearer of a particular class identity bounded Soviet attitudes toward Yugoslavia. The arguments of Khrushchev and Mikoyan in particular, on the one hand, and Molotov, on the other, reflected the domestic divisions over difference and deviance. The inescapability of class identity is evident in the understandings of those most willing to tolerate deviation from that ideal class ally. Even they identified certain practices by Yugoslavia that bore watching and indicated a danger of its drifting off into deviance and degeneration into a bourgeois identity as an ally of the United States.

Although geopolitical concerns were an important understanding of Yugoslavia, these considerations were not sufficient to generate Soviet interest in an alliance. Had class identity had more political resonance (which itself was contingent on the domestic identity politics at the time that favored difference over idealization), Soviet interest in Yugoslavia would not have been as a potential ally but as a dangerous potential enemy, which it had been from 1948 to 1955. Moreover, Soviet great power identity opened the way for an alliance not just through balance of power considerations—it was the Soviet acknowledgment of its violation of its own normative commitments that permitted an alternative understanding of Yugoslav deviance. Instead of seeing deviant Yugoslav behavior as solely diagnostic of Yugoslav identity, Soviets understood these undesirable practices to be partly the product of interaction with Soviet deviations from acceptable normative conduct.

The Soviet understanding of itself as Russian implied an understanding of Yugoslavia as a relative of some kind, as partly us, regardless of conduct. This apprehension of similarity reduced Soviet expectations of danger from difference, Yugoslavia having become imagined as a non-Russian republic of the Soviet Union, a Ukraine abroad. This allowed the Soviets to understand Yugoslav nationalist deviation as partly a response to an incorrect application of Leninist nationality policy, just as it had been misapplied at home. But this ethnonational understanding of Yugoslavia also entailed the application of hierarchy, with the Serbs and Croats being understood as Ukrainian little brothers that were less advanced on the socialist evolutionary ladder than any of the Soviet Union's more authentic socialist allies.

In short, the Soviet Union sought an alliance with Yugoslavia in 1955 because the predominant discourse and its constitutive identities made it possible. The adherence to a variant of class identity more tolerant of difference, recognition of the Soviet Union's own violation of international norms of sovereignty and domestic nationality policy, and appreciation of geopolitical advantage from an alliance combined to enable this particular Soviet alliance choice.

China, the Soviet Union's Closest Other

China occupied a most ambiguous position in the Soviet understanding of itself. China was the one state in world politics that came closest to being the Soviet Union. China's size, revolutionary and antiimperialist history, devotion to Marxism-Leninism, and appeal to other revolutionary movements around the world gave China features that resonated with Soviet class and great power identities. But the closest Other is often the most threatening identity for any Self because, as differences are erased, as distance is closed, expectations for and from similarity grow. Difference that once could be ignored as trivial becomes a challenge to the Self's own claims of authenticity. As the Soviet Union came to see China as a great power building socialism, just as it was, the questions about the identity boundaries between them became increasingly problematic. Differences that could easily be countenanced in eastern European countries or, even more so, in Yugoslavia, could only be tolerated at much higher cost. The more China was like the Soviet Union, the less China could deviate from the Soviet model without bringing that very model into question. This tension was alleviated by the Soviet understanding of China as underdeveloped, like central Asia. A premodern China's deviations were attributed to this less-developed status. But this was a remedy that forced an uncomfortable trade-off between Chinese equality and Chinese underdevelopment, Chinese progress on the road to socialism and Chinese subordination to its older Soviet brother.

Chronology

October 1954, the Khrushchev delegation to China traded foreign policy unity for economic aid and the return of Port Arthur.[141]

December 1954, the United States signed a bilateral security treaty with Taiwan. The treaty did not include defense of offshore islands.

January 1955, Chinese soldiers occupied the northernmost island of the Tachen group off Taiwan.

January 28, the U.S. Congress passed almost unanimously a resolution granting the president full power to commit U.S. troops to defend Taiwan and the Pescadores.

January 30, the Soviet Union introduced a UN resolution condemning U.S. behavior on Taiwan.

March 16, at a press conference, Dwight Eisenhower mentioned the possibility of using tactical nuclear weapons to defend Taiwan from attack.[142]

[141] George D. Embree, *The Soviet Union between the 19th and 20th Party Congresses, 1952–1956* (The Hague, 1959), 155.

[142] This description of the Quemoy-Matsu crisis is derived from Alexander L. George and Richard Smoke, *Deterrence in American Foreign Policy: Theory and Practice* (New York, 1974), 266–92.

April 27, the Soviets signed an agreement to provide China with all the assistance necessary to build a nuclear weapon.

China occupied an extraordinary position in Soviet apprehension of the world. Three Soviet identities—class, modernity, and nation—implied a hierarchical relationship between Self and Other, with the Soviet Russian Self in a superior position vis-à-vis all others. But China presented a unique Other. When understood in terms of class and great power identities, China approached the Soviet Union's own understanding of itself as a vanguard of socialism and great power. Indeed, Khrushchev once referred to the Soviet Union and China as if they were partly each other, a mutually constitutive moment. He was explaining to Burma's Prime Minister U Nu that a prime objective should be to become a truly independent country. He then said that "with friends like China, we have even greater possibilities to become more independent."[143] In other words, mutual dependence, or interdependence, between two socialist powers such as China and the Soviet Union would produce independence with respect to the rest of the world, making possible the seemingly counterintuitive position that dependence was actually the road to independence. But such an achievement was possible only if the Self and Other were understood as being partly one another.

Molotov told the Supreme Soviet that there existed a "world camp of socialism and democracy, headed by the USSR, or, it would be more accurate to say, by the Soviet Union and the Chinese People's Republic."[144] Khrushchev, at the July plenum, referred to China and the Soviet Union as heading the socialist camp together.[145] Moreover, during the relentless attack on Molotov over Yugoslavia, Khrushchev interrupted the proceedings to question why Molotov thought the Chinese could not correct the CPSU in matters of Marxism-Leninism; Khrushchev said, "they can."[146] Yet another sign of equality was China's participation at the May conference in Warsaw that formalized the creation of the Warsaw Pact. In perhaps the most public and official of venues, in an article in *Kommunist* marking the fifth anniversary of the treaty of friendship, alliance, and mutual aid between Moscow and Beijing, Kapitsa, author and foreign ministry counsellor, immediately identified China as one of "the two greatest powers of the socialist camp." The "cooperation of the Soviet Union and China is the backbone of the socialist camp."[147]

---

[143] TsKhSD, f. 5, op. 30, d. 116, p. 230.

[144] Vyacheslav Molotov, speech reproduced in *New Times*, no. 7 (February 12, 1955).

[145] CC Plenum, July 9, 1955, morning session, 19. Suslov used the same formulation at the July 11, 1955, evening session, 29. N. M. Pegov, secretary of the Presidium of the Supreme Soviet, also used it at the celebration of the sixth anniversary of the Chinese revolution. *Pravda*, 1 October 1955, p. 1.

[146] CC Plenum, July 11, 1955, morning session, 18.

[147] Mikhail Kapitsa, "The Great Friendship of the Peoples of the USSR and China—

China was also given equal billing in its relevance as an exemplar for those pursuing "agrarian, anti-feudal, and anti-imperialist revolutions."[148] The language used here was not markedly different from Soviet descriptions of a similar exemplary role for its central Asian republics. And although seemingly a gesture granting equality to the two socialist great powers, in fact, the Soviets reserved to themselves, if only through omission, sole leadership of proletarian revolutions in the capitalist world. Nevertheless, Soviet regard for China's place in the Third World was very high. The Chinese experience "furnishes conclusive proof that Asian countries, with their virtually inexhaustible natural resources and manpower, can independently, without foreign capital, advance by leaps and bounds."[149] In the many articles surrounding the fifth anniversary of the treaty between Moscow and Beijing, Nikolai Tikhonov wrote that the People's Republic of China (PRC) "had turned itself into a mighty factor of the liberation struggle of all oppressed peoples against imperialist reaction and colonial enslavement."[150]

China's equality was established on more than class grounds. Soviet geopolitical understanding recognized China as a sovereign great power. The Soviet alliance with China had to be differentiated from alliances among capitalist great powers, which, according to official Soviets, always were determined by "power differentials," unlike the Chinese-Soviet alliance, in which "the parties are equal."[151] Materially speaking, China had the largest population (as Khrushchev told his Indian hosts, China was a "state which, as the saying goes, you cannot step over without noticing"[152]), it was richly endowed with natural resources, and it was situated on Soviet borders.[153] At a public meeting celebrating the fifth anniversary of the treaty, Professor

---

Bastion of Peace and Security," *Kommunist* 1 (January 1955): 25. Suslov and Molotov, for example, recommended that the Soviet Union consult with China before developing its plans for economic aid for North Korea in January. TsKhSD, f. 5, op. 120, p. 2.

[148] N. Tropkin, "On the Strategy and Tactics of Leninism," *Kommunist* 1 (January 1955): 108.

[149] B. Bolotin and G. Kuzmin, "China's New Role in the Asian Economy," *New Times*, no. 21 (May 21, 1955): 14. For China as the paradigm for "popular-democratic revolution in a backward, semi-colonial, semi-feudal country," especially for the popular-liberation movement of the East, see I. Tugarinov, MFA Information Committee report, July 16, 1955, in AVPRF, f. 100, op. 48, d. 127, p. 395.

[150] Nikolai Tikhonov, "The Power of Our Peoples Is Inexhaustible and Insuperable," *Pravda*, 14 February 1955, p. 3. In a lead editorial marking China's first five-year plan, its successful execution was called an example for all those still under colonial domination, the "peoples of the East." "First Five-Year Plan of the People's Republic of China," *Pravda*, 3 August 1955, p. 1.

[151] N. Sudarikov and P. Fandikov, "The Great Friendship," *New Times*, no. 7 (February 12, 1955): 4.

[152] Nikita Khrushchev, speech reproduced in *New Times*, no. 52 (December 22, 1955): 19.

[153] For this conclusion, see I. Gerasimov, "Soviet Geographer in China," *New Times*, no. 35 (August 25, 1955): 20.

A. I. Denisov, chairman of the board of the Society of International Cultural Relations, exulted in how much power the Beijing-Moscow alliance enjoyed. He said that together they had "enormous human resources, inexhaustible natural riches, enormous territories with a common border, a really mighty and invincible force. The history of mankind has never known such power."[154]

Understood geopolitically, China was regarded as a great power ally in an antiimperialist coalition led by Moscow. But because China was regarded not merely as a member of the socialist community or as an important ally against the United States, but also as part of the Soviet Self, aid to China, including military aid in the areas of the design and production of atomic weapons, was not regarded purely as aid to another state, but in fact as aid to oneself.[155] As Khrushchev later related in his memoirs, the Soviets regarded the strengthening of China as the strengthening of the socialist camp and as "the securing of our eastern borders."[156] This geopolitical understanding of China found its way into Soviet arguments for awarding the Beijing government the Chinese seat on the UN Security Council. Molotov, at the General Assembly session in New York in September, faced with the task of making the case, began by drawing the General Assembly's attention to China's size and economic potential.[157] In identifying China as a great power, as Bulganin did at the August 1955 Supreme Soviet session, the Soviets acknowledged China's global place.[158] China was not only a player in Asian security, but participated in European affairs as well. The Chinese

[154] *Pravda*, 13 February 1955, p. 1.

[155] For just a small example of the comprehensiveness of the military cooperation between Soviet agencies and Chinese colleagues, see the instructions given by Ivan Kurdiukov, deputy head of the MFA Far Eastern Department to Ambassador Iudin pursuant to the Council of Ministers' decisions on these matters in March, in AVPRF, f. 100, op. 48, d. 61, pp. 16–18.

[156] Nikita S. Khrushchev, *Vospominaniia: Izbrannye Fragmenty* (Moscow, 1997), 346. I do not use this rich source of evidence for Soviet policy in 1955 unless there is corroboration from other sources. In this case, see Kapitsa, "Great Friendship," 34. The MFA archives are revealing on this point as well. Dozens, perhaps hundreds, of Chinese aid requests, including those for military equipment, training, and advisers, were handled by the ministry in the most routine and automatic of fashions, implying an almost natural relationship of material power flowing from the Soviet Union to China. See, in particular, AVPRF, ff. 100, 179, 243, 253, 270, 275, 312, 313.

[157] Vyacheslav Molotov, speech reproduced in *Pravda*, 21 September 1955, p. 3.

[158] Nikolai Bulganin, speech reprinted in *New Times*, no. 33 (August 11, 1955): 5–20. See also Kapitsa, "Great Friendship," 36, who declares that China's performance at Geneva proves that "one cannot resolve important international problems" without Beijing. See also Sudarikov and Fandikov, "Great Friendship," 7, who write of China as a "genuine Great Power" with global interests. E. Zhukov identifies the Soviet Union and China as "two Great Powers standing side by side." "Moscow, Peking, Delhi," *New Times*, no. 45 (October 3, 1955): 16. The official slogans for the thirty-eighth anniversary of the Bolshevik Revolution termed China a "mighty world power," less than a great power, but still a country of global rank. *Pravda*, 25 October 1955, p. 1.

newspaper, *Zhenmingzhibao*, promised that if war were to come to Europe, China would not stand on the sidelines.[159]

China was also an equal when understood as a sovereign state. And this international normative identity was ubiquitous in 1955, if for no other reason than that the main Other, the United States, forcefully denied China that identity, refusing to recognize the Beijing government and denying it the China seat on the Security Council. In this way, daily international practice, more precisely the violation of normative practice, implied a China that was the sovereign equal of the Soviet Union and all other states in world politics.[160] U.S. efforts to deny a sovereign identity to China ensured that the Soviet Union regarded China as a sovereign state in every way equal to the Soviet Union in that domain. When Molotov was asked by visiting U.S. journalists William Randolph Hearst and Kingsbury Smith to elaborate on the Soviet position on Taiwan and the offshore islands, he began by appealing to the texts of relevant international treaties, the Cairo and Potsdam declarations of 1943 and 1945 and the Japanese surrender documents.[161] China's rights as a sovereign great power were embedded in international legal discourse.

But China was not understood solely as an equal to the Soviet Union. Although a great power for material reasons, a sovereign equal for international normative reasons, and a revolutionary equal for class reasons, China remained at the same time a premodern periphery in need of a vanguard in Moscow. The predominant Soviet discourse on modernity equivocated on China's identity. On the one hand, its size and natural resources made it a great power; on the other hand, it remained a primitive, rural, agricultural periphery in comparison to the industrialized modern Soviet center. In its hierarchy of socialist allies, the most common location for China was between the Soviet Union and the "other people's democracies"; that is, China was positioned above Moscow's eastern European allies, but below Moscow itself.[162] Although China was on the path of "socialist construction," the

---

[159] Kapitsa, "Great Friendship," 37–38. Involving China in European affairs apparently strained popular conceptions of China as a great power. Yekaterina Furtseva, when reporting to the CC on party *aktiv* meetings around Moscow, related that one of the more frequent sources of confusion for these Moscow communists was grasping how China could help European states preserve peace, in TsKhSD, f. 5, op. 30, d. 90, p. 51.

[160] Cynthia Weber has shown how violations of an international norm can fix the meaning of that norm. In her cases, military interventions constitute the meanings of sovereignty. Cynthia Weber, *Simulating Sovereignty: Intervention, the State, and Symbolic Exchange* (Cambridge, 1995).

[161] Unpublished conversation of January 29, in AVPRF, f. 123, op. 39, d. 1, p. 7.

[162] Such a position was maintained through understandings such as Molotov's. On Bulganin's promotion to prime minister, many congratulatory telegrams arrived. Molotov suggested replying to those from eastern Europe en bloc, but sending China one separately. TsKhSD, f. 5, op. 30, d. 119, p. 53. See Tropkin, "On the strategy," 103.

USSR alone was building communism. Like all socialist states, China was on the road to becoming the Soviet Union.

It was reported that Anshan was "one of the first big Chinese cities rapidly acquiring socialist features." These included the trappings of Soviet urban modernity: "new residential buildings, clubs, schools, and kindergartens. Most of the shops are state-owned or cooperative and there are almost no pedicabs in the streets."[163] Although "in a few years, China will become a mighty *industrial* and agricultural socialist power,"[164] in the meantime it was subordinate to the Soviet Union, which was already both. Khrushchev placed China in the development hierarchy under the GDR. In his summary speech to the July plenum Khrushchev ridiculed Molotov's request to take twenty-five buses with him to the GDR. Molotov responded by pointing out that Khrushchev had brought tractors to China. Khrushchev's response illuminated China's position: "Dear Viacheslav Mikhailovich! China is a destroyed peasant country. We are ambassadors of an industrially developed country. . . . In giving these tractors to our Chinese friends . . . , they will learn from us. . . . But imagine if you take buses with you to Germany. . . . After all, we learned how to build buses from the Germans. What will they say?"[165]

Chinese were seen as less developed intellectually and technically, as well. "The Chinese people see in the world-historical experience of the Soviet Union a rich source of knowledge. . . ." At factories in the Soviet Union an observer could find many Chinese "trying to master the operation of complicated machines."[166] All progress in agronomy was attributed to Chinese visits to Soviet institutes or the appearance of Soviet lecturers in China.[167] A member of a Soviet dance troupe visiting China observed that "the ballet, as we know it, does not *yet* exist in China."[168] D. Zaslavsky, a Soviet journalist, reporting his experiences in China proudly tells how Chinese children on the street greeted them with smiles and shouts of "Hello, older Soviet brother." What is more, these children were only repeating what they heard at school, on the street, and at home, implying its utter penetration of Chinese society and daily life.[169] This replicated the hierarchy at home between senior Russian brothers and less-developed, but beloved, non-Russian re-

---

[163] G. Astafyev, "Anshan Today," *New Times*, no. 40 (September 29, 1955): 18–19.

[164] Gerasimov, "Soviet Geographer in China," 20. Emphasis added.

[165] CC Plenum, July 12, 1955, 35.

[166] Kapitsa, "Great Friendship," 29.

[167] N. Fedorenko, "Peking Diary," *New Times*, no. 10 (March 6, 1955): 21–25. See also Lin Tan-Chiu, "Springtime in China," *New Times*, no. 18 (April 30, 1955): 13–14.

[168] Asaf Messerer, "Folk Talent in People's China," *New Times*, no. 41 (October 6, 1955): 22. Emphasis added to stress the Soviet expectation that someday China will achieve a higher level of development. The same was said for symphonic music, 24.

[169] D. Zaslavsky, "We Go Together," *LG* (February 15, 1955): 4.

publics. This evolutionary understanding of China as being on its way to the position the Soviet Union already was found a place in an official secret history of Chinese-Soviet relations. The decision to close the joint stock companies was explained as "the young China" finally "acquiring the necessary expertise to manage these enterprises."[170]

This view of China as the less developed younger brother was reflected in official Chinese requests for Soviet aid. A typical letter to the Soviet embassy in Beijing from the Chinese foreign ministry began, "Taking into account the absence of people capable of operating the Iliushin-14s [we] ordered, the Chinese Civil Aviation Ministry appeals to the Soviet government to send six Iliushin-14 crews. . . ."[171] Through the daily identification of itself as the Soviet Union's dependent in its ministerial contacts with Soviet counterparts, China reproduced for Moscow an identity already resonant with discursive possibilities. In a conversation with Bulganin and Mikoyan on March 19, Chinese ambassador Liu Shao-chi requested that Soviet economic advisers in China "prompt their Chinese comrades, and not be embarrassed to point out their inadequacies and give advice. . . ."[172] But Moscow's younger brother was at least an able pupil. On October 1, *Pravda* devoted much of the paper to the celebration of China's sixth anniversary. Among the commemorations were testimonials from Soviets who had worked on Chinese projects. Characteristic was the tribute of A. Mervelov, a foreman at the Kirov machine tool factory in Tbilisi. He recalled how "Anshan workers not only rapidly learned to independently run our machine tools, but also introduced a number of substantial improvements."[173] Just as Russians could learn some things from non-Russians at home, the Soviets might even learn something from China. Kapitsa acknowledged that Soviet citizens were enriched by Chinese culture and were interested in Chinese medicine, especially Tibetan folk medicine, in particular the use of ginseng, and methods of healing in use since ancient times.[174]

Once an Other is regarded as very much like the Self, as the Soviet Union regarded China as another socialist great power with sovereign rights, dif-

---

[170] The history was drawn up by Fedorenko and Kapitsa. AVPRF, f. 100, op. 48, d. 39, p. 9. The joint stock companies were vehicles for Soviet investment in Chinese industries.

[171] AVPRF, f. 100, op. 42, d. 5, p. 110. For similar self-subordinating language, see AVPRF, f. 100, op. 48, d. 1, pp. 3, 15.

[172] AVPRF, f. 100, op. 48, d. 5, pp. 82, 83. Bulganin replied that sometimes Soviet comrades needed to be more restrained. In the same vein, Rumiantsev reviewed a documentary film on collectivizaton made for Chinese consumption. In his memorandum to the CC on the film, he criticized it, saying that its "many pompous phrases and bragging about Soviet aid to China and other people's democracies, and the role of the Soviet Union as teacher and philanthropist is tactless." TsKhSD, f. 5, op. 17, d. 548, p. 126.

[173] A. Mervelov, "Unity of Purpose," *Pravda*, 1 October 1955, p. 3. See also A. Orlov, "High Labor Heroism," *Pravda*, 1 October 1955, p. 3.

[174] Kapitsa, "Great Friendship," 33. Myra Redina describes how Soviets taught Chinese

ference becomes very hard to justify or difference becomes that much more meaningful in a context in which its existence has unsettling implications for the understanding of Self as well as the Other. As Khrushchev told his colleagues at the July plenum, pursuing good state-to-state relations with Yugoslavia would be "more difficult, of course, than with bourgeois states like Austria or India, whose leaders do not say they are Marxist-Leninists."[175] Because China was much farther along the socialist road than even eastern European CPDs, let alone Yugoslavia, Khrushchev's sentiment went double for China. Similarity can promote discord because disputes over authenticity are possible only with actors that are understood as partly oneSelf. At the same time, difference can promote good relations because claims about fundamental constitutive principles of one another's identities are moot.

China was close enough to the Soviet Union's understandings of itself that Chinese differences from the ideal were the object of the closest official Soviet attention. The Soviet Amassador to China, P. F. Iudin, expressed displeasure with how China had characterized the Chinese-Soviet relationship at the April 1955 Chinese party conference, which Iudin summarized in a memorandum to Molotov and Khrushchev. He complained in particular about Liu Shao-Tsi's speech on the international situation, which did not pay enough attention to Chinese-Soviet relations or "to the aid the Soviet Union gives China. For example, in the section on Taiwan, nothing was said about Soviet support for China's position. Only a single sentence was given to our idea of an international conference." The speech also failed to mention how Soviet aid had increased the PRC's international prestige and defense capabilities. Then Iudin cited some particular passages that he believed were veiled attacks on the Soviet Union. "Since, in reality, most aid to socialist countries is given by the Soviet Union, then bewilderment could be evoked by the following: 'one shouldn't think that once you've helped someone, you can deal with them unfairly. . . .'" Finally, Iudin offered the following quotation to demonstrate China's less than acceptable performance at the conference. Liu Shao-Tsi listed relations with Vietnam and North Korea as an example of "mutual aid," ignoring the Soviet Union again.[176]

The Soviets also observed that China's class identity as a site of a proletarian revolution was problematic, given the level of class conflict still under

---

dancers classical choreography in Beijing and Soviet artists learned the "tea-gathering dance" in exchange. Myra Redina, "Forever with China," *New Times*, no. 7 (February 12, 1955): 10.

[175] CC Plenum, July 9, 1955, morning session, 14.

[176] AVPRF, f. 100, op. 48, d. 127, pp. 16–17. Iudin's interpretation did not go unchallenged in Moscow. Nikolai Fedorenko and I. Kurdiukov, Fedorenko's successor as Far East Section chief, produced a memorandum to Molotov on May 12, less than three weeks after the Iudin analysis. In that memorandum, they claimed, contrary to the ambassador, that plenty of attention had been paid to Soviet foreign policy in the world and that Iudin's interpretation of Liu Shao-Tsi's comments as a veiled attack was wrong—the countries referred to were Vietnam and North Korea, not the Soviet Union (228–31).

way in China. This assessment both subordinated China to its more developed Soviet vanguard and raised the prospect that the Chinese revolution was not as secure as Chinese colleagues claimed. Soviets observed that class struggle was continuing in China,[177] and because antagonistic class relations had been eliminated in the Soviet Union China was in a subordinate developmental position. At the March party conference, Chinese leaders "smashed" the Gao Gan–Zhao Shu-shi bloc. Commenting on this, the Soviet Union was proud that it no longer had class contradictions of this magnitude.[178] Soviet diplomatic personnel in China sent back a steady stream of reports attesting to the domestic political weakness of China relative to the Soviet Union. The Soviet consul in Canton, I. Kriuchkov, wrote to deputy foreign minister and Far East Section head, Nikolai T. Fedorenko, that approximately 400,000 Chinese left the country through Shanghai legally every year and many who returned had been recruited by Taiwanese intelligence. Kriuchkov's information came from a local Chinese police official.[179] In an August report from the Soviet embassy in Beijing to Fedorenko, Kurdiukov, and the Information Committee, it was revealed that a "counter-revolution" persisted in China, with agents having penetrated all links of the party and state apparat, and some of them even "occupying responsible posts in leading organs." The authors, N. Chekhanov and A. Borunkov, reported that Chinese security organs had registered more than 1 million people suspected of ties with the Kuomintang. Molotov blue-penciled this entire section of the report.[180]

Chinese economic reforms were understood as if they were being carried out within the Soviet Union. The Iudin memorandum on the Chinese party conference pointed out that Chen Iun's report on the Chinese economy omitted many key issues, including economization, labor productivity, rationalization, labor competition, single authority, and profitability.[181] Chinese political deviations also drew on Soviet understandings of Self. Individualism, conceit, daily moral degradation of communists, aspirations to a bourgeois way of life, selfishness, inadmissible relations with women, and various state crimes were all part of the Chinese reality against which the party was

---

[177] This particular deviation is something that is not reported by Soviet observers of the eastern European allies. For example, see Suslov, speech in East Berlin on the sixth anniversary of the GDR, in *Pravda*, 7 October 1955, p. 3.

[178] The Chinese report about the conference was published in *Pravda*, 6 April 1955, p. 3. Soviet Ambassador Iudin's analysis of the conference is in AVPRF, f. 100, op. 48, d. 127, p. 15. Soviet recognition that their closest socialist Other, China, was still experiencing meaningful class conflict, while socialism in the Soviet Union was far more secure, strengthened those who tolerated difference at home.

[179] AVPRF, f. 100, op. 48, d. 128, p. 1.

[180] Ibid., 91. N. Chekhanov was the embassy's second secretary in Beijing, and A. Borunkov was his aide.

[181] AVPRF, f. 100, op. 48, d. 127, p. 6.

struggling.[182] Parallels with Soviet deviations in less developed parts of the Soviet Union were manifest. Finally, Chinese agricultural reforms were understood through the Soviet experience of the 1930s. A Soviet consular official in Mukden reported to Fedorenko that Chinese policy relied on poor, cooperative, and reeducated middle peasants, deferring the destruction of the *kulaks* until 1957. Just as in Soviet times, the "excesses" of coercion against middle peasants were condemned.[183]

In one respect, China was not unlike Yugoslavia—the Soviet Union understood its difference from itself, its deviation from the single true model, as it understood such phenomena at home, as temporary, episodic, nondiagnostic, and anomalous. Difference did not threaten China's socialist identity. But such understanding did not remove the Soviet attitude of superiority toward China because of China's place on the ladder of modernity. In July 1955, the MFA Information Committee produced a report on the Chinese Communist Party's (CCP's) policy toward private capital, authored by I. Tugarinov and sent to Kurdiukov for distribution to the CC Presidium. He began by enumerating the ways in which private capital was deliberately allowed to operate freely in China and the economic rationale for such a policy, including increased consumer goods production, rural commerce, state accumulation of tax revenue, less unemployment, and more worker training. But it was the political rationale that connected the appreciation of difference to Soviet reality and to foreign policy. Tugarinov wrote that private capital must be used to strengthen the united popular democratic front. And this broad alliance was especially important because of the tense international situation in the Far East, in particular, around Taiwan.[184] In other words, as tension increased abroad, a country must broaden its domestic base, not narrow it by writing people off as deviants. The working class and peasant identity of China was, however, put at risk by this strategy. The Information Committee analysis observed that the Chinese communists expected to recruit more supporters from the bourgeoisie through developing state capitalism. Meanwhile, "direct counterrevolutionary resistance" was continuing by part of the bourgeoisie. What is more, there were "insufficiencies and extremes" in the execution of CCP policy that included the bourgeois degeneration of cadres. The report concluded that Chinese officials too frequently stressed the "bloodless and peaceful" quality of the transition in China, ignoring the inevitable aggravation of the class struggle.[185]

---

[182] Ibid., 274. This is from a Soviet embassy officer in Beijing who wrote a report on the internal party work of the Chinese Communist Party for Kuznetsov, Fedorenko, and Kurdiukov. It is dated July 9.

[183] Ibid., 398–401.

[184] Ibid., 366–69.

[185] Ibid., 380–87. See also D. Zaslavsky, "The Soul of a Rabbit," *New Times*, no. 1 (January 1, 1955): 22.

In other words, China was behind the Soviet Union on the path of socialist development, and Chinese comrades did not fully recognize how much more secure socialism was in the Soviet Union than in China.[186]

China was the Soviet Union's ally and more in 1955. Although China was the revolutionary equal of the Soviet Union, a most powerful exemplar for the decolonizing world, it also suffered from unfinished class struggle at home. Although China, geopolitically speaking, was a great power, just like the Soviet Union, it also was a premodern country, not yet even an industrial-agricultural power, let alone a modern industrial power like the Soviet Union. Instead, it was subordinate to Moscow and had to rely on it for the knowledge, technology, and capital equipment to enter the modern world. Finally, China's sovereign equality was both unquestioned and championed by the Soviet Union. As was the case with Yugoslavia, Soviets recognized that it had violated these sovereign rights in the past. Khrushchev recognized that China's understanding of itself as a postcolonial state, the previous object of imperialist exploitation, had been rudely ignored by the policy of establishing joint-stock companies in China under Stalin.[187] The combination of the Soviet Union's self-understandings and its related appreciation of China as both subordinate and equal added up to a set of contradictions and tensions that ultimately would have to be resolved.

India, the Soviet Union's First and Biggest Little Brother in the Zone of Peace
Difference made the Soviet alliance with India possible. India was the closest that another state could get to being understood as part of the Soviet periphery at home. India fit perfectly into the hierarchy of modernity that dominated Soviet discourse on how its own peoples were arranged vis-à-vis Moscow and Russians. India's position necessitated a vanguard role for the

---

[186] A Soviet graduate student in the Institute of Eastern Studies who did not recognize this difference got the attention of the CC itself. In a March 25 memorandum to the CC, Rumiantsev reported that the graduate student, I. Iliushechkin, "committed a serious theoretical and political error," arguing that China's socialist revolution started in 1927. Worse, this meant that he "equates the October socialist revolution with the Chinese revolution." Rumiantsev excoriated the institute's director and his deputy for allowing the discussion to proceed after the error had been made. The student was ordered to write a paper correcting his mistake. TsKhSD, f. 5, op. 17, d. 518, pp. 144–45.

[187] Nikita Khrushchev, *Vospominaniia, Izbrannye Fragmenty* (Moscow, 1997), 345. The MFA was a site for the production of a geopolitical view of China. See the report that Fedorenko and Kapitsa prepared, a history of Sino-Soviet relations for the previous five years, in which they do not begin with a class analysis of China, a review of its revolutionary exploits, or an analysis of the ties between the two ruling communist parties. Instead, the document opens with a legal construction of the relationship derived from the text of the February 1950 Treaty of Friendship and Cooperation between the two governments. AVPRF, f. 100, op. 48, d. 39, pp. 1–2.

Soviet Union to help its biggest little brother progress on the road toward industrialization, urbanization, and maybe even socialization. But such prospects for India, and for a Soviet-Indian alliance, were unthinkable without the turn toward differentiation that the Soviet Union experienced at home in 1955.

Chronology

June 1954, Indian Prime Minister Nehru and Chinese Foreign Minister Chou En-lai announced *dasa shila*.

September 1954, SEATO was formed by the United States, Cambodia, Laos, Pakistan, Thailand, and the Phillipines.

February 2, 1955, the Soviet Union agreed to help India build the Bhilai steel plant. The U.S. Senate ratified SEATO the same day.

February 24, the Baghdad Pact was formed, with Turkey and Iraq as its charter members.

April 6–10, the Asian Conference for Relaxation of International Tension was held in Delhi, with eighteen delegations present, including one from the Soviet Union.

April 18–24, the Bandung conference was held without a Soviet delegation.

June, the CIA overthrew the Arbenz government in Guatemala.

June 7–23, Nehru visited the Soviet Union.

July 1, Pakistan announced its decision to join the Baghdad Pact.

September, a Egyptian-Czech arms deal was concluded.

October, Soviet relations were reestablished with Saudi Arabia.

October 10, in speech to an American Legion convention, Dulles declared that neutrality was obsolete.[188]

October 11, Iran joined the Baghdad Pact.

October 20, Burma's U Nu visited the Soviet Union.

November 7, Kaganovich gave the Great October Socialist Revolution Day speech in which he introduced the zone of peace.

November 18–December 18, Khrushchev and Bulganin visited India, Burma, and Afghanistan.

November 21, the first meeting of the Baghdad Pact was held.

End of 1955, Soviet aid programs were either under way or under negotiation in India, Afghanistan, Yugoslavia, Burma, Indonesia, Jordan, Ceylon, Ecuador, and Pakistan.

Khrushchev made the case for difference during his stay in India, asking his audience, "why should we clarify the questions on which we don't agree? It

---

[188] Quoted in John Lewis Gaddis, *Strategies of Containment: A Critical Appraisal of Postwar American National Security Policy* (New York, 1982), 154.

is much more important to affirm that upon which we do fundamentally agree."[189] At the July plenum on Yugoslavia, Mikoyan digressed to a discussion of India, accusing Molotov of writing off yet another potential ally. Mikoyan argued that classifying India according to Molotov's ideal class criteria would make India as much an Other as Pakistan or Iran. Mikoyan lamented the costs of such a homogenization of difference. "Just how carelessly, often ignorantly, we pin labels on states not in the socialist camp is evident in the example of India. In connection with the arrival of Nehru in Moscow, the MFA distributed to Presidium members a memorandum on India characterizing the Indian government as a 'bourgeois-landlord state' and saying that the economic policy of the Government of India is determined by the interests of the big bourgeoisie and landlords."

In fact, Mikoyan said, India was pursuing agrarian reform and antifeudal measures, and "elementary democratic norms are observed in India, something one cannot say about Iran or Pakistan." And here was the reason why getting this right was important: "To not note the difference means depriving ourselves of the opportunity to have the right policy." Mikoyan's recommendation was to search for difference among those relegated to the camp of the Other: "One must search for the particular in each country, distinguish one country from the other and not in order to simply push aside these peculiarities, but to have an accurate policy."[190]

India's status in the decolonizing zone of peace did not exempt it from being examined from a class standpoint. This analysis situated India in the Soviet hierarchy in a relatively low position. But the examination revealed that India was at the very least not a dangerous Other, if still a long, long way from the Soviet Self. Class identity implied an allied subordination to an older brother in Moscow. Khrushchev positioned India in the hierarchy when he observed, after singling out China, and then the Asian and European people's democracies, that Nehru had said that India, too, would follow the socialist path and while "that is good, our conceptions of socialism differ. But we welcome this statement and this intention."[191] India would be socialist when Moscow said it was.

By prevailing Soviet standards, India's political leadership, including Nehru, did not pay appropriate attention to the role of class struggle, the working class, the peasantry, and the Communist Party during the national liberation struggle.[192] On the eve of Khrushchev's and Bulganin's arrival in

---

[189] *Pravda*, 23 November 1955, p. 1.

[190] CC Plenum, July 11, 1955, morning session, 6. See also Kaganovich's remarks on India, CC Plenum, July 11, 1955, evening session, 36.

[191] Nikita Khrushchev, speech reprinted in *New Times*, no. 52 (December 22, 1955): 19. Bulganin also acknowledged that India was "creating a society according to a socialist model" during Nehru's stay in the Soviet Union. *Pravda*, 22 June 1955, p. 1.

[192] These observations are made by N. Pastukhov in his review of Jawaharial Nehru, *Otkry-*

Delhi, an accompanying journalist, Iury Zhukov, observed that although the Indians had different opinions about the origins of their economic difficulties and how to overcome them, the main thing was that they agreed that economic development must proceed.[193] Agreement on so little implied that Indians did not sufficiently appreciate the class content of their economic plight. Until imperialists, capitalists, and the local bourgeoisie were identified as the cause, the socialist solution would not be available to India. But Khrushchev was more bullish about what Indian leaders understood about the threat from capitalism. In his speech before the Indian parliament, Khrushchev welcomed "the perspicacity of Indian leaders who understand the danger to the independence of India" that arises from foreign capital.[194]

India's identity, although not that of imperialist ally or stooge, as it had been in Soviet thinking only a few years before, was still distilled through an understanding of India that related it to its colonial metropole, the current imperialist alliance, and its continuing ties with Britain. For example, India's foreign policy on China and Taiwan differed somewhat from that of Beijing and Moscow. These differences, although apparently unimportant to the forward course of Soviet-Indian relations,[195] did reveal that official Soviets understood these differences in terms of their relationship to the positions of Washington and London, as if India could only be apprehended in relation to its colonial past and imperialist present, not on its own terms or on terms independent of Soviet relations with the imperialist Other. Although Moscow backed Beijing's position that all U.S. military forces, including the Seventh Fleet, be removed from Taiwan and that the Kuomintang government was not the legitimate authority there, India foresaw international, rather than Chinese, control of Taiwan after the departure of the Kuomintang government and supported a plebiscite on Taiwan to resolve its future.[196] The Indian chargé in Moscow even supported the U.S. position of

---

tie Indy; the Russian edition of this book had come out just before Nehru's visit to the Soviet Union. "From the History of the Indian People," *Pravda,* 5 June 1955, p. 5.

[193] Iury Zhukov, "Yesterday in Dehli," *Pravda,* 18 November 1955, p. 3.

[194] *Pravda,* 22 November 1955, p. 2.

[195] A long report from the MFA's Information Department, prepared for Khrushchev and company's November visit to India, laid out numerous foreign policy differences between China and India. Whereas China regarded India, Indonesia, and Burma as being still too much under the thumb of imperialism and too conservative at home, India was trying to insinuate itself into the leadership of the National Liberation Movement in the Third World. India also continued to provide aid to Tibetans and Taiwanese operating from Indian territory. Their borders remained unsettled, and they exported the same kinds of goods. V. Solodovnik, in TsKhSD, f. 5, op. 30, d. 120, pp. 136–43.

[196] On India's position, see a report to deputy foreign ministers Zorin and Fedorenko, AVPRF, f. 100, op. 48, d. 128, p. 11. See also the May 28 memorandum on Nehru's upcoming visit signed by Fedorenko and I. F. Kurdiukov.

allowing Chiang Kai-shek to participate in talks with China, the United States, and India.[197] B. Volkov and V. Solodovnik identified the United States as holding the position Indian adopted. Kudriukov and Kapitsa claimed that India's position on Taiwan "reflects the positions of England. . . . The conversion of Taiwan into an autonomous demilitarized region fully corresponds to the position of England. . . ."[198] These readings of India through London did not go over well in India. The Indian chargé in Moscow, Iriloki Kaul, met with Molotov on February 23 to complain about a recent *Pravda* article in which Nehru was said to have fallen under the influence of Anthony Eden and Winston Churchill on the question of Chiang Kai-shek's participation in talks on Taiwan.[199]

It may prove significant that foreign policy difference with states such as India could be understood only through references to the position of the United States and its allies. It was as if difference from the Soviet or socialist position on an issue necessarily entailed some identity with a dangerous Other. This kind of tethering might prove limiting in Soviet appreciation of its alliances in the decolonizing world, making difference always vulnerable to becoming danger. This boundary, this bias toward turning difference into deviance, could constrain how deeply any alliance with the Third World might develop for the Soviet Union. If it understood any deviation from its own policy preferences as necessarily creating a relationship with the class enemy, rather than mere difference from itself, this made the Third World state an Other, perhaps foreclosing possible relationships. Such are the costs of binarization.

India was understood as part of the Soviet Self, the premodern Soviet Union —the agrarian, preindustrial, raw-material-producing, rural, religious part dependent on world capitalism for economic survival. India was central Asia before the Bolshevik Revolution. What movement India was making away from this peripheral identity was understood by the Soviets through its own experience in central Asia.[200] Consequently, the Soviet Union was India's

---

[197] B. Volkov and V. Solodovnik, May 31, 1955, memorandum to the CC Presidium on the Indian position on Taiwan, in AVPRF, f. 100, op. 48, d. 128, pp. 31–32.

[198] In Ibid., 70. Other Indian "waverings" included entertaining a proposal made by U.S. Senator Hubert Humphrey and Supreme Court Justice William O. Douglas that would have given India a permanent seat on the UN Security Council, in exchange for which China and Taiwan would have agreed to seats in the General Assembly. Ivan Kurdiukov and Mikhail Kapitsa, report on China and the UN, in AVPRF, f. 100, op. 48, d. 55, p. 38.

[199] AVPRF, f. 100, op. 48, d. 5, pp. 40–41a. That perhaps Soviets understood that Indians were insulted by such references could be inferred by Molotov's ultimate deletion from his February Supreme Soviet foreign policy address of remarks to the effect that India was still tied to Britain. This February 5 draft is in AVPRF, f. 6, op. 149, d. 51, p. 85.

[200] For example, when representatives of the Soviet Peace Committee traveled to India on March 31 to attend the pre-Bandung conference there, they brought with them the movie

vanguard, its more experienced ally, in the long trek toward a more progressive, perhaps socialist, future.

India's premodernity was widely remarked on. It was reported that President Rajendra Prasad had signed a bill on marriage granting women the right to divorce for the first time in history. TASS noted that religious strictures had held women back all these centuries.[201] Bulganin understood India through the premodern Soviet past in his speech in the Indian Parliament in November 1955. There he said that the Soviet Union had accomplished the task of reconstructing its country economically and culturally. And "you too are faced with the problem of converting your country . . . into an advanced state, with a developed national economy. . . ."[202] In other words, India was at last on the path of modernity.

What progress was noted was progress recognizable to a Soviet observer of modernization. For instance, D. Kraminov, a member of a Soviet cultural delegation, observed that as far as he could tell, Indians watching the National Day parade, although they applauded for each of the many delegations from parts of India, "especially liked" a big picture of a new hydroelectric plant.[203]

Khrushchev, in a speech in Agra, congratulated Indians on their recent liberation, but then warned them their freedom was insecure without industrialization, "especially a machine-building industry."[204] Khrushchev's commitment to industrialization as coeval with modernization and progress was so strong that he publicly disagreed with the governor of Madras, who had said that industrialization and socialization "are no salvation from all misfortunes."[205] Industrialization as modernization was linked to a class analysis that foresaw a growing industrial proletariat ensuring a socialist future and the production of the means of production as reducing dependence on world market capitalism. And the latter was a problem, despite the fact that India had nationalized the airlines and the railroads and was financing heavy industry through the state. Still, private capital was given free rein in all other areas, and foreign capital, especially British and U.S., was most welcome.

That the Soviet Union understood itself as India's vanguard was evident from the fact that the Soviets, with few exceptions, did not speak of any exchange of experience with India, only a one-way flow of superior knowledge

---

Holiday of the Tajik People to show the other delegates, most of whom were from decolonized countries. TsKhSD, f. 5, op. 17, d. 548, p. 63.

[201] *Pravda*, 21 May 1955, p. 3.

[202] Nikolai Bulganin, speech reprinted in *New Times*, no. 52 (December 22, 1955): 4–8, quotation on 8.

[203] D. Kramov, "On India," *Pravda*, 26 March 1955, p. 3.

[204] *Pravda*, 21 November 1955, p. 1. State ownership of heavy industry is also hailed as a step away from premodernity by Iurii Zhukov, "Yesterday in Delhi," 3.

[205] Reported in *Pravda*, 30 November 1955, p. 1.

and technology from the Soviet Union, just as Russian culture flowed from Moscow to non-Russian areas of the Soviet Union and modernity flowed from Moscow to the periphery more generally.[206] When V. Yakovlev reported about the Soviet cultural delegation to India led by Aleksei Surkov of the Soviet Writers' Union, he noted that "the composer of our delegation," Ashrafi, had many "passionate arguments with Indian musicians, insisting that they could not ignore European musical achievements."[207] Ashrafi conducted himself as a carrier of modernity to the less-privileged Indians. This hierarchical understanding was manifest during Khrushchev's tour of India. During that trip in November and December, at virtually every stop, it was reported that Khrushchev magnaminously invited whichever Indian worker, factory manager, or farmer with whom he was conversing to come to the Soviet Union to learn how to do whatever it was he was doing, but better.[208] In Bulganin's summary of the the tour for the Supreme Soviet, he spoke of all that Soviet experience could offer India, adding that India's "age-old culture," if not its modern achievements, could offer an experience useful to the Soviet Union.[209]

Finally, India was understood as a multinational country. When M. P. Tarasov, the deputy chair of the Presidium of the Supreme Soviet, welcomed his Indian parliamentary counterparts to Moscow, he began by observing that their stay in the "multinational Soviet Union would allow [them] to become familiar with . . . the culture of our republics."[210]

In Molotov's survey of the nonsocialist world before a session of the Soviet parliament, India was clearly at the top of the list, with Indonesia and Burma

---

[206] Exceptions included an appreciation of Indian forestry techniques from the Fourth World Forestry Congress held in Uttar Pradesh, in V. N. Sukachov, "World Forestry Congress," *New Times*, no. 12 (March 19, 1955): 28–30; and an appreciation of Indian contributions to science, in M. Rubinstein, "Science in India," *New Times*, no. 24 (June 11, 1955): 11–14.

[207] V. Yakovlev, "India Today," *New Times*, no. 23 (June 4, 1955): 21–22.

[208] See, for example, Iury Zhukov, O. Orestov, and O. Skalkin, "Soviet Guests in India," *Pravda*, 29 November 1955, p.3. These three reporters covered the Khrushchev-Bulganin tour daily, and in each article is usually an instance of Khrushchev telling his new Indian friends that they had already done that in the Soviet Union and done it better, while offering to share the Soviet experience if they wished. Khrushchev's offers of advice were limited neither geographically nor thematically. In Rangoon, for example, he invited his Burmese hosts to Moscow to study waterproofing. Iury Zhukov and O. Orestov, "Soviet Guests in Rangoon," *Pravda*, 3 December 1955, p. 3.

[209] *Pravda*, 30 December 1955, p. 2. A Supreme Soviet deputy for Azerbaijan, M. A. Ibragimov, made the direct case for the relevance of non-Russian experience in the Soviet Union for India (7). Soviet leaders also remarked on the architectural similarities between central Asia and Mughul India.

[210] *Pravda*, 8 May 1955, p. 4. See also Khrushchev's address before the Indian Parliament in November, reprinted in *New Times*, no. 52 (December 22, 1955): 9–15. Bulganin, when welcoming the U Nu delegation from Burma, spoke for the "entire multinational Soviet peo-

occupying a position just below it. Asia in general compared favorably to the Near East, and Africa and Latin America were well off the map.[211] The relative importance of India was reflected in Bulganin's delivery of a speech about the trip to India before the Supreme Soviet on December 29, a public report given only for such events as the Geneva summit and the Austrian State Treaty. At his UN General Assembly speech, Molotov singled out India as being most influential in Asian policy matters.[212] By the end of his stay in India, Khrushchev observed that although "it is customary to count among the great powers the Soviet Union, the US, China, France, and Britain, . . . why isn't India considered to be a great country?" And so, on that day, Khrushchev declared that "we believe India is a great power."[213] Much more than in the case of China, Soviets regionalized India's great power status to Asia.[214] As in the case of China, India's size mattered.

The compatibility of interests between India and the Soviet Union was significant. They broadly agreed on peaceful coexistence, disarmament, the Bandung principles, and opposition to regional military blocs. But this concord could not be mistaken for class identity, the basis of understanding for both Yugoslavia and China. Bulganin told the Supreme Soviet in December that India's interests rested on the "character of the development of the Indian state," its interest in economic development, which required peace.[215] India's premodernity, its location on the lower rungs of the modern development ladder, and its need for a peaceful environment in which to pursue these aims explained its support for broad foreign policy goals compatible with those of the Soviet Union.

Toleration of difference at home made India imaginable as a Soviet ally. The possibility of an Indian ally lay in its difference from the Soviet Union. There was no danger of its being close enough to be dangerous. India was part of a

---

ple," not a Soviet identity that appears when speaking to European audiences. *Pravda*, 4 November 1955, p. 2.

[211] Viacheslav Molotov, address before the Supreme Soviet, reprinted in *New Times*, no. 7 (February 12, 1955): 13. See also Miller, "Friends," 15. P. Yeronin began his survey of Latin America, for example, by writing that the changes "that followed the second world war have been least conspicuous on the American Continent." "Under the Iron Heel," *New Times*, no. 25 (June 18, 1955): 13.

[212] *Pravda*, 24 September 1955, p. 4.

[213] Nikita Khrushchev, speech reprinted in *New Times*, no. 52 (December 22, 1955): 29. He included India as a great power in a December draft of his speech for the Twentieth Party Congress held in February 1956, in TsKhSD, f. 1, op. 2, d. 3, p. 42. India is referred to as a great power in an article kicking off Bulganin and Khrushchev's tour to India. Zhukov, "Yesterday in Delhi," 3.

[214] As in Khrushchev's draft of his Twentieth Party Congress speech, in TsKhSD, f. 1, op. 2. d. 3, p. 51.

[215] *Pravda*, 30 December 1955, p. 2.

new class of allies, allies whose meanings were far less, far shallower, than prior Soviet allies in the socialist community. Indian class deviation was expected, and tolerated, to a point. Indian declarations of allegiance to a socialist future were welcome, as were a number of dramatic practices that pointed in that direction, such as the construction of the Bhilai steel complex slated to produce 1 million tons of steel a year. India was further limited as an ally by its colonial past; Soviets still understood India through that past, as if India had to be measured by its distance from it. But high hopes for the alliance rested in the fact that the Soviet Union had already experienced the long transition India was pledged to embark on, the noncapitalist path of development so brilliantly exemplified by the central Asian republics. This personal experience of peripheral progress and geopolitical compatibility combined to give Soviets robust expectations that alliances in the zone of peace were a new growth industry, with India being the flagship for all others.

Austria as Neutral Exemplar

The Soviet Union did not appear to consider Austria a potential ally. Instead, the question in 1955 was whether Austria was preferable as an occupied country or as a formally neutral and demilitarized European state. There were three broad themes in the Soviet consideration of this question. The first was geopolitical. How would Austria's neutrality affect the balance of power in Europe and how could Austria's new status play into Germany's reunification as a neutral demilitarized state? This question could be asked only because the Soviet Union had begun to ask itself about neutrality at home, that is, about the possibility of deviance from the new Soviet ideal being an acceptable difference. As far as Austria was concerned, the question was whether a neutral identity for Austria, despite not being remotely close to an ally of the Soviet Union, could still be distant enough from the West to be an acceptable difference. Finally, a most consequential identity for Austria emerged from the Soviet Union's most recent history, the war with Germany just a decade before. In short, the Soviets understood Austria through Germany. Analyses of Austrian neutrality were not simply calculated with respect to Germany but were embedded in an understanding of Austria that deprived that country of meaning apart from Germany. This peculiar ontology underlay Soviet geopolitical calculations.

Chronology

October 22 and November 13, 1954; January 15 and February 8, 1955, in response to the prospect of the FRG joining NATO, the Soviet Union suggested a reunified Germany within a collective security framework.

January 1, 1955, Malenkov announced that nuclear weapons had made peaceful coexistence both necessary and possible.

February 9, Molotov announced that the Warsaw Pact would be formed if the FRG joined NATO.

March 12, *Pravda* published records of Molotov's conversations with Austrian Foreign Minister Bischoff in which Moscow delinked an Austrian settlement from the German question. Molotov also agreed to Soviet troop withdrawals independent of a peace treaty with Germany.

March 22, the MFA announced that Albania, Bulgaria, Poland, the GDR, Hungary, Czechoslovakia, and Rumania had agreed to create the Warsaw Pact if the FRG joined NATO.

April 12, the Austrian delegation arrived in Moscow.

May 15, the Austrian State Treaty was signed and the Warsaw Pact was created.

June 7, the Soviet Union offered to recognize the FRG.

July 18, the Geneva Four Power Summit began.

September 12, FRG Chancellor Adenauer went to Moscow. It was agreed to release all German prisoners of war.

September 17, the Soviet Union announced its withdrawal from the Porkkala naval base in Finland.

October 27 to November 16, Molotov attended the Geneva Four Power Foreign Ministers Meeting.

November 22, the Soviet Union tested a 1.6-megaton superbomb.

Soviet apprehensions of Austria were complicated and problematic. Austria was still a capitalist country; hence, neutrality aside, it had the inherent potential to become hostile to socialist countries in the future. Aleksandrov-Agentov recalled that Khrushchev, Malenkov, and Mikoyan were agreed on the need to create a strong alliance of communist countries in central and eastern Europe, the first step being the Warsaw Pact. The second prong of the strategy was to create a buffer between the Pact and NATO.[216] Sweden and Finland provided this cushion in the north; Austria and Yugoslavia were seen as additional buffers in the west and southwest.[217] In Khrushchev's original proposal to the CC Presidium in early 1955, it was acknowledged that Austria would remain a bourgeois state.[218] And, geopolitically speaking, "Austria is a small country whose geographic position and natural wealth have made her very attractive to the latter-day exponents of aggression."[219]

[216] Aleksandrov-Agentov, *Ot Kollontai do Gorbacheva*, 89.
[217] CC Plenum July 9, 1955, morning session. Khrushchev's report contains an exposition of this strategic rationale.
[218] Aleksandrov-Agentov, *Ot Kollontai do Gorbacheva*, 93–95.
[219] "The Austrian Example," *New Times*, no. 20 (May 14, 1955): 6.

Mikoyan spoke about the strategically untenable position of Soviet troops remaining in Austria while speaking at the July plenum. Mikoyan pointed out that Soviet forces had been in Austria for more than ten years. Every year there was a holiday to mark Austria's liberation by Soviet troops. But recently, Mikoyan reported, "there was an attempt to hold a demonstration on that day demanding the liberation of Austria from our occupation, that is how far matters have gone, that we have found ourselves in a losing political position in the eyes of the Austrian working class and the entire population. . . . And if tomorrow Austrians throw stones at us, what will we do? Do we have to shoot them?" Mikoyan went on to point out the strategic advantages of having U.S. troops off the Dunai and behind the mountains in Italy, or even in the United States.[220]

The power of international practice to reproduce geopolitical identity and discourse was evident in Molotov's negotiations with Austrian Foreign Minister Bischoff. In order to communicate effectively with the Austrians, Molotov was compelled to use the geopolitical language and understandings that dominated international and European discourse, rather than his own class-based views of Austria, Europe, and the West. Geopolitical discourse also governed the instructions generated by the Foreign Ministry for Ambassador Ilyichev in Vienna in May 1955.[221] The MFA was the institutional site of geopolitical understandings of the Austrian question. The Gromyko draft of instructions for Ilyichev was circulated to the CC and was written entirely in the language of geopolitics.[222]

The Soviets trumpeted the Austrian example as significant for "international relations generally."[223] The centrality of Austria as a neutral exemplar is found in an April 7 draft by Molotov of the Soviet position on upcoming talks with Austria in Moscow. There he wrote that if Austria refused to include the word neutrality in the treaty itself, this would result in the suspension of negotiations until consultations with the CC could be conducted.[224] The Soviets suggested that the FRG, on its way to rearmament within NATO at this time, should consider the Austrian example and perhaps even the examples of other capitalist countries in Europe.[225]

---

[220] CC Plenum, July 11, 1955, morning session, 19.

[221] AVPRF, f. 06, op. 14, d. 110, p. 56–60.

[222] Ibid., 72–76.

[223] "Austrian Example," 6.

[224] AVPRF, f. 6, op. 14, d. 110, p. 84.

[225] For example, "The Significance of Austrain Neutrality," *New Times*, no. 21 (May 21, 1955): 7–9. Italy's possible departure from NATO, inspired by the Austrian exemplar, was noted by the editors of *New Times* in "A Legitimate Desire," *New Times*, no. 23 (June 4, 1955): 4. See also a memorandum from Gromyko and Semenov to Molotov on the draft Soviet position on Austria, April 6, 1955, in AVPRF, f. 06, op. 14, d. 110, p. 50. The idea, or ideal, of German neutrality should perhaps not be interpreted as a Soviet pipe dream. Dozens of private conversations with French officials contained a common dread of the Paris Agreements

One geopolitical theme was mostly absent. Soviets rarely argued, or even understood, their actions in Austria as a bold concession that would go a long way toward dispelling western images of the Soviet Union as a hostile expansionist enemy. A rare exception was Khrushchev's assessment at a meeting of industrial workers in the Kremlin. He pointed out that "bourgeois propaganda insistently and malevolently argues that the Soviet Union wants to seize all of Europe." But the treaty with Austria, especially the withdrawal of Soviet forces, according to Khrushchev, was "the strongest possible proof that the Soviet Union is not preparing to capture Europe, or conduct war in general. Who withdraws his forces if he is getting ready to attack?"[226] Although the Soviet Union hoped the Austrian model of neutrality could have a corrosive effect on NATO, especially on the FRG, it did not understand its actions in Austria as foreboding a western reevaluation of Soviet intentions in the world. One self-understanding the Soviets did not have, at least with respect to other great powers, was as a potential threat. This was not true with respect to Yugoslavia, India or other smaller or weaker powers.[227]

Independent of geopolitical considerations, Austrian neutrality was a departure from Soviet understandings of other states. Just as Yugoslavia could be an ally with a difference and India could be a potential ally with a great deal of difference, Austria could avoid being part of the western Other by establishing distance between itself and the West through neutralization and demilitarization. The Soviets compared a neutral Austria favorably to other western countries, referring to Austria as "another Switzerland," which had enjoyed the fruits of neutrality for 150 years. Austria was compared to other European countries, most notably NATO members, and the FRG, whose sovereignty and independence suffered from its alliance relations, whereas both Austria and Switzerland enjoyed both peace and prosperity.[228] Austria presented the Soviets with a new kind of actor in world politics. Austria had a "new international status," one of "honest neutrality."[229]

Neutrality within the Soviet Union was no less novel, and potentially dangerous, than being situated between the two camps abroad. Just as Molotov

---

and a common desire to keep Germany disarmed and divided. MFA Information Committee memorandum to Suslov, July 1955, in TsKhSD, f. 5, op. 28,d. 283, pp. 21–26.

[226] *Pravda*, 19 May 1955, p. 2.

[227] We might add here that if this interpretation of Soviet self-understanding is correct, then arguments that the West missed a chance to reciprocate Soviet flexibility in this period are not necessarily correct. Because the Soviet leaders expected no such reciprocity, its absence could not have taught them that their accommodative actions went for naught. Deborah Welch Larson, "Crisis Prevention and the Austrian State Treaty," *International Organization* 41, no. 1 (Winter 1987): 27–60.

[228] "The Soviet Austrian Negotiations," *New Times*, no. 17 (April 23, 1955): 1–3. See also the lead editorial the day the Moscow agreements were signed, in *Pravda*, 16 April 1955, p. 1.

[229] "In the Interests of Preserving Peace in Europe," *Pravda*, 16 May 1955, p. 1.

feared the effects of Yugoslavia's difference on the authentic meaning of socialism within the Soviet alliance, he feared the effects of Austrian neutrality on Moscow's eastern European allies.[230] Molotov's question was if Austrian neutrality was expected to exert an influence on Germany and other western European countries, why would not the logic apply as well to people's democracies? Could or should only capitalist states become neutral? Indeed, it had been pointed out that the Austrian example had particular peace-enhancing effects for the security of Czechoslovakia, Hungary, and Yugoslavia.[231] So, why would the neutrality of other neighbors not have similar salutary effects? Just as in the case of Yugoslavia, as in all cases where toleration of difference was an issue, the answer revolved around how secure the Soviet Union believed socialism to be at home, particularly how secure it was from difference there. Khrushchev's reply to Molotov addressed both sides of the question. He argued that these states were people's democracies, and hence the Austrian experience was not a relevant precedent. Khrushchev understood socialist allies of the Soviet Union to be something meaningfully different than ordinary western European states. Just as at home, deviant practices could never push true socialist men and women from the Soviet path, the existence of a neutral Austria could not possibly sway the minds of socialist allies in Europe.[232]

The last way in which Soviet Union understood Austria in 1955 was through its understanding of Germany or, more precisely, Hitler's Germany. At the popular level, the Soviet leadership received many letters from ordinary Soviets expressing concern about allowing Austria to become neutral and free of Soviet occupation. The argument was that Austria, through the Anschluss, had already proven incapable of preventing hostile German actions against itself, let alone against countries to the east.[233] Molotov shared these concerns. In a March 22 memorandum to the CC about his talks with Austrian Foreign Minister Bischoff in February and March, Molotov understood the issue of the Austrian treaty entirely through Germany. The threat from a neutral Austria becoming dominated by pro-German political forces, the threat from Germany to a neutral Austria, and U.S. prospects for taking

---

[230] Kurt Steiner, "Negotiations for an Austrian State Treaty," in *U.S.-Soviet Security Cooperation: Achievements, Failures, Lessons*, ed. Alexander L. George, Philip J. Farley, and Alexander Dallin (New York, 1988), 75. Molotov's fears were John Foster Dulles's hopes, wishing for the creeping liberation of eastern Europe.

[231] "Significance of Austrian Neutrality," 8.

[232] Steiner, "Negotiations for an Austrian State Treaty," 75.

[233] On October 13, 1955, just after Adenauer's visit to Moscow, Defense Minister Zhukov sent Shepilov dozens of letters to *Pravda* on relations with Germany. In particular, Soviet writers reacted badly to the release of German war criminals, fearing that fascism had not been eradicated in Germany, that Germany had been aggressive since at least 1870, and that these criminals would go home and infect the FRG armed forces with fascism. TsKhSD, f. 5, op. 30, d. 90, pp. 113–34.

advantage of a neutral Austria were all read through Molotov's view of Germany as a potential threat. This Germanization of the Austrian problem helps explain why Molotov insisted on a clause in the Austrian State Treaty that gave the Four Powers the right to return to Austria in the event of another Anschluss.[234] Other members of the Presidium opposed Molotov on this issue once it became clear it would be a deal killer. At the negotiations with Bischoff, Molotov told him that Austria must acquire some kind of guarantee against a future Anschluss.[235] Reflecting this fear of German influence, a late amendment to the Soviet negotiating position was developed by Molotov; this ban on German investment in Austria was accepted by both the Presidium and Austria.[236]

Molotov shared his views of Germany with West Germans. In his September meeting with Adenauer in Moscow, Molotov asked West Germany to remember that it was the Soviet Union, the United States, and Britain that had saved and liberated the Germans from Hitler. Germans had proven themselves incapable of doing it.[237] Adenauer's response was to try to create a different identity for Germany. He first observed that Hitler was not Germany, that "one cannot identify Hitler with the entire German population." He then suggested it would be better if both sides did not spend so much time examining the past because "too many obstacles" to better relations would arise. This is ironic because the Soviet understanding of Germany in 1955 was precisely of the German Hitlerian past. Finally, Adenauer suggested that Hitler had been successful because the great powers failed to unite against him, but today Germany wanted great power cooperation in Europe; it wanted a "system of European security."[238]

Khrushchev, at his first meeting with Adenauer in Moscow, also let the West Germans know that the Soviet Union understood Germany through its recent past.[239] The next day Khrushchev connected this understanding to Soviet fears of a rearmed FRG within NATO. After laying out Germany's many crimes during the war, Khrushchev summed up:

Germany has entered NATO, an organization aimed against the Soviet Union. That means the army is being prepared for war against

[234] AVPRF, f. 6, op. 14, d. 110, pp. 3, 52, 61.

[235] AVPRF, f. 6, op. 14, d. 193, p. 4. In a February 28 conversation with Bischoff, Molotov tried to trade a reduction in the time for Soviet troop withdrawals for more concrete measures to be taken by Austria to prevent another German absorption. AVPRF, f. 100, op. 48, d. 5, pp. 41–47.

[236] AVPRF, f. 6, op. 14, d. 110, pp. 114, 183.

[237] AVPRF, f. 6, op. 14, d. 205, p. 14. This was in a draft of his remarks. In a later draft on September 10, he removed any references to the U.S. or British role in freeing Germany of Hitler (37).

[238] AVPRF, f. 6, op. 14, d. 206, pp. 25–27.

[239] Ibid., 50.

the Soviet Union . . . and you expect some kind of magnanimity. Allow me, but who do you take us for? You treat us too rudely. . . . All this gives us the right, our delegation, government, and people to say that apparently the government of the FRG has not learned the lessons of history, which only just happened.[240]

The Soviet withdrawal from Austria was enabled by Soviet toleration of difference at home. Establishing the neutrality of Austria, however, was understood as a geopolitical act aimed primarily at Germany, whose Hitlerian past was the only way that Soviets understood the meaning of Austria in 1955.

CONSTRUCTING ALLIES AT HOME: THE IDENTITY POLITICS OF DIFFERENCE AND DEVIANCE

The case studies and other examples reviewed in this chapter suggest some general propositions about the relationship between identity and foreign policy.

Identities imply interests. How did Soviet identities in 1955 imply state interests? The relationship is between a particular understanding of Self and the understandings of Others that are thereby made thinkable and, so, possible. The Soviet understanding of itself as Russian enabled an understanding of Yugoslavia as a member of the Slavic family, a little brother. This understanding, in turn, created a particular interest in Yugoslavia that would have been absent had the Russian national identity not existed for the Soviet Union. This ethnonational relationship with Yugoslavia reduced the level of difference between Moscow and Belgrade on other identity dimensions. It created a meaningful similarity between them that would not have otherwise existed. This understanding discouraged the generation of this kind of similarity with non-Slavic Soviet allies in eastern Europe, such as Rumania and Hungary, denying them this particular Soviet interest.

Different identities imply different interests. The Soviet class identity meant that Soviet interests in China included ensuring that that socialist power would pursue domestic political, economic, and social policies recognizable to a Soviet communist. The Soviet Union had interests in the domestic sociopolitical and social order in countries such as China, people's democracies, and Yugoslavia because of its own understanding of the Soviet Union as a vanguard of socialism, the international proletariat, and the world revolutionary movement. It was not possible for any other country in the world to have precisely these kinds of interests in any of these countries. Only the Soviet Union, with its particular domestic identity terrain, could have un-

[240] Ibid., 75.

derstandings of Self and Other that implied such interests. And only the Soviet Union could have the kind of interests it had in the decolonizing world in 1955. Soviet interest in industrialization; agrarian reform; state control of banking, insurance, wholesale trade, and agricultural marketing; secularization of education; and so on in India and the rest of the decolonizing world is unfathomable without reference to Soviet identity in its own periphery, especially central Asia.

Identities function to make some actions more probable than others. The Soviet choice to pursue an alliance with Yugoslavia in 1955 was made more probable by the understanding of Yugoslav identity made possible by the Russian national component of Soviet identity. Soviet willingness to provide China with unprecedented access to its military production, training, and technology was made more probable by Soviet understandings of China as part of itself. The Soviet Union's enthusiastic desire to help India build a steel plant at Bhilai was based on Soviet understandings of its own peripheral identity in central Asia and precommunist Soviet Russia, where modern industrialization was regarded as a precursor to socialist development. The Soviet decision to establish neutrality in Austria was made more probable by a Soviet geopolitical identity that required balancing efforts against West Germany's imminent rearmament within NATO.

Identities entail the social practices that constitute them. Soviet class identity was constituted when Kaganovich visited Czechoslovakia and held it to the standards of ideological and practical orthodoxy that were his directives from the Presidium. The modern Soviet identity was reproduced in the itineraries of the many foreign delegations to the Kursk hydroelectric complex. The Russian national identity was constructed at the Second Congress of the Soviet Writers' Union, where all proceedings were in the Russian language. Difference was instantiated in the official recognition of Yugoslavia's path of socialism. Soviet great power identity was constituted by the Soviet government's Statement on the Middle East, in which the Soviet Union's geographical position was argued to confer special status for Soviet concerns and sovereign rights were demanded for all states in the region.

Identities stand in certain relations to one another. The relationships among multiple Soviet identities were clearly played out in Yugoslavia. There, as we have seen, the Soviet class identity championed by Molotov in play with a Russian ethnonational identity was advanced not only by foreign policy elites such as Khrushchev and cultural figures such as the Soviet writers at their congress, but through incidental contact with ordinary Yugoslavs and Russians in those two countries. At the same time, through an understanding of the Soviet Union as a great power and Russia as the center to the non-Russian Soviet periphery, the Soviets understood Yugoslav national sensibilities toward Moscow as a problem that could not be understood by segregating domestic from international aspects. Without appreciating the multiperspective aspect of Soviet identity, it is impossible to apprehend the Yugoslav-Soviet relationship in 1955.

Understandings of Self and Other are mutually constituted. Soviet understandings of itself as the modern Russian vanguard of peripheral areas of the globe were only possible when understood with respect to Others. Soviet modernity was reflected in the lower levels of development characteristic of China, India, and other parts of the decolonizing world. Soviet Russian ethnonational identity was reproduced in the interaction with Slavic Yugoslavia and historically implicated Germany. Soviet vanguard class identity was triggered by the interaction with others that claimed the same commitment to class identity and socialist construction, as in China. Soviet geopolitical identity was evoked over Yugoslavia when the U.S. interest in Yugoslavia as a player in the struggle against communism became the center of attention. International normative concerns were immanent in Soviet relations with lesser powers whose sovereign equality was problematic for the Soviet great power status.

State institutions participate in the reproduction of identity. The MFA was the primary site for Soviet great power identity. Considerations of balance of power politics, as well as international normative obligations and rights, were concentrated in this institutional setting and were reproduced in daily interactions with the agents of other governments.

Constructivist accounts may offer limited predictions about future state actions. The identities that constrained and enabled Soviet understandings of its potential allies in 1955 provide an account of how Soviet relations developed with Yugoslavia, China, India, and Austria in that year. But they also have some predictive potential beyond 1955. To the extent that the tension between class orthodoxy and tolerated difference continued to obtain the following year, Soviet reactions to events in Poland and Hungary may be understood in an entirely different light. To the extent that the Twentieth Party Congress ushered in the beginning of the Sino-Soviet rift, the Soviet understanding of China as closest Other may provide new insights into how that relationship deteriorated over the next years and decades. If Soviet understandings of India as the central Asian periphery are relevant to the decolonizing world more generally, the Soviet pursuit of allies in Africa, Asia, and Latin America over the next thirty-five years may be understood through this domestic dimension of Soviet identity. The Soviet great power identity in its relation to modernity implies an abiding tension between an acknowledgement of great power status and the need to maintain a balance of power vis-à-vis the West and the anxieties this raised with countries whose sovereign equality was openly asserted.

The predictive potential of identity arises in thinking about 1999. We might expect that issues of modernity, given the collapse of the Soviet project, and of the Russian nation, given its inheritance of the multinational Russian state, would both figure prominently in 1999 Russian understandings of Self and Other. On the other hand, class identity, at least as understood by Marxism-Leninism, would not be expected to have survived the collapse in recognizable form. The same might be said about the toleration of difference, the public and the private, and the individual and the collective. It could be hypothesized that these particular identities were so closely associated with the Soviet project and its unique identity, that their capacity to endure the Soviet collapse was quite limited. They never enjoyed the kind and volume of daily social practical reproduction as either modernity or nation. Finally, Russian geopolitical identity would be expected to bear a recognizable similarity to the Soviet construal, not least because of the institutional continuity provided by the MFA. Of course, the unearthing of the 1955 identities cannot predict which new and unique identities emerged in 1999 Moscow.

4/

Historical, Internal, and External Others
Russian Identity in 1999

When we left Moscow in 1955, there was a dominant discourse on modernity that featured a mild but significant contestation over the identity relations between Russians and non-Russians, center and periphery, and difference and deviance. The urban Russian working class in Moscow was the center of centers; the peasantry in the countryside and non-Russians anywhere within the Soviet Union were the periphery in need of their more modern class vanguard to take them into the future. With the advent of the Thaw, difference from the modern Soviet ideal was understood by some as a mark of Soviet maturity and security, not dangerous deviance. Individualism and personal space was presented as no challenge to the more totalizing New Soviet Man (NSM). In other words, a version of innocuous liberal and, most important, private pluralism was part of an official collection of discourses still mainly dominated by the homogenizing modernizing Soviet project.

The identity topography of Moscow 1999 was very different from 1955. The collapse of the Soviet Union had not simply permitted the deep structure of essential Russian national identity to emerge from its marginalized status because that Russian national identity had been ubiquitous in 1955 Moscow and even reified as the Soviet national identity. Although we expect 1999 identities to differ from those of 1955, there is probably no agreement on how they would differ. Here I show these particulars, relating them to the past and connecting them to implications for Russian foreign policy choice.

Despite the comparative nature of the research in this book, I offer comparisons of the identity terrains in 1955 and 1999 only in passing. An explicit treatment is not warranted on methodological grounds. The objective here is to describe and analyze Russia's understandings of itself in 1999; this task requires the presentation of how the various identitities of Russians in Moscow in 1999 related to one another, not how Russians related to the identities of 1955. Only in the event that Russians themselves understand 1999 through 1955 will such comparisons be offered.

AN OVERVIEW OF MOSCOW 1999

Moscow was dominated by three events in 1999: the recovery from the shock of the August 1998 collapse of the ruble; the renewal of the war in Chechnia; and the seemingly endless shuffling of the political elite, with the replacement of Prime Minister Evgenii Primakov by Sergei Stepashin and then of Stepashin by Vladimir Putin, who was elected president in December to replace Boris Yeltsin.

The currency crisis seemed to have put the last nail in the coffin of liberal market reforms in Russia. The war in Chechnia was brought home to Muscovites through a series of bombings in the new and resplendent shopping area in Manezh Square; the Inturist hotel on Tverskaya, just off the Manezh; and a couple apartment houses in outlying areas of the city. The (s)election of Putin seemed to have put an end to Boris Yeltsin's political career in a way satisfying to both liberals and communists; both supported his initial program in the state Duma. From just this thumbnail sketch we might infer that three main axes of Russian identity were the market, the Caucasus, and democracy. We would be right, but short of the mark.

AN OVERVIEW OF IDENTITY IN MOSCOW 1999

Figure 3 shows a map of the identity terrain in Moscow in 1999, the collection of identities in the relationships to one another that result from the contextualization and intertextualization of their meanings. The Russian Self in 1999 constituted itself with respect to three kinds of Others: Historical, External, and Internal. Each of these identity relationships was embedded in a discourse on modernity that, as a metanarrative, situated it both with respect to modernity and with respect to one another. The identities that appear below, above, and between the three Others in the figure are the fundamental identities induced from the texts. They are the substantive content of the different identities and are the most inductive, least theorized units of analysis. The identification of different kinds, or locations, of Others is an intertextualizing move to render the collection of identities more meaningful in a theoretical sense. A still more theoretically ambitious move is the rendering of these identities into the four discursive formations that I discuss in this chapter.

Figure 3 is a map of Russian identity formations, not a reproduction of a Russian's identity. It is an abstraction based on readings of texts, not a calculation of relative importance based only on a quantitative weighing of appearances in those texts. It is an effort to reconstruct a deeper, not so apparent logic or coherence from the appearance of a particular collection of identities read from a particular, even if broad and numerous, collection of Russian texts being read by Muscovites in 1999. I do not claim that any in-

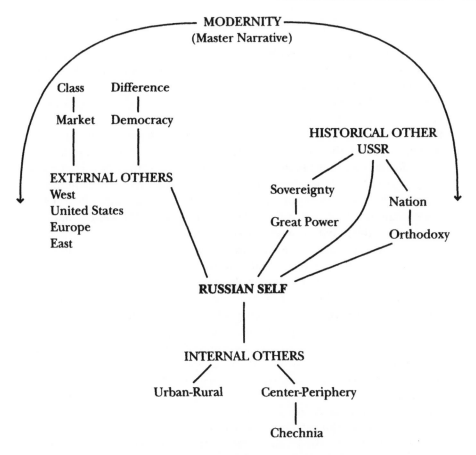

Figure 3   A Map of Russian Identity: Moscow 1999

dividual Russian or large group of Russians, in fact had a cognitive map in their minds that is identical to the conceptual map laid out in figure 3, but the cognitive map should be derivable from it. Moreover, I do claim that this map could be understood as a representation of a deeper, more comprehensive, more fundamental or foundational web of meaning within which any Russian had to negotiate her daily representations of being Russian, including a Russian decision maker in the Kremlin.

I derive four discursive formations, with four sets of hypotheses about 1999 Russian foreign policy from the identities in figure 3. Indeed, each of the four discourses has a different position within them with regard to these identities, thus rendering each differentiable from the others and thereby yielding distinct expectations for Russian understandings of other states. With the collapse of the Soviet Union, Russia found itself between two different modern identities—that of the Soviet past and that of the western present.

Four different discourses characterized Russia's position with regard to these two modernities. The first two, the New Western Russian (NWR) and the New Soviet Russian (NSR), explicitly adopted an identity read through the External Other of the West and the Historical Other of the Soviet Union, respectively. The third discourse, the Liberal Essentialist (LE), rejected both the western present and Soviet past as the authentic Russian future, instead finding in Russia, the West, and the East elements that together might constitute Russia's genuine identity.[1] The fourth discourse, the Liberal Relativist (LR), rejected all identity projects as modern—their fixity, their homogenization, their determination that there was an essential authentic Russian to be found out there somewhere—in effect equating the western and Soviet modernities as both noxious to life as lived.[2]

In table 2, I summarize the four discourses in relationship to one another and the substantive identities that constitute them. This table orders the findings of this chapter, but it may also serve as a preliminary guide. The most straightforward reading of the table is to see how it specifies areas of discursive consensus, the nearly unanimous understanding of the meaning of the Soviet past, both its positive and negative aspects. The only exception was the NSR's high regard for Soviet economic performance. The other areas of consensus were a high regard for European attributes and agreement that the Federal Center must be strengthened if it was to deal with the legitimate demands of the regions and address the illegitimate and unlawful separatism in Chechnia and the Caucasus.

Another straightforward reading is to see how the four discourses relate to one another. First, the LR discourse is very much an outlier. Although it was not infrequently in agreement with the consensual positions of the other three discourses, it more rarely was allied with another discourse as a constituting element of Russian identity. Two of these bridging operations were the LR's agreement with the NSR in its negative attitude toward western mar-

---

[1] For those readers who are familiar with the Eurasianist discourse in contemporary Russia, the LE discourse subsumes it. For those expecting a *derzhavnost* or statist discourse, some of its elements appear in the LE discourse, but most are more accurately attributed to the Leftist NSR collection of identity relationships. When I use the Left as a political label in this book, I have in mind the communists, the agrarians, and sometimes their nationalist fellow-travelers, whom in the West we would most often call the neofascist superpatriotic Right. I do so to keep this collection of political tendencies separate and distinct from the Right, for which I have in mind the liberal marketeers most closely associated with Yabloko and other economically liberal parties. The Center I reserve for the LEs. Please excuse any initial confusion and trust that it will dissipate with further reading.

[2] An interesting parallel can be drawn between this LR discourse and the romanticist discourse of the late-nineteenth-century Russian intelligentsia. I thank Darius Toltschik and Jeff Rossman for raising this very intriguing possibility for further research.

Table 2
Four Russian Discourses and the Identities That Constitute Them

	New Western Russian	New Soviet Russian	Liberal Essentialist	Liberal Relativist
Historical Other, Soviet Past				
Authoritarianism	− − −	− − −	− − −	− − −
Corruption	− − −	− − −	− − −	− − −
Individual passivity	− − −	− − −	− − −	− − −
Anti religious	− − −	− − −	− − −	− − −
Great Power	+ + + +	+ + + +	+ + + +	
Democracy	+ + + +	+ + + +	+ + + +	
Culture	+ + + +	+ + + +	+ + + +	
Youth	+ + + +	+ + + +	+ + + +	
Economy	− − − −	+ + + +	− − − −	
Decentered Russia	+ + + +	+ + + +	+ + + +	+ + + +
Moscow Center	+ + + +	− − − −	+ + + +	
Essentialist				
Nationalism	− − − −	+ + + +	+ + + +	− − − −
Religion	+ + + +	+ + + +	+ + + +	
Orthodox Church	− − − −	+ + + +	− − − −	− − − −
Orthodoxy	− − − −	+ + + +	+ + + +	
External Others				
United States				
Economy	+ + + +			+ + / − −
Individualism	+ + + +			− − − −
Nationalities	+ + + +			
Culture				− − − −
Europe				
Economy	+ + + +		+ + + +	
Culture	+ + + +		+ + + +	
Democracy	+ + + +		+ + + +	
Markets				
Abstract Western	+ + + +	− − / + +	+ + / − −	− − − −
Real Russian	− − − −	− − − −	− − − −	− − − −
Class				
Middle	+ + + +	+ + + +	− − − −	
Intelligentsia	+ + + +	+ + + +	− − − −	
Rich	+ + + +			
Poor	− − − −	+ + + +		
Oligarchy/ nomenklatura	− − − −	− − − −	− − − −	− − − −
Democracy				
Western	+ + + +	− − − −	+ + + +	− − − −
Russian	− − − −	− − − −	− − − −	− − − −

(*continued*)

Table 2 (*continued*)

	New Western Russian	New Soviet Russian	Liberal Essentialist	Liberal Relativist
Internal Others				
Strengthen center	++++	++++	++++	
Center responsible/ regions not	++++	++++	++++	
Chechnia to blame	++++	++++	++++	
Rural periphery value	– – – –	++++	++/– –	

Plus signs (++++) in a row indicate that the particular identity is present or is positively valued by that discourse. A minus sign indicates a negative evaluation of that identity. A combination (++/– –) indicates a mixed evaluation of that identity within the particular discourse. If there is neither sign, that discourse did not include that identity.

kets and democracy. Another was its agreement with the NWR in its opposition to an essentialist understanding of Russian national identity.

The second most inert identity is the NSR. It was alone in lauding Soviet economic performance and the Orthodox Church and in sympathizing with the poor, the rural, and the peripheral. On the other hand, the NSR was a fellow traveler with the LE discourse in an appreciation of the uniqueness of the Russian nation and of the value of Orthodoxy and the traditional countryside in constituting the same. As already noted, the NSR was also in agreement with the LR in declaiming western markets and democratic practices.

The LE and NWR were most frequently in discursive alliance with one another. Most notably, they opposed the NSR's appreciation for the Soviet economic experience, its valuation of the periphery, its support for the Orthodox Church, its opposition to western markets and democracy, and its lack of regard for Russia's middle class and intelligentsia as engines of modernity and reform. The areas in which the two were in opposition are the essentialization of the Russian nation, the value of nonwestern market and democratic experiences, and the importance of rural verities in constituting an authentic Russian future.

In the rest of this chapter I present Russia's relationship to its three Others—Historical, External, and Internal—while developing the four discursive formations and their different relationships to these identities. The chapter closes with the development of a set of hypotheses about Russian foreign policy in 1999 based on the four alternative discourses.

RUSSIAN IDENTITY AND THE HISTORICAL SOVIET OTHER

A simple dichotomization of 1999 Russian reality into a struggle between those who wanted to become the West and those who either wanted to return to Soviet rule or to some authentic Russian past is possible only if we focus on the most extreme tails of the narrative distribution. On the other hand, there was a large expanse of Soviet identity that all four discourses rejected, there was a fair amount that each regarded with a level of respect, and there was the Left's singular esteem for some aspects of the Soviet identity shared by no one else. Moreover, there was a discourse of ironic complexity offered by the LR.

Several aspects of the Soviet experience were unanimously decried by Russians in 1999. Stalinist terror and the arbitrary use of police and prosecutorial powers were at the top of the list of evils attributed to Soviet modernity.[3] As Vavilen Tatarsky, Viktor Pelevin's protagonist in *Generation "P"* puts it, "like mushrooms after the rain, coffins follow leaders."[4] The level of corruption and favoritism shown to party elites and the nomenklatura was condemned.[5] Colonel Lev Gurov, Nikolai Leonov's fictional cop, describes witnessing the hypocrisy of party meetings in the 1980s at which "everyone was railing at capitalism, while each pilfered what he could" from the state.[6] Related to both the terror and the corruption was the consequent passivity and acquiescence of the Soviet people before this arbitrary power. Dmitrii Zabolitskikh makes this point while comparing the American cartoon icons Tom and Jerry to the characters in the Soviet cartoon classic "Hey, Wait Up!" He observes that Tom the housecat, despite the relentless abuse suffered at the hands of a lowly mouse and a demanding mistress of the house, never gives up and always resists. In contrast, the equally hapless wolf in the most popular Soviet cartoon "would begin to empty his pockets with embarrassment before the police motorcycle even approached him. . . ."[7]

The inability of Soviet modernity to produce material prosperity was reflected in the following joke: "Is it possible to build socialism in the Sahara? Of course, but then there will of course be a shortage of sand."[8] The mod-

---

[3] Every high school history textbook that I surveyed includes such condemnations. At the level of mass popular fiction, Leonov's hero, a Russian cop named Lev Gurov, declaims the Soviet state for not prosecuting its malefactors. Nikolai Leonov, *Ment Vernulsia* (Moscow, 1998), 157. See also Sergei Notichkin, "Union? Only Not a Communist One," *Moskovskii Komsomolets* (*MK*), 29 October 1998, p. 3.

[4] Viktor Pelevin, *Generation "P"* (Moscow, 1999), 32.

[5] Aleksandr Khinshtein, for example, wrote a detailed analysis of how state-owned *dachas* were distributed in Soviet times, in "Dachas without Rent," *MK*, 29 October 1998, pp. 1–2.

[6] Leonov, *Ment Vernulsia*, 213.

[7] Dmitrii Zabolotskikh, "Fairy Tale of Times Past: The Cartoon 'Nu, pogodi!' as a Mirror of the Epoch of Developed Socialism," *Iskusstvo Kino* (*IK*), no. 10 (1998): 84.

[8] Nitochkin, "Union?" 3. See also the editorial "Dead State," *Izvestiia*, 24 November 1998,

ern Soviet project's contempt for religion and repression of believers was also unanimously condemned.[9] The public acknowledgement by Gennady Ziuganov, chairman of the Communist Party of the Russian Federation (CPRF), that the Soviet project "was darkened by violence, senseless struggle against God [*bogoborchestvo*] and ideological dogmatism" was significant.[10] The isolation of the Soviet Union from the rest of the world and its quest for autarky were also regarded as misguided and costly delusions.[11]

These views of Russia's relationship to the Soviet past come from a wide variety of texts, including high school textbooks, popular novels, serious monographs for the intelligentsia, film reviews, and articles from a variety of newspapers. There is no particular distribution of these negative views of the past, which, after all, were held by Ziuganov himself. This list of Soviet ills can be interpreted as how Russia wished not to understand itself through the modern Soviet project. These were aspects of the emergent Russian Self that should be suppressed if they ever reappeared. Without this relationship with itelf through this Soviet Other, these particular aspects of Russian identity might not have been raised and rejected.

But Russia in 1999 did not reject its Soviet past altogether. In five ways, Russians valued the Soviet experience—they appreciated the Soviet Union's status as a great power in world affairs, they recognized that democracy was already emergent under Soviet rule, they fondly recalled the high quality of Soviet mass culture, they acknowledged the superior conditions the Soviet government created for young people, and last, but touted only by the Left, they acknowledged Soviet economic performance, especially in agriculture.

Every high school history textbook that I surveyed identifies Soviet great power status as a major accomplishment of the seventy years of communist rule. In these same textbooks, it is argued that democratization had begun

---

p. 1. In Koretskii's pulp detective novel, the narrator prefers the current system of mafia ownership of stores to the Soviet model, in which nobody owned anything. Danil Koretskii, *Operativnyi Psevdonim*, vol. 1 (Moscow, 1998), 177–78. See also Valerii Ostrovskii and Aleksei Utkin, *Istoriia Rossii XX Vek: 11th Klass*, 3rd ed. (Moscow, 1998), 240. This text was recommended by the Russian Ministry of General and Professional Education. Mikhail Vozdvizhenskii, "They Are Completely Different," *Literaturnaya Gazeta* (*LG*), 20–26 October 1999, p. 7.

[9] See, for example, Igor Chubais, *Ot Russkoi Idei—K Idee Novoi Rossii, Kak Nam Preodolet Ideinyi Krizis* (Moscow, 1997), 36.

[10] This remark was not made before some liberal or western group who would have appreciated its enunciation. Instead, Ziuganov delivered it in his keynote speech before the Popular Patriotic Union of Russia, an umbrella group including the communist, agrarian, and other Left organizations in Russia. Gennadii Ziuganov, "Political Report of the Chairman of the PPUR at the 2nd Congress of the Popular Patriotic Union of Russia," *Sovetskaya Rossiia* (*SR*), 24 November 1998, p. 2.

[11] For example, by Chubais, *Ot Russkoi Idei*, 16.

in the Soviet Union as early as the 1950s, during the Thaw, and had accelerated greatly under Mikhail Gorbachev.[12]

In the area of mass culture, a love for Soviet film was shared not only by 1999 Russian critics,[13] but also by the head of the Duma faction of the Agrarian Party, Nikolai Kharitonov, who told a reporter that he had videos of Tikhii Don and Krasnaya Kalina at home, calling Vasilii Shukshin, the director-actor of the latter, a man "from God, from the land."[14] It was reported that showing Soviet films on Russian TV in Moscow had provoked a "deafening avalanche of phone calls," and not just from "nostalgia-seeking old men and women, but from a crowd of young people" who understood these films not as Stalinist or Soviet, but as a kind of "genre."[15] Instead of the expected binary between the scorned Soviet past and the promise of the new Russian future, 1999 Russian youth transcended this dichotomizing trope, permitting the recovery of a more complex and ambiguous view of that Soviet past.

The commemoration of the eightieth anniversary of the Communist Youth League, or Komsomol, in October 1998 provided an occasion to look at contemporary Russian youth through the perspective of that Soviet organization. It was not shocking that Boris Pastukhov, former first secretary of the Komsomol in the early 1980s, recalled "the sincerity of the young people who left for the front, who went to till the virgin lands . . . " to work on the construction of the Baikal-Amur railroad in Siberia. To doubt in their sincerity "would be a completely criminal action." Without all these "fools, idiots, and suckers, as they call them now," no problems in Russia could be solved.[16]

But it was not only former Komsomol dignitaries reminiscing about the idealism of youth who celebrated the eightieth birthday of this Soviet institution. Others lamented the passing of the idealistic energy of Soviet youth, if not the Komsomol itself.[17] The newspaper Vremya devoted most of its Oc-

---

[12] For example, Vladimir Dmitrenko, Vladimir Esakov, and Vladimir Shestakov, Istoriia Otechestva XX Vek: 11th Klass (Moscow, 1996), 518. This textbook was also on the Russian Ministry of Education's recommended list. See also Mikhail Zuev, Istoriia Rossii: XX Vek (Moscow, 1995), 376.

[13] For example, Elena Stishova, "Alone," IK, no. 10 (1998): 31. See also Vladimir Krainev, "Russia—Motherland of Little Walls," Moskovskie Novosti (MN), 18–25 October 1998, p. 15.

[14] Nikolai Kharitonov, interviewed by Aleksandr Mitrofanov, "I Love People for Free," Vecherniaia Moskva (VM), 23 October 1998, p. 3.

[15] V. Kisunko, "So Who Needs Kinopravda?" IK, no. 10 (1998): 48.

[16] Aleksandr Artyomov, Viacheslav Kopyov, and Boris Pastukhov, "I Will Not Part with the Komsomol," MK, 29 October 1998, p. 3. Pastukhov organized contruction brigades for the Baikal-Amur Mainline railroad project and at the time of the interview was the Russian minister for the Commonwealth of Independent States (CIS) affairs. See also Viktor Mishin, interviewed by Vladimir Chuprin, "Golden Spike," MK, 29 October 1998, p. 3. Mishin was first secretary of the Komsomol from 1982 to 1986.

[17] For instance, Nitochkin, "Union?" 3.

tober 29, 1998, issue to reporting on how the Komsomol's anniversary was being celebrated all over Russia, not just in the "red belt" of south-central Russia.[18] And former Komsomol officials did not only understand the Komsomol as a site for building the NSM, but also praised it for making them more adept businessmen in the new Russian economy. Aleksandr Artyomov, at one time head of the Moscow Komsomol under Gorbachev and in 1999 chairman of the Russian version of the Chamber of Commerce, testified that the Komsomol taught him how factories and financial relations worked and introduced him to the cooperative movement and that, consequently, many businessmen have emerged from the ranks of the Komsomol.[19]

The Left was alone, however, in recalling the Soviet economic past with fondness. Mikhail Lapshin, a leader of the Agrarian Party, spoke in favor of the collective farm system at the Popular Patriotic Union of Russia congress in November 1998.[20] The head of agricultural administration in one of the *raions* (townships) of the red belt attributed his success in growing grain to the fact that he continued to operate by Soviet economic principles of *kolkhoz* organization, "undemocratic" requisitions of feed grain from farmers, and "socialist competition."[21]

The ingredients from the Soviet past that constituted a new Russian identity without serious contestation include a concern for the younger generation, a commitment to raising the level of popular culture, a nurturing of democratic institutions, and a restoration of great power status. In looking at the Soviet past, the new Russian identity rejected authoritarianism, arbitrary police powers, corruption, individual passivity before the state, ideological homogenization, atheism, and autarky. From this list, only the Soviet economic model became an issue of contestation.

"Today there are no crowds in the department store like in olden times, but then again, unlike then, there are now goods for any taste and fat wallets."[22] Ambivalence implies the capacity to see the Self in the Other in a multidimensional polyvalent fashion. In these words of Dmitrii Koretskii's fictional

[18] For the example of Tatarstan, see Elena Taran, "Tataria: Komsomol Members Have Been Shaken by the Days of Yore," *Vremia*, 29 October 1998, p. 3. For events in Novosibirsk, see Vasilii Polevanov, "Construction Detachment Mess Kits Have Become Museum Exhibits," *Vremia*, 29 October 1998, p. 3.

[19] Artyomov, Kopyov, and Pastukhov, "I Will Not Part," 3.

[20] Zhanna Kasianenko, "Under Banners of Patriotism," *SR*, 24 November 1998, p. 3. See also Aleksandr Trubitsyn's comparison of the merits of the Soviet project to the unpaid workers, rampant syphilis, and unchecked criminality characteristic of a Russia where Galina Starovoitova could be assassinated while entering her apartment in Petersburg. Aleksandr Trubitsyn, "A Purely 'Democratic' Murder," *SR*, 24 November 1998, p. 4.

[21] Nikolai Kotov, interviewed by Valentina Nikiforova, "A Peasant Committed to the Land to the Point of Stupefaction," *Pravda*, 10–13 September 1999, p. 2.

[22] Koretskii, *Operativnyi Psevdonim, vol. 1*, 87.

intelligence agent hero, Sergei Lapin, are found the two minds with which Russians understood the Soviet experience: things were worse, but better. The 1999 Russian realized that what seemed good was actually bad—full stores were a sign of insufficient demand, not satisfied shoppers; and full shelves were a sign of customer satisfaction, but only for those with plenty of money.

There was also the recognition of some good in the Soviet bad. Khrushchev's stabs at "a certain democratization of society" beginning in the 1950s were appreciated, but also acknowledged to "naturally not mean free elections."[23] Igor Chubais, for example, in his search for an "idea of a new Russia," applauds the ability of communist ideology to "unite an enormously variegated country" because all people need a "unifying system of values."[24] But Chubais rejects the content of communism, although claiming that the modern idea of a totalizing and partially homogenizing authoritative set of guiding ideas is necessary for any society. This exemplifies the LE belief in the need for a genuine Russian identity, but not one with Soviet totalizing features. Most important, the LE condemned the idea of any single ideology again dominating Russia or, still less so, the world.[25]

Viktor Pelevin names his main character Vavilen Tatarsky in *Generation "P."* This name is an ironic combination of the exiled Soviet dissident writer Vasilii Aksenov who represented the "ideals of the [19]60s generation" and Lenin, the founder of the exiling state, demonstrating an abiding "faith in communism." In a single name Pelevin manages to combine the idealistic young hope of true believing communists (like the admirers of Komsomol virtue previously mentioned), with those (like Aksenov) who suffered exile for their deviation from that truth.[26]

Soviet Nationality Policy and the Place of Nation in Russia in 1999

The Russian nation was the Soviet nation in 1955. It was the center to the non-Russian periphery, at the top of a hierarchy of Ukraine and Belarus, the Baltic states, the Caucasus, and, finally, central Asia. It was the center of modernity, class consciousness, and culture and other nations were expected to acquire the attributes of Soviet Russian modernity as already embodied by the citizenry of Moscow.

---

[23] Zuev, *Istoriia Rossii*, 311.

[24] Chubais, *Ot Russkoi Idei*, 48.

[25] Kamaludin Gadzhiev, *Vvedenie v Geopolitiku* (Moscow, 1998), 170. See also Maksim Belozor, "Ambitious Devotees," *Segodnia*, 5 October 1998, p. 2. The teacher he interviews cannot choose between the "romantic and sincere" boys he taught in Soviet times and those now, who were "smarter and more pragmatic."

[26] Pelevin, *Generation "P,"* 12. The name Tatarsky is a contradiction in that it evokes a non-Russian background for the character in the novel who is given the task of developing a new Russian idea.

In 1999, much was different in Russian conceptualizations of the nation, the Russian nation, and its relationship to other non-Russian nations. Russia was now its own nation; it no longer served as the surrogate nation for a state without a usable history of its own. Russia had become dramatically decentered, no longer understanding itself as a center to non-Russian peoples and nations. The syntax of hierarchy had all but disappeared in the apprehensions of other, non-Russian nations. Moscow still understood itself as the center of Russia, even while understanding Russia as the center of very little.

What had replaced the Russian national center was an endangered Russia in a state where essentialized national identities abounded in pluralism. Difference reigned and was accepted as natural, not feared as a premodern atavar against which battle must be waged, as was true during the modern Soviet project. The danger came from an Other within and without Russia's boundaries—the Caucasus.

To treat the Russian nation as a single text in Moscow 1999, we begin with a general theory of LE nationalism, such as presented by Leonid Bogoliubov and colleagues in their sociology textbook. They stipulate that every society and culture is unique, that the interests of ethnic and national groups are often in conflict, and that this situation is good for humankind because diversity is inherently good.[27] This was the LE core: differences are hard-wired into bodies and minds and that is good, as long as these differences are respected and not subject to homogenizing projects of any kind. The Soviet project understood itself as just such a project. But in 1999, Russians remembered Soviet nationality policy differently.

In the most comprehensive treatment among the texts I have collected, Vladimir Dmitrenko, Vladimir Esakov, and Vladimir Shestakov, in their history textbook, argue that Soviet conduct toward non-Russians was both good and bad,[28] that imperial Russia was also both good and bad,[29] and, perhaps most important for understanding how Russians understood non-Russians, that Russians themselves were as much the victims of Soviet modernity as any of the non-Russian peoples.

Soviet discrimination against Russians, in this view, included the absence of a Russian Commissariat in the People's Commissariat of Nationalities, al-

---

[27] Leonid Bogoliubov, Liudmila Ivanova, and Anna Lazebnikova, *Chelovek i Obshchestvo*, 3rd ed. (Moscow, 1998), 85, 115, 313–18. This textbook for tenth and eleventh graders had a very high production run of 150,000. See also Gadzhiev, *Vvedenie v Geopolitiku*, 180, 226.

[28] For instance, the Bolshevik liberation of nationalities was good; Stalinist deportation of, often, the same nationalities was bad. Dmitrenko, Esakov, and Shestakov, *Istoriia Otechestva XX Vek*, 21, 359–61.

[29] For example, peoples of the empire enjoying a "feeling of fellowship" was good; pogroms, Russification, and Orthodox prosyletization was bad. Ibid., 178.

though Poles, Jews, Moslems, and so on had theirs; the same was said about the Communist Party, Trade Union Council, Komsomol, and Academy of Sciences. Russia had no capital city of its own, yet its budget subsidized the rest of the country.[30] This apprehension of Self as historical victim, in addition to the self-absolution it offered, permitted a decentering of Russia vis-à-vis non-Russians and, indeed, the acquisition of a certain equivalence to them in relation to the oppressive Soviet center.

But Russians were not able to escape their past as that Soviet center "[i]n the eyes of the non-Russian population of Russia and the Soviet Union. Precisely Russians were the cause of mass genocide and all misfortunes . . . since, as a rule, Russians implemented Stalinist policies."[31] This interpretation is consistent with how Russians considered themselves to be the vanguard and center for the less-developed non-Russian periphery in 1955 and how, especially at the Second Writers' Congress, voices from the periphery declaimed this brand of centrism. Given the Russian understandings of itself as victim and non-Russian understandings of this Russian victim as villain, it is not surprising that Dmitrenko and his colleagues report to their readers that "national-patriotic feelings," Russian "national self-assertion," "tendentious arguments" about Russian superiority, and the "absurd" idea of an ethnically pure Russian nation have appeared in public discourse, especially in periodicals such as *Nash Sovremennik*. But this textbook reassures its readers that these ideas are held only by extremists and are "decisively" rejected by "the democratic forces of Russia who justifiably consider them to be dangerous."[32] They conclude that Russia is a "polyethnic" country that must respect the rights of non-Russian minorities.[33] This combination of acknowledging the identities of ethnonational groups as natural and fixed with equal rights characterizes the LE discourse in its relationship to nationalism and its decentering potential.

Both the liberal and the essentialist components of Russian apprehensions of other nations was manifested in Russian understandings of the peoples of the Caucasus. The essentialism that took the form of ethnic stereotypes was most evident in popular novels. The more benign instances of this are Koretskii's moustachioed Armenians, who apparently cannot pronounce Russian correctly because the text of his novels is studded with misspelled Russian words, somewhat phonetically related to the apparently intended word, whenever Armenians speak to one another. Koretskii's Caucasians wear "black patent leather shoes, black pressed pants, a white shirt, and black bowtie"; his Azerbaijanis have "dark skin, thick black hair with an

---

[30] Ibid., 104, 451.
[31] Ibid., 452.
[32] Ibid., 577–79.
[33] Ibid., 597.

oily shine, and a characteristic hook nose"; and "characteristic of Caucasian men," they are both the object of women's attention, as well as "having a weakness" for them.[34] Less benignly, Koretskii treats Caucasians as obviously criminal in appearance.[35]

Koretskii offers us a "half-breed," an organized crime boss who is the son of a Russian (modern/European/western) father and an Azerbaijani (non-Russian) mother. The dynamic between the two identities promises hybridity in the Russian understandings of Self. According to Koretskii's narrator, Elkhan Takhirov is not comfortable among either Azerbaijanis or Russians. (His hybridity transcends an additive identity, becoming instead a new identity with incommensurable features.) He "remained between faiths; he was neither circumcised, nor baptized. . . . By conviction he was an atheist." (Although denying both, he does not remain in a state of uncertainty but becomes a denier of God altogether, a very modern move.) He eats "European-style breakfasts, drinking tea in a national-style glass."[36] What kind of attitudes toward nation and modernity does this hybridity yield? These are implicit in how he handles an argument within his criminal organizaton.

"Listen, Elkhan," Hussein said, "Velikan has hired two Armenians. . . . The bastards work there and rake in the money."

"But what have they done to you?" Elkhan asks.

"What? They murdered our brothers in Karabakh!"

"Exactly those guys?"

"What difference does it make! We must drive them to hell! Let the Armenians work with each other!"

"But do you have Azerbaijanis to replace them?"

"We'll find them!"

"This means that the place will be closed until you find them? And then what, you'll drive me out because I am not a full-blooded Moslem?"

(Note how tolerance for the Armenians is implied both by Elkhan's appreciation of the market as the final arbiter of identity and his own personal appreciation of liberalism's implications for personal survival in this complicated world.) There is a long pause in which Hussein exchanges glances with Mekhman, thinking to himself, "He does support Russians more." Elkhan goes on to say that nationality has no significance in business. (Is this not redolent of the modern Soviet project's claim that national identity would disappear in the face of class consciousness?) But Hussein and Mekh-

---

[34] Koretskii, *Operativnyi Pseudonim*, vol. 1, 98, 111–13, 188.

[35] Koretskii, *Operativnyi Pseudonim*, vol. 2, 120. For an ironic subversion of this stereotype of danger, see Pelevin, *Generation "P,"* 249.

[36] Koretskii, *Operativnyi Pseudonim*, vol. 1, 188, 311.

man fall silent. Elkhan, realizing he has "ruined their moods," reassures them that "soon the Russians themselves will piss on the Armenians. And we will stand aside and let them."[37]

The essentialization of national identity in itself has no determinate consequences for the relationship between Self and Other except to create difference. In a hierarchical syntax, however, it might lead to the oppression of national minorities, as was the case in modern Soviet Russia. But the LE leveled hierarchy, decentered Russia, made difference acceptable without entailing domination. But not all essentializations are equivalent. Attributing danger to an essentialized Other necessarily entails the construction of a threat to the Self from that Other. Finally, the effects of hybridity on identity are evident in the fictional Elkhan Takhirov, Russo-Azeri crime boss. His acceptance of western modernity in the form of the market inoculates him from acting on national difference, essentialized or not. Acceptance of the market entailed a liberal attitude toward national difference.

Russian Orthodox Difference

The modern Soviet project of 1955 declaimed religious beliefs as premodern, while acquiescing to social religious practice.[38] The predominant discourse on religion in Moscow in 1999 was that a belief in God in general was good and that the official Soviet policy toward religion was execrable.[39] One effect of this consensus was to make it harder for Russians to countenance the Soviet modernity project as their future. But this consensus went no farther than that. Although religion in general was valued, Russian Orthodoxy and still more so the Russian Orthodox Church (ROC) were contested territory.

In general, with the exception of the Left, the ROC was harshly criticized. The church was discredited by its association with Soviet rule,[40] by its continued relationship with the Russian state,[41] by its close association with commercial ventures and money-making schemes,[42] and by its self-interested hostility toward all competing faiths.[43] On the church's relationship to money, Pelevin has Tatarsky appeal to God for forgiveness for his sins by of-

---

[37] Ibid., 340–41.

[38] This section benefitted from discussions with Doug Perkins.

[39] See, for example, Gadzhiev, *Vvedenie v Geopolitiku*, 172–73, in which he argues both that religion and modernity are compatible and that the West is not at all as secular as critical theorists have argued.

[40] Zuev, *Istoriia Rossii*, 355.

[41] Chubais, *Ot Russkoi Idei*, 63–64.

[42] Evgenii Krutikov, "You Yourself Are a Wahhabite . . . ," *Izvestiia*, 13 October 1999, p. 3. This article was particularly damning because it was a warning to Moslems in Russia not to go down the same road of corruption as the Russian Orthodox Church and the Vatican.

[43] Anna Astakhova, "If You Don't Like This, You're No Patriot!'" *Segodnia*, 23 November 1998, p. 2.

fering to do God's advertising campaign on Earth. He says in his prayer to God, "I'll write you a good one, honest. It is all about positioning." He criticizes the latest media buy of the church that shows a babushka with a bag into which a hand from a rolled-down Zaporozhets car window puts a one-ruble note. And then a $100 bill comes from a Mercedes. Tatarsky tells God that "it is the Mercedes we need to target." He begins to sketch on a poster "a long white limousine in front of the cathedral of Christ the Savior outside the Kremlin walls. The rear door opens; a light glows. We see only the light, legs, and an arm. The pitch: Christ the Savior. A solid Lord for solid citizens." Tatarsky ends his prayer by asking God how He likes it.[44]

The church was consensually condemned, but Orthodoxy or the Orthodox religion was not. The disagreement was over the relationship between Russian national and Orthodox religious identities and Russian Orthodoxy and other faiths in Russia. In this collection of possible relationships between national and religious identities, there was no dominant discourse, but rather a number of distinct themes. Many considered being Russian and being Orthodox to be equivalent. The society section of the daily newspaper *Segodnia* published a "How to Celebrate Easter" guide, in which the author identifies all the Soviet customs of marking Easter, such as "going to the cemetery," that were inappropriate to an authentically practicing Russian.[45] Orthodox practice provided a bridge across the Soviet interruption to "historic Russian civilization."[46] Sergei Shoigu, Russian Minister for Emergency Affairs, in his speech at the Fifth Russian Orthodox Synod, spoke of this religion as the main creative force uniting all Russians.[47] Here we observe the essentialist view that an authentic Russian identity required a fixed Orthodox faith.

But no less prominent than the view that Orthodoxy was a carrier of Russian identity was the view that Russians could remain authentic Russians even if they were believers in other faiths. Because even the Communist Party chairman, Gennady Ziuganov, asserted that citizens of Russia could practice whatever religion they chose, at the Congress of the Left in November 1998,[48] it is superfluous to enumerate other, more expected sources. But his formulation implied something narrower: Russian citizens (*rossiane*) were entitled to freedom of faith, but other faiths were not necessarily constitutive of the identity of Russians (*russkie*). But, some asked incredulously, "how is it possible to not consider old believers as one of the 'traditional'

---

[44] Pelevin, *Generation "P,"* 158–59.

[45] Aleksandra Tolstikhina, "Easter Is a Holiday of Disobedience: One Can March in the Holy Procession All Week," *Segodnia* 10 April 1999, p. 6.

[46] Maksim Shevchenko and Ivan Rodin, "The President and the Patriarch Greeted Russians Differently on New Year's Day," *Nezavisimaia Gazeta* (*NG*), 11 January 1999, p. 3.

[47] Sergei Shoigu, "The Power of Russia Is in Unity," *Krasnaya Zvezda* (*KZ*), 10 December 1999, p. 3.

[48] Ziuganov, "Political Report," 2.

confessions of Russia?"[49] The occasion for concern was the law adopted by the Duma in 1997 "on freedom of conscience and religious associations," which was aimed at not only "old believers," but also Jehovah's Witnesses, evangelical Lutherans, and other Protestant "totalitarian sects."[50]

Writers such as Anna Astakhova defended religious pluralism, but rejected not only the ROC and its role behind the elimination of competing faiths, but also the binarization of Orthodoxy and the West. Maksim Shevchenko and Ivan Rodin imply such a binarization in remarking on the church's growing role in the resurrection of Russian civilization, positioning it as an antidote to the market, which is unable to be part of such a project.[51]

Summary

The NWR was most consistent in its rejection of the Soviet past, but even it held some aspects of the Soviet past in high regard, such as Soviet superpower status and developed mass culture. It did not consider the Russian nation to be a privileged identity within the Russian Federation or see Orthodoxy as singularly constitutive of some more authentic Russian identity. The LR, as well, shared an agnostic attitude toward any given, fixed Russian identity with any particular essential and genuine components. But it did not assume the kind of wholesale critical attitude toward the Soviet past as did the NWR because relativists did not discern much difference between competing Truths. The NSR was most respectful of the Soviet past, but still was significantly critical of several of its failings, with the important exception of economic performance. The Left's acceptance of diverse forms of religious worship in Russia denied Orthodoxy an exclusive constitutive place in the Russian nation. The LE, on the other hand, although sharing a mixed view of the Soviet past, did consider the Russian nation to have essential characteristics that necessarily identified a Russian as Russian, but only within tolerant relations toward other equally essentialized nations, with equal rights within the Russian Federation.

RUSSIAN IDENTITY AND EXTERNAL OTHERS

The External Others through which Russia understood itself in 1999 were the United States, Europe, and, to a far lesser degree, the East. The western

---

[49] Mikhail Dziubenko and Aleksandr Soldatov, "Old Belief: Moscow, Pokrovsky Synod, Saint's Day," *MN*, 18–25 October 1998, p. 12.

[50] Astakhova, "If You Don't Like This," 2.

[51] Shevchenko and Rodin, "President and the Patriarch," 3. The historical binary relationship between Russia and the Orthodox Church and the West is investigated by Iurii M. Lotman and Boris A. Uspenskii, "Binary Models in the Dynamics of Russian Culture to the End of the Eighteenth Century," in *The Semiotics of Russian Cultural History*, ed. Alexander D. Nakhimovsky and Alice Stone Nakhimovsky (Ithaca, 1985), 33–49.

Other itself was often reduced to Europe, excluding the United States. NWR discourse identified Russia most closely with the United States, NSR and LR discourse with no one, and LE discourse with parts of each.

Two aspects of the United States resonated with Russian understandings of Soviet modernity: economic performance and individual rights. Aleksandr Danilov and Liudmila Kosulina illustrate the decline of the Soviet Union for their high school student audience by comparing the 17 million personal computers in operation in the United States by 1985 to the tens of thousands of obsolete models in the Soviet Union.[52] Leonov's characters conclude that some new U.S. machine can fix someone's crippled leg because, after all, "Americans can invent what they want."[53] In his otherwise scathing critique of U.S. life, Mikhail Vozdvizhenskii extols U.S. "rational economic laws of society."[54]

The second aspect of U.S. modernity that linked to Soviet failings was the 1999 Russian appreciation for the self-confident individual, an integral part of U.S. identity. We have already seen how Tom of "Tom and Jerry" was compared to the wolf in "Hey, Wait Up!"[55] Aleksei Venediktov, a history teacher and main editor of Echo Moskvy radio, said "Russia lags behind the West" and went on to say that "Americans have, first of all, I, a personality, and then the state. American school children are taught their rights, civil liberties, and humanitarian values. Here this is only beginning."[56]

Finally, U.S. nationality policy was appreciated when compared to the equally modern Soviet effort. According to Chubais, success in the United States is evident in the fact that "every citizen [there] calls himself an American," not an ethnonational name.[57] The 1999 liberal understanding of the Russian nation, in both its NWR and essentialist formulations, was associated with this understanding of the U.S. civic nationalism.

What was admired in America was also close to being what was reviled. Anti-Americans were not only in the Left; they were heavily represented among the critical intelligentsia. Valentin Eshpai, for example, in his review of the U.S. movie *The Truman Show*, quotes Henry Miller to the effect that life in American suburbia, presumably one of the achievements of economic modernity, was in fact "a comfortable hell" and that the population of the

---

[52] Aleksandr Danilov and Liudmila Kosulina, *Istroriia Rossii: XX Vek*, 3rd ed. (Moscow, 1997), 313. This text, which is on the Ministry of Education's recommended list, was intended for ninth graders.

[53] Leonov, *Ment Vernulsia*, 381.

[54] Vozdvizhenskii, "They Are Completely Different," 7.

[55] Zabolotskikh, "Fairy Tale of Times Past," 84.

[56] Belozor, "Ambitious Devotees," 2.

[57] Chubais, *Ot Russkoi Idei*, 69.

United States had been largely "cretinized."[58] Although appreciating the material wealth produced by the U.S. economy, Bogoliubov and colleagues remind their readers that this has been achieved at a price: "the market economy makes harsh demands on a man. . . . People have to work a lot and vigorously. The average work week gets longer and longer in the US and according to American specialists, the majority of Americans don't sleep enough and suffer from nervous stress. And of course it gets worse, the poorer you are."[59] The fact that "the entire nation identified with Forrest Gump" spoke to its spiritual vacuousness. And in contrast to the appreciation of U.S. individualism previously documented, Eshpai, quoting Jacques Lacan, writes that "the individual is emptiness, filled by the matrix of culture." And what kind of culture? Not the multicultural utopia of liberals but rather just the "monotonous hopelessness of a comfortable existence."[60] In other words, individuals who believed they had power vis-à-vis the state were just deluded liberals. Eshpai's stream of thought situated the LR alternative offered in Moscow. Individualism was really a naive delusion of empowerment, and the false promise of U.S. economic performance was rampant materialism.[61]

Not only was the United States absolutely execrable, but, more important from the perspective of Russian identity, Americans were Russia's "complete others. It would be hard to imagine more dissimilar people. Our thinking is absolutely the opposite, we have contrary views on one's personal life, on the sense and essence of labor, on the state, and on an individual's way of life."[62] A visit to the United States revealed that American democracy did not produce justice:

A woman sat down in a New York cab and told the driver to stop in front of Rockefeller Center. Since it wasn't easy for him to do this, the driver asked her to take another taxi. However, the passenger rudely insisted. . . . She threatened to complain to his company, hinting for effect that she would accuse him of trying to rape her.

And so she did. But the driver had been broadcasting their exchange on his radio. His boss decided to give the recording to her boss. . . . He offered the driver $300 for moral injury. After which he called the woman to his office to fire her. . . . Once again justice has

[58] Valentin Eshpai, "From TV to the Boundaries of Our World," *IK*, no. 10 (1998): 33–35.
[59] Bogoliubov, Ivanova, and Lazebnikova, *Chelovek i Obshchestvo*, 299.
[60] Eshpai, "From TV," 35.
[61] Inna Tkachenko, "Enemy of the People American-style," *IK*, no. 10 (1998): 36–37. On the American obsession with investments, see Vozdvizhenskii, "They Are Completely Different," 7.
[62] Ibid., 7. The Russian for "complete others" is *nachisto inye*, which could also be translated "utterly different."

triumphed! A beautiful, truly democratic turn, with the killing of a lie. All so, but the woman's lawyer revealed the course characteristic for democracy. It turns out the driver didn't have the right to record the conversation without the woman's consent.[63]

The spiritual emptiness afflicting the United States described by the film critic Eshpai was linked to America's inevitable decline. An academic at the Russian Academy of Education, a professor of history at the Moscow State University, Dr. Igor Bestuzhev-Lada argues that "in the only remaining superpower, its prosperous inhabitants are overtaken by the greatest unhappiness: they have resolved all their day to day problems and have fallen into despair over a problem-free life. And to where this will lead is well-known— to the same decay . . . "[64] experienced in the Roman, Byzantine, and Ottoman Empires. A binarization of the material and the spiritual emerged from a discussion of the United States.

A different source of ambivalence about the United States came from the professional tennis player Anna Kurnikova. The *Kommersant* reporters who interviewed her set up the piece by describing her popularity as not based "on her tennis success, but on her vivid Americanized image." Attempting to unmask her inauthenticity, they asked her which language she speaks most frequently. She replied, "About tennis in English, but with my parents and friends, of course in Russian." Unconvinced, the reporters objected, "But you are almost never in Russia." Seeing where the conversation was going, Kurnikova replied, "I am Russian and never will become an American." "But didn't you want to get American citizenship?" asked the correspondents. Instead of denying it, Kurnikova replied enigmatically, "I have not thought of it." But then she reminded them, "you need to live several years in the US for that."[65] A bona fide Russian star risked losing her bona fides by living in Florida, speaking English, and achieving success through Americanization.[66]

In *Generation "P,"* Dmitrii Pugin, an advertising agency executive in Mos-

---

[63] Ibid.

[64] Igor Bestuzhev-Lada, "From Colossus to Collapse. And back? That Which Beautifies a Woman Still Is Insufficient for an Entire Civilization," *LG*, 13 January 1999, p. 5. The author is further identified as a well-known futurologist.

[65] Anna Kurnikova, interviewed by Aleksei Zhuk and Aleksei Dospekhov, "I Fight for Every Point," *Kommersant*, 24 October 1998, p. 11.

[66] As a fortunate, and of course on the job, witness to the Kremlin Cup tennis tournament in Moscow in October 1998, I can attest to the ambivalent reception given Kurnikova during her performance on court, as well. The only exception to the polite applause at her introduction and departure was mostly silence during her rather desultory first-round loss. A much more supportive reaction from the Russian crowd, for example, was provoked by the authentic Americans Serena and Venus Williams and the apparently more authentic Russians Elena Likhotseva and Elena Dementieva. But, in appreciation of the power of Kurnikova's Americanization, the Kremlin Cup was marketed all over Moscow with glossy posters of

cow, confesses to having lost his "Soviet mentality by working as a cabdriver in New York." He is now "infected with an irresistible attraction to success." He compares New York to Moscow: "in New York you understand that you can spend your entire life in some small fetid kitchen looking out over a dirty courtyard, while chewing on a wretched piece of meat. . . . But in New York you understand that life is passing you by, in Moscow you don't."[67]

Pelevin situates Russia with respect to the United States and Europe very deftly in a discussion of technological needs. "By American standards" our computer graphics capability is already old, "but it is enough for us." This is a rendering of Russia's relationship to the United States that is neither admiring nor scornful but diffident recognition of irrelevance or incommensurability. The United States may need this kind of technology, but why should we feel inferior because we do not have what we neither want nor need? What follows deepens this point. "After all, even all of Europe uses them."[68] If it is good enough for Europe, surely it should be good enough for us. He even concludes with the judgment that Russia will never catch up with the United States in the development of graphics capacity. This is utterly contrary to the other three Russian discourses. Both the NWR and NSR expected to become equal to or better than the West, respectively. And the LE at the very least held out the possibility of catching up. Only the LR refused to be measured by U.S. modernity.

Pelevin provides a rich example of Russian-U.S. identity relations in the following excerpt. Tatarsky, the hero in *Generation "P,"* was a philology student in the 1980s who could not find a job in his field after the Soviet collapse. He finds himself working as an ad man for a series of high-powered Moscow firms. In this vignette, he is being introduced to the new relationship between Russia and the United States after the Cold War. Pugin introduces Tatarsky to the center of the machine:

> "Americans treat us like shit." "How?" asked Tatarsky. "In megahertz. After Chechnya they reduced us to 200mhz." [The United States controls the world's supply of bandwidth.] Pugin, continuing: "We, of course, accelerated our nighttime use, but they also watch our TV in their embassy. As soon as we would raise the frequency just a little bit, they would send a [weapons] inspector around to cut it. In general, it is a disgrace. We are a great country, but we sit now on 400mhz. And after all, those are not even ours."

Kurnikova in action on, it seemed, every lamppost. No pictures of authentic Russians were in evidence, presumably because it was the inauthentic NWR who had the rubles necessary to attend the event.

[67] Pelevin, *Generation "P,"* 33.

[68] Ibid., 214.

Tatarsky, still puzzled, asks, "Do the Americans have the same thing?"

"Of course, and it began much earlier. Reagan by his second term was already animated. [All important political figures in both the United States and Russia are the creation of virtual graphics technology, hence the importance of the megahertz gap.] And Bush. . . . Remember when he would stand at his helicopter and his hair combed back over his bald spot would fly up in the wind? That was simply a masterpiece. I think that in computer graphics nothing comes close to them. America. . . .

"But isn't it true that copywriters work for their politicians?"

"That's nonsense. . . . That country is without a soul. [Again, the binary between material/technological/economic achievement and spirituality/culture/depth.] The creators they have in politics are complete shit. There are two candidates for president but one team of screenwriters. And they are Madison Avenue rejects. . . . Their election materials are simply awful. If one starts speaking about a bridge to the past, then in two days the other one has to start speaking about a bridge to the future. Bob Dole simply redid the Nike ad: from just do it to just don't do it. And they cannot think of anything positive, except blowjobs in the Oval Office. . . . [And here is the claim to Russian superiority, again not on material or technological grounds.] No, our scenarists are ten times sharper. Look at what kind of eminent characters they have come up with: Yeltsin, Ziuganov, Lebed. . . . We have here such talents that we have no need to be embarrassed before anyone."[69]

In sum, the United States was understood along two binaries: material and technological abundance versus spiritual and cultural superficiality, on the one hand, and genuine individual power in the public sphere versus a recognition that such an idea can only be self-delusional.

Europe was understood as being far closer to the meaning of Russia than was the United States. This identification with Europe occurred at all levels of discourse. Writers for the intelligentsia valued how European legislators "serve the interests of European business, . . . creating the legal conditions for economic growth" while decrying the opposite chain of command in Russia—from bureaucrats to entrepreneurs.[70] Vishnevskii reassures his readers that Russia's similarity to Europe was not "imitative" but rather the "natural consequence of the similarity of society's needs

---

[69] Ibid., 214–16.
[70] Chubais, *Ot Russkoi Idei*, 59.

themselves,"[71] an essentializing move linking European and Russian identities.

"European style" meant the highest quality, Vladimir Paperny argues.[72] When Natalya Volchok instructs young girls on how to conduct themselves at a party, she advises them to behave in the "English-style, quietly; don't make a spectacle, make your way out unnoticed."[73] A new word had emerged in Russia, "evroremont," which meant to redecorate or modernize one's apartment or house. When Aleksandr Korzhakov describes the fight over office space in the Kremlin during his time with Yeltsin, he claims that Viktor Ilyushin had scoped out the best office, the one recently vacated by Evgenii Primakov, because it had been decorated in the European style, with modern furniture.[74] In effect, Europe provided a most welcome alternative route to modernity to the one exemplified by the United States.

Aleksandr Lebed's press secretary faulted his boss for not being sufficiently European. Aleksandr Barkhatov reports quizzing a Frenchman about the impression created by a Lebed interview aired in France and finding out that the presidential aspirant's apartment was "too glaringly Asiatic" and that his holding a toy monkey with a banana in his lap made him look like an idiot.[75] Barkhatov was told by a Siemens representative that Lebed should have left his military uniform at home when visiting Germany because it "strongly recalled Hitler's generals" and that Lebed's public criticisms of Yeltsin's health were perceived as unworthy of a respectable politician. Lebed's declaration that he was no democrat only left the impression in Germany that he was not fit for public office.[76] Barkhatov tried to convince Lebed that the "sympathies of Europeans are not found by politicians easily; they should be carefully collected."[77]

The incidental normalcy of Europe is evident in a conversation between two cops in *Ment Vernulsya*. Detective Gurov asks his buddy Kryachko why he is toasting Christmas because it does not come until January 7. Kryachko replies that "all of Europe observes it today, the 25th. Well, let's do it the way they do in Europe then," agrees Gurov.[78] Leonov's fictional oligarchs extol the European way of life as "guaranteeing quiet work and normal human re-

[71] Anatolii Vishnevskii, *Serp i Rubl, Konservativnaya Modernizatsiya v SSSR* (Moscow, 1998), 26. Here he is quoting the late-nineteenth-century Russian publicist Pavel Miliukov.

[72] Vladimir Paperny, *Kultura Dva* (Moscow, 1996), 96.

[73] Natalya Mikhailovna Volchok, *Sovremennaya Entsiklopediya dlya Devochek* (Minsk, 1998), 331.

[74] Alekandr Korzhakov, *Boris Yeltsin: Ot Rassveta do Zakata* (Moscow, 1997), 119.

[75] Aleksandr Barkhatov, *General Lebed ili Moia Lebedinaia Pesnia* (Moscow, 1998), 199. Barkhatov was Lebed's press secretary during Lebed's service as Yeltsin's national security adviser in 1996–97.

[76] Ibid., 215–16.

[77] Ibid., 245.

[78] Leonov, *Ment Vernulsya*, 259.

spect" while they are planning the assassination of a high government official.[79]

In a college textbook on geopolitics, Kamaludin Gadzhiev distinguishes between the U.S. and European models: "The West European model has stronger communitarian, solidaristic, and paternalistic elements, a greater role for the state in the definition of social and economic strategy. . . . Something common unites the peoples of Europe—historical fates, value systems, cultural legacies, etc. . . ." The consequence is that for the many peoples of the former Soviet Union, the "rush to Europe was not dictated so much by geographical proximity, but by the fact that for many of them it is becoming a 'city on the hill,' a role which the US singularly pretended for many generations."[80]

Europe was a modern alternative to U.S. modernity, a preferred alternative because of what it shared with Russian conceptions of Self. And these differentiations were distributed in all the media: books for the intelligentsia, high school textbooks, popular crime novels, and memoirs of political figures.

Russians admired in themselves that which was already understood as European. An essentialist brand of philo-Europeanism is evident in Volchok's encyclopedia for young Russian women. In chapters devoted to art and music appreciation, the author introduces European, mostly French and Italian Renaissance, painters as the first artists about whom Russian teenage girls should develop passing knowledge. The great Russian artists are those who have mastered all that Europe has to offer plus "do not sever [their] spiritual ties to national folk art."[81] Classical music is presented in the same manner. Mikhail Glinka's genius was that he "did not lose his national uniqueness" while attaining Europe's level of development.[82] Volchok's review of Russian culture is an example of LE pastiche. Although acknowledging the value of Others, there still existed a Self whose essence must be preserved in any combination with those Others. Nonessentializing LR discourse, on the contrary, did not value Europe for its apparent connection to some fixed Russian authenticity.

[79] Ibid., 312.

[80] Gadzhiev, *Vvedenie v Geopolitiku*, 274–79. Gadzhiev also identifies Asia, especially east Asia, as a source of democratic and economic values more compatible to Russia's reality than those of the United States (170, 236–45). The only other significant, and positive, treatment of Asian civilization, society, history, and culture with respect to Russian reality is in Bogoliubov, Ivanova, and Lazebnikova, *Chelovek i Obshchestvo*, a sociology textbook. It is of theoretical interest that the features Gadzhiev attributes to western Europe are very similar to those cross-cultural psychologists find in Asia when comparing subjects to their U.S. counterparts. Alan Page Fiske, Shinobu Kitayama, Hazel Rose Markus, Richard E. Nisbett, "The Cultural Matrix of Social Psychology," in Handbook of Social Psychology, ed. Daniel T. Gilbert, Susan T. Fiske, Gardner Lindzey (New York, 1998), 919–25.

[81] Volchok, *Sovremennaya Entsiklopediya dlya Devochek*, 123.

[82] Ibid., 158.

Anti-Europeanism was missing from the Russian identity topography of 1999. This absence implies a deconstruction of the West into its U.S. and European parts. The Russian Left was significantly absent altogether from any discussion of Europe; its External Other was the binarized United States. Europe became the West in Russian understandings of that identity. Russians, when considering the West, treated the United States as a different and excludable subcategory.

Vladimir Magun and his colleagues, in multiple surveys in Russian cities and towns, found that youth were attracted to the West by its economic promise;[83] Dmitrenko and colleagues' textbook consistently compares Soviet and Russian economic developments to western standards;[84] Leonov's fictional detectives observe that even though "patriots work in the special services, they do not respect their own country's technology, preferring imports";[85] and in surveys of Russian youth who were asked what famous person they would like to be, Russian teenage boys chose western movie and rock stars and Russian girls chose western models and actresses.[86] In all of these texts, the West was understood as a desirable Other, and the United States was meaningfully absent from this West.

The LR position on Europe was one of irony, refusing to grant either Russia or Europe a fixed identity on which to build a meaningful relationship. Instead, there was the veneer of ridicule aimed at demonstrating both the unacceptability and inevitability of the situation described.

Let us take a look at Pelevin's treatment of Russia's attachment to the West.

> Several security guards sat around in black uniforms. They looked far more serious than a conventional cop. . . . Cops simply weren't fit for comparison—their blue uniforms with all the ranks and buttons . . . [Europe and Russia]. The black uniform struck a blow: the designer had ingeniously combined [pastiche] in it the aesthetic of the SS [Europe], motifs of anti-utopian films about a totalitarian society of the future and nostalgic themes of the gay-style times of Freddy Mercury [Europe and sexuality]. Cotton-wadded shoulders, deep cut in the breast and Rabelaisian cuffs were combined in such a cocktail [West] that one wouldn't mix with people dressed like that. That was obvious even to an idiot.[87]

[83] Vladimir S. Magun, ed. *Revoliutsiia Pritiazanii i Izmenenie Zhiznennykh Strategii Molodezhi: 1985–1995 Gody* (Moscow, 1998), 33–34.

[84] Dmitrenko, Esakov, and Shestakov, *Istoriia Otechestva XX Vek*, 420, 457, 461, 471.

[85] Leonov, *Ment Vernulsia*, 91.

[86] Iuliya S. Arzhakova, "Objects of Sympathy and Identification for Upper Classmen," in Magun, *Revoliutsiia*, 92–95.

[87] Pelevin, *Generation "P,"* 186–87.

Pelevin presents Europe as more powerful than Russia by dint of the fact that cops are not "fit for comparison" to the western-aping private security forces, but simultaneoulsy points out how the more powerful Russians at home only absurdly attempt to literally wear that European identity. But the presumed power relations remain concealed beneath the irony, while in fact being the oblique targets of that device. Consider a less verbose example: "On the floor sat an elderly obese man with the face of a retired cop. He wore sweatpants and a t-shirt that said 'Sick my duck.'"[88] Pelevin ridicules Russia's efforts to translate the West into Russian.

Western Markets and New Russian Classes

Understandings of markets partially constituted each of the four discourses at work in 1999 Russia. The NWR extoled the virtues of Russian pursuit of markets; the NSR disagreed; the LE grafted the idea of the market onto putatively inherent characteristics of Russian reality; and the LR ridiculed the very idea that markets could operate the way they were abstractly represented by western liberals. But the four shared a contemptuous attitude toward the real Russian market as it operated in Moscow in 1999. The differences were over what to do about the markets' perversion.

The working class and its vanguard, the Communist Party, were the core of class analysis in Moscow in 1955. In 1999, this central analytical space was filled by a far wider array of classes, although the most prominent were the oligarchs and nomenklatura at one pole and the middle class and intelligentsia at the other. Despite the fact that these identites were part of Russia's Self, they were read through Russia's relationship with the West, Europe, and the United States and so stood in a mutually constitutive relationship with the external world, the Soviet past, and the Russian present.

Russian understandings of 1999 markets can be usefully categorized in several different ways. The NWR generally understood the market in the West as the ideal aim of Russia. Those who valued the Soviet past generally favored a hybrid state market, as did the LE, which saw no contradiction in combining elements of the unfettered market with state protection, as was done, in its view, in east Asia and Scandinavia.[89] Discourses that conceived the market as naturally regulated by the state were more likely to understand

---

[88] Ibid., 210. For a more sympathetic portrayal of Russia's efforts to remain true to its Self while accepting "years of retreating to the West," see Roman Volobuev, "Not Children's Reading Material," *LG*, 13 January 1999, p. 8. This article points out the impossible line walked by current issues of *Rovesnik*, the magazine of the Komsomol in Soviet times; it now combines commercial kitsch with superior prose.

[89] Gadzhiev argues that "the very concept of the 'West' has lost its sense" because values misleadingly attributed solely to the West, such as democracy, markets, and law are amply represented in east Asian polities. *Vvedenie v. Geopolitiku*, 170.

Europe as the West and the United States as some unique form of lesser relevance.

There was also an important differentiation between the market in the abstract, or in western reality, and the real Russian market in 1999. The latter was almost unanimously reviled or ridiculed, whereas the former received the polarized attention already mentioned. Although the Russian market was reviled by statists and liberals alike, only the Left read it through the hostile external Other, the United States.

A reporter for *Kommersant*, at the time a voice for liberal economic policies, ridiculed then Prime Minister Evgenii Primakov's speech before the Union of Russian Industrialists and Entrepreneurs on the grounds that it had too many "paradoxical sentences." These included the view that "privatization must create new jobs," when in the rest of the world the reverse happened, and the idea that "bankruptcy does not improve anything." If Russia waited until the state maintained order in the country for markets to appear, as Primakov maintained, then markets would never appear.[90] But Nikolai Kharitonov would have found nothing paradoxical about Primakov's remarks. In an interview the same month, he praised Ziuganov for being able to understand that "without a market under state control, there will be no future."[91] The LE also accepted hybridity as the norm.[92]

The market in the abstract, which was, after all, how Russians experienced the western market, polarized into the critical discourse of the Left and everyone else.[93] Uniting the Left and everyone else was the very low regard for the real Russian market that they did experience. This consensus was powerfully reinforced because of the August 1998 currency crisis that wiped out the savings of millions of Russians overnight. With the exception of Yegor Gaidar, who proclaimed the "market economy in Russia stable" because Primakov had already pledged to not "touch private property or foreign investments,"[94] the rest of Russia had nothing good to say about it.

Gaidar was a Ziuganov target when he called Russia's market economy a "liberal chimera" hatched by the "Chicago Boys and Russian-speaking bankers." (Note the connection of the United States with Russia's market failure.) Look what the "sweet-talking sirens of the free market" have brought the overwhelming majority of Russians to whom "they promised a capitalist paradise."[95] Although the ascription of blame to the West and un-

[90] Konstantin Levin, "Congress of Victors," *Kommersant*, 21 October 1998, p. 1.

[91] Kharitonov, "I Love People for Free," 3.

[92] See, for example, the textbooks Bogoliubov, Ivanova, and Lazebnikova, *Chelovek i Obshchestvo*, 139–40; Zuev, *Istoriia Rossii*, 426.

[93] Everyone else included, for example, Chubais, *Ot Russkoi Idei*, 71.

[94] Yegor Gaidar, "In Russia It's Time to Take a Risk," *MN*, 18–25 October 1998, p. 8. This was a speech delivered at a corporate symposium in Berlin, perhaps accounting for its reassuring words aimed at attracting western capital back to Russia after the August 1998 crisis.

[95] Ziuganov, "Political Report," 2. It has been suggested to me that "Russian-speaking

patriotic Russians was more or less isolated to the discourse of the Left, that was about all that was so isolated.

Aleksandr Khinshtein, for example, in his report on state *dachas*, turns *privatizatsiya* (privatization) into *prikhvatizatsia* (a neologism for plundering). He concludes his survey with the following observation: "In 1941 Konchalovsky sketched a portrait of Aleksei Tolstoy; the writer is sitting at a desk filled will all kinds of food. A scandal broke out: in a country at war, children are hungry, but Tolstoy feasts. Today living in a state dacha is like feasting in 1941...."[96] Daniil Goncharov, reporting on a privatized coal mine in Ekibastuz, comments that even "true monetarists and market liberals" should realize that privatization is hardly necessary if it leads, as in the case here, to the "squandering of state property, cessation of tax payments, and months-long delays in wages."[97] Aleksandr Gelman, considered to be part of the liberal 1960s generation, reflects that the "reformers were much better at imagining what a market economy is than at understanding . . . our native sick economy. They hired consultants for the alien economy after which they lusted. . . ."[98]

Fictional characters such as Sergei Lapin in Koretskii's crime thriller also describe the absurdity of privatization. At a local electronics factory, the director and other members of the "ruling fraternity suddenly are wondrously converted from wage labor into owners of controlling shares. . . . Sergei knew they would get nothing for their stock, but not because they were wise in the ways of privatization; they were simply used to simple people always being ripped off, spit on, and trampled—people exist so bosses can ride their backs to paradise. And what happens to the honored proletariat? They end up as cashiers, pedicurists, prostitutes and security guards."[99]

The liberal market was unthinkable in those discourses that looked to Soviet and Russian history for Russia's identity. It was accepted by those who looked to the West. But the real Russian market was rejected and ridiculed by all. The really existing western market was the most imagined part of a Russian identity in 1999.

The issue of the market was tied closely to the emergence of new social groups. In 1955, it was expected that class analysis be a central part of Marxist-Lenin-

---

bankers" is code for Jews, but I have not found a consensus on this interpretation. For additional critiques from the ranks of the Left, see Larisa Yagunkova, "Long Live the Blessed Path! Picketers Demand a Dictatorship of Conscience," *Pravda*, 18–19 May 1999, p. 3.

[96] Khinshtein, Dachas without Rent," 1.

[97] Daniil Goncharov, "Privatizing 'Yourself'," *Trud*, 29 October 1998, p. 5. The Russian word for squandering here is *razbazarivanie*, literally to sell out of a bazaar. Bazaars in Russia are not considered to be markets, or *rynki;* they have the connotation of a place where people try to swindle and take advantage of one another, not a place where the laws of supply and demand are operating fairly.

[98] Aleksandr Gelman, "Feet without a Path," *LG,* 21 October 1998, p. 5.

[99] Koretskii, *Operativnyi Psevdonim,* 37–39.

ist discourse. But the use of class identities to make sense of the social world was also widespread in 1999. Textbooks, in particular, discussed world civilizations, prerevolutionary Russia, the Bolshevik Revolution, and colonialism from this perspective.[100] Class appeared to provide an intelligible ontology for these authors, but not any particular theoretical content. Class identities were used to simplify the social terrain into analytical categories, but were not employed according to Marxist, let alone, Leninist theories. This continuing attachment to class identity was another link that reinforced the Russian identification with Europe over one with the United States.

In 1955, the class at the top of the hierarchy was the working class, which was in a binary relationship with the bourgeoisie and more ambiguous relations with the intelligentsia and peasantry. In 1999, the relevant class identities had changed, the axis of binarization had changed, and the hierarchical syntax had been eliminated. If we were to spatially arrange the class identity terrain of 1999 Russia, it might look like:

Middle Class   Intelligentsia   Rich   Poor   Oligarchy/Nomenklatura

The middle class and the oligarchy were the two poles. The intelligentsia was close to the middle class, both being in binary opposition to the oligarchy. The rich and the poor formed the hinge between the two poles. The rich were more closely associated with the middle class than with the oligarchy. This was because they were understood as the part of the middle class who had made it, but without the criminalized identity of the oligarchy. Meanwhile, the poor, whom we might expect to have been associated with the middle class, were not identified so straightforwardly; instead, they were often criminalized rather than being credited with sympathetic qualities. The rich, on the other hand, were treated with a combination of scorn, emulative desire, and irony, differentiating them from the criminal rich, the oligarchy, and its official henchmen, the nomenklatura.

With the exception of the peasantry, a most important element in the center-periphery identity, the 1955 classes were absent and hence no longer meaningful identities in Russia.[101] This was a fundamental move away from the Soviet identity because part of the ontological moorings of that project had all but disappeared from the public discourse.

In Koretskii's novel about the intelligence officer with amnesia, Sergei

---

[100] These discussions are found, respectively, in Bogoliubov, Ivanova, and Lazebnikova, *Chelovek i Obshchestvo*, 193–232; Danilov and Kosulina, *Istoriia Rossii*, 10–109; Zuev, *Istoriia Rossii*, 13–73; Gadzhiev, *Vvedenie v. Geopolitiku*, 84.

[101] In fact, the working class was so marginalized that a newspaper presumably sympathetic to its interests reported that no party (not the Communist Party?) represented them in the Duma, unlike agricultural and business concerns. Svetlana Alekseeva, "In the Kuzbass Again, like 100 Years Ago, a Worker's Revolution is Maturing," *Komsomolskaia Pravda* (*KP*), 10 November 1999, p. 6.

Lapin, the ambiguous identity of the rich emerges. The narrator, observing the slum in which Lapin has ended up after years of forgetting he was an elite operative in the KGB, remarks on the "eternal hatred of the poor for the rich bloodsucker."[102] The inevitable consequence is armed violence. The rich are criticized for squandering their money,[103] for buying "improbably expensive dry wine which, as everyone knows, is impossible to drink—it has neither flavor nor strength."[104]

But, on the other hand, "new clothes, money in his pocket, and the patronage of such an influential man as Tereshchenko [local oligarch], made Sergei a completely different man—cheerful, self-confident, and energetic."[105] Being rich transforms in a western direction. Now Lapin can become an "example and symbol of hope for someone."[106] Being rich, Sergei Lapin comes to notice the slum in which he lived, ironically called the Bogatianovka (*bogat* means rich in Russian). "Having lifted himself up the steep and slippery slope (separating the poor from the rich) Lapin had fallen into another world. Wide sidewalks, restored facades, rich store windows, streams of cars [NWR modernity]. They cleared the snow and didn't piss directly onto the street. And people looked different: cleaner, better groomed and dressed, healthier. . . ."[107]

Perhaps rich was to oligarch as West was to the United States. Both the oligarchs and the United States were disrespected subtypes of the more generic classes of rich and West. Pursuing this logic, the middle class was the Europe of the West, that is, the positively evaluated rich-to-be, the new respected class in formation.

This textual picture of the rich is incomplete without looking at how unsympathetically the poor were understood. The editors of *Kommersant Vlast* (KV) asked six prominent Russians whether they gave money to the poor. Here are their answers:

> Sergei Dorenko, TV personality: "In principle, I never give the poor money. Simply because the majority of them work for bandits."
> Sergei Stepashin, former Russian Prime Minister: "Not often, but I give. . . . It seems to me that I can recognize by their external appearance or at a glance those who are really needy. . . . Let this re-

---

[102] Koretskii, *Operativnyi Pseudonim*, vol. 1, 62.

[103] Ibid., 59, 125.

[104] Ibid., 143. See also Korzhakov's delight at finding that his new U.S. Secret Service buddies drink 700 grams, just like he does, and have strong alcohol right out in plain sight in their offices, not hidden away as it is in the Kremlin. *Boris Yeltsin*, 225. If the rich do not know how to drink, are they real Russians, after all?

[105] Ibid., 89.

[106] Ibid., 115.

[107] Ibid., 170–71.

main not on the conscience of those who give, but on those who
take. . . ."

Aleksandr Zhukov, chairman of the Duma budget committee: "I
try to solve these problems more broadly, by being a Duma deputy."

Petr Aven, President of ALFA bank: "Sometimes I give, although
as a liberal economist, I don't advise others to do so."

(This is like U.S. political scientists who vote in elections, but teach their students that it is irrational to do so.)

Boris Berezovsky, entrepreneur: "Before, yes, I gave this question
a lot of attention. But too many people ask. . . . And over time it has
become clear that many don't need contributions. . . ."

Aleksandra Marinina, writer: "Never. I don't trust them. When I
was a criminologist, I received a mountain of information about organized bands of these poor people. They hardly ask for bread
crumbs, but for a dacha for their leader."[108]

The rich and the poor were in binary opposition, but with values opposite to the expected ones of reviled rich and righteous poor. Instead, the rich
enjoyed a fair amount of admiration and the poor received a great deal of
suspicion from a wide variety of Russian society.

It is no exaggeration that the Russian intelligentsia carried much of the
discursive load in producing an image of the intelligentsia as the respected
conscience of Russia. In more popular renditions, it was vouchsafed a certain level of conscience, but equally matched by its impotence as a political
force in the real Russian world. In Leonov's novel, it becomes clear that
someone is plotting to overthrow Yeltsin's government. When it is suggested
that the intelligentsia would oppose such an outcome (that such a group
even exists as an actor is significant), Lieutenant Elanchuk replies: "The intelligentsia is in its usual state of confusion" about politics.[109]

Perhaps Ekaterina Dyogot, a regular contributor to both *Kommersant Vlast*
and *Literaturnaya Gazeta*, makes the most comprehensive case for the intelligentsia:

Nations cannot get along without minds, without important representatives of the human sciences who possess weight both in the eyes

---

[108] "Five Questions about Money," *Kommersant Vlast* (*KV*), 46 (November 16, 1999): 50–
51. The titles were provided by the editors of *Kommersant Vlast;* Berezovsky, at this time in ac-
tuality owned a controlling share of this newspaper.

[109] Leonov, *Ment Vernulsia*, 235. See also, Barkhatov's conclusion that "the intelligentsia in
general can just go to hell. Of course, I am softening the language." *General Lebed ili Moia Lebedinaia Pesnia*, 254.

of professionals and of society, and are able to mentally stimulate the latter—such as Kristeva, Bourdieu, Said, Jameson, and Paglia [*sic*]. . . . Our best minds have either left for the other world— Bakhtin, Lotman, Mamardashvili, Likhachev—or are somewhere abroad—Averintsev, Ivanov—and they are there in part because they don't feel needed here.

What is worse, the intelligentsia's authority had been replaced by a new one: "To call someone an authority now means implying his criminal connections. . . . In the eyes of society, authority is possessed only by those who have taken it by force." Moreover, what intelligentsia Russia did have, if it was highly regarded in the West, it was "strongly criticized and even disdained in Russia," and this was incomprehensible because often it was the most vociferous critic of the West. If Russia does not wake up, "the organ of our highest mental exertions will be *Zavtra*" (a jingoistic, neofascist circular).[110]

If the rich were the internal West, then the oligarchy and nomenklatura were the internal United States for Russia. The nomenklatura the collection of state-associated figures whose positions gave them privileged access to the fruits of that state and its citizens, was an invention of Russian czars. But Russians in 1999 identified it with Soviet times and not with fondness. Perhaps Koretskii provides the most positive spin on the Soviet nomenklatura. He writes, "in former happy nomenklatura times, bosses of various calibres went to the capital to 'resolve questions,' having filled up the cuchette with boxes held together with straps, of Don delicacies inaccessible to the average person. . . . Drinking began long before departure and meanwhile white and black Volgas (BMWs, Mercedes, and Volvos at that time had only been heard about and, if heard about, were considered attributes of treachery and espionage, in general, the vices of harmful western life) rushed along" to pick them up.[111] Less ironically, the Soviet nomenklatura was a "state within the state." The ability to *dostat* (literally, to achieve the acquisition of, not merely to get or buy) through connections with this elite "naturally stratified society; parasitic feelings developed, and the desire to work was crushed."[112]

The nomenklatura in Russia was understood largely, and negatively, as the agents of the oligarchy, "the bankers, politicians, and sometimes even hired managers who . . . have their own significant capital, and who, with this capi-

---

[110] Ekaterina Dyogot, "Grief without Brains," *KV* (November 9, 1999): 51. For additional valuation by the intelligentsia of themselves, see Dmitrenko, Esakov, and Shestakov, *Istoriia Otechestva XX Vek*, 450, 504, 542; Ostrovskii and Utkin, *Istoriia Rossii XX Vek*, 102.

[111] Koretskii, *Operativnyi Psevdonim*, vol. 2, 185–86.

[112] Dmitrenko, Esakov, and Shestakov, *Istoriia Otechestva XX Vek*, 504.

tal, manage to aid the resolution of political tasks."[113] The oligarchs were differentiated from the just plain rich, who were admired, because the oligarchs by definition had accumulated their wealth illegitimately through "so-called popular privatization" and through not just ownership of property but of the "rules themselves."[114] Andrei Borodin, a banker, pointed out that oligarchs, even after the financial crash, despite enormous losses, still possessed the political capital of "contacts, connections and possibilities for influencing political decisions" through the nomenklatura.[115] Some of the disdain for the oligarchs was captured in the popular applause for their not infrequent clashes when *kompromat* (inside dirt, or, literally, compromising material) came forth, revealing more than the "so-called democratic press," which of course was in the pockets of the same oligarchs. Even Korzhakov's memoirs were valued, insofar as they revealed what was really going on behind the scene being staged for the Russian viewers by the bought-and-paid-for media.[116]

This close relationship between money, capital, connections, and the state is reflected in Pelevin's perhaps not so deeply imagined Russian present.

> "Listen," Tatarsky said, "I cannot understand something. Let's allow that the copy writers write all the texts for the politicians. But who answers for the texts? Where do we get the themes? And how do we figure out where national politics should go tomorrow?" [Note that Tatarsky has naively assumed that real power lies with his ad agency.]
>
> "Big business," answered Morkovin [the chief of the ad agency; his name is best translated as dickhead]. "Haven't you heard of the oligarchs?"
>
> "Well of course, but who writes scenarios about the oligarchs?"
>
> "Copy writers, but on a different floor."
>
> "But how do we choose what these oligarchs decide?"
>
> "Depends on the political situation. There's no choice. There is one iron need all around. Both for them and for those. Indeed also for us." [Notice how all interests collapse into the oligarchy's interests.]

[113] Andrei Borodin (then president of the Bank of Moscow), interviewed by Andrei Denisov, "Bankers Will Find a Political Niche," *MN,* 18–25 October 1998, p. 2. Denisov identifies Borodin as "one of the new oligarchs."

[114] Chubais, *Ot Russkoi Idei,* 58–59.

[115] Borodin, "Bankers Will Find a Political Niche," 2. For a contrary view, that politicians dictated the fate of bankers, see Denisov's conclusion in Boris Borodin and Liudmila Telen, interviewed by Andrei Denisov, "Oligarkhi: Second Hand," *MN,* 18–25 October 1998, p. 3.

[116] Ironically, this argument appeared in that same media. Vladimir Nadein, "The Enormous Flaw of the Oligarchs," *LG,* 11–17 August 1999, p. 4.

"So, there aren't any oligarchs? . . . I understand, er, it seems I understand. Those define these, but these. . . . These define those. But
how then. . . . Wait. . . . But on what does all this rely?"

Morkovin punches him in the face.

"You don't ever think. Never, understood?"

"But how am I not to think?"

"The principle is very simple. Everything in society must be normal. We must regulate only the volume of money we have. And all
the rest follows as if on rails. So, one need not interfere for any reason." [Market identity?]

"But someone must command all this, no?"

"You so quickly want to understand everything," Morkovin
grinned. "I say wait a bit. To understand who commands all this is a
big problem. It is not who rules the world, but what."[117]

Big material power stood behind the economic, political, and social order of Russia, masked by the media, who were in the employ of some shad-
owy structure connected to the oligarchs. Pelevin's fictional world differs
little from the story told by newspaper correspondents, other novelists, and
academic textbook writers.

If the nomenklatura and its oligarchic patrons were in binary opposition
to another class, it was to the small Russian middle class, not the poor or the
intelligentsia. The Russian middle class, perhaps because of its absence in
Russia's past, had become an object of precise definition. For example, in
the second half of September 1998, 16 percent of Russians identified themselves as members of the middle class. Youth were more likely to so identify
themselves, as were people with higher education and relatively high income. Over one-quarter of the young, more educated, and relatively well-off
nationwide, as well as residents of Moscow and Petersburg more specifically,
identified themselves as middle class. Owning property and a car were associated with this identity, as well as a certain social status. In the opinion of
the general public, members of the middle class "have good education, a stable job, and confidence in the future."[118]

But the really existing Russian middle class was not considered to be real
enough, at least in terms of the western model on which its desirability was
based—desirability not just in terms of effecting market reform, but as a
constituent part of a democratic Russia. Elena Petrenko, a sociologist and
director of the Public Opinion Foundation in Moscow, writes that "not one

---

[117] Pelevin, *Generation "P,"* 218–21.

[118] "Sixteen Percent of Russians Count Themselves as Middle Class," *Segodnia,* 5 October
1998, p. 3. See also Aleksei Lazarev, "The Number of Unemployed and Job Openings in
Moscow Are Approximately Equal," *KP,* 26 October 1998, p. 4.

person is really in the middle class in Russia." It meant owning private property and means of production, not just a *dacha* or a car. Only when Russia became "normal" would this class fully emerge. (This language is reminiscent of Soviet Marxist-Leninist theorists in 1955 enumerating all the many conditions necessary for the creation of a true proletarian.) The people who the previous analysis called middle class, Petrenko calls only "optimists" about the future: young, well-educated, actively employed people, approximately 12 percent of the population, reduced by one-half after the August 1998 crisis, she estimates.[119]

Although there was disagreement about what the middle class actually was, there was a consensus that more of it was desirable for a prosperous, politically stable, and democratic Russia. The middle class was the link between the market and democracy, and not only for this discussion. It was the absence of the middle class, "the real buttress of democracy in all developed countries,"[120] that hindered democratic consolidation in Russia. If, in the West, the middle class was understood as situated between the upper and lower classes, or the rich and the poor or perhaps working class, then this was not how Russians understood the word. Instead, it referred to the *meshchanstvo*[121] of nineteenth-century Russia, who, despite being "unattractive, limited, selfish, and vulgar . . . played a stabilizing role in modern societies." Their business interests demanded a law-governed state and defense of individual rights, both ideals of democracy. Anatolii Vishnevskii goes on to argue that it was the absence of this mediating class in the Soviet Union that made it "stable" only when mobilized or stagnant. What Russia needs is that "cautious middle who avoids extremes." (Note that the Soviet project made Russians absolutely intolerant of any totalization of modernity, whether Soviet or western.) Even though a Russian middle class was technically absent, Vishnevskii concludes, there was enough of a "proto middle class" that the state or the oligarchs, presumably, would not find it "so simple to shove society around."[122]

The emergence of a real middle class was prevented by the oligarchy and nomenklatura's hijacking of the privatization process. Instead of a new class

[119] Elena Petrenko, "Middle Stratum or Middle Class?" *LG*, 21 October 1998, p. 2. On the August 1998 crisis's devastating effect on the middle class, see also Iurii Zapol, president of VideoInternational (one of the two biggest ad agencies in Russia), interviewed by Anton Charkin, "Snickers Is a More Reliable Candidate for President," *Izvestiia*, 24 November 1998, p. 6.

[120] Dmitrenko, Esakov, and Shestakov, *Istoriia Otechestva XX Vek*, 576.

[121] This word, whose root means "mixture," not "middle," refers to a class of urban retailers, traders, artisans, and semiprofessionals in czarist Russia. It could be considered a liminal class connecting the bourgeoisie and the working class. Its second meaning is wholly pejorative, equivalent to "Philistines."

[122] Vishnevskii, *Serp i Rubl*, 107–8, 420. Recall that this work was funded by a group associated with middle-class interests.

of "owner-shareholders," of property owners, there was bribery, the tyranny of bureaucrats, corruption, and crime.[123] Significantly, Gennady Ziuganov singled out the middle class for sympathy and attention. At the PPUR congress, he said "we fully understand the drama of the so-called middle class, who, like all the rest, were harshly deceived by the disaster-reformers. From the beginning, they flattered them, calling them the national elite, the locomotive of reform and bulwark of progress. But then they ruined them and threw them out on the street from banks and offices on the eve of a severe winter."[124]

Ziuganov set up the emerging class binary in Russia in 1999: the middle class versus the oligarchy and nomenklatura. The intelligentsia, although ruthlessly critical in their contempt for the oligarchy, were deemed to be minor players overall. The working class's meaningfulness had disappeared; the poor were distrusted; and the rich had transcended, symbolically at least, their probable origins within the oligarchy and nomenklatura. Russia's aspired identity was largely a market economy protected by a law-governed state with a burgeoning and prosperous middle class providing the stability only a liminal class can provide between the poor, who could erupt at any time, as Koretskii reminds us, and the oligarchs, who were roundly reviled, as all the texts remind us.

These understandings of class connected to the identities of the West, the United States, and Europe. If the oligarchs lost power in Moscow, the United States would be less associated with market failure; the more the middle class grew and was associated with market success, the more Russian identity would shift toward an understanding of itself through the United States. This was so if the middle class was associated by Russians more with U.S. than with European reality. If the oligarchy remained entrenched, the European identity would remain stronger because extra-market excesses appeared more remediable via the version of regulated market capitalism offered by Europe.

Democracy: The West's Already Existing Present, Russia's Already Perverted Present

Democracy was a universal aspiration in all Russian discourses in 1999. It was also nearly universally held that what democracy had existed in Russia had lasted, at most, only from late in Gorbachev's rule to early in Yeltsin's, from approximately 1987 to 1993. It was also universally held that Russian reality since 1993 had been only a most perverse form of democracy and that true democracy was some distance down the road. The critical dissensus was between the Left and everyone else. There was a sharp dichotomy be-

---

[123] Zuev, *Istroiia Rossii*, 425.
[124] Ziuganov, "Political Report," 2.

tween the Left's understanding of democracy as partly embodied by the Soviet past and the Center and Right's understanding of democracy as most
fully identified with the West and the East. The ironic treatment of democracy by a part of the relativist intelligentsia, perhaps most ironically, linked
them to the Left they reviled.

The four discourses answered the question of whether Russia was a
democracy differently.

> NWR: "No, but it could be if it borrows from the West."
> LE: "No, but it could be if it selects the right combination of intrinsic
> identity characteristics of East, West, and Russia."
> NSR: "No, it is not and cannot be until it recovers elements of the So-
> viet past.
> LR: "No, but so what? There is no such thing; the distribution of mate-
> rial power drives it all in any case."

And what should Russia become?

> NWR: "The western present."
> NSR: "The idealized Soviet past."
> LE: "What we are, our true Self, along with other elements from East
> and West compatible with our authentic Russian Self.
> LR: "It doesn't matter, there is no Russia."

The discourse on democratic identity further accentuated the division
between those, mostly liberal, Russians who identified their future with the
External Other, Europe, and those, the Left, who identified their future with
the Historical Other, the Soviet past. We can see the connection between a
democratic Russia appreciated as such by the public and its strengthened
identification with Europe. But this did not mean that the failure to attain
the democratic ideal would result in identification with the Left's alternative. Not at all—they were denials of one another. Instead, the most likely
result of failing democratization was a liberal pastiche or a relativist ironization of the western present, Soviet past, and Russian unreality.

With the exception of the Left, Russians understood democracy to be
the antithesis of the Soviet past. As Nikita Struve put it, "to not be a plural-
ist means being a totalitarian."[125] Aleksandr Gelman, after cataloguing the
"mismanagement" and "avarice" of the "shameless" hijackers of Russian
democracy under Yeltsin, still concludes that "despite all the errors, inadequacies, and even crimes, which I consider the Chechen war to be, I do not

---

[125] Nikita Struve, interviewed by Viacheslav Repin, "The Church Awaits Its Reformers,"
LG, 10 February 1999, p. 1.

understand why, instead of this unsuccessful leadership, communists should come to power. And, not instead, other proponents of reform and democracy. . . ."[126]

The Soviet-democratic binary was not only the understanding of liberals, but was shared by the Left, although, of course, with the valence reversed. Aleksandr Trubitsyn, writing immediately after the murder of Galina Starovoitova, a Duma representative and one of the icons of liberal Russia, elaborates on the binary West/criminality/democratic present versus the Soviet past:

> The entrance to the apartment building, a big sum of American and Bulgarian money in a bag, waiting murderers, shots from an American weapon, blood, corpses, escape in a car. Could you imagine such a thing in peaceful Soviet times? No, one could not. This is a purely "democratic" murder. All this is precisely the product of "democracy," the product of the regime, for the establishment of which Starovoitova fought. Precisely by the efforts of this regime the country was ruined, industry stopped, morals trampled, and people corrupted. It is completely natural in this atmosphere created by "democrats" that organized crime, terrorism, seizure of hostages, rackets, kidnapping, and other crimes so unthinkable under Soviet power that even words for them in the Russian language were not found, could not help but emerge.
>
> This is a Frankenstein monster made up of the many corpses killed by the creator himself. Criminal-mafia world, a beast with the brain of a banker/usurer, with the raking in hands of a privatizer, with the tongue of the hired TV personality, with the gluttonous belly of the speculator, and with the empty gaze of the hired murderer, all created by "democrats." They sometimes assault their own creators, when they fall under foot. This is a sad and tragic story, but maybe it will serve as a lesson for those, who, for the sake of seizing power, allied with criminals, who legalized speculation, calling it "business," usury, calling it "banking," robbery, calling it "privatization," and even hired murderers have been elegantly renamed "killers" ["killers" is in English].[127]

"Democracy" in quotation marks signified the Left's appropriation of that identity for themselves and the placement of the Soviet past in binary oppo-

[126] Aleksandr Gelman, "Old Age Is the Youth of Wisdom," *Moskovskie Vesti* (*MV*), 18–25 October 1998, p. 27. On the Soviet past as an illogical, unnecessary, and undesirable alternative to democrats, see also "Dead State," 1.

[127] Trubitsyn, "Purely 'Democratic' Murder," 4. For more views of the Left, see Ziuganov, "Political Report," 2; Vasilii Safronchuk, "Political Boomerang," *SR*, 24 November 1998, p. 3.

sition to the perverted democracy in Russia in 1999, with its violence, corruption, miserable economic situation, and immorality. But this characterization of the really existing Russian democracy was not the monopoly of the Left. The entire discursive spectrum seconded and thirded this critique; however, the alternative they saw was not the Soviet past but the western present, or a democratic ideal, collected from the essentials of West, East, and Russia itself.

According to non-Left Russians, the perversion of contemporary democracy was manifest, its causes lay in the absence of some necessary preconditions that were are yet to form,[128] but there was hope because, approximately from 1987 to 1993, there had been signs of real democracy developing.

Korzhakov writes in his memoirs that after the failed August 1991 *putsch* against Gorbachev, "it seemed to [Korzhakov] as if Russia had received a lucky lottery ticket." Democrats had come to power and the country "thirsted for changes." But, instead of democracy, the result was the maximizaton of not "state, national interests, but those of commerical structures, foreign investors, and bandits."[129] Lev Gurov, the cop who returns to work in *Ment Vernulsya*, observes that "things have gotten out of hand with this democracy. In the good old [Soviet] days, a cop would never have gotten so close to the holy of holies," referring to the capacity of state security forces to collect *kompromat* on important politicians.[130] Aleksandr Gelman describes Russian democracy as a giant deception, not unlike Pelevin's account of virtual politics. "Political parties differentiate themselves basically by deceiving different groups of the electorate. Each party specializes in the deception of 'its' contingent. The party of power deceives businessmen. Communists deceive working people. Yabloko deceives the skeptically-inclined intelligentsia. And fascists deceive various types of lumpen."[131]

In his memoirs, Yeltsin's main bodyguard, not widely or highly regarded as part of democratic Russia, periodicizes Russia's movement from post-Gorbachev democracy to its corrupted present. He writes that "Yeltsin's first speechwriters helped him a lot in the first presidential elections. They worked selflessly, for an idea. Now this sounds funny, but there was a time when many believed in the imminent democratic future of Russia."[132] Korzhakov describes how Yeltsin's government willingly denied itself superior government housing, because "after all, in 1992, democrats at least exactly corresponded to their label."[133] But by 1993, that is, after the Yeltsin gov-

---

[128] For example, the absent civil society in Chubais, *Ot Russkoi Idei*, 60. He also dwells on the absent middle class.

[129] Korzhakov, *Boris Yeltsin*, 359.

[130] Leonov, *Ment Vernulsia*, 177–78.

[131] Gelman, "Feet without a Path," 5.

[132] Korzhakov, *Boris Yeltsin*, 120.

[133] Ibid., 135.

ernment had strafed the White House with artillery fire to quell a putative coup by Ruslan Khasbulatov and other parliamentarians, Korzhakov reports how "strange" it was to hear Sergei Filatov and Gennadii Burbulis, two "consistent democrats and humanists," discuss using lasers to blind demonstrators outside the Ostankino TV studio.[134] Khinshtein's reporting on the fate of Soviet dachas narrates the same recent history of Russian democracy. "At first, in the thick of the fight against privileges, Yeltsin was categorically against free housing. In the beginning of his government, he even signed an order abolishing state dachas. But, as is the custom [now], the document was successfully nullified and forgotten. . . ."[135]

Hope for Russian democracy was also found by the non-Left in the fact that western democracy was only an ideal. It also did not work as advertised; indeed, it worked in ways quite familiar to Russians. For example, Elena Chinyaeva finds that Tony Blair's New Labor mission to find a "new national idea" and the "increasingly common domination of legislatures by lobbyists" were common to Russia. But "the difference is that they resolve them with dignity, maintaining respect for themselves and for their countries, through open democratic procedures." She identifies Russia's potential to become a functional flawed West if it accepts the bottom line that democracy is "electoral turnover."[136]

The boundaries of discourse between the NWR and LR can be seen in the following conversation between Gurov and the Duma member Doronin in *Ment Vernulsia:*

> Gurov—"The motives of a man who wants to serve in the Duma are incomprehensible to me."
>
> Doronin was indignant—"Yes, a man won't sleep nights, will destroy himself to the end, only to end up in the Duma."
>
> [Gurov:] "Even more incomprehensible. In my view there is no more boring and thankless task."
>
> "Precisely thankless," agreed Doronin. "Doesn't someone have to serve?"
>
> "An interesting thought," Gurov began to feel uncomfortable: precisely by this 'someone must' argument he had justified his own service in the police. "The majority of people, as I understand it, rush to become deputies from a feeling of inadequacy, for privileges, from an aspiration to set oneself up for the future, to work less and get more."

---

[134] Ibid., 165. On the devolution of democratic Russia, see also Zuev, *Istoriia Rossii,* 380–403.

[135] Khinshtein, "Dachas without Rent," 2.

[136] Elena Chinyaeva, "They Are Not Choosing Democracy," *KV* 49 (December 14, 1999): 19.

[Doronin:] "And the minority? Perhaps an aspiration to change life for the better, from a love for Russia?"

[Gurov:] "I can't deny such elevated and naive motives."[137]

Although a pale version of Pelevin's more deliciously cynical and ironic writings, Gurov is the embodiment of the skeptical LR, assuming that hidden configurations of power in fact run Russia and that the accoutrements of democracy are more decorative than real, things like parliaments and newspapers. Doronin, a new Russian liberal, is face to face with the new Russian relativist.

The only area in which the real Russian political order had apparently made great strides was marked by meaningful silence. Recall that in 1955 there was a vigorous discussion of whether difference from the ideals of the New Soviet Man would inevitably give rise to dangerous deviation; in 1999, this discussion was absent. Difference was instead accepted as a natural fact of everyday life, not a foundational element of identity evoking contestation. That the silence did not mean precisely the opposite—that all difference was naturally deviant, and so there was no need to speak of it—is most unlikely given the discourse on democracy in the External Others; also there was one deviant roundly identified as such in Moscow: the homosexual.

Koretskii's narrator lumps homosexuals together with drug addicts, but not with men having extramarital sex;[138] Korzhakov devotes an inordinate amount of space to the tale of a Yeltsin press secretary's "homosexual orgies," which included both sadomasochism and defenestration;[139] and Tatiana Maksimova reports on the fear of homosexuality in a Petersburg military academy.[140]

Other concerns with deviance included Lebed's refusal to go on a TV program on which prositutes had appeared earlier because they were "abnormal";[141] a film critic's lament that the Cannes film festival was dominated by "the abnormal—the schizophrenic, the paralytics, and the perverts";[142] and Tatarsky's ironic observation that communists in Russia today must be schizophrenic because the textbook definition of that disorder is a faith that is not shared by others.[143]

---

[137] Leonov, *Ment Vernulsia*, 147–48. Elsewhere Gurov has to be reminded that not all the media are just "for sale" (280–81).

[138] Koretskii, *Operativnyi Pseudonim*, vol. 1, 159, 279.

[139] Korzhakov, *Boris Yeltsin*, 252–53.

[140] Tatiana Maksimova, "Girls to the Right! Boys to the Left: No Gay Princes Will Come from Today's Cadets, The Missing Beautiful Sex Will Not Interfere with Studying!" *KP*, 11 September 1999: 10.

[141] Barkhatov, *General Lebed ili Moia Lebedinaia Pesnia*, 98.

[142] Andrei Plakhov, "Horror before History," *IK*, no. 10 (1998): 93.

[143] Pelevin, *Generation "P,"* 14.

Summary

The NWR discourse understood Russia through its high regard for the West, including the United States. Of the four Russian discourses, this one evaluated U.S. individualism, civil liberties, and economic achievements through the market most highly. This is not to say that the political and economic systems of Europe were not preferred for their greater attention to social justice, equality, and noncommercialism. But it is to say that alone among the four alternatives the NWR identified itself at least partially with the U.S. present, as well. The NWR, despite its uncritically high regard for the market, shared the angry and anxious disappointment of the other Russian discourses with the perverted Russian market as it really existed. What differentiated it from the others was its understanding of the solution: become the West. If it is possible to establish the class identities of these discourses, the NWR's constituency was the most middle class of all the formations, but included the rich and, implicitly, the oligarchy, as well.

The NSR discourse identified with neither the U.S. nor the European alternatives of the western market and democratic order. The NSR condemned market reforms in Russia today, but its remedy, a return to the Soviet past, left it isolated. The NSR embraced the poor, the peasantry, and the working class, such as it still existed.

The LE discourse was more inclined than the NWR to identify both with Europe over the United States and with aspects of the Soviet past. Its understanding of Russians as endowed with certain collectivist sentiments implied a certain identification with European modifications of U.S. market individualism. What the NWR, NSR, and LE shared was a rather close agreement on what constituted modernity: material and technological progress, democratic governance, and cultural and spiritual achievements. What separated them, beyond the niceties of what they precisely were, was how they expected to get there: through the western present, Soviet past, or authentic Self. The LE was situated between the NWR and NSR in their understandings of how to get beyond the perverted market of 1999: through the adoption of those economic practices, both market and nonmarket, both Russian and non-Russian, that were genuinely Russian in essence. This was how the East was read onto Russian realities. The LE encompassed the intelligentsia, the middle class, and the rich.

The LR discourse, with its refusal to grant the West any of its claims to the achievement of the good life, whether democratic or material, found itself in a contiguous, although not overlapping, relationship with the NSR. They are fellow-travelers. This discourse considered mythological the idea that citizens in the West exercised any real power in politics, developed any genuine individual differentiation from the mass, or had developed beyond the crudest of material consumers. Because the LR was antiessentialist, denying that any identity had any fixed meaning, it did not buy into the LE understanding of Russians as inherently possessing any particular characteristics. Instead, the world was one of material power configurations, masked by the cynical manipulations of the NWR, NSR, and LE, alike. To relativists, the market was a disaster, but so was any alternative; it all added up to domination by the powerful, no matter what it was called.[144] Unlike the other three formations, the LR had no fixed view of modernity, but it reflexively responded with irony to others' conceptions. It can be said that the LR was the intelligentsia, pure and simple. Although relativism appeared in the popular novels of the day, implying perhaps some link to the poor, it was mostly concentrated in the texts by and for the educated classes of Moscow.

RUSSIA'S INTERNAL OTHER: THE FEDERAL CENTER AND ITS REGIONAL OTHERS

We have looked at how Russia identified itself through its Historical Other, the past and the associated discourses of Orthodoxy and the nation. We have also looked at how Russia identified itself in the External Other of the West and its associated identities of market, class, democracy, and difference. Now we turn to the third and final axis of Russian identity: its Internal Other. This dimension articulated itself as the relationship between the center, Moscow, and the periphery, all that was not Moscow. It mapped onto the urban-rural differences familiar from our discussion of this 1955 binary. And, perhaps most critically, it operated through the contemporaneous rebellion, invasion, and war in Chechnia.

In general, Russia had become decentered, compared to Soviet days, as the discussion of the Russian nation has made clear. But that does not mean that Russians in Moscow did not consider themselves still to be the center of Russia, only that being the center had a different meaning. Meanwhile, events in Chechnia had pushed Russian identity toward the center, in a way predicted by more than a few theorists of conflict, beginning with Georg Simmel and not ending with experimental social psychology.

Marina Davydova connects the differences between the NWR and NSR to differences between the center and the periphery in an article comparing the clientele at two Moscow theaters, the Chekhov and the Gorky.

> Everything was different at the holiday parties. . . . But the main
> thing was the completely different electorate. . . . You go to the
> Chekhov and the elite is strolling around in furs—TV stars, film

---

[144] The Russian LR was most like western poststructuralists. See Anne Norton, *Reflections on Political Identity* (Baltimore, 1988); Nancy Fraser, "The Uses and Abuses of French Discourse Theories for Feminist Politics," *Theory, Culture, and Society* 9 (1992): 22; Allison Weir, *Sacrificial Logics: Feminist Theory and the Critique of Identity* (New York, 1996).

barons, aging theatre idols [the rich are part of the NWR con-
stituency]. . . . You approach the Gorky and you see typical representatives of the "marginal strata of society," who, in their free time,
trade vodka and smoked fish near the Revolution Square metro station, or patriotic literature a little farther, near the Lenin museum
[the poor are part of the NSR]. . . .

The Chekhov is visited by Gaidar, Shokhin, Shabdurasulov—in
general, representatives of the "antipopular regime." Tireless fighters against this regime visit the Gorky—Ziuganov, Baburin, and also
some of the "former ones," Yazov, Kriuchkov, and others. . . . At the
Chekhov the artists nobly sprawl behind little tables on the stage—
drinking and eating, behaving casually. . . . On the stage from time
to time, pathos was replaced by irony [the intelligentsia's method is
not part of the Left's discourse]. . . .

The moral look of the fighters for everything good against everything bad didn't allow the representatives of the Gorky to hold a
New Russian party on stage. In the Gorky, if they drink, then only after a solemn party. . . . They would rarely joke [remember Rumiantsev's attitude toward the LitGaz parodies of the Writers'
Congress]. . . . By the penury of their party at the Gorky I was reminded of a party of independence in some desolate province [as if
the Left was the periphery to the NWR center]. . . . At the party in
the Chekhov there was so much bungling, so much non-seriousness
[again, the intelligentsia as good-hearted incompetents]. . . . But
there was no spite, and this is very significant. Some of our intelligentsia love to say: ah, politics, it is so dirty, and after all, aren't they
all the same, Yeltsin and Ziuganov, democrats and communists? . . .
To be convinced there is a difference, just go to the theatres, and
feel the difference.[145]

In her last lines, Davydova continues the liberal attack on the relativists who
recklessly, in her view, equate the Left and the West. This is directly parallel
to the excerpt from *Ment Vernulsia* wherein Gurov the relativist spars with
Doronin, the liberal Duma member.

Urban Center, Rural Periphery

Absent in Moscow in 1999 was the hierarchical syntax characteristic of
the identity terrain of 1955, dominated by class and the Russian nation. At
that time the working class was both the center and the apex; the Russian
nation was the center of all Slavic and non-Russian peoples, the apex of all
their accomplishments; and the Soviet Union itself was the center of the

[145] Marina Davydova, "Feel the Difference," *Vremia*, 29 October 1998, 7.

world revolutionary movement and socialist community. But the syntax of hierarchy remained in 1999 embodied in the relationship between the Moscow center and its periphery in the Russian Federation. And it was further distilled in the age-old tension between the urban, industrialized, modern center and the rural, agricultural, premodern, traditional periphery. Indeed, if there was a single identity formation that emerged intact and as predominant in 1999 as it had been in 1955, it was the hierarchy between the superior urban and the inferior rural.

These binaries map themselves onto the four discourses along the axes of modernity and the market. The NWR was perhaps most open in its understanding of the rural and the peasantry as backwater, obstacles on the path toward modernization according to the market model. The NSR, as nonmarket modernizers, trumpeted the peasantry as embodying authentic Russian ideals, just as Davydova sketches the celebrants at the Gorky Theatre. This essentialization of Russian peasant characteristics connected the Left with the LE, which also considered these rural idealizations to be constitutive of a genuine Russian identity. Only the LR escaped from the modernist trap of dichotomizing the rural and the urban, the modern and the traditional, although of course it was of the urban modern project, if only as a daily resident.

The urban-rural identity was polarized in Russian discourse, positioning the NWR against the Left and the LE. As an empirical matter, L. S. Shilova and Vladimir Magun report that young people living in Moscow and Petersburg were more than twice as likely to support the market as those living in provincial cities.[146] Magun writes that even when those past high school were surveyed, there was still a "certain lag" in provincial cities when it came to accepting western "aspirations."[147] Although Shilova and Magun only identify differences between the rural and the urban, most others go on to establish a clear hierarchy between the two.

Memoirs and novels are the place to find incidental subordination of the rural to the urban because these authors are not trying to make any deliberate arguments about it. Korzhakov, Yeltsin's bodyguard, for example, attributes former Prime Minister Viktor Chernomyrdin's conservative suits to the influence of his wife, "who grew up in a peasant family and hasn't, to this day, lost the signs of her class membership."[148] Peasants have "coarse faces"; a person gets singled out if he is not "one of the eternally hung-over muzhiks"; "provincials streaming out of the metro stop immediately to ask

[146] L. S. Shilova and Vladimir S. Magun, "The Connection of Goals and Life Strategies," in Magun, *Revoliutsiia*, 72.

[147] Magun, *Revoliutsiia*, 39. See also Elena Berezina, "Without a Right to Return to Life," *LG*, 11–17 August 1999, p. 7.

[148] Korzhakov, *Boris Yeltsin*, 309.

where GUM is"; "Kriachkio answered with the open-hearted smile of a village fool"; and in a "car sat counterintelligence operatives dressed for the provinces."[149] This off-handed essentialization of rural inferiority is reminiscent of the Moscow sophisticate (who had just arrived in Moscow herself some years before) greeting her new country cousin with a knowing smile of condescension in Leonov's *Russian Forest* in 1955.[150] When Barkhatov writes about traveling with the presidential candidate Lebed, he refers to even the *oblast* centers, the provincial capitals, as glubinka (the sticks; literally, the depths).[151]

But as powerful as daily textual practice was in subordinating the rural to the urban, and it was a very powerful engine for that binarized, hierarchicized identity, there were far more deliberate treatments that made the argument more starkly. A. I. Sogomonov, for example, would not have been out of place in Moscow in 1955 when he declaims the countryside as an obstacle to Soviet and now Russian modernity. He argues that people in the countryside adhered to the "traditionalist doctrine of a guaranteed income," an impediment to modern market reforms. Russia has remained a transitional state because it is still partly an "agrarian state," because Russian peasants who migrated to Soviet cities had only become "quasi-urbanized," resisting "social and technological innovation . . . and the historically inevitable rational individualism. . . ." If we replace individualism with collectivism, this would be consistent with high Soviet modernity in 1955. Sogomonov goes on to claim that what prevailed in Russia was a "neopeasant world," a world where active state control, state insurance against risks, and just redistribution of goods was expected. Sogomonov concludes by calling this neopeasant identity a sign of "simple modernization," which must be replaced by "high modernization" that looks a lot like the NWR.[152] Indeed, if the "passivity of the individual" was one of the features of the historical Soviet Other that was roundly rejected in 1999 Russia, then Sogomonov connects that malady to the "peasantry who subordinate themselves to their fate" and who consequently understand the success of others as "either dis-

---

[149] Koretskii, *Operativnyi Pseudonim*, vol. 1, 63, 65; vol. 2, 317; Leonov, *Ment Vernulsia*, 291, 268.

[150] Another direct parallel with 1955 is the fact that the countryside knew it was being humiliated, and objected, as was the case at the Second Writers' Congress. See Korzhakov's description of Yeltsin's resentful attitude toward the city-slickers. *Boris Yeltsin*, 55. See also the revealing survey of how the center's presidential candidates, to wit, Ziuganov, Luzhkov, and Primakov were received in the provinces. "Internal Voice," *KV* 46 (November 16, 1999): 31–32. It is interesting that *vnutrennii*, referring to the provinces, also means "inside, the depths," which apparently makes Moscow and Petersburg the *vneshnii* or "outside, the heights"? At the very least, they were the parts of Russia most openly exposed to the outside world as Russia.

[151] Barkhatov, *General Lebed ili Moia Lebedinaia Pesnia*, 268.

[152] A. Iury Sogomonov, "The Phenomenon of Revolution of Expectations," in Magun, *Revoliutsiia*, 115–26.

honorable or exploitation." The only hope for Russia, as it had been for many Soviet analysts in 1955, was for the peasantry to die off and be replaced with a younger generation steeped in market relations.[153]

Sogomonov was not alone in seeing rural peasant values as continuing obstacles to modernity in Russia in 1999. Vishnevskii, for example, argues that urbanization elsewhere in the world was associated with the development of the market. In the Soviet Union, however, urbanization was not accompanied by the development of the market, so peasants who moved there never benefited from the modernizing effects of market relations. Instead, they remained attached to "old patriarchal family values," rather than asserting themselves as individuals. He connects this insufficiently marketized population to the absence of a true middle class, and to the lack of support for Gorbachev's "liberal, democratic reforms."[154]

This market-modernizing discourse of the NWR parroted the predominant Soviet modernizing discourse of 1955; both saw the premodern peasant in his rural milieu as an obstacle to true modernity. They only differed on what this entailed. Also familiar was the counter to this predominant derogation of the peasantry, its celebration. In 1955, this was a marginal voice; in 1999, it formed the other pole of the conversation. Recall that those Russians who were most critical of the West, the United States in particular, pointed out the spiritual and cultural vacuum that existed out there where there was material and technological plenty. The peasantry and rural life were understood by those Russians who appreciated it as a primary source for Russia's spiritual depth and meaningfulness. Vladimir Krainev, the piano virtuoso, for example, argues that city-dwellers found it harder to "appeal to something higher" than did those living in "the provinces." In the city "there is no time, no time to get deeper into oneself . . . and through the Self, arrive at God."[155] Otar Ioseliani, the prize-winning film director, asserted that loneliness never existed in the countryside. Extended families protected the elderly from being thrown into a home; the entire community watched over you; this was "the normal experience of humankind."[156]

Korzhakov implies in conversation with Viktor Chernomyrdin that Igor Malashenko and Viktor Gusinksy were not real men, because they did not have real men's hands. "When you meet Gusinsky next time, look at his little hands. What stuffed little pillows and cultivated little fingers. My wife saw his hands on TV and said: These are vile hands for a muzhik." Then, look-

---

[153] Ibid., 115–16, 120–29. On "traditional conservatism of the provinces," see also Aleksandr Kinsburgskii and Alla Semchenko, "Leading Politicians," *LG*, 19 May 1999, p. 1.

[154] Vishnevskii, *Serp i Rubl*, 100–111, 137, 157. See also Dmitrenko, Esakov, and Shestakov, *Istoriia Otechestva XX Vek*, 502; Ostrovskii and Utkin, *Istoriia Rosii XX Vek*, 88.

[155] Krainev, "Russia," 15.

[156] Otar Ioseliani, interviewed by Ekaterina Tarkhanovaia, "Otar Ioseliani," *Kommersant*, 27 June 1998, p. 7.

ing at Chernomyrdin's hands, Korzhakov pronounces them "normal, having held a hammer not that long ago."[157] Moreover, Russians from the *glubinka* were considered to be more authentic Russians, more genuine carriers of the essentials of being Russian.

Kharitonov, not surprisingly, as the Agrarian faction head in the Duma, declares that city-dwellers "are less patriotic" than those who "live and work on the land," because for them, the concepts "my motherland and my land are not abstractions." Indeed, the "spiritual-moral roots of Russia are on the land, in the countryside." Attesting to his own authenticity, Kharitonov brags about being able to milk a cow by hand."[158]

The discursive boundaries between countryside and city, peasant and urbanite, and tradition and modernity were tightly drawn. On one side were those who saw the true essence of Russia at work on a daily basis, and on the other were those who also saw these daily practices at work, but as the bane of the eternal modernization project of Russia. Just how fixed these two views were perhaps was revealed by the fact there was no room for irony in this discourse. The best that even Pelevin can come up with was a crude joke about whether a cesspool in the Moscow suburbs backed up into the city or out into the countryside.[159] And Kharitonov, explaining why the *Kukly* TV show had not made a satirical puppet out of him, said: "It is very hard to put a peasant in a funny situation."[160] The NSR and LE shared a view of the countryside that the NWR scorned.

The Weakening Federal Center

The predominant understanding, shared by the Left, NWR, and LE alike was that the center was losing its influence and authority over the regions and that this trend should be stopped. But, at least until the advent of the second Chechen war, this tension between the center and the regions was not ethnonationalized. Russians in Moscow did not grasp the situation as one in which non-Russian republics were at odds with the Russian capital. Instead, they were at odds with the Federal Center, understood as the juridical, sovereign, institutional center of a sovereign federal state, with all the rights and obligations that flowed therefrom. Moreover, the Federal Center did not treat the regions as Others for the simple reason that, by and large, the center blamed itself for the regions' desires for more autonomy and local power.

We must begin in 1917 to appreciate how Russians in 1999 situated re-

---

[157] Korzhakov, *Boris Yeltsin*, 385.

[158] Kharitonov, "I Love People for Free," 3. See also Dmitrenko, Esakev, and Shestakov, who argue that until Stalin crushed them, the "peasantry had been the creator and preserver of popular culture and traditional daily life for centuries." *Istoriia Otechestva XX Vek*, 452.

[159] Pelevin, *Generation "P,"* 46.

[160] Karitonov, "I Love People for Free," 3.

gional unresponsiveness to central legislation and decrees. It is the concept *dvoevlastie* (literally, dual powers) that captured for Russians what was happening in 1999. *Dvoevlastie*, in terms of Soviet history, at least, was the period in which the provisional revolutionary government (PRG), which had replaced the czar in March 1917, was challenged by the Soviets, councils of workers, sailors, soldiers, and peasants, especially in Petersburg and Moscow. The PRG's failure to consolidate its authority was seen as a primary reason for the later success of the Bolshevik coup in November 1917.[161] This explanation for political chaos, collapse, and revolution was offered time and time again for 1999 Russian politics.[162]

The battles between Yeltsin's Russia and Gorbachev's Soviet Union in 1990–91 and between Yeltsin's executive and Khasbulatov's Duma in 1992–93 were both described as instances of unsustainable *dvoevlastie*.[163] In 1999 Russia, organized crime was understood as a parallel power structure, challenging the state's authority.[164] This was not merely an academic understanding. Korzhakov argues that *dvoevlastie* between Moscow and the union republics led to the Soviet collapse.[165] It is a "textbook certainty" that Russians sensed that there was a "dangerous state of dvoevlastie, both in the center [between the executive and Duma] and in the regions" [between the center and local authorities]."[166]

There was a consensus that the regions were gaining too much autonomy from the center and, more important, that it was the center's dereliction of duty, primarily its inability to provide the necessary economic resources to sustain an acceptable standard of living in the countryside, that was responsible for this dangerous drift toward chaos. And, because the Federal Center was blamed, the regional governors, legislatures, and citizens were not branded rebels, traitors, malcontents, or Others. They were simply responding to the center's impotence[167]—and how they responded! Novosibirsk's teachers understandably went on strike over nonpayment of wages for eight months.[168] In the province of Khanty-Mansiisky, an oil-producing

---

[161] Danilov and Kosulina, *Istoriia Rossii*, 116; Ostrovskii and Utkin, *Istoriia Rossii XX Vek*, 130.

[162] For example, Aleksandr Boreiko, "Holding at Any Price," *Segodnia*, 24 November 1998, p. 4; Aleksandr Oskin, "Only Bad News," *Trud*, 11 February 1999, p. 2.

[163] Dmitrenko, Esakov, and Shestakov, *Istoriia Otechestva XX Vek*, 585–603.

[164] Bogoliubov, Ivanova, and Lazebnikova, *Chelovek i Obshchestvo*, 49.

[165] Korzhakov, *Boris Yeltsin*, 128.

[166] Zuev, *Istoriia Rossii*, 374–412, quotation from 411.

[167] Korzhakov uses a double entendre: he calls it impotence in a whorehouse, or *bardak*, which is also Russian for "mess" or "chaos." *Boris Yeltsin*, 158. There was even the sense that the regions would have liked more order imposed on them from the center. See Kinsburgskii and Semchenko, "Leading Politicians," 1.

[168] Iurii Trigubovich, "There's Money in the Oblast! So Thinks the RF Government, but They Think Otherwise in the Regions," *NG*, 11 January 1999, p. 4.

donor to Moscow's federal treasury, they justifiably wanted more financial help from the center in dealing with their indigenous population's educational, training, cultural, and environmental needs.[169]

The center was understood to be so inept and incapable in the face of legitimate regional demands that even peripheral appeals beyond Moscow, to the international community, for salvation, were reported with at least understanding, if not outright sympathy. In Kamchatka, for example, "since there is no hope with Moscow" dealing with the energy crisis there, they appealed to the UN directly for humanitarian aid in the form of fuel oil.[170] Vladimir Zema, the administrator of the southern Kurile islands, territory claimed both by Japan and Russia appealed directly to Yuri Luzhkov, Moscow mayor and presidential candidate, to send financial assistance for food and fuel. Several months before, the Shikotan *raion* assembly, having received no response from Moscow, voted to lease parts of its territory to Japan on a long-term basis, effectively preempting the center's MFA.[171] Sergei Pasko, chairman of the Baltic Republican Party in Kaliningrad, offered to rent some of its territory to NATO for military exercises. Some in that party even proposed German annexation of the territory, the joke being "Yes, sell us finally to the Germans. Maybe they will at least restore order."[172]

It might seem that regional efforts to cut separate deals with foreign powers would lead to Russian views of them as potentially hostile Others, but this did not happen. The reason for this was the existing Russian Self, its own economic and political perversions, so clearly elaborated in the previous sections on markets and democracy. Evgenii Anisimov summarizes where Russia was heading if the center could not come through with the economic performance counted on by the regions. The "economic crisis has put a cross on a united and indivisible Russia." And it was not a more powerful or coercive center that was needed, but rather one that "can feed families." Anisimov predicts that the army would break up along the lines of "local authorities" because they could feed, clothe, and house them. Local militias and regional special forces would acquire new importance. Regional responses to the August 1998 currency crisis were an omen for Russia's future. *Oblast* governors banned food exports, stopped paying taxes to the center, and imposed price controls on daily necessities. If events con-

---

[169] "Plague on a Drilling Background," *Trud*, 29 October 1998, p. 5.

[170] Sergei Borovkov, "Kamchatka Sends an SOS," *Trud*, 29 October 1998, p. 2.

[171] Dmitrii Latypov and Kseniia Chebysheva, "Kuriles for Rent," *Trud*, 29 October 1998, p. 1.

[172] Vladimir Emelianenko, "Republic of Queens," *MN*, 20–27 September 1998, p. 7. Krasnoyarsk Governor Aleksandr Lebed's failure to consult with Moscow about unilaterally increasing the charges to Ukraine for storing its nuclear waste was reported without critical comment, despite its effects on Ukrainian-Russian relations. Andrei Vaganov, "The Nuclear Card of the Krasnoyarsk Governor," *NG*, 11 January 1999, p. 3.

tinued in this direction, we would expect to see special food detachments, as in the days of war communism in the first years of Soviet rule, clashing along regional lines. War would become interrepublican in nature; the center would be an impotent bystander. Moreover, under these conditions, the heretofore dormant ethnonational identities would emerge to exacerbate the fundamental "economic factors that today are ripping the country into parts."[173]

To the extent that the regions were understood as Others, or deviant Others, they were apprehended to be criminals, law-breakers, violators of the center's legal and sovereign authority.[174] Although this became more obvious in the case of Chechnia, criminalizing deviant regions also reinforced the NWR identity because it connected to the international discourse on sovereign rights, which was understood as being the domain of western powers.

Chechen Effects

The second Chechen war, commonly understood, retrospectively, as beginning with the May 1999 attack by Chechen rebel forces on Daghestani interior ministry forces in the mountains separating the two republics, but entailing as well the September 1999 bombings in Moscow, had discernible effects on Russian understandings of the relationship between the center and the periphery.

First, Russia, experienced a recentering, a recognition that it was too weak and incompetent on economic, military, and political dimensions in all discourses. Second, and in contradiction to my previous arguments about the center-periphery identity in general, the center was blamed far less for the Chechen war than were the Chechens themselves, thus opening up the possibility for a Chechen Other, something that had been foreclosed in many other regions whose independent actions were excused by the center's economic and political incapacity.

Finally, Chechnia was mostly dichotomized along nonethnonational axes. Instead of Russians understanding Chechens as an essentialized ethnic Other in opposition to the Russian ethnonational Self, the binary opposition was the lawless criminal Chechen Other versus the legally authorized sovereign Russian center. Nor was Chechnia positioned along the religious binary opposition of Islam versus Orthodoxy. In fact, Orthodoxy was almost never invoked as a way to make sense of the conflict; instead Islam itself was differentiated between the good, traditional, authentic Chechen Islam versus the fanatical, alien Islam imported from abroad. This differentiation of Islam was repeated in the distinction between good and bad Chechen

---

[173] Evgenii Anisimov, "Spring Will Not Come in Russia," *KP,* 24 November 1998, pp. 1, 3.
[174] For example, Bogoliubov, Ivanova, and Lazebnikova, *Chelovek i Obshchestvo,* 49.

leaders, good Chechen people and bad Chechen field commanders, and good and bad Moslem clergy.

Russian reporters, in the months before the war, lamented that military operations were impossible, and economic resources were unavailable, so the center could deploy neither carrots nor sticks.[175] During the war itself, the center's "paralysis of will and impotence" became an issue.[176] And the war "is not Moscow's fault. . . . By all their behavior, the field commanders demonstrate that they just cannot live without an enemy."[177] If the center was to blame, it was because it had not been vigorous enough in defending the center's prerogatives in Chechnia and in the Caucasus region more generally. Moscow was accused of having "turned its recent allies" in the region into "nonentities, criminals, and corpses."[178] Critiques of the center called for a more powerful and effective center to address whatever responsibility it had for Chechnia spinning out of control, but nobody suggested this exculpated the Chechens themselves for the war. Even reporters in the media of the Left who accused the Kremlin of being allied with Shamil Basaev, one of the field commanders, did not conclude this was a reason to weaken the Center.[179]

Even before the second Chechen war, Chechnia and the Caucasus more generally was the criminalized Other to the Russia's legally constituted sover-

---

[175] Emil Pain, "What Stands behind the Elite Reshuffling in Chechnia: Neither Carrot nor Stick," *LG*, 21 October 1998, p. 3. Pain and other observers were responding to the reported murder of Akmal Saidov, Yeltsin's official representative in the Chechen capital of Grozny. His predecessor, Valentin Vlasov, had been kidnapped in May. See also Nikolai Ivanov, "They Haven't Taken a General Hostage, but Russia," *Segodnia*, 10 March 1999, p. 2. He was writing about Moscow's inability to punish Chechnia for the kidnapping of the MVD's Grozny representative, Major General Shpigun.

[176] Nikolai Kozhanov, "Does Khasaviurt Really Threaten Dagestan?" *Pravda*, 10–11 August 1999, p. 1. Khasaviurt is the treaty concluded between Moscow and Grozny in December 1996, ending the first Chechen war. See also Milrad Fatullaev, "Russia Continues to Attack the Robbers," *NG*, 10 August 1999, p. 1; Sergei Ishchenko, "The Caucasus: Dress Rehearsal for a Big War," *Trud*, 10 August 1999, p. 1. But no one other than the Russian commander of the Federal Center's forces in Chechnia, Major General Viktor Kazantsev, rejected this criticism, asserting that "both the president and the prime minister showed resolve, occupied a very clear position, and posed concrete military missions for the armed forces." Viktor Kazantsev, interviewed by Sergei Ishchenko, "'I Will Go to the End in Chechnia'," *Trud*, 10 November 1999, p. 1.

[177] Petr Karapetian, "Uneasy Neighborhood," *KZ*, 10 July 1999, p. 3.

[178] Milrad Fatullaev, "Russia Continues to Attack the Robbers," 4. Among the center's lost allies Fatullaev identifies Bislan Gantamirov, who by November was slated by the center to replace Aslan Maskhadov, Chechnia's besieged president.

[179] Artur Ruslanov, "Heavy Price of Betrayal," *Pravda*, 10–13 September 1999, p. 1. Ruslanov, like Fatullaev, enumerates ways in which the "Kremlin" had betrayed Russia's friends in the region.

eign Self.[180] This meant that Russia was fighting separatists, rebels, bandits, kidnappers, hostage-takers, terrorists, and slave-traders in Chechnia, not Moslems or even Chechens, per se. If the last, it was a fanatical strain of Islam, alien to the authentic Chechen Moslem identity, against which Russia and good traditional nationalist Chechens were fighting.

The criminalization of Chechnia came in many guises. Pain summarizes the situation as benignly as anyone in October 1998:

> The present status of Chechnia in no small measure provokes its criminalization. After all, a territory which has legal connections with all regions of the Federation and the external world, but is not subordinate to the laws of Russia, literally attracts streams of not only stolen cars and criminals on the run, but also the most dangerous forms of criminal enterprise: the production of counterfeit money and documents, narcotics, the wholesale arms trade, the slave trade, etc.[181]

Prior to the bombings in Moscow in September, Chechens were regarded as just generic criminals. But after those bombings, it became commonplace to identify Chechen Others more specifically as terrorists, committing *terakty* (terrorist acts) against civilians in Chechnia, the Caucusus, Russia, and Moscow proper.[182] The Russian center's legal right and constitutional obligation to fight kidnappings, car-theft rings, and narcotics trafficking was hardly questionable,[183] but fighting terrorism also resonated with international legality, centering Moscow still more in the West, the keeper of international law in the post–Cold War world. This was so regardless of whether Moscow was fighting its war in Chechnia according to western understandings of international law or not. What matters was that the Russians themselves understood their Chechen Others as authorized targets of Russian military force, authorized not only by Russia's place in the federation, but by its membership in a broader western community.

[180] It is interesting that news about Chechnia in the daily *Kommersant* appeared neither in the international nor the domestic section of the paper but in the section devoted to the Commonwealth of Independent States.

[181] Emil Pain, "What Stands," 3. See also Ilya Maksakov, "New Old Conflicts in Chechnia," *NG*, 11 January 1999, p. 5.

[182] For examples not already cited, see Bella Lyaub, "Berezovskii Has a Plan for Chechnia," *Kommersant*, 17 November 1999, p. 3; Iurii Gavrilov, "There Is No Place for Terrorists on Our Land," *KZ*, 8 October 1999, p. 1. (an interview with General Kvashnin); Boris Gromov, "Authority and War," *LG*, 8–14 September 1999, p. 1 (Gromov is a Duma deputy, Hero of the Soviet Union, and retired major general who had overseen the Soviet withdrawal from Afghanistan in 1989); Konstantin Petrov, "Moskva. Gurianova, 19," *KZ*, 10 September 1999, p. 1.

[183] See, for example, Dmitri Nikolaev, "Intelligence Battle In Dagestan," *NG*, 4 June 1999, p. 5. Indeed, terrorism, banditry, and the transport of explosive devices were all explicitly punishable under the Russian criminal code.

There were good Chechens and bad Chechens, so the ethnonational features of Chechens were not essentialized.[184] Aslan Maskhadov himself, for example, was initially understood to be a good Chechen, an ally of Russia against the bandit-terrorist field commanders led by Shamil Basaev and Salman Raduev. This was true roughly until July 1999.[185] In that month, Maskhadov was typified as a good, but weak and hence ineffectual, Chechen ally.[186] By August, he was being accused of complicity with the terrorists.[187] By September, he was "essentially the protege of Wahhabis and separatists. . . ."[188] And by November, Russia was looking for a new Maskhadov, a new good Chechen, in the personage of the former mayor of Grozny, Bislan Gantamirov, who had just been released from a Russian prison.[189]

There were also good and bad Moslems, or, more precisely, authentic and alien ones. It was clear to Russian observers long before the onset of the war that "whatever support there is for Islamic rule in Chechnia is clearly inspired from above," by "Islamic extremists." The "regular" clergy, on the other hand, cautioned people against such radical acts.[190]

> Even in the citadel of Wahhabism—Urus-Martan—traditional
> Chechen communities, the kupy, are beginning to squeeze out the
> alien [*chuzhak;* it is hard to get more Other than that] Wahhabis
> from public life. Among the Chechen intelligentsia who remain
> faithful to national traditions and customs, it is understood that only

[184] I confess that this argument, that there is little evidence of racialization of Chechens in Russian discourse in 1999, has attracted by far the most skeptical responses from readers of earlier drafts of this work. Although I do not retreat from my position here, I do acknowledge that, perhaps, had more ethnographic methods been employed, that kind of ethnonational understanding might have appeared to be more prominent than in the texts alone.

[185] The rough end points are Pain, "What Stands," 3, published in October 1998, and Nikolaev, "Intelligence Battle in Dagestan," 5, published in July 1999.

[186] For example, Karapetian, "Uneasy Neighborhood," 3.

[187] Aleksandr Veklich and Anatolii Stasovskii, "They Are Involving Russia in a War in the Caucasus," *KZ*, 10 August 1999, p. 1.

[188] Ruslanov, "Heavy Price of Betrayal," 1.

[189] Marina Shirokhova and Maksim Stepenin, "Created by the UVD in Grozny," *Kommersant*, 17 November 1999, p. 1.

[190] Nikolaev, "Intelligence Battle in Dagestan," 5. See also Andrei Krasnov, "By the Laws of a Military Tribe," *KV* 7 (February 16, 1999): 22–25. He interviews Dr. Aleksei Malashenko, a member of the Carnegie Scientific Council and a researcher at the Russian Academy of Sciences Eastern Studies Institute, who assured him that Islamic law could not be introduced into Chechnia "because the corresponding social context is absent; their pre-Islamic, montane traditions have great weight" (23). See also Shoigu, "Power of Russia," 3. Shoigu, the Russian Minister for Emergency Affairs, delivered this speech to the Fifth Universal Russian Popular Sobor, held in the Danilovskii Monastery, Moscow, entiled "Russia on the Eve of the 2000th Anniversary of Christianity: Faith, People, Authority."

traditional communities [as opposed to the dangerously Other inauthentic aliens] can become the foundation of Chechen statehood.[191]

Good Daghestani, and then Chechen, people resisted the terrorists. Chechens, appalled by the taking of hostages, cooperated with the local police and security forces.[192] The Chechen community in Moscow also condemned the actions of Basaev and his forces.[193] Measures aimed at punishing Chechen terrorists in fact were criticized for unfairly affecting Chechen businessmen in Moscow.[194]

Summary

There was a great deal of discursive consensus on Russia's need to reestablish a Federal Center as the single authorized legal embodiment of the Russian state. Because the center's political and economic failings were blamed for regional moves toward autonomy, if not outright independence, the regions themselves avoided becoming Others. Instead, the Russian center's Other was its own Self because market and democratic realities were understood as perversions of a desirable abstraction situated in the West. Moreover, Chechnia, although a criminalized Other, was not binarized along religious or ethnonational axes of identification.

There were two interesting differences among the four discursive formations. The first was the greater constitutive part played by the rural and the peasantry for the NSR and, to a lesser but still significant degree, for the LE. Indeed, it could be said that the Left understood itself as part of an impoverished periphery put upon by the urban NWR rich, out of touch with rural and authentic Russia. And the NWR was contemptuous of the passive and traditional peasantry, apprehending them as obstacles on the road to modernizing progress. Meanwhile, the LE perceived elements of the Russian peasantry and rural life as fundamentally constitutive of an authentic

---

[191] Igor Zadvornov and Aleksandr Khalmukhamedov, "Moscow Has No Choice," *NG*, 10 August 1999, p. 5. Chechnia was presented to a European audience as "medieval" by Sergei Kovalev, the eminent Russian human rights activist. For the contrary view that Basaev and the field commanders and Wahhabism in general enjoyed significant authority among the good Chechen people, see Leonid Berres and Andrei Krasnov, "Hot Caucasus," *KV* 32 (August 10, 1999): 5, 10.

[192] Nikolai Gritchin, "Raid on the Slavetraders," *Izvestiia*, 29 October 1998, p. 2. On good Ingushetians, see Ilia Maksakov, "Chechnia's Borders Are Reinforced," *NG*, 10 April 1999, p. 5.

[193] Aleksandr Tolkachev, interviewed by Igor Andreev and Margarita Popova, "The Chechen Diaspora in Russia: Indignation and Fear," *LG*, 17 March 1999, p. 5. Major General Tolkachev was the head of the Section on Regional and Social Communications, Ministry of Internal Affairs.

[194] Natalia Kalashnikova, "Putin Has Closed the Caucasus," *Segodnia*, 10 November 1999, p. 1.

Russian and so was at least contiguous, if not overlapping, in identity with the Russian Left.

The second interesting element of discursive dissensus was the absence of any LR ironization of the relationship between the Federal Center and the regions, the rural and the urban, Chechnia and Moscow. It can be speculated, as was the case with European identity attributes, that those identities that were not relativized were so deeply essentialized and naturalized that not even relativists attended to them as power configurations to be challenged through ridicule or revelation. If this interpretation of missing irony is correct, then it only underlines the deep consensus in Moscow in 1999 about the need to resurrect the center as an economic and political power vis-à-vis the regions.

IDENTITY'S IMPLICATIONS FOR RUSSIA'S
UNDERSTANDINGS OF OTHER STATES

I derive testable predictions for Russia's understandings of other states based on the four discursive formations. These include each of the four formations separately, as well as the NWR-LE, NSR-LE, and NSR-LR combinations. This yields seven identity configurations on which to base expectations for Russian interests in other states, predictions that are evaluated in chapter 5.

Each identity formation had a different answer to the question of who was the Russian Self. This has implications for Russia's apprehending of other states. Which states in international politics constituted threats, which constituted potential allies, and which were irrelevant are derivable from these self-understandings. At the most general level, because of Russia's de-centering, the flattening of hierarchy, the muting of binary oppositions, and the all-round acceptance of Russia's place in a global metanarrative of modernity, there was much less threat to any of the four discursive understandings of the Russian Self. The consensus on modernity also militated against an identification with any Third World country as a potential ally.

A decentered identity alleviated the pressure on Moscow to come to the aid of its outlying parts, to help the less able, or to ensure the security and prosperity of others like it around the world or even the region. This was the opposite of the highly centered Soviet identity. The absence of hierarchy implied that Russia was not on top of an order of states whose subordination was constitutive of Russia's identity. This, too, was the opposite of the Soviet Union's position in 1955, when it was at the top and center of the world revolutionary alliance, the socialist community, and, at home, Russia and Moscow were at the top and center of the Soviet Union itself. The lack of binary opposition in the world reduced the threat to Russia's existence, both ideationally and materially. There was no imperialist Other whose raison d'etre was the destruction of the socialist camp. This reduced threat would be expected to reduce the Russian demand for allies or interest in other states as allies. Finally, Russia's place in the global metanarrative on modernity reduced any interest in states that could not contribute to Russia's transformation into a fully modern identity. Consequently, interest in the developing world approached nil. This, again, was the exact opposite of the Soviet identity, which understood the developing world as the soft underbelly of its binarized imperial Other and hence of great interest.

Given these consensual points of departure, I hypothesize that the four discursive formations have the following implications for Russian interests in other states:

- The NWR identified most closely with the United States and/or Europe, but experienced no external threats. The NWR, if predominant, would prefer to ally with those most like its understanding of itself.
- The NSR identified most closely with China or nobody and was most threatened by the United States and, to a lesser degree, Europe. The NSR would also like to ally with states most like it, but they were few and far between in the 1999 international system. The closest facsimile was China, but it had abandoned the Soviet economic system most admired by the NSR while holding onto the political system abandoned by the NSR. And certainly no alliance with Europe or the United States would be expected because they were the most extreme external Other for the NSR.
- The LE identified mostly with Europe and less so with China, but felt most threatened by the U.S. totalizing project. The LE would prefer to ally with Europe and then China over the United States because of the qualities understood to be intrinsic to authentic Russian identity that were more widely found in Europe and Asia than in the United States.
- The LR identified with nobody, but was most fearful of any totalizing, homogenizing project, such as the one emanating from Washington. The LR would ally with nobody because there was no fixed identity, either for the Self or for Others, around which a preference could be formed.
- If the predominant Russian discourse became a combination of the NWR and LE, it would still be expected that Europe would supplant the United States as the most desirable Other.
- If the predominant discourse became a combination of the NSR and LE, it would be expected to push Russia closer toward an alliance with China and then with Europe, perhaps the Orthodox European states, but not with the United States or the developing world. A NSR-LE

combination would have the most complicated implications. Transitivity would push it toward China because that is all the two discourses agreed on. But shared understandings of Russian nationalism would push it toward Europe as a second choice and shared ideas about Orthodoxy constituting the Russian nation would impel it toward choosing Orthodox allies in Europe. There would be no alliance with either the United States or countries in the developing world.

• If the predominant discourse became a combination of the NSR and LR, it would be expected to result in no alliances—a kind of isolationism punctuated by ad hoc relationships with individual states aimed at achieving narrow material, economic, military, or technological objectives, such as arms sales, nuclear technology contracts, and the provision of raw materials.

One final important observation is that the U.S. project was understood as threatening by three of the four discursive formations. Its totalizing homogenizing potential, so reminiscent of the Soviet past, alarmed the relativists; its universalizing claims worried the essentialists, who were convinced of an irreducible Russian uniqueness; and its idealized view of an unfettered market was rejected by the Left.

To the extent that a discourse values some aspect of the Russian Self, say high mass culture, an Other that threatened that value should be devalued and treated as more hostile than those other states that did not pose such a danger. Two additional examples are probably most relevant. All four discourses appreciated the Soviet past for the great power status attributed to the Soviet Union during the Cold War. Presumably, states that accorded Russia that kind of status in 1999 would be considered more favorably than those who denied such an identity. To the extent that the consensually reviled oligarchy was identified with the United States, the United States should expect to be understood as dangerous. If Europe escaped guilt by association with the United States, this should imply a closer Russian affinity with Europe than the United States.

Given the discursive consensus on the need to strengthen the center vis-à-vis the rebellious peripheries such as Chechnia, we should expect Russia to identify more with those states who were either experiencing refractory republics or who supported the sovereign right of legally constituted states to maintain their territorial integrity against such threats. This should, perhaps, push Russia closer to Yugoslavia and China, on the one hand, but also perhaps toward Europe over the United States. One way to tell that I am wrong about Europe would be if Russians in fact identified more with either Orthodox or eastern European countries than they did with either Europe more generally or western European countries.

5/

The Unipolar World
Recentering a Peripheral Russia in 1999

In 1999 Russia pursued only a fraction of the opportunities available to it to resist U.S. hegemony in the world. It did not balance against the United States in any fundamental way, not even after the expansion of NATO brought a presumably proximate military threat right up to its western frontiers. But, on the other hand, Russia did not ally with the hegemon either. It did not jump onto the unipolar bandwagon as, it might be argued, Europe and Japan more generally did; or, at least, they made no effort to get off it. What can explain this ambiguous position, between enemy and ally, neither enemy nor ally? In general, it can be said that Russia's Internal and Historical Others, the center-periphery axis, and the Soviet past elucidate Russia's ambiguous situation.

First, Russia had only five formal allies in 1999: Tajikistan, Belarus, Kyrgyzstan, Kazakhstan, and Armenia. These relationships were formalized in the 1992 Tashkent Treaty, which is often referred to as the Collective Security Treaty because each state was obliged to come to the aid of the other in event of war.[1] The findings here, unlike those about 1955, are not based on archival sources. Instead, the sources are public newspaper and journal accounts, including speeches and addresses by political elites. The four discourses discussed in chapter 4 are here associated with particular media outlets. So, the NWR discourse was most likely to be found in *Kommersant* and *Kommersant Vlast;* the LE in *Nezavisimaia Gazeta, Izvestiia, Segodnia,* and *Trud;* the NSR in *Pravda* and *Komsomolskaia Pravda;* and the LR in *Literaturnaia Gazeta.* The last was also a home for the NWR. *Krasnaia Zvezda,* although obviously a place for the military point of view, was an additional forum for the LE and, to a much lesser extent, NSR. The characterization of these newspapers according to identity formation is based on the discourses in chapter 4, not on the foreign policy implications discussed here. The separation between domestic Russian identities and their implications for con-

---

[1] This pact, which originally included Russia, Uzbekistan, Kyrgyzstan, Kazakhstan, Tajikistan, and Armenia, came into effect in 1994 for an initial period of five years and so was up for renewal in 1999. In the interim, Belarus, Georgia, and Azerbaijan had joined. But in 1999, Georgia, Azerbaijan, and Uzbekistan withdrew.

sequent Russian understandings of their external world is maintained here, as it is in the 1955 case, although the task is made more difficult, but by no means impossible, by the absence of separate archives.

Second, in 1955 the Soviet Union was in an alliance with China and the members of the Warsaw Pact, considering alliances with Yugoslavia and Egypt, and exploring a qualitatively different relationship with India. In 1999, Russia had only a handful of allies, and these were inherited from Soviet times. It was not actively seeking to form alliances with any other state. This being the case, what can be analyzed here is not so much Russia's alliance behavior as Russia's understandings of other states and how these understandings are, or are not, shaped by domestic identity discourses.

Finally, although there is enough empirical material on Russian interests and understandings to assess the hypothesized effects of the different identities and discourses on Russian apprehensions of External Others, I can only offer predictions for alliance choices per se. Although certainly falsifiable in principle, they are falsified not by the evidence presented in this book but only by future events.

Three domestic discourses, NWR, NSR, and LE, articulated themselves in the foreign policy arena as well, and these are elaborated in greater detail. Specific international episodes are interpreted from the viewpoints of the three discourses, in particular, U.S. foreign policy toward Russia, NATO's war against Yugoslavia, and Russia's union with Belarus. Concentrated attention is given to Russia's Internal Other, Chechnia, and how this relationship between the center and periphery at home was mapped onto understandings of world politics.

Chronology

August 17, 1998, the Russian ruble is devalued.

September 11, 1998, Sergei Kirienko is succeeded as prime minister by Foreign Minister Evgenii Primakov. Igor Ivanov succeeds Primakov.

December 9, 1998, Russia is invited to attend NATO'S fiftieth-anniversary celebrations to be held in Washington in April 1999.

December 18, 1998, Russia withdraws ambassadors from London and Washington to protect U.S. and British airstrikes against Iraq.

February 26, 1999, Tajikistan becomes the fifth member of the CIS customs union, joining Russia, Kazakhstan, Belarus, and Kyrgyzstan.

March 12, 1999, Hungary, Poland, and the Czech Republic join NATO.

March 20, 1999, NATO's airstrikes against Serbia begin.

April 14, 1999, Yeltsin appoints Viktor Chernomyrdin as special Russian envoy on Yugoslavia.

May 13, 1999, Sergei Stepashin replaces Primakov as prime minister.

May 13, 1999, during visit to Moscow, French President Jacques Chirac joins Yeltsin in calling for a multipolar world.

June 10, 1999, Russian troops begin to participate in the multilateral peace-keeping force in Kosovo (KFOR).

June 18, 1999, Stepashin and Yeltsin represent Russia at the Cologne G8 summit.

July 23, 1999, first meeting of Russia-NATO Permanent Joint Council since it was boycotted by Russia in March.

August 4, 1999, Russia sends troops to counter Chechen rebel incursions into Daghestan.

August 14, 1999, Vladimir Putin replaces Stepashin as prime minister.

September 9, 1999, apartment house bombings in Moscow occur.

October 1, 1999, Russian troops re-enter Chechnya in force.

December 8, 1999, Presidents Aleksandr Lukashenko and Boris Yeltsin sign Russian-Belarussian Union Treaty in Moscow.

December 31, 1999, Yeltsin resigns as president, end Putin becomes acting president of the Russian Federation.

There are six dimensions on which the different 1999 Russian foreign policy discourses significantly differed:

1. How an ethnonational Russian identity articulated itself in the understanding of Others in the world.
2. What Russian possession of nuclear weapons meant for Russia's identity and security.
3. Where Russia was situated in the center-periphery continuum of global politics.
4. The role that international law, norms of sovereignty and territorial integrity, and institutional membership played in constituting Russia's external identity.
5. The extent to which the syntax of binarization operated in a discourse.
6. The extent to which the United States and Europe were separable western Others.

There are in addition three dimensions on which there was discursive consensus:

1. NATO's war against Yugoslavia was a greater threat to Russian security than either the U.S. deployment of ballistic missile defense (BMD) or the consequences of NATO expansion.
2. Russia was the natural and legitimate center of the CIS.
3. Russian military technology and its performance continued to inspire confidence in Russia's capacity to secure its borders from attack.

THREE DISCOURCES AND THEIR FOREIGN
POLICY PREFERENCES

The New Western Russian and the Desire to Become the West

The NWR did not ethnonationalize Russian identity at home and so did not understand Others through that set of discursive markers. The absence of this identity ensured that the NWR would not have an interest in Yugoslavia or the Serbs as Slavic brothers. Moreover, it would not understand a union with Belarus as a gathering of Slavic lands, instead regarding Belarus as a Soviet artifact, both economically and politically. The NWR regarded nuclear weapons, and the deterrence they guaranteed against foreign attack, as promising a very high level of fundamental security for Russia. Membership in the nuclear club implied that Russia would be a coparticipant with the United States, France, and Britain, in the resolution of questions concerning the Comprehensive Test Ban Treaty (CTBT), and the nonproliferation of weapons of mass destruction (WMD).

Although all discursive formations wished to see Russia returned to the center of international politics, the routes were different. The NWR expected that economic reform and democratization alone would restore Russia to its rightful place in the world. Russia would not reach the center by allying with Belarus; instead, the development of a solid material economic foundation would result in Russia's restoration. But this outcome presupposed the closest possible relationship with the United States and Europe, a relationship so close it is fairer to regard it not as an alliance, but as a fusion of identity horizons, a sublimation of the Self in a closest Other—becoming the West, not allying with it.

The NWR also expected that Russian participation in international institutions, such as the UN Security Council (UNSC), the Organization for Security and Cooperation in Europe (OSCE), the Council of Europe (CE), and the G-8 would confer great power status on Russia and increase its security, as would the international norms of sovereignty and territorial integrity and norms against terrorism. This bundle of affiliations and expectations pointed toward the NWR interest in an alliance with the United States and Europe, the powers that dominated these insitutions and defended these norms.

The binarization of the External Others was notably absent from NWR discourse, as was the deployment of any kind of hierarchy of states beyond the expectation that Russia was a modern great power or on the way to that status. The absence of binarization reduced greatly the NWR perception of threats to Russian security.

The NWR was the only discourse that denied any difference between the United States and the West. It alone totalized the West into a universal teleology of democracy and liberalism. Ironically, the NWR was most like Molotov in 1955, who denied the existence of any differences within the Soviet and socialist identity, thereby denying Moscow of alliance opportunities. The NWR also denied Russia of alliance opportunities by not seeing Europe or the European countries as individual agents capable of autonomous interests and alliance preferences. This underlines the crucial similarity between Soviet and western modernities: they both homogenized difference; they both reduced choice. For the NWR, the United States and Europe were equivalent.

The absence of binarization and the conflation of the United States and Europe implied the NWR disregard of geopolitical calculations of the balance of power. With no binarized Other, there was no need to calculate one's power relative to that Other; there was no need to search for allies to balance against that Other. The only Other against which the NWR balanced was the Internal Other of Chechnia and the Historical Other of the NSR.[2] Both of these could be balanced against by allying with the same External Other: the West. The NWR believed in a benign unipolar world, led by the United States and Europe, which Russia would be only too welcome to join if it could get its economic and political identity in order at home.

According to the LE and NSR discourses, the NWR discourse had its chance to direct Russian foreign policy and failed miserably. It failed because the West was more interested in Russian weakness than in Russia's return to the center. Begun under Gorbachev and wrapped up by 1993 (these years are exactly the lifespan attributed to true democracy in Russia by Russian observers), this policy of becoming the West was associated with Gorbachev and his foreign minister, Eduard Shevardnadze, and Yeltsin and his foreign minister, Andrei Kozyrev. It was discredited by the lack of results. Russia did not become the West, either politically or economically, and the West, whether by NATO expansion or by restrictive trade practices, demonstrated an unwillingness to accept Russia's new western identity.

This discourse was finally done in by the one-two punch of the August 1998 currency crisis, which effectively discredited Russia's pursuit of the western liberal economic model, and the April 1999 NATO war in Kosovo, which discredited Russia's pursuit of a relationship with the United States and NATO as an equal partner rather than an acquiescent subordinate. These two events, combined with the continual deterioration of democratic practice within Russia since 1993, left the NWR discourse in 1999 in a state of profound crisis and isolation.

The New Soviet Russian and the Irrepressible Cold War

The NSR, identified with an essentialized ethnonational Russian and understood other states along this dimension. Consequently, the NSR was most

---

[2] I address this issue in more detail in chapter 6; it is important to note here that balancing against the Internal Other is consistent with Steven David's concept of "omnibalancing." Steven R. David, *Choosing Sides: Alignment and Realignment in the Third World* (Baltimore, 1991).

supportive of an alliance with Yugoslavia and a union with Belarus. In a move reminiscent of 1955 when Khrushchev invoked the Slavic connection to bolster his case for a rapprochement with Tito, contemporary Russian Leftists lobbied for an alliance with Belgrade on the grounds that they were members of the same Slavic brotherhood. This ethnonational connection was only redoubled in the case of Belarus. The union with Minsk was natural, not only on ethnonational grounds but also because of the common positions against western conceptions of democratization and liberalization shared by the NSR and Belarussian President Aleksandr Lukashenko.

The NWR presumed nuclear weapons made the country secure. The NSR was far less likely to understand nuclear weapons in the technical sense of bolstering Russian security through the doctrine of deterrence but instead interpreted them geopolitically, as elevating Russia's great power status and helping push it closer to the center of global affairs. This was in stark contrast to the NWR expectation that domestic westernization and international legal institutionalization and alliance with the West would have this recentering effect. The NSR credited none of these possibilities.

The NSR conceived of itself as the internal periphery of Russian politics, its rural, essentialist, ethnonational, Orthodox periphery, in opposition to the urban, western, liberal center in Moscow. Whereas the NWR understood recentering in the world as coming about through assimilation to western ways, the NSR saw it as resulting from the restoration of Russia's great power status, its reconquest of lost positions, its reemergence as a geopolitical center. One way of achieving this was through the restoration of the Union. Whereas the NWR pointed out the economic costs of such a union, the NSR trumpeted the geopolitical gains. The NSR calculated Russian interests vis-a-vis an incalcuably threatening External Other: NATO and the United States. The NWR argued that it was economically unsustainable; the NSR argued it was geopolitically rewarding. It was as if the NSR wished to resort to Leninist command-administrative methods of restoring the center and the NWR were orthodox Marxists concerned with reconstructing a material base before embarking on any new superstructural projects.

The value of Belarus to the NSR was also closely related to the fact that it constructed the world in binary terms. Not only did it see the NWR at home as the enemy (and this view was reciprocated), it saw enemies abroad—the United States, NATO, and the West more generally, in that order of threat. Indeed, the NSR regarded the NWR at home as a kind of fifth column, in alliance with the enemy abroad. Once the unipolar power was regarded as the enemy, Belarus becames a geostrategic asset. Binarization explains the NSR interest in Yugoslavia. Once the United States and NATO had arrayed themselves against Serbia in Kosovo, NSR interests in allying with Milosevic and Belgrade were intensified. (Note the utter absence of such hydraulic logic for the NWR who wish to become the West.)

The NWR did not differentiate between the United States and Europe, believing they were equivalent; the NSR did differentiate, but without consequence, believing that the United States dominated Europe, coercing it into foreign policy actions it would not otherwise undertake. It is ironic that both these perspectives denied Russia the possibility of allying with Europe against the United States, although via different logics—the NWR could not ally with Europe against the United States because they were the same; the NSR could not because European countries were under the thumb of their transatlantic hegemon.

The NSR employment of binary oppositions to situate the Russian Self and the U.S. Other ensured that geopolitical construals of the balances of power were a primary way to understand global politics. This was more or less the opposite of the NWR, for which Russia was already a candidate member of a splendidly unipolar world under benign U.S.-western hegemony. For the NSR, on the other hand, the world was bipolar: us versus them, or the United States versus Russia and, potentially, the rest of the undominated world, including China, India, Iran, Iraq, Cuba, North Korea, and the periphery more generally. For the NSR, union with Belarus and allying with Yugoslavia were balancing against the United States.

The NSR discourse on foreign policy had as much political effect as did its discourse on Russia's domestic order. It was stronger than the NWR, but it was seriously weakened by its high regard for the Historical Other's economic program. The NSR foreign policy was in large part a return to the Cold War. The allies appeared to be the same, the rhetoric was almost identical, and the theory about how the world worked was very familiar. All this worked to the disadvantage of this discourse by invoking aspects of the Historical Other, the Soviet Union, which had already been discredited.

Liberal Essentialism and the Appreciation for Legitimized Difference
Simply put, the NWR wanted to become the West; the NSR wanted to resist the West, and the LE wanted the West to let Russia be Russia. It is important to resist the reductionist temptation to merely situate LE discourse between its NWR and NSR rivals. Although the LE shared the NSR regard for the ethnonational component of Russian identity, the LE had more in common with the Left than with the NWR only on this particular dimension; the meaning of ethnonational identity for the LE was very different from its meaning for the NSR.

The absence of an ethnonational component to its identity made the NWR discourse less interested in uniting with Belarus or allying with Belgrade; the presence of an essentialized Russian identity made the NSR very interested in both union and alliance. But the essentialized Russian identity of the LE made the Slavic identity of the Serbs and Belarussians of no determinant meaning because the LE assumed that Russian ethnonational identity was unique—it might be in the same general family as other Slavs, but it was essentially incomparable to these Others. So, although it might appear as if the NSR and LE shared an ethnonational Russian identity, the meanings of this identity and the implications for alliance choices were quite at odds.

The LE expected Russian recentering in global affairs to come about through a combination of means. As did the NWR, the possession of nuclear weapons instilled the LE with confidence about Russia's fundamental security. But restoration would come through neither retreat before the West nor the reconquest of the positions held by the historical Soviet past. Instead, recentering would occur by becoming an authentically modern Russia, economically and militarily robust, spiritually and culturally genuine. In this respect, LE was not situated between the NWR and NSRs; it was orthogonal.

The LE had no binary relations with Others in international politics, but it did not occupy this nonantagonistic position because it understood Russia to be a part of a more universal western project. There were no binary relations because Russia was unique and hence not comparable, or opposable, to any other state. Russia was understood as a unique sovereign state among other unique sovereign states. There was no hierarchy of states, although implicitly great powers such as Russia were on top of a large heap of unremarked subordinate units. Its equality was assured through international legal norms of sovereignty, nonintervention, territorial integrity, and antiterrorism. Unlike the NWR, which expected these international legal guarantees to be enforced by the United States, the LE expected these norms to be community standards shared by all great powers, not subject to the unilateral interpretation of a single power. Whereas the NWR world was one of benign unipolarity and the NSR world one of binarized bipolarity, the LE world was a multipolar collection of unique, equally sovereign great powers.

Neither the NWR nor NSR saw any possibility of allying with Europe against the United States, but the LE admitted to the possibility of such an alliance because it alone appreciated the differences that separated Europe and the United States. Just as in 1955, difference in 1999 produced alliance opportunities. An interest in any particular alliance presupposes the capacity to imagine that sort of relationship with another state. The NWR and NSR discourses did not permit such imaginings; the LE discourse did.

Essentialized difference implied that alliances would not be entered into on the basis of common identity because all identities were fundamentally unique. But this did not mean the absence of a rationale for alliances; the LE felt threatened by Others in the world who could undermine Russia's identity at home. This meant that the United States was the single greatest potential threat in the world. And this implied an effort to protect Russia from both modernities—the one offered by the NWR in the form of becoming the West and the one offered by the NSR, in the form of a return to

Soviet modernity. Although protection against both these threats was primarily a domestic matter of reconstructing a genuine Russian daily life, help in the form of tactical alliances with Europe, China, Japan, or Iran was not foreclosed. But they would not be alliances of identity; they would be alliances for identity.

The LE was the discursive formation dominating Russian domestic and foreign policy in 1999. It was navigating a course that, while bluntly rejecting the NSR apprehension of the United States and the West, treated the United States and not Europe as the most likely threat to Russian identity in the world. In doing so, it sought tactical alliances in Europe (over BMD), China (over international institutional support for norms of sovereignty and non-intervention), and Iran (over a mutual interest in providing a market for Russian military technology and materiel).

Liberal Relativism, the Discourse That Did Not

The LR discourse was limited almost solely to the intelligentsia. Its ironic treatment of both modernities, the NSR and NWR, made it an implicit ally of the LE. But its rejection of all essentialisms made it the ally of no one. The LR treated both Russian allies and the threats that these relationships were supposed to mitigate as equally ridiculous and irrelevant. This discourse is not treated in a sustained manner in this chapter because it so rarely manifested itself in foreign policy. Its ironic and contrarian attitudes toward Russian interests in Serbia, its union with Belarus, and its position within the CIS are noted in passing, but these did not add up to more than a discourse of bemused indifference to the efforts of other Russians to regain the center. An important methodological lesson can be learned from the absence of LR discourse on Russian foreign policy. It shows that an interpretivist discursive analysis of domestic identity and foreign policy is falsifiable—not all discourses matter, and it is possible to show that some do and others do not.

DISCURSIVE CONSTRUCTIONS OF THREAT AND SECURITY

At the risk of reducing the complexities of the three primary discourses to a homogenized list, I offer table 3 as a comparative guide to each discourse and its implications for foreign policy themes.

The Russian Nation and Russian Foreign Policy, 1999

That Russian nationalism accounted for Russian interests in the world is too vague a claim about the role that Russia's ethnonational identity played in Russia's self-understanding and, consequently, its understanding of Others in world politics. Moreover, the most nationalistic of the discourses, the NSR, did not imply an automatic hostility toward non-Russian Others. Instead, its self-identification with an ethnic Russia only implied that some

Table 3
Three Discourses, Six Themes

	New Western Russian	Liberal Essentialist	New Soviet Russian
Russian nation	Irrelevant category of analysis	Russian uniqueness	Slavic fraternity
Nuclear weapons	Russian security guaranteed	Russian security enhanced, great power status assured	Enables great power behavior vis-à-vis the U.S.
Centering Russia	Become the West	Become the real Russia	Restore as much of the USSR as feasible
International institutions	Route to great power status	Route to great power status and security	Poor substitute for military power
Binarization and balance of power	No external binary; Russia is part of a unipolar coalition	No binaries; Russia is part of an irreducibly multipolar world	Binaries at home and abroad; bipolar competition prevails
The West	West = U.S. + Europe	West = Europe	U.S. controls the West

states, such as Ukraine, Belarus, and Yugoslavia, were more likely allies than others, say China or India.[3] It was not ethnonational identity itself that produced the binarized hostility toward the West and the United States that was so deeply characteristic of NSR discourse. This dangerous differentiation instead came from reading Russia through its internal Historical Other, the Soviet Union, and its binarized relationship with the United States.[4] Because of its overbroad usage, I do not use the word "nationalism" in this book. Instead, the idea of nation is considered a constitutive part of Soviet, and now Russian, identity, its importance and meaning intelligible only within a discursive context, whether the NSM or NSR.

The Russian Left's reporting from Yugoslavia during NATO's bombing of that country is reminiscent of Soviet reporting from there in 1955. The two Slavic brothers enjoyed a natural affinity, cemented still more by sharing the danger of NATO's assault from the air.[5]

[3] On the boundaries of a Slavic fraternity, see Sergei Pletnev, "Minsk Will Help Belgrade," *Nezavisimaia Gazeta (NG)* 10 March 1999, p. 5; Valentin Zaitsev, "Once Again about the Justice of Punishing Aggressors," *Pravda,* 10–11 August 1999, p. 3.

[4] This kind of synthesis of Soviet and ethnonational identity is apparent in Tretiakov's report on the Russian fulfillment of its "internationalist" (Soviet) duty to supply its "Yugoslav brothers" (ethnonational) with natural gas that winter. Mikhail Tretiakov, "Washington Defends Terrorists," *Pravda,* 11 November 1999, p. 3.

[5] Nikolai Varsegov, "'Around Nighttime Belgrade,'" *Komsomolskaia Pravda (KP)* 10 June 1999, p. 3.

Those who denied any ethnonational affinity between Russia and Serbia had a different understanding of Russia's interests there, its policy toward the Kosovo war, and its relations with the West and with Yugoslavia. Reflecting this official government viewpoint at the end of the war, Maksim Iusin, writing in *Izvestiia*, ridicules the fact that while Belgrade was ready to accept the cease-fire terms worked out by Yeltsin's special envoy, Viktor Chernomyrdin, Russian communists in the Duma accused Chernomyrdin of perpetrating a "second Munich," a "betrayal of our Serbian brothers." Iusin observes that the logic of the Duma "patriots" implied that Russian and Serbian national interests demanded a continuation of the war, the full destruction of the Yugoslav economy, more refugees, the complete annihilation of Yugoslav ground forces, and a crisis between the West and Moscow. Iusin accuses Ziuganov and "his comrades" of a bizarre double standard: they wanted Milosevic to continue his war in Kosovo, but where Russian interests were really threatened, in Chechnia, they wanted to impeach Yeltsin for prosecuting that war.[6]

Although Russian nationalism might seem superficially adequate to explain Russia's actions in the Kosovo war, its opposition to the United States air strikes and its support for Belgrade, in fact, ethnonational Russian identity implied a far more aggressive Russian policy over Kosovo than actually was chosen by the Yeltsin government. Instead, the failure of this very discourse to dominate and the presence of a LE self-understanding permitted Russia to participate in the endgame designed to stop the war and involve Russian peacekeeping troops on the ground in Kosovo, in alliance with NATO.

What is missing from the nationalist account of Russian foreign policy and Kosovo is the consideration of other sources, in this case discursive, of Russian interests in Yugoslavia. One such basis was the international institution of sovereignty. To the extent that sovereignty was an identity that afforded Russia great power status and the right to protect the interests of the center in Chechnia, NATO's violation of that principle in Yugoslavia was understood as a threat to Russia's interests. No ethnonational identity was necessary to imply these interests against NATO bombing of Serbia. Indeed, resorting to that "slogan in defense of brother-Slavs and Orthodox co-religionists" implied no less than "declaring war on different civilizations on the grounds of racial and religious difference. . . . Russia, comprised of different tribes [*raznoplemennaya*] does not defend Serbs, but rather the right of the peoples of Yugoslavia to freedom and independence, including Kosovan Albanians."[7] The LE and NWR alike understood that the consequences of

---

[6] Maksim Iusin, "The War in Yugoslavia Has Ended," *Izvestiia*, 10 June 1999, p. 1.

[7] Grigorii Vanin and Aleksandr Zhilin, "The Results of the War in the Balkans Are Clear Even Today," *NG*, 10 April 1999, p. 6. The equation of the right of Serbs and Kosovars is also made by Leonid Zhukhovitskii, "Russia Has Betrayed No One," *Literaturnaia Gazeta* (*LG*), 8–14 September 1999, p. 7.

basing Russian interests on an ethnonational discourse would be the multiplication of Russian interests and commitments. Instead, Russian interests should be based on a more defensible set of principles.

The NWR alone did not understand Russia's interests as being in opposition to NATO's in Yugoslavia on either ethnonational or great power grounds. Because Russia's supreme interest was to become the West, Russian opposition to NATO's bombing only undermined Russia's interests. "The orgy of nationalism with an anti-Western face in Russia" had only pushed more eastern European countries to accelerate their plans to join NATO. But the grounding of interests on Slavic brotherhood was a concept from yesterday. Instead, today in 1999, according to the NWR, interests must be based on socioeconomic categories, not geopolitical or ethnonational ones. In other words, material considerations must prevail. Finally, the NWR understood the global balance of power differently, as well, condemning "basing policy on the myths and stereotypes of the times of bipolar confrontation," this, of course, being constitutive of NSR discourse. Instead, Chernomyrdin had it right when he "took into account existing international realities" in helping to end the war.[8]

The effects of ethnonational identity, and its absence, were manifest in Russian preferences for or against an alliance with Belarus. Those who understood Russia and Belarus to be "a single nation" enthusiastically supported reunification on those grounds.[9] Opponents of this reunion, especially the NWR, understood the opposition discourse very well. It was a combination of ethnonational Russian identity and a binarized hostility toward the United States and its fifth column in Russia, the NWR. "The theme of an alliance with Belarus in political discussions has become a sacred cow—no one can dare criticize or condemn it. Immediately you will turn out to be an enemy of the 'brotherhood of Slavic peoples,' and you will get a reputation as a 'hireling of the West.'"[10]

The Roads to Recentering Russia

There were four broad avenues to recovering Russia's great power identity in world politics: military power, economic recovery, international institutional validation, and resurrection of the Union. The NWR stressed the first three, the NSR the first and last, and the LE all of them (see table 4).

---

[8] Tatyana Parkhalina, "Real Results and Imaginary Gains," *NG*, 4 June 1999, p. 3. Tatyana Parkhalina is the deputy director of the Institute for Scientific Information in the Social Sciences at the Russian Academy of Sciences; until April 1999 she was director of the Center for NATO documentation in Moscow.

[9] For example, Pavel Voronin, "There Will Be a Single State!" *Krasnaia Zvezda (KZ)*, 10 November 1999, p. 3.

[10] Aleksei Ryabov, "Sleep Enormous Country," *Kommersant Vlast (KV)*, 50 (December 14, 1999): 24–26. See also Viktor Ivanov and Vadim Bardin, "Money for the Boss!" *KV* 50 (December 14, 1999): 28.

Table 4
Three Discourses and Their Primary Paths to Russia's Recentering

	New Western Russian	Liberal Essentialist	New Soviet Russian
Military power	No	Yes	Yes
Economic recovery	Yes	Yes	No
International institutionalization	Yes	Yes	No
Recovery of the Union	No	Yes	Yes

The binary positions of the NSR and NWR were manifest, as too was the pivotal location of the LE. Table 4 shows only the primary routes; it is a matter of emphasis and degree in certain cases. For example, the NWR did not deny the effectiveness of nuclear weapons in making Russia secure; it simply did not value them as highly as economic growth or membership in the international community. Similarly, the NSR hardly opposed economic recovery; it simply placed more stress on reconstructing the remnants of the Soviet Union and maintaining Russia's military capacity.

Russians equated being in the center of world politics with being a great power. Some believed that having nuclear weapons made Russia a great power.[11] Some believed Russia was a great power by definition. As Aleksandr Meshkov, a political scientist and publicist, puts it, "Russia cannot help but conduct itself in the world as a great power. . . . Russia is fated for this role by history." As evidence for this status, Meshkov cites Russia's military technology, educated technical cadres, and natural resources.[12] A few, especially the NSR, acknowledged that Russia was not a great power, but, rather, was in the periphery.[13] The Left went further, however, accusing the United States and its fifth-column henchmen, the NWR, of deliberately consigning Russia to this peripheral status. This international position resonated with the Left's domestic position, construed as being in the rural periphery while

[11] These included a former Soviet nuclear weapons scientist and the chairman of the Duma International Affairs Committee. Boris V. Litvinov, interviewed by Vladimir Gubarev, "Warhead Sickness," *Trud*, 12 January 1999, p. 2; Vladimir Lukin, interviewed by Dmitrii Privalov, "Anti-missile Umbrella for the Entire Planet," *Trud*, 11 February 1999, p. 4. Lukin is a Yabloko member of the Duma.

[12] Aleksandr Meshkov, "About Face," *NG*, 10 April 1999, p. 3. See also Anatolii Vishnevskii *Serp i Rubl* (Moscow, 1998), 15, 405–15; Gennadii Ziuganov, interviewed by the Agency of Patriotic Information, "'Russia Is Concentrating," *Pravda*, 9–12 July 1999, p. 2.

[13] For example, Aleksandr Grigorievich Yakovlev, "Constructive Ambitions and Irrational Interests," *NG*, 12 May 1999, p. 14. He is a professor and senior scientific worker at the Russian Academy of Science's Far East Institute.

the oligarchs plundered Russia's center. Oleg Stepanenko, a reporter for *Pravda*, makes the connection between the domestic and abroad very clear: "The most dangerous are those who betray Russia while masking themselves like robbers, like Yavlinsky with his various Nemtsov props. . . . The West is trying to make us into a colony, a raw material appendage for the civilized world." What the NWR planned to do at home is "clear a place for the political, military, and financial institutions of the West" because to "stay in power," "to maintain their plundered wealth," the West must control state power here in Russia.[14]

One important area of near-consensus was the view that nuclear weapons, even if they did not necessarily make Russia a great power, did nonetheless provide a certain heightened level of physical security, especially against the United States. This confidence in Russia's ultimate security was most widely expressed in the military, but appeared also in the writings of the Right, Left, and Center. The Russian defense minister, the commander of Russia's strategic nuclear missiles, the general in charge of drafting Russia's new military doctrine, the text of that doctrine itself, a retired weapons scientist, and a host of military commentators all endorsed the notion that strategic nuclear deterrence still worked and made Russia more secure.[15] Authors associated with the Right, Center, and Left all supported this consensual position. The NSR writer even went so far as to argue that Russia's nuclear doctrine must be effective because it was so similar to that of the United States![16]

This consensus on Russia's nuclear security might help explain, along with the Chechen dimension, why United States plans to deploy BMD were not treated as anywhere near as threatening to Russian security as NATO's war against Yugoslavia. Although of course U.S. BMD would be better left

[14] Oleg Stepanenko, "First Step toward a Fraternal Union," *Pravda*, 9 December 1999, p. 3. Note that the language Stepanenko uses to describe Russia's current fate, "raw material appendage," is precisely the language used in Soviet times to describe the decolonized world's place in imperialism's grasp. See also Richard Ovinnikov, "Imperialism Will Get on the Rack," *Pravda*, 9–12 July 1999, p. 3; Viktor Onuchko, "Scottish 'Hawk' Changes His Nest," *Pravda*, 10–11 August 1999, p. 3.

[15] Igor Sergeev, "Two Weeks Ago Russia Used Nuclear Weapons," *NG*, 10 July 1999, p. 2. Defense Minister Sergeev's press conference reported by Vladimir Georgiev. Viktor Smirnov, interviewed by Ilshat Baichurin and Aleksandr Dolinin, "Does Russia Have a Cosmic Vision?" *KZ*, 8 October 1999, p. 2. Colonel General Smirnov is the deputy chief of staff of the Strategic Rocket Forces for Missile Space Defense. Valerii Manilov, "Russia's New Military Doctrine," *KZ*, 8 October 1999, p. 1. Colonel General Manilov is first deputy head of the General Staff of the Russian Federation Armed Forces and was the director of the commission on developing the new doctrine. "Military Doctrine of the Russian Federation," *KZ*, 9 October 1999; available from http://news.eastview.com/oo/KZV/10/data/217kz31.htm, Litvinov, "Warhead Sickness" *Trud*, 2.

[16] Marina Eratova, "So That There Won't Be a Command to Fire!'," *Pravda*, 9 December 1999a, p. 2; Ilya Bulavinov, "Hawk Song," *KV* 15 (April 13, 1999): 24–25; Iurii Golotiuk, "Orbital Defense of Russia," *Izvestiia*, 10 November 1999, p. 1.

undeployed, this preference was largely borne of concern for the additional costs of countering it, not for fear of Russia's being stripped of its second strike capability in the event of nuclear war. At worst, its deployment would show Washington's continuing unipolar arrogance, rather than a direct threat to Russia's security.[17]

International institutionalization did not so much refer just to membership in particular organizations, such as the World Trade Organization (WTO) or the G-8. What was more important to the constitution of Russian identity as a great power were the international norms that were embedded in these institutions, norms such as sovereignty, territorial integrity, juridical equality, multilateral decision-making, and the like. Each of these norms, and more, helped maintain Russia's great power status, its position in the center of world politics. With the exception of the NSR, these institutions and their associated norms were highly valued in Russian foreign policy discourse in 1999. Moreover, it was through the U.S. violation of these valued norms that Washington became a threat to the NWR and LE because of NATO's war against sovereign Yugoslavia. It was the parallel between Chechnia and Kosovo, their identities as part of the periphery riddled with terrorists, their challenge to a sovereign, legally constituted center, that turned NATO into a threat to Russia, not BMD deployment, not NATO expansion, and not binarization through the Soviet past.

Russian interests in the Kosovo conflict ran through its identity in Chechnia, the legitimate, although weakened center fighting against the illegitimate rebels, the terrorist separatists who were violating international law and challenging the norms that constituted Russia as a sovereign state with inviolable boundaries. Recall from chapter 4 that the Chechen rebels were understood as terrorists. In a similar fashion, the Kosovo Liberation Army (KLA) was not infrequently referred to as terrorists, and not, as might be expected, exclusively by the Left.[18] The effects of Chechnia were sufficiently dangerous to warrant inclusion in the new Russian military doctrine adopted in October 1999. "The strengthening of national-ethnic and religious extremism and separatism" are both identified as "main features of the military political situation." Organized crime, terrorism, and the illegal arms and drug trade, all activities normally identified with Chechen rebels, are identified as one of the "main destabilizing factors of the military political situation." Interference in Russia's internal affairs, that is, foreign support

---

[17] See, for example, Vladimir Lukin, "Anti-missile Umbrella for the Entire Planet," *Trud*, 11 February 1000, p. 4; Iurii Pankov, "America Says Good-bye to Disarmament," *KZ*, 10 August 1999, p. 3.

[18] Iurii Pankov, "Five Occupation Zones in Kosovo," *KZ*, 10 June 1999, p. 3; Mikhail Tretiakov, "We Should Not Be in Kosovo for Nothing," *Pravda*, 9–12 July 1999, p. 1; Vanin and Zhilin, "Results," 6.

for the Chechen rebels originating in Afghanistan, Pakistan, and Saudi Arabia, is "one of the main external threats" to Russian security. The language in the doctrine links this external threat to "one of the main internal threats," separatism and terrorism.[19] Chechen rebels were terrorists, the KLA was a terrorist organization, and terrorism threatened Russia's security. But Russians were heartened by the fact that another great power, the United States, was also threatened by terrorism. Indeed, the very same terrorist, Osama Bin Laden, putatively threatened both countries.[20] This common interest against terrorism only made U.S. support for the terrorists in Kosovo that much more threatening to Russia. If the United States acted against its own interests there in Kosovo, might it not do so as well here in Chechnia?

In general, it was expected that international law would work in favor of maintaining and elevating Russian status as a great power in the world. The Russian military repeatedly voiced support for a "world of sovereign equality, balance of interests, international legal norms" and adherence to established decision-making procedures in the UNSC and the OSCE. Valerii Manilov, in particular, in introducing Russia's new military doctrine, contrasts this model of international politics to one "based on the dominance of one superpower and the military resolution of global problems." Manilov singles out "NATO aggression against sovereign Yugoslavia" as an example of the disfavored "tendency."[21]

Russia felt the constraining effects of the UNSC and OSCE had been violated by United States and NATO actions in Yugoslavia.[22] These institutions were to substitute for material Russian power in affecting U.S. and NATO decisions to use force in Yugoslavia and elsewhere. The concern with U.S. unilateralism, with U.S. circumvention of the influence that Russia

---

[19] "Military Doctrine of the Russian Federation," 3–7. The doctrine's text itself makes no explicit mention of Chechnia, but it is no great stretch to see the close similarity in language. Moreover, when Colonel General Manilov held a news conference to unveil the new doctrine his team had authored, he explicitly identified Chechnia as the reason for these passages and others. See Manilov, "Russia's New Military Doctrine," 1.

[20] The equation of Russian and U.S. interests against terrorism was common and widespread across discourses. For example, see Anatolii Andreev, "The MVD and FBI Will Cooperate," *Trud*, 10 September 1999, p. 4; Elena Tregubova, "Istanbul Waits for Yeltsin and Extremists," *Kommersant*, 17 November 1999, p. 1; Vladislav Dunaev, "America Is in the Gun Sites of Terrorism" *NG*, 10 February 1999, p. 6; Oleg Moroz, "Foreign Countries Are Again against Us," *LG*, 20–26 October 2000, p. 3; Dmitrii Gornostaev, "The State Department Has Given Us an Order?" *NG*, 10 November 1999, p. 3; Pyotr Aleksandrov, "Russia Should Not Lose Its Own Dignity," *Pravda*, 9 December 1999, p. 3.

[21] Manilov, "Russia's New Military Doctrine," 1. See also Leonid Ivashov, "We Succeeded in Defending Russian Interests," *KZ*, 10 December 1999, pp. 1, 3. Colonel General Ivashov is chief of the Section on International Military Cooperation in the Russian Defense Ministry.

[22] See, for example, Dmitrii Privalov, "Russia and China Are as Close as Ever," *Trud*, 10 December 1999, p. 1.

could exert within these multilateral institutions, was fixed in Russia's new military doctrine. Russians also recognized that they could recover a more central position vis-à-vis the former Soviet republics, at least on one issue—the Russian diaspora's citizenship rights, especially in the Baltic states. Even military commentators, in criticizing Latvia's language law, did so in the context of what European institutional obligations implied for Latvian behavior, not what the Russian government, itself, desired.[23] Indeed, what consequences awaited the Latvian government for violating "international and European legislation"? Not Russian action—instead, Russian interests would be served by suits brought in the Human Rights Court in Strasbourg and the "redoubled attention" of the CE human rights monitors.[24]

But there was a tension among the rights that international institutions conferred on Russia in its fight against Chechen terrorism, separatism, and trade in narcotics, arms, and hostages; the constraints these insitutions promised against unilateral U.S. military actions; the normative protection offered to Russians living in the near abroad; and the obligations those same institutions imposed on Russia. We can see this tension in Russia's new military doctrine. On the one hand, it explicitly bound Russia to adhere to UNSC resolutions and Russian Federation treaty obligations when deploying and using Russia's armed forces within the CIS; moreover, it pledged to create special peacekeeping forces designed to meet Russia's UN, OSCE, and CIS obligations. On the other hand, the doctrine is silent about Russia's international obligations when using its military forces within the Russian Federation in its domestic periphery, in places such as Chechnia. Apparently, it is denied that the international institutions that promised to empower the Russian center might, as well, reduce its capacity to tame its rebellious periphery.[25]

But many recognized not only the contradiction, but the danger embodied in the U.S. actions in Kosovo—that the international norms used to justify the "humanitarian intervention" in Kosovo could threaten Russian efforts to control its Chechen periphery. Richard Ovinnikov cites no less an authority than former U.S. Secretary of State Henry Kissinger on the subject, reporting that Kissinger realized that as a result of NATO's war against Kosovo "countries concerned that they could end up the target of unilateral NATO actions can distance themselves from us [the United States]. . . . They will be stimulated to acquire weapons of mass destruction as the most reliable deterrence against American conventional superiority."[26] Although Kissinger was referring primarily to states without nuclear, chemical, or bi-

---

[23] Aleksei Lyashchenko, "Riga Has Ignored Europe," *KZ*, 10 July 1999, p. 3.

[24] Svetlana Sukhova, "My Tongue Is My Enemy," *Segodnia*, 10 July 1999, p. 3. See also Karen Markaryan, "Now in Latvia One Must Hold One's Tongue in Russian," *KP*, 10 July 1999, p. 2.

[25] "Military Doctrine of the Russian Federation," 18–21.

[26] Ovinnikov, "Imperialism Will Get on the Rack," 3.

ological weapons, Ovinnikov justifies Russian concerns over the adequacy of its deterrent based on these remarks.

Vadim Markushin, a military analyst, writes wistfully about the good old days of NATO, when its mission of collective defense was grounded in accepted international law. But in 1999, after Kosovo, the new mission of "humanitarian intervention" only "gives carte blanche to the use of force for practically any reason—[such as] separatist squabbles" of the kind going on in Chechnia. And, just as Ovinnikov concludes that Russia needed to take military measures against this new threat, so too does Markushin.[27]

Valeriya Sycheva brings the threads of Russian concern together, noting that NATO had published a new textbook on its fiftieth anniversary in which "the concept of sovereignty is practically diminished" and NATO arrogated to itself the "right to severely punish any violator of democratic principles in any country." She rhetorically asks, "Are public whippings now inscribed in international pedagogy?" She differentiates between the UNSC, which had "also resorted to such instructive methods," and NATO on the grounds that the latter had few members. "Following the logic of NATO," Russia would find itself in the periphery, "the map of the world could easily become a mosaic of dwarf-states next to the US and Europe." But she concludes, unlike her communist and military colleagues, that meeting this challenge "in the military area for Russia is pure suicide."[28]

Consistent with the NWR discourse that found security in becoming the West, Leonid Sborov points out helpfully that as long as Russia was ruled by people who the West cannot consider "odious figures," Chechnia would not become Kosovo. He writes that the world community supported the Iraqi Kurds, Kosovars, and Congolese because it had its Saddam Hussein, Slobodan Milosevic, and Laurent Kabila. But "Chechens, Kashmiris, and Turkish Kurds share the absence of odious figures in the camp of their enemies." Moreover, the international community would only support "secular, non-communist, non-authoritarian movements." Therefore, Chechens, Islamists, Turkish Kurds, indigenous Mexicans, communists, and Afrikaaners would not be supported.[29] In sum, as long as the Russian Self became or remained close to the western Other and Chechens remained Others to the western Self, Russia need not fear Chechnia becoming Kosovo.

It is revealing to see how the different discourses reacted to the threat to Russian security posed by the U.S. violation in Yugoslavia of the norms of

---

[27] Vadim Markushin, "NATO Abolishes 'Non-offensive Defense'," *KZ*, 10 June 1999, p. 3. See the interview with Colonel General Ivashov, who was involved in the Chernomyrdin mission to convince Slobodan Milosevic to accept NATO's peace terms, wherein he expresses concern about the fate of sovereignty as a principle of international law after Kosovo. Ivashov, "We succeeded in Defending Russian Interests," 1.

[28] Valeriya Sycheva, "Geopolitics Textbook for Bomber Pilots," *Segodnia*, 10 April 1999, p. 3.

[29] Leonid Sborov, "He Who Can, Separate!" *KV* (April 13, 1999): 32–35.

the sovereign right of a nation to fight separatism and terrorism within its borders without fearing violations of its territorial integrity. Those most alarmed were the Left; all except the NWR stressed the military capacity of Russia to prevent a repetition of Kosovo in Chechnia, although the Left was most consistent in holding out the threat of such a U.S. action. Only the NWR expressed confidence that Kosovo was not Chechnia because Chechens were not Kosovan Albanians but rather Moslem terrorists, whom the United States and Russia both were interested in destroying. We can infer from these writings that the NWR expected Russian security to come from Russia's becoming the West, that is, by its participating in the punitive actions against states deemed to have violated the hegemonic norms. The NSR preferred to rely on increasing Russian military capacity. The LE, on the other hand, found solace in Russian nuclear capacity, but was not at all as enthusiastic about beefing up the Russian military in general, and was far closer to the NWR in believing in the need for Russia's place in international institutions, if not in becoming the West.

The Left desired the reconstruction of the center through retrieving the Union, whereas the NWR and LE preferred constructing a material economic basis for great power status. The differences among the discourses were most apparent in the treatment of a union with Belarus. There were three ways in which Belarus was understood as an ally: as a part of the Soviet Union that never should have ended its relationship to Moscow, as a strategic military asset in the binary competition with the United States, and as a natural ethnonational brother.[30] Oleg Stepanenko, and other authors in the communist press, argues that union with Belarus not only was a "vital need" for Russia, but connected Russian domestic opposition to a union to the West and, hence, to unpatriotic fifth-column actors. As evidence, he relates that when Russian and Belarussian negotiators discussed a common currency, representatives of Russia's central bank said, "we can't; we have IMF [International Monetary Fund] obligations. Essentially, Russian leaders . . . operate under the diktat of the West."[31]

The Left wished to strengthen the center by accumulating more subordinate peripheries, whereas the Right and Center wished to strengthen the center itself. The collection of themes for the Left is familiar: ethnonational identification, a binarized enemy necessitating a military asset, and a historical illusion as contemporary ally.

The opposition to the union with Belarus shared none of these ways of

---

[30] Natalya Airapetova, "Russia and Belarus Are Entering the New Century in a Single Union," *NG*, 9 December 1999, p. 1; Smirnov, "Does Russia Have a Cosmic Vision?" 2; Voronin, "There Will Be a Single State!" 3.

[31] Oleg Stepanenko, "Hard Path to Union," *Pravda*, 10–13 September 1999, p. 3.

situating itself. Instead, the argument was against the union on the grounds that Belarus would be an economic burden, that it was undemocratic, and that its inclusion in a special relationship with Russia would only instigate other subjects of the federation, in particular Tatarstan, Bashkiria, and Daghestan, to demand similar arrangments, thereby setting off a centrifugal weakening of the center.

Unlike the NSR advocates of union, who almost never acknowledged any costs associated with the joining of Russia and Belarus, its opponents recognized that although increased territory and more efficient transportation routes to the West would be nice, its economic cost outweighed any foreseeable gain.[32] The Belarussian economic policies that the NSR found attractive as resonant of a Soviet past were seen by the NWR and LE alike as being "too Soviet" and hence incompatible with Russia's present, let alone future, economic order.[33] The mismatch between base and superstructure is pointed out by Grigorii Yavlinskii, who calls the idea of union "a thoughtless political adventure. . . . A political merger cannot supercede the economic realities."[34] Yavlinsky expresses a logic that was precisely contrary to his binary opponent, the NSR, which wished to put the political cart, union, before the material horse, economic reform. The idea that Belarus could ever carry out effective measures, especially under Lukashenko, was met with derisive ridicule, which yielded the hope that the union was impossible.

Konstantin Smirnov reports that

> to introduce the economic reforms agreed to by the Russian Federation Central Bank deputy head Oleg Mozhaiskov, who developed the plan for a common Russian-Belarussian currency, including complete market reforms, monetarization of the economy, affirmation of legal order in economic life, full mutual convertibility of both currencies, and the reduction of budget deficits and government debt to levels required for Euro membership, will take not 8–10 years, but no less than 100.[35]

It was further sarcastically observed that it might be cheaper to have Belarus in the union because there it would be just another hapless claimant on the federal budget, whereas now it was free to buy subsidized Russian oil and natural gas and resell it at world market prices, pocketing the difference.[36]

---

[32] Elena Yermolenko, "Union of Soviet Socialist Illusions," *LG*, 13 January 1999, p. 2.

[33] Semen Novoprudskii, "Impossible Happiness," *Izvestiia*, 9 December 1999, p. 1.

[34] Grigorii Yavlinskii, "'SoBeRus' Left until Fall," *Segodnia*, 10 July 1999, p. 2. Reported by Sergei Mulin.

[35] Konstantin Smirnov, "Friends, Our Union Is Horrible," *KV* 28 (July 13, 1999): 38.

[36] Ivanov and Bardin, "Money for the Boss" 28. For an ironic treatment of Russian's ethnic ties to Lukashenko, see Ales Myakina and Andrei Bagrov, "Minsk Dynamo," *KV*, 13 July 1999, p. 5.

Whereas the NSR expected that a union with Belarus would strengthen the Russian center, the NWR and LE expressed the fear that it would instead lead to its weakening. "According to Russian and Belarussian political scientists, economists, and lawyers who have studied unification in detail, it will provoke in Russia a centrifugal process which will lead to the disintegration of the Federation. . . ."[37] More specifically, both Mintimer Shamiev, Tatarstan's president and Salman Aushev, Daghestan's president, demanded that their autonomous areas receive the same level of autonomy that Belarus received in any union. They were joined by Murtaz Rakhimov, the Bashkir leader.[38]

Although opposition to the union was situated more in the LE concern with economic cost than in the NWR concern with democracy and human rights, at least one Russian opponent of union, Anatolii Kozlovich, reported that the International League of Human Rights and Amnesty International had both comdemned the arrest and jailing of demonstrators against the union in Minsk.[39] There was just too much difference between Russia and Belarus to countenance a union of Others.

The pragmatic arguments for and against union, strategic gains versus economic cost, were embedded in the various discourses. Whereas the NSR wanted the union despite Belarus's economic problems, or perhaps because the Belarussian economy was closer to its understanding of what Russia's economy should be, both the NWR and LE opposed or were wary of the union precisely because of the Belarussian economy's weakness and vestigial Soviet features. The NSR understood Belarus through its own Historical Other, the Soviet past. But so too do the NWR, which rejected that Other and, further, situated Belarus in a binary opposition to its own western Self. The LE also understood Belarus through a partially rejected Soviet Historical Other, but were affected by its economic pragmatism. The actual outcome, the policy adopted by the Primakov, Stepashin, and Putin governments in 1999, rejected both the NSR identification with Belarus and the NWR anathemization of Belarus; instead, the LE position was adopted, one of slow and methodical merger, but only as long as Belarus became more like Russia, which, to a significant degree, meant becoming more like the West, at least in economic terms.

Binarization and the Balance of Power: Three Discursive Alternatives
A discourse's reliance on binary oppositions to situate Self and Other inheres to a dichotomized view of the world, one that admits to no gray areas, one in which another state is either Self or Other with no intermediate definitions permissible. This was what made the differences between Molotov,

---

[37] Anatolii Kozlovich, "Slaughter in Minsk," *LG*, 20–26 October 1999, p. 1.

[38] Evgenii Krutikov, "Unequal Marriage," *Izvestiia*, 9 December 1999, p. 1.

[39] Kozlovich, "Slaughter in Minsk," 1.

on the one hand, and Khrushchev and Mikoyan, on the other hand, so palpable in apprehending Yugoslavia's place in the Soviet world in 1955. In
1999, the same differences were clear. The NSR had binarized the world
into Russia, understood through the Soviet Historical Other, versus the
United States and its subordinated West. It was a strictly bipolar world, one
in which a (neo)realist account of world politics would not be out of place.
But it was only one interpretation of the world and not the one that dominated Russian foreign policy.

The NWR had a binarized Other too, but it was at home—the NSR. In foreign affairs, there was a closest Other, the West, which the NWR wanted to
become. Hence, a unipolar western, or U.S., hegemony was not a threat but
a club whose membership Russia should seek. The LE, confident in the ontological security of a single Russian Self, along with multiple nonthreatening Others (including other Russian Others) understood the world as a place
of multiple great powers, each meaningfully different from one another.

In its most elaborate articulation, the world was divided between the United
States and its western subordinates, on one side, and Russia, with its Eurasian
geopolitical responsibilities, on the other. Aleksandr Dugin, a Gosduma
member from the National-Bolshevik Party and a well-known geopolitician,
argues that "any conflict . . . must be connected to those global forces which
compete at the planetary level." These words could have begun any *Kommunist* article on foreign policy in the Soviet Union from 1949 to 1989. "We
are talking about the competition of the Atlanticist pole with the Eurasian
pole. . . . " Whereas during the Cold War there was a real bipolar competition, in 1999 the conflict was between "a real Atlanticist pole and a potential Eurasian one," Russia. It is a very short step from understanding the
world in these binary terms to attributing threatening intentions to the
other pole. According to this view, the United States aspired to prevent
a Russian-Chinese alliance because this would strengthen the Eurasian
pole.[40] Pursuant to this concern, the United States aimed to "create chaos
on Russia's southern border," including supporting Chechen rebels, although indirectly through Saudi Arabia and Pakistan. China's position as a
potential ally against the United States was strengthened by NATO's bombing of Yugoslavia. Understanding China through Chechnia led Russian analysts to see China as equally threatened by NATO's intentions to impose
"humanitarian interventions" on other states suffering from separatist
groups. Here China would have in mind Taiwan and Sinkiang, at least at
first.[41] At Yeltsin's meeting with Chinese president Jiang Zemin, they agreed

---

[40] Aleksandr Dugin, interviewed by Igor Yadykin, "Caucasus Footprints of Atlanticism,"
KZ, 10 September 1999, pp. 2–3. On this point, see also Yakovlev, "Constructive Ambitions
and Irrational Interests," 14.

[41] Aleksandr Reutov, "'Anti-western' Visit of Yeltsin," *NG*, 9 December 1999, p. 1.

in a joint statement condemning those who aspired to unipolar hegemony.[42]

To see how binarization produced an understanding of the Self through an Other, we need only look to Dugin's strategic advice: "We must answer with completely symmetrical tactics, i.e., support Eurasian Islam. . . . and since Atlanticists continue to see us as their main geopolitical opponent, we need to introduce into our military doctrine and national security concept the completely symmetrical formulation . . . which fully reproduces—only with the reverse sign—the Western model." Dugin moves quickly to the domestic binary and its foreign policy analogue. The "pro-Atlanticist craze which existed in our society, [the NWR], began with the boundless Gorbachev admiration of the West, continued with the collapse of the Soviet Union, and ended practically with the complete renunciation of our territory, when many representatives of the intelligentsia and politicians took openly pro-Chechen positions." In other words, the NWR advocated the continued weakening of the center, its surrender to the periphery. Its adherents at best, were the unwitting allies of the enemy, the West. Dugin concludes that fortunately NATO's war against Kosovo had discredited the NWR and, in general, spurred a "process of geopolitical enlightenment" at home. This effort was aided by the candid pleas by Zbigniew Brzezinski in his book, *Global Chessboard,* that the United States encourage Russia's dismemberment.[43] It always helps to binarize the Other when it cooperates by providing evidence of its malign intentions.

This binary logic ended up in the new Russian military doctrine. The significant difference was that the United States itself was not identified as the Other but rather its collection of unipolar practices were. The Soviet gloss to the document was manifest: "The main contradictions of the contemporary epoch [this is the language used by general secretaries of the CPSU when delivering their addresses at party congresses] . . . consists of the contradiction between two tendencies: the first model is based on the dominance of a superpower and military-forceful resolution of problems of world politics." The examples offered by Manilov included Yugoslavia. "The second is equality of peoples and nations, consideration and guaranteeing the balance of interests of states, and the observation of fundamental norms of international law."[44] Note the absence of the Dugin or NSR formulation of Eurasia headed by Russia versus the United States. Instead, there were prin-

---

[42] Privalov, "Russia and China," 1.

[43] Dugin, "Caucasus Footprints," pp. 2–3. Like Brzezinski's writings, William Wohlforth's article, "The Stability of a Unipolar World," *International Security* 24:1 (summer 1999), 5–41, is cited by Richard Ovinnikov as evidence that the U.S. believes it has already "achieved irreversible domination of the globe." In "View of the World through a Gun Sight," *Pravda*, 11 November 1999, p. 3.

[44] Manilov, "Russia's New Military Doctrine," 1. See also "Military Doctrine of the Russian Federation," 3.

ciples of international relations held by some states, mostly the United States, and other principles held by other states, including Russia. Clearly, the alliance opportunities for the second characterization, especially within the West, were available in this conceptualization, but not in the binarized world assumed by the NSR.

U.S. actions in Yugoslavia led Russians who were not so radically situated as Dugin to adopt a binary way of thinking about the situation. Dmitrii Gornostaev writes, even if regretfully, that "unfortunately, when NATO brandishes its arms, then Russia must do the same thing. . . . Moscow has only two choices: either recognize its impotence [its decentered position] or make threats which can exert a moderating influence on NATO's leadership." The author advocates that Moscow remind NATO of its nuclear potential, if only as a bluff.[45]

Binarization was associated with a focus on the global balance of power, geopolitics, and the global effects of events not on Russian borders as long as they could be associated with U.S. actions. According to *Pravda*'s Marina Eratova, Russia and China were the real targets of NATO's war in Yugoslavia. Why? Because "only these two states can resist US expansion." The very next NATO military operations would unfold against Belarus, then Iran and Iraq, she opines.[46] Russia's mission must be to maintain the balance of power in Eurasia, Ziuganov says.[47]

One of the critical differences between the NSR and LE was in their reaction to this U.S. bid for unipolar hegemony. Whereas the NSR understood the situation as one of bipolar binarized hostility beween the Russian-led Eurasian bloc and the United States, the LE suggested the world was essentially multipolar. No Russian leadership, no Russian location on top of some hierarchy, at the head of some vanguard, was assumed. This was most unlike the NSR, which continued to strongly remind everyone of Soviet identity in 1955.

The emergence of unipolarity was an anathema to the NSR, and was opposed by the LE, too. Only the NWR accepted unipolarity with aplomb. This was because the hegemon was understood as the NWR itself; its binary Other was at home, in the form of the NSR. It was happy to have the United States set the tone for the world because that was the future of Russia. As we have seen from Dugin's writings, the NSR returned the favor by binarizing the NWR and their U.S. allies as the Others for Russia.

Instead of a binarized, polarized world of dichtomous denial, the NWR tended to understand the time as one of *vseobchchee mezhdunarodnoe slizhenie*

---

[45] Dmitrii Gornostaev, "The Cuban Missile Crisis Can Be Repeated in the Balkans," *NG*, 10 April 1999, pp. 1, 3.

[46] Marina Eratova, "Everything Is Going According to Plan," *Pravda*, 11–14 June 1999, p. 3.

[47] Ziuganov, "'Russia Is Concentrating'," 2.

or (overall international convergence).[48] Essentially, the U.S. version of modernity had won. It was time for Russia to join the bandwagon and benefit from the embrace of the United States, NATO, and Europe. Resistance was not only futile and pointless; it was completely unnecessary because Russia would become precisely what it should become in any case—the West.

In what might be called a foreign policy manifesto of sorts for the NWR, Boris Semin and Abdul-Khakim Sultygov, both economics graduate students in Moscow, published a full-page article in *Nezavisimaya Gazeta* in July, entitled "Unconstructive Ambitions or Rational Interests," in which they laid out the program for becoming the closest Other, the West. As the first major departure from the NSR discourse,[49] these two scholars embrace Brzezinski's prescriptions for Russia, rather than citing it as evidence of U.S. hegemonic aspirations. They cite the inveterate cold warrior's opinion approvingly that Russia should concentrate on being recognized as democratic with a "full-fledged market economy." Semin and Sultygov infer the following foreign policy tasks for the achievement of this identity:

1. Initiate a strategic economic and military-political partnership with the United States and Britain and an all-encompassing partnership with Germany and Japan.
2. Support NATO expansion and a U.S. military presence in Europe.
3. Develop a strategic partnership with Ukraine.
4. Integrate Russia into European institutions.
5. Initiate joint nuclear forces with the United States.
6. Escort or accompany U.S. influence in the world, including in the CIS.
7. Transform Russian in its relations with post-Soviet states from a geopolitical player into a geopolitical center, following the example of Japan, to operate under the protection of the United States, having become a geopolitical extension of U.S. power.[50]

With the exception of allying more closely with Ukraine, these foreign policy positions would be rejected *tout court* by the NSR. They reflect an al-

[48] Nikolai Dolgopolov, "Quiet Wars," *Trud*, 12 January 1999, p. 4. Dolgopolov was not necessarily a NWR adherent himself.

[49] It is as if Francis Fukuyama's popular and controversial arguments about the triumph of liberalism at the end of the Cold War had found a very receptive audience among NWR adherents.

[50] Boris Semin and Abdul-Khakim Sultygov, "Unconstructive Ambitions or Rational Interests?" *NG*, 10 March 1999, p. 14. Selim is the director of an expert council at the A. Avtorkhanov Institute of Humanitarian-Political Technologies and Sultygov is the director of the institute. Both are economics graduate students there. For a detailed NSR rebuttal of this NWR manifesto, see Yakovlev, "Constructive Ambitions and Irrational Interests," 14.

most absent external Other for the NWR. But there was still the NSR, the Internal Other, which, in combination with western neglect, was thwarting Russia's desire to become the West. Semin and Sultygov write that the "Clinton Administration has thrown out the baby with the bath water, democratic Russia with communism." Citing George Soros, they agree that "Western countries have missed the opportunity to aid the transition of Russia from socialism to capitalism." They compare generous U.S. aid to Germany after World War II with the miserable pittance Russia has received, but they place the primary blame on the Historical Other, the communists, who should have been banned after the Soviet collapse, just as the Nazis were after Germany's defeat.[51]

This understanding is further manifest in how the balance of power, and geopolitics more generally, fit into NWR discourse. Roughly speaking, the balance of power in world politics was a working ontology for all discourses, even the LR. The NSR saw the balance of power almost exclusively in material military terms, with two predominant poles, Eurasian and Atlanticist, vying for control over the international system. But this was not how the NWR comprehended it. First of all, power to this discourse was primarily economic and institutional, not military. As Tatyana Parkhalina writes in the context of NSR geopoliticians calling for Russian intervention in Yugoslavia, "geopolitics is yesterday's concept. Russia needs to form its national state interests not in geopolitical, but in socioeconomic categories. The 'grandeur of power' is defined not by the quantity of missiles, planes, and tanks, but by rates of economic growth, quality of life, and cultural influence, i.e., qualitative, not quantitative characteristics."[52] Second, there is no *balance* of power because there already was only one predominant, and legitimate, hegemonic pole in world politics, the United States and the West. Further, the NWR understood the balance of power as a way to measure just how weak Russia was and so just how necessary it was to become the West. So, while the NSR was declaiming as *capitulationist* Chernomyrdin's efforts to end the war in Kosovo, the NWR hailed his efforts as the most sensible of policies given the prevailing balance of power.[53]

That the world was multipolar and not unipolar appears both in LE texts and in the new Russian military doctrine.[54] The LE was well aware that the

---

[51] Semin and Sultygov, "Unconstructive Ambitions or Rational Interests?," 14.

[52] Parkhalina, "Real Results and Imaginary Gains," 3.

[53] Ibid.

[54] "Military Doctrine of the Russian Federation," 3–4; Manilov, "Russia's New Military Doctrine," 1; Kamaludin Gadzhiev, *Vvedenie v Geopolitiku* (Moscow, 1998), 267–72; Andrei Kokoshin, interviewed by Aleksandr Tsipko, "Not Everything Is Lost Yet . . . ," *LG*, 8–14 December 1999, p. 1, 6. Kokoshin was first deputy defense minister from 1992 to 1997 and secretary of the Defense Council and deputy secretary of the Security Council from 1997 to

main discourse with which it was competing was the NSR. Anatolii Vishnevskii singles out the NSR for special attention in *Serp i Rubl:* "In Russia
there is great power revanchism, voices which do not want to give up their
customary [Soviet] resistance to the West. They do not attach significance
to the growing multipolarity of the world or . . . they dramatize the danger
of returning to a unipolar world where, in their opinion, the USA will dominate without constraint." He accuses them of trying to replicate the old ideology of "proletarian internationalism and national liberation struggle" with
"national-patriotic chauvunistic" ideas. Geopolitical thinking in terms of traditional bipolar balance of power politics was being "called upon to replace
Marxism."[55]

But why was the LE so confident that the NSR fears of unipolarity were
overblown? After all, it rejected the NWR's embrace of the West as Russia's
natural and only identity. And "obviously, the US, if it wishes, can use its first-
class economic, military, and political potential to maintain order in the
world." And "of course its former main enemy has suffered defeat and is on
the ash heap of history." There were three obstacles to a unipolar world: difference, institutions, and the death of the Soviet Union. The world, contrary
to NWR belief, was not a unified civilization under U.S. hegemonic sway, ex-
pectantly waiting in the anteroom of that hegemony, or even likely to experience a coercive U.S. hegemony. Instead, there were many independent
states, whose vast variety of essential characteristics made the U.S. capacity
"to unilaterally resolve the fate of all the countries and peoples of the globe
. . . " nothing more than a fantasy, one held by the NSR in Russia and obtuse
strategists in Washington. Moreover, U.S. material capability was further
constrained by the sovereign and legal rights accorded to these other states,
and U.S. participation in institutions whose decision-making practices reduced the potential for unilateral U.S. adventurism.[56]

But perhaps the main reason for LE confidence in the U.S. capacity to
pass up the temptation of unipolarity was the loss of the U.S.'s defining External Other, the Soviet Union. In his textbook on geopolitics, Gadzhiev
writes, "The American idea and the American mission acquired new param-
eters during bipolarity: almost all the most important of their constitutive
elements were rethought and reoriented through the prism of anti-Sovi-
etism and anti-communism." But now this defining Other had disappeared,

---

1998. He now heads the Center for problems of National Security at Moscow State University is a corresponding member of the Russian Academy of Sciences, and a member of the
Coordinating Council of the Fatherland—All-Russia bloc. He was also one of the most influential "new thinkers" under Gorbachev who reconceptualized Soviet, and then Russian,
security needs under the rubric of defensive sufficiency.

[55] Vishnevskii, *Serp i Rubl,* 397–402.

[56] On the danger of the United States operating outside these multilateral constraints, see,
for example, Leonid Gankin, "Missile Strike at the UN," *KV* 3 (January 19, 1999): 26.

and indeed one could argue that NSR fears could be realized, in this view, only if that discourse became dominant in Russian life. The disappearance of the Soviet Other had resulted in a new phenomenon, a U.S. need to examine the "insufficiencies of the American model and the American idea" in light of different, non-Soviet axes of understanding. Gadzhiev concludes, "one can say that the Soviet empire carried with it into the archives not only the communist idea, but possibly another idea, the idea of a pax Americana."[57]

Unipolar U.S. dominance was made far less likely not through the operation of a material balance of power; indeed, if this were the way the world worked, U.S. hegemony would be guaranteed. Instead, U.S. material power was balanced by the existence of a number of essentially different independent states whose sovereignty and territorial integrity were protected by international normative constraints and whose joint membership in international institutions with the United States reduced its capacity to act unilaterally. Finally, and perhaps most significantly from the perspective of discursive politics, the LE understood the absence of a Soviet Other for the U.S. Self to be a strong guarantee against the reemergence of another bipolar binarization of global politics.

Gadzhiev's enunciation of LE ideas about polarity most clearly differentiated that discourse from the NSR. But the LE discourse was also very different from the NWR denial of a material balance of power, essentialized difference with other states, and need to restore Russia's central position in the post-Soviet space. One of the critical differences between the NWR and LE was in their understanding of the meaning of, and hence Russian interests in, the CIS, the former Soviet space, the near abroad. The LE discourse implied a different source of threat to Russian interests in the former Soviet space than either NWR indifference or the NSR conviction that the United States and its henchmen were out to drive Russia from the area. The LE source came from within, especially Russia's own weakness. This paralleled the consensus of all three discourses at home that Moscow's economic weakness accounted for peripheral drives for autonomy. But only the LE discourse translated this understanding of center-periphery relations to CIS affairs. The NWR had no meaningful source of threat, given that the West was their closest Other, if not already partly Self. The NSR, dominated by the binarization of identity with the United States, saw all territory beyond Russian borders as contested with Washington; moreover, at home the NSR saw the West in Moscow in the form of the NWR. In sum, for the LE, the former Soviet space was Russia's to lose; for the NSR it was what the United States was trying to dominate; and for the NWR it was irrelevant.

Consequently, the LE stressed the need to get Russia back on its economic feet in order to guarantee a multipolar world in which Russia was one of the

---

[57] Gadzhiev, *Vvedenie v Geopolitiku*, 267–72.

poles. This was consistent with the previous discussion of roads to centering, but here the connection between economics and polarity was made explicit. Andrei Kokoshin declares that Russia must follow China's example of market reform in "order to turn ourselves into a superpower, firstly economically. This is our most important national goal."[58] As Stepan Sulakshin, the chairman of the Gosduma committee on oil, construction, transportation, and energy puts it, "if our economy is not put in order, then Russia can be deprived of its sovereignty." So, worse than dropping out of the ranks of the great powers, Russia's physical security was at stake. Moreover, if Russia wanted "to return the world to multipolarity," it must address its economic weakness.[59]

What follows could be a LE manifesto on Russia's interests in the former Soviet space, derived primarily from Gadzhiev's textbook on geopolitics. We might call it balance of power without binarization. On the one hand, Russian weakness had created a power vacuum that other great powers naturally tried to fill. But the intentions of these Others were not considered to be hostile or threatening to Russia per se, despite Russia's vulnerability and strong claims to influence in these areas.

According to Gadzhiev, the post-Soviet space was the single most important area for Russia's foreign policy. It had "vitally important interests" affecting Russia's economy and national security.[60] None of the main threats to these interests that Gadzhiev identifies were attributed to the other great powers—the proliferation of WMD, national and religious fundamentalism, ecological catastrophes, the drug trade, and international terrorism. Russia's primary aim was to prevent conflicts in the area. Russia's security depended on stability and good relations with the former Soviet republics. Reflecting the essentialist view of Russia's ethnonational identity, Gadzhiev singles out the 25 million Russians living abroad as both a source of tension with some CIS countries, and also possibly "a firm bridge between Russia and its new neighbors." In other words, it was the ethnonational identity that might bind; but note that it was the other Russians abroad that signified a common identity, not non-Russian Slavs such as Ukrainians or Belarussians.

In a formulation far closer to the NSR than to the NWR, Gadzhiev declares that "Russia is the strategic axis for the entire post-Soviet space." Its size, human capital, and military "potential *objectively* make it the regional leader."[61] After all, "Russia is not only the past [unlike the Soviet Union, we might add], but is also the present of these countries, from which there is

---

[58] Kokoshin, "Not Everything Is Lost Yet," 1. This sentiment is reproduced in Russia's new military doctrine, "Military Doctrine of the Russian Federation," 5.

[59] Stepan Sulakshin, "Russian Oil for Serbian Tanks," *NG,* 12 May 1999, p. 3.

[60] Gadzhiev, *Vvedenie v Geopolitiku.* See also Svyatoslav Perfilov, "The Economic Union Is Dead, Long Live the Union?!" *NG,* 4 June 1999, p. 5.

[61] Gadzhiev, *Vvedenie v Geopolitiku.* Emphasis added. See also Vishnevskii, *Serp i Rubl,* 404–5.

nowhere to hide. . . ."[62] Gadzhiev observes that the initial identifications of the former Soviet republics with the "West and the Islamic world in the Caucasus and Central Asia has been replaced by sobering and disppointment," a LE observation. These new states were naturally part of a Russian-centered community, Russia being their "natural center of gravity."[63] Efforts to graft their identity onto the West (this of course would put paid to NWR expectations) or Islam were objectively unavailing.

Gadzhiev criticizes the NWR failure to see to Russian interests in the near abroad, noting that not until 1993 "did Russia expand its political, military, and economic influence" there.[64] The consequences of this LE understanding of interests and threats were the need for Russia to "resist the strengthening of the influence of other great powers on the post-Soviet space."[65] But this was not a binarized threat emerging from the most dangerous Other, as in the NSR discourse. Instead it was a diffuse threat emerging from all or any essentialized Others in world politics that happened to try to take advantage of Russia's temporary weakness in its natural and essentialized sphere of interests.

Constructing Allies: United, Dominated, and Differentiated Wests

Each discursive formation made available a different collection of potential allies. In 1999, there were three distinct possibilities associated with the NWR, NSR, and LE. The NWR, due to its identification of Russia with the United States and the West (United West), saw no reason to ally with any state against their imminent Selves. But to call the United West an ally of the NWR was a gross understatement of the degree of the NWR identification with it. It wanted to become it, not form a partnership with it. With the exception of welcoming its aid in resisting the NSR at home, the NWR understood the United West as far more than merely a strategic ally; it was the very closest Other, bordering on the Russian Self, if all went well. The belief that the world had a universal civilization and Russia had a place in it resulted in happiness in unipolar splendor. There were very few alliance possibilities under unipolarity.

---

[62] Gadzhiev, *Vvedenie v Geopolitiku*. See also Rakhim Khasanov, "Russian Interests in Tadzhikistan," *NG*, 10 April 1999, p. 5. Khasanov is a professor of political science.

[63] Gadzhiev, *Vvedenie v Geopolitiku*. See President Putin's identification of Turkmeni and Russian strategic interests as the same. Iurii Chernogaev and Boris Volkhonskii, "Rakhmanov Is Also Our President," *Kommersant*, 17 November 1999, p. 11. These authors treat Putin's visit as entirely farcical, a neo-Soviet carnival of sorts.

[64] Gadzhiev, *Vvedenie v Geopolitiku*, 325–32. Mikhail Nikolaevich Zuev also argues that not until the end of 1993 did Russia "declare itself to be a great power with independent [of the West] geopolitical and national interests." Mikhail Nikolaevich Zuev, *Istoriia Rossii: XX Vek* Moscow, 1995), 430. Note how this periodization of Russian foreign policy coincides with the discussion of democracy and liberalism in chapter 4.

[65] Gadzhiev, *Vvedenie v Geopolitiku*, 362.

And this was precisely the eventuality the NSR wished to prevent. Locked in a binarized bipolar world, NSR allies were those states that were opposed to the United States and were not under its domination. These included China, India, Iraq, Iran, and Cuba. Although not a long list of potential allies, it was far longer than that of the NWR. But it was also bounded by the binary metric and by the historical view that the United States controlled the West (Dominated West) and that the West was not meaningfully separate from it. Because they were not separate, the European countries and Japan, for instance, were not available allies for the NSR. This was a syntactic analogue to Molotov's denial of the capacity to be an ally to Yugoslavia in 1955.

The LE, on the other hand, was open to a wide array of alliances, but they were of limited depth and meaning. Unlike the NWR, which was willing to lose itself in its western counterparts, the LE did not understand any other state as so similar (let alone essentially similar) as to allow for this kind of fusion of identity. Although clearly understanding some Others as being closer to Russia's essential Self, such as Europe over the United States, this did not portend the erasure of enduring essential difference under any circumstances. Critically, and contrary to the NSR, the LE differentiated between U.S. and European Others, understanding the latter to be essentially more compatible with Russia's own Self and its consequent interests.

The NWR spent no discernible time thinking about Russia's allies in the world because there was only one and it had Russia's identity, too. The NSR found no meaningful difference between the United States and Europe, not because it did not notice such differences,[66] but because they were rendered moot by the U.S. military, economic, and political domination of Europe. What would be the use of trying to ally with any European country against the United States if no Europeans were capable of autonomous action? "Today the global contradiction along the Western-nonWestern line on choosing a path of existence is already immeasurably more powerful than the differences among Western centers of power. . . ."[67] In other words, the binarization that ordered the NSR worldview trumped any evidence that the West might not be as monolithic and undifferentiated as this discourse implied. This is the way that the NSR discourse operated in the case of NATO's war in Yugoslavia. In the face of party Secretary Ziuganov's warnings that it was a "war for American interests and domination" in Europe, "Europe will play the music ordered by Washington."[68] More globally, Washington's use

---

[66] Although sometimes it did not, as in U.S. and British interest in Yugoslavia. Onuchko, "Scottish Hawk Changes His Nest," 3.

[67] Yakovlev, "Constructive Ambitions and Irrational Interests," 14.

[68] Ziuganov, "Russia is Concentrating," 2; Sergei Illarionov, "Washington Aspires to World Domination," *Pravda*, 11–14 June 1999, p. 3. Illarionov is a retired Soviet ambassador.

of NATO in Yugoslavia, rather than European decision-making mechanisms, only repeated the pattern of the United States "maneuvering the European Union out of" various parts of the globe, including the Middle East; a few years earlier the United States had compelled Europe to agree to NATO's security plans for the Mediterranean.[69] The United States was happy with the outcome in the war in Kosovo not only because it weakened Serbia, covered U.S. deployments of military personnel to the Balkans, and demonstrated European dependence on the United States, but also because it was an occasion to demonstrate Europe's need for NATO and Washington's dominant position within it and, so, in Europe.[70]

The LE understandings did not fit under the rubrics of union and domination. Instead, it was a discourse of difference—different states with different interests ending up in various positions of alliance with the United States, some more immutable than others, depending on circumstances. This analysis implied both greater and lesser alliance opportunities for Russia. The LE was alert to the differences that emerged between Washington and its European allies during the Kosovo war. Italian, Greek, and Hungarian preferences for a suspension of bombing early in the war in response to Belgrade's declaration of a unilateral ceasefire were contrasted with Washington's demurral.[71] Shortly before the war's conclusion, an article focusing on the German Green Party opposition to the war; antiwar demonstrations in Belgium and Italy, where some parliamentarians were demanding an end to the bombing; and growing French intellectual resentment (Belgrade was compared to Guernica on the front page of *Le Monde*) presented these phenomena as evidence of growing differences between the United States and its European allies.[72] After the conclusion of the war, as NATO continued to celebrate its fiftieth anniversary, Europeans successfully insisted, as a consequence of the war and over Washington's objections, on maintaining adherence to the UN charter as part of NATO's strategic concept, implying European concerns with the legality of actions such as Kosovo.[73] This supported the LE belief that international institutions were a critical path to Russia's global recentering and hence that European support for this, if only conceptually, was an opportunity to empower Russia.

The exploration of European-U.S. differences over the Kosovo war made the LE discourse different from the homogenizing NWR discourse, but it did not differentiate it from the NSR. But how did the LE discourse account for Europe's behavior in Kosovo, despite these differences? We know the

---

[69] Richard Ovinnikov, "The US and the EU: Friendship Is Friendship, but . . . " *Pravda,* 12–13 October 1999, p. 3.

[70] Markushin, "NATO Abolishes 'Non-offensive Defense'" 3.

[71] Anatolii Fedorov, "NATO Has Lost Count of Its Losses," *Trud.* 10 April 1999, p. 4.

[72] Vladimir Katin, "Europe Is Rethinking the War in Yugoslavia," *NG,* 4 June 1999, p. 6.

[73] Pankov, "America Says Good-bye to Disarmament," 3.

NSR answer: U.S. domination. But this was not the LE answer; indeed, there were a variety of answers.

The United States had exerted its "influence" to bring its NATO allies into line on Kosovo.[74] The Europeans were "involved in this military adventure largely because they are dependent on the US for their own actions in their own European home."[75] Kokoshin describes the European states as "quasisovereign" having ceded their sovereignty voluntarily to first the EU and now the United States. But in order to preserve European unity it was sometimes necessary for individual European states to act contrary to their own interests.[76] Or perhaps the Europeans had their own interests in the Balkans and Kosovo that they were pursuing independently of the United States, but whose advancement the war against Yugoslavia favored.[77] In the simplest explanation of all, Aleksandr Yakovlev suggests that perhaps Europeans just wanted to be allies of the United States, in "an established and time-tested alliance" led by the only superpower, even if it involved some adventures that each would not have agreed to on its own.[78]

The LE also placed hope in European institutions, especially the OSCE. The Istanbul OSCE summit in December 1999 was reported to have "in general re-established the character of relations which existed in Europe prior to NATO's aggression against Yugoslavia." There, an understanding was reached that political means, not military force, would be used to build security in the future. The OSCE's "principle of unanimity or consensus" would "serve as a real obstacle to the realization of the NATO conception of 'humanitarian interventions'." The meeting in general pushed the idea of "NATOcentrism," advocated by the United States, to the back burner.[79]

Lest it be thought that NWR philo-Americanism had been replaced by LE philo-Europeanism, rather than a more general appreciation for difference, it should be noted that the LE realized that on one issue, Chechnia, the United States was less hostile than either the Europeans or Canadians. Whereas the United States said it would not reduce aid to Russia because of Chechnia, harsher warnings had been issued by the British foreign minister,

---

[74] Gornostaev, "Cuban Missile Crisis," 3.

[75] Aleksandr Ptashkin, "'They Will Answer for This'," *Trud*, 12 May 1999, p. 5.

[76] Kokoshin, "Not Everything Is Lost Yet," 1.

[77] Sergei Karaganov, interviewed by Sergei Maslov, "The War in Yugoslavia Is Worse than a Crime. It Is a Mistake," KP, 15 May 1999, p. 2. Karaganov is the head of the Council on Foreign and Defense Policy. This is Aleksandr Yakovlev's explanation for NATO expansion, too— Europeans had their own interests in expanding NATO eastward, independent of U.S. rationales. Yakovlev, "Constructive Ambitions and Irrational Interests," 14.

[78] Yakovlev, "Constructive Ambitions and Irrational Interests," 14.

[79] Ivashov, "We Have Succeeded in Defending Russian Interests," 1, 3. See also Tregubova, "Istanbul Waits for Yeltsin and Extremists," 1; Pankov, "America Says Good-bye to Disarmament," 3.

the EU Foreign Affairs representative, the German foreign minister, and the Danish prime minister. Even the Swedish defense minister cancelled his trip to Moscow because of Chechnia. But, in the aftermath of Kosovo, western policymakers, including NATO General Secretary George Robertson, reassured Russia that "the problem of Chechnia is not seen like the problem in Kosovo."[80]

Constructing Threats: Nil, Moderate, and Dire

Each of the three discourses interpreted NATO's war in Yugoslavia. Each assessed the adequacy of Russia's foreign policy with respect to Yugoslavia; which side, Yugoslav or U.S., bore responsibility for the onset of the conflict; read Kosovo more or less through Chechnia; and finally, inferred just how threatening the United States was to Russian security and interests based on its actions in Yugoslavia. Based in large part on evidence from Kosovo, but also from the world more broadly, each discourse offered summary judgments about the kind of danger presented by the United States to Russia. The NWR saw virtually no threat; the NSR saw mortal danger; and the LE understood the United States as a disappointment, a manageable threat but a threat nonetheless.

Given that the NWR considered the West to be Russia's imminent Self, the West was not blamed for the war in Kosovo but rather the hardline foreign policy of Russia "whose peacemaking initiatives could have brought much more effect had our country from the very beginning acted jointly with the West, and not resisted it. . . . even the bombing might not have occurred."[81] The NWR praised Chernomyrdin's moderate approach on Yugoslavia. Indeed, some adherents argued that had the Left been in power, Russia would have been at war with NATO by now.[82]

Although on the whole blaming Milosevic for the war in Kosovo, the NWR also criticized the West, or at least its KLA allies, who should not have resorted to force. And "carpet bombing? This is a resolution of the problem?" Instead, "NATO could have been a serious mediator in the conflict."[83] The West was also taken to task for trying to censor reporting from Yugoslavia that revealed NATO's bombs killing innocent civilians.[84]

---

[80] Dmitrii Gornostaev, "The EU Is Considering Whether to Impose Sanctions against Russia," *NG*, 9 December 1999, p. 6. For an unfavorable comparison of Canada's position to that of the United States, see Maksim Iusin, "'Crusade' against Moscow," *Izvestiia*, 9 December 1999, p. 4.

[81] Parkhalina, "Real Results and Imaginary Gains," 3.

[82] Rostislav Larionov, "Great Misfortune of Russian Weapons," *KV* 25 (June 22, 1999): 26.

[83] Igor Serkov, "Catastrophe," *LG*, 7 April 1999, p. 1.

[84] Dushan Relich, "The Best Censor Is Death," *LG*, 19 May 1999, p. 8. Relich is a Yugoslav journalist who in 1991 was chosen as the main editor of the official Yugoslav information agency, TANIUG. As a result of persecution by the secret police, he left for Germany.

The only threat that NATO's war in Kosovo posed was not to Russia's national security but rather to the political and discursive security of the NWR itself. The NWR discourse was severely discredited by western actions in Yugoslavia. The August 1998 currency crisis had pushed the NWR discourse further to the margin on issues of Russian identity; NATO's war in Yugoslavia squeezed it almost off the social text altogether. The only NWR response to this further deterioration of its position was to ironicize Russia's LE policy in Yugoslavia in an editorial in *Kommersant Vlast*. The bitter truth that needed to be turned into more digestible irony was the fact that Primakov's anti-Americanism during the crisis was more effective in bringing about closer ties with Washington than the full-body embrace advocated by the NWR. "Russians have won the Kosovo conflict," said the *Washington Post* and other American publications. How? By taking an anti-American position. Primakov turned his plane around over the Atlantic; NATO representatives were sent packing from Moscow; and Russia loudly supported Milosevic, boycotted the NATO summit in Washington, and sent a naval intelligence vessel into the Adriatic to observe. But, most surprisingly and worrying to the NWR, the U.S. responded with "flattering remarks about the constructive role of Russia. . . . Albright abandons everything and rushes to a meeting with Igor Ivanov in Oslo. . . . International forces replace NATO forces in Kosovo, with Russian participation of course. . . ."

The Russians came out of the conflict "glorified as diplomats and mediators. . . . The voice of Russia in NATO, weakened since 1991, will become louder . . . " But "most important, Primakov will prove to the world, and more important, to pro-Western Russians [the NWRs], that an anti-American foreign policy has returned Russia to its legitimate place in the world [to the Center]. . . . " The editorial ends with an effort to take back with sarcasm that which has already been granted through straightforward narrative: "We [the NWR] support Primakov's vision of Russia as leader of the opposition to the US, and ally and representative of the foulest regimes— Serbian and Iraqi."[85] Here the authors have engaged in some binarization of their own: Primakov's LE policy cannot simply be anti-American, or simply not so pro-American, it must also entail allying with odious Others.

On the broader issue of American foreign policy toward Russia, the NWR related a most benign view of U.S. intentions with respect to Russia and their effects on Russian security. The expansion of NATO toward Russia's western borders, for instance, was no threat. Moreover, the decision to expand and the demand from eastern European countries for such an expansion "is of course a response to the continuation of [our] imperial policy. If a threat from Moscow wasn't sensed, there wouldn't be unease in Tallinn, Warsaw, and Budapest. . . ."[86] As we know from the Semin and Sultygov NWR mani-

---

[85] "Russians Won in the Kosovo Conflict," *KV* 19 (May 5, 1999): 32.

[86] Igor Chubais, *Ot Russkoi Idei—K Idee Novoi Rossii* (Moscow, 1997), 74.

festo, U.S. unipolarity was no threat.[87] Recent post-Soviet history showed that the West, "Americans, Germans, and Danes," and not those supposed allies, Cuba, Iraq, and North Korea, "delivered bread, medicine and milk for children in that horrible winter of 1991 after the August putsch. . . ."[88] The only issue on which the United States had defied Russian interests was one on which the NWR agreed with the U.S. opposition—how the war was being fought in Chechnia.[89]

The NSR discourse constructed an understanding of the threat from the United States that was the precise opposite of the interpretation offered by the NWR. The NSR considered the United States to be completely responsible for the war in Kosovo, aided and abetted only by the NWR and LE traitors who managed Russian foreign policy. By appeasing the United States in Belgrade/Munich, the Russian center had opened the door to the ultimate destruction of Russia itself.

If only Yeltsin had been impeached, Yugoslavia might have been spared having its "civilization trampled like ancient Huns had done."[90] Chernomyrdin's peace mission, praised by the NWR for its realistic appraisal of Russia's possibilities, was condemned for "pursuing a pro-NATO policy." Viktor Iliukhin, chairman of the Duma committee on security declared that "Russia has betrayed the interests of Yugoslavia and Russia. . . . there will be more aggression from the US. Betting on Chernomyrdin—a mediocre politician and ungifted diplomat, but true advocate of Vice President Gore—was doomed to failure from the beginning. . . . We will be America's puppet in Kosovo. . . ."[91] Matters had deteriorated to the point that the NSR looked to other states to advance Russia's interests because the current leadership in the center could not. "Unfortunately, unlike the Soviet Union, contemporary Russia, with a regime acquiescent to the West, is hardly able to become the initiator of resistance to recolonization." (Recall that the NSR situated Russia in the periphery.) Instead of Moscow, the NSR called for reliance on China, India, and the nonaligned movement in general.[92] If Belgrade was seen as Munich, then Primakov, Yeltsin, and Chernomyrdrin were "contemporary Chamberlains, who, by calling for passive contemplation of NATO's outrages . . . in fact increases the threat of a new war." Why? "Because the subordination of Europe to American hawks creates a direct military threat to our country." Sergei Illarionov, the former Soviet ambassador who wrote this comparison, goes on to wistfully recall what a real power had

---

[87] Semin and Sultygov, "Unconstructive Ambitions or Rational Interests?," 14.

[88] Zhukhovitskii, "Russia Has Betrayed No One," 7.

[89] Moroz, "Foreign Countries Are Again against Us," 3.

[90] Mikhail Tretiakov, "Battle in the Town of Korisha," *Pravda*, 18–19 May 1999, p. 1.

[91] Eratova, "Everything Is Going According to Plan," 3.

[92] Ovinnikov, "Imperialism Will Get on the Rack," 3.

done in the past—in Spain and China in the 1930s, in Vietnam, and in Egypt in 1956."[93] In sum, the NSR understood its own goverment as part of the threat emanating from the United States.

Kosovo was read through Chechnia. The KLA was referred to as a terrorist organization, as were the Chechen rebels.[94] The expectation was that just as the Clinton Administration had tried to save the terrorist separatists in Kosovo, it would try to do the same in Chechnia, snatching away a Russian military victory just when the rebels were on the run.[95] At the barest minimum, NATO's war in Yugoslavia was evidence that the United States intended to establish its domination over the Balkans.[96]

More commonly, U.S. actions were construed as a confirmation of NSR expectations that the United States was trying to establish unipolar domination of the globe.[97] And the instrumentality for this bid for global dominance was the creation of a new international norm: humanitarian intervention. This norm would permit the United States to unilaterally decide whenever and wherever it wished to use military force in the world, including of course in Russia and in Chechnia. This would open the way for the "destruction of Russia, the main annoyance in the eyes of the West, and the fundamental goal of NATO. But [Russia] is too big a chunk, so it is better to divide it into parts so it can [be] more easily swallowed."[98] In this way, Yugoslavia was considered just a dress rehearsal for Chechnia, and Chechnia for other vulnerable parts of the Russian Federation.

The threat from the United States, according to the NSR, was total and relentless. It was aimed at nothing less than the destruction of Russia through its further disintegration.[99] Issues such as BMD and NATO expansion, although of course understood as threatening, were nothing compared to the U.S. license to intervene militarily, as demonstrated in Kosovo.

The LE held the vast middle in Russian identity politics. Although critical of U.S. actions in Yugoslavia, it also recognized that its own ally in Belgrade left a lot to be desired. Although reading Kosovo through Chechnia, it also expected there to be limits on the applicability of the experience. Although

---

[93] Illarionov, "Washington Aspires to World Domination," 3.

[94] Tretiakov, "We Should Not Be," 1.

[95] Tretiakov, "Washington Aspires to World Domination," 3.

[96] Ovinnikov, "Imperialism Will Get on the Rack," 3.

[97] Eratova, "Everything Is Going According to Plan," 3; Ziuganov, "Russia Is Concentrating," 2; Ovinnikov, "Imperialism Will Get on the Rack," 3.

[98] Ovinnikov, "Imperialism Will Get on the Rack," 3.

[99] Tretiakov, "Washington Defends Terrorists," 3; Anatolii Chekhoev, interviewed by Valentina Nikiforova, "The Problems in the Caucasus Must First be Solved in Moscow," *Pravda*, 12–13 October 1999, pp. 1 2. Chekhoev is a Gosduma deputy, deputy chair of the Committee on CIS affairs and Relations with Fellow Countrymen (diaspora Russians), and a communist. Ovinnikov, "Imperialism Will Get on the Rack," 3.

NATO's aggression in Yugoslavia was evidence of the possibility of international institutional support being overridden by raw power, the LE did not appreciate this evidence as ratifying the views of the Left, but did use it to discredit the NWR on the Right. Russian foreign policy restraint in Yugoslavia was valued. Although a real United States threat, including to Russian territorial integrity in the Caucasus, was acknowledged, it was not treated as inevitable or as being equivalent to a threat to Russia's very existence.

The overwhelming majority of the LE agreed that what the United States and NATO were doing in Yugoslavia was a barbaric outrage.[100] But just as common in LE discourse was for the critique of the United States to be leavened with the recognition that "Slobodan Milosevic of course is also no little gift." This was said after comparing the KLA to Chechen terrorists and calling Ibragim Rugova "the local Gamsakhurdia."[101] Even the patriarch of the Russian Orthodox Church, which, recall, is a constituent part of the ethnonational identity of the NSR, in his appeal for an Easter cease-fire, asked that the leaders of Yugoslavia secure a "peaceful and dignified life for all, including ethnic Albanians in Kosovo. . . ."[102] First Deputy Minister of Foreign Affairs Aleksandr Avdeev granted that "both Yugoslavian authorities and the extremist wing of the Kosovan Albanians—the KLA . . . bear responsibility for the ethnic conflicts in Yugoslavia which had begun in 1995."[103]

Atrocities committed by Serbs while leaving Kosovo were also reported, such as a mass grave of Albanians who had been shot and then set on fire.[104] After the conflict was over, it was reported that Serbian authorities were not fulfilling their obligations to hand over maps of their minefields to the UN Kosovo Force (KFOR), the multinational peacekeeping force of which Russia was a member.[105] Serbian threats to reintroduce military forces into Kosovo after their withdrawal were criticized for justifying KLA activity and

---

[100] See, for example, "Let's Help Stop the War," *Trud,* 10 April 1999, p. 1; Vyacheslav Samoshkin, "Great Resettlement of Illegals," *NG,* 10 April 10 1999, p. 6; Iurii Pankov, "NATO: Changing of the Guard," *KZ,* 8 October 1999, p. 3; Ekaterina Glebova, "Those Who Supported NATO Have Become Victims of Trickery," *Izvestiia,* 10 November 1999, p. 4.

[101] Vanin and Zhilin, "Result," 6. That Milosevic "has blood on his hands" for pursuing a civil war in the first place was acknowledged by Karaganov, "War," 2.

[102] Evgenii Strelchik, "'To the Blessed Grief of This Day Is Added the Pain of Human Sufferings'," *NG,* 10 April 1999, 2.

[103] Aleksandr Avdeev, interviewed by Nikita Shevtsov, "'Tomahawks' Chase People," *Trud,* 10 April 1999, p. 4. In this interview, Avdeev even said that although the Americans were now pursuing a military solution to the Kosovo problem, "they do not exclude the possibility of a political settlement."

[104] Taras Lariokhin, "A Bayonet from the Time of World War I and a Gun from a Water Pipe," *Izvestiia,* 10 July 1999, p. 4.

[105] Vladimir Abarinov, "Kosovo Will Remain Dangerous in Both Direct and Figurative Senses," *Izvestiia,* 10 July 1999, p. 4.

undermining Russian diplomatic support for Belgrade.[106] By the time the KFOR operation was under way, NATO forces were being lauded for their "maximally correct" behavior, the fact that "local people simply worship them," and their good relations with non-NATO contingents.[107] Not two months after the end of the war, Marina Kuvashova, a Russian military commentator, was differentiating between the "disobedient" KLA, whose members had attacked KFOR soldiers, and the NATO soldiers, "who are now the main obstacles to the KLA's achievement of independence. So, a new war could come about in Kosovo between NATO and the separatists."[108] This was certainly a far cry from any NSR analysis, and even LE considerations, just months before. Because Russia was part of KFOR, it found itself in an alliance with NATO against the KLA and, more implicitly, against Belgrade.[109]

No doubt because of this ambivalent or balanced view of the two opposing sides in Kosovo, the LE strongly supported Russia's efforts to end the war as quickly as possible. This was seen as a way of saving Milosevic from himself and rescuing the Serbian people from being relentlessly bombed by U.S. forces. Not only did Moscow get the war over as quickly as possible, but it did so despite Russia's material weakness. In short, Russia did as well as it could with a bad hand, its own weakness and Milosevic as its ally. Moreover, this peacemaking policy showed the utter bankruptcy of the two alternative discursive positions: NWR appeasement and NSR warmongering, the latter of course with the use of Serbian blood, not Russian.[110]

Kosovo was read through Chechnia, but the implications were bounded long before Russian disintegration. Grigorii Vanin and Aleksandr Zhilin warn, for example, that the "legal" basis of humanitarian intervention could be applied to any former Soviet republic, including Russia. Yugoslavia and Russia were similarly placed. They both had terrorist separatists, the KLA and the Chechen rebels, that were not recognized as terrorists by the United States; instead the United States held Belgrade and Moscow responsible for both "humanitarian catastrophes." This reconfiguration of the international sovereignty norm "will permit the dismemberment and destruction, behind the mask of peacemaking, of any state . . . even such giants as India and China." So far, so NSR. But these LE authors do not attribute complete and total responsibility for Russia's weakened center to the United States. Instead, it was "Russia's falling economic and military potential" that was to blame. Again, it was the LE theme of domestic recentering first, getting eco-

---

[106] Maksim Iusin, "Yugoslavs Threaten to Take Kosovo Back from NATO," *Izvestiia,* 10 September 1999, p. 3.

[107] Vadim Solovyev, "A Month after the War," *NG,* 10 July 1999, pp. 1, 6.

[108] Marina Kuvashova, "A Real War Goes on in Kosovo," *KZ,* 10 August 1999, p. 3.

[109] Dmitrii Privalov, "End of the Honeymoon," *Trud,* 10 August 1999, p. 3.

[110] Pankov, "America Says Good-bye to Disarmament," 3; Iusin, "War in Yugoslavia Has Ended," 1.

nomic and material resources in order first, to counter external threats. But the authors conclude on an even rosier note, pointing out that "candidates for the role of victims of humanitarian catastrophes are most probably Crimean Tatars, Abkhazians, Adzhartsy, and Gagauztsy," none of whom live on Russian territory. Why was Chechnya not on the list? "Chechens, being part of a nuclear power, have a different fate."[111]

The greater confidence in the possibilities of nuclear deterrence encouraged the LE to be less alarmed about the kind of threat the United States had demonstrated to Russia in Yugoslavia. Even Colonel General Leonid Ivashov, who was reported to have dissented from Chernomyrdin's moderating mission to Brussels and Belgrade, invokes international institutions to explain why NATO could not repeat in Chechnia what it had done in Kosovo. First, "no matter what anyone in NATO wants, the alliance and its leader, the US, are compelled to recognize that Chechnia is part of Russian territory. . . . " What compels them? Nothing other than the international institution of sovereignty, apparently, because Ivashov mentions nothing more material. Second, the fact that terrorists operated in Chechnia meant that NATO and the United States must recognize Russia's "full sovereign right to destroy them, to defend its territorial integrity."[112] In sum, the threat emanating from Kosovo founders, according to Ivashov at least, on the shoals of international law and norms of sovereignty, territorial integrity, and the legitimate right to fight terrorism.

The fear that NATO's war on Kosovo inspired in the LE was borne of two elements, one material and the other not. The first was Russia's own material weakness, its own physical incapacity to protect its own center. But the second was not the material capacity of the external Other, the United States but rather its stupidity or myopia, its inability to realize that its own interests were best served by a multipolar world where it acted authoritatively according to consensual international institutions.[113]

So far the discussion of LE constructions of threat from Kosovo has differentiated this discourse most dramatically from that of the NSR. But in fact, the LE inferred from Kosovo that the NWR discourse on Russian foreign policy was just as bankrupt. The full indictment was offered by Aleksandr Meshkov, a political scientist writing in *Nezavisimaia Gazeta* at the outset of the war. He observes that even NWR leaders, such as Gaidar, Boris Nemtsov, and Anatolii Fedorov, had been forced to condemn NATO's bombing. They did so because, if for no other reason, they could not help

---

[111] Vanin and Zhilin, "Results," 6.

[112] Ivashov, "We succeeded in Defending Russian Interests," 1, 3. See also Gornostaev, "State Department?" 3.

[113] See, for example, Gornostaev, "Cuban Missile Crisis," 1.

but understand that the growing "patriotic and anti-American feelings in the country will practically reduce their influence to nothing and make their political futures impossible." But what was happening here was no simple tactical adjustment but rather a wholesale subversion of the NWR discourse. "Before our eyes is collapsing the house of cards woven from classical postulates of liberalism and the seemingly unshakeable truths about the 'democratic' and 'humanistic' West." Note how U.S. foreign policy actions ended up undermining the very identity of the NWR by making a mockery of their revered external Other, the Other that Russia was supposed to aspire to.

Meshkov describes a discursive turn we have encountered before. Russia was democratic until 1993; Russia was governed by NWR foreign policy until then. "After all, there was a time when it seemed that its walls were firm." Prior to Yeltsin's shelling of the White House, the NWR discourse appeared natural, as unassailable as Russia's future. "Who would have tried then to say anything about the 'aggressive' essence of NATO or the unseemly behavior of the US!" Meshkov recalls how in the NWR days, it was impossible to argue that Russia should be a great power. Instead, in this age of "general human values" (Gorbachev's formulation, as discrediting as a communist cliche), "Russian nihilism" reigned, expressed in the poetic lines: "How sweet it is to hate one's country and greedily await its destruction!" But something changed to de-naturalize these kinds of sentiments. "With the aggression of NATO against Yugoslavia the mainsprings of the 'new world order' were revealed. For many Russians, the scales fell from their eyes." On the one hand, the "wild project" to become the center of world revolution, the NSR discourse, had been rejected, and Kosovo led to the rejection of the NWR project of becoming the West. Instead, "before our eyes is occurring an about face. . . . The time has come to re-establish our geopolitical influence, raise the economy from the ruins, and defend our spiritual and cultural values . . . " (an essentialist credo against the NWR embrace of the United States). Meshkov ends this post-Kosovo manifesto with an essentialist plea to go back and reread Berdyaev, Ilyin, and Danilevskii to rediscover the Russian idea and its embodiment in civilization.[114]

In terms of the overall LE judgment about the threat emerging from the United States, it would be accurate to say that a threat was recognized, but that its limits were established and tolerable. The LE discourse on the U.S. threat after Kosovo looks more like the NSR understanding than the NWR understanding, but it was still very different from both. On the one hand, there was the inference that the United States was in favor of Russian disintegration, but in general this was limited to the Caucasus, not a fear of

---

[114] Meshkov, "About Face," 3.

the wholesale destruction of the Russian Federation, as the NSR declared.[115]

But Gadzhiev, one of the LE manifesto writers, was closer to the NWR discourse on the U.S. threat—NATO expansion was no threat, the United States was not interested in Russian disintegration or collapse, and a continued U.S. military presence in east Asia was welcome as a stabilizing influence there.[116] NATO expansion was no threat because Gadzhiev explored explanations for Washington's behavior other than the binarized one of malign intentions toward Moscow. He suggests that the end of the Cold War meant that NATO either had to radically transform itself, or collapse in the face of an absent threat. There were "powerful forces who are vitally interested in NATO's" survival, including the United States, for which NATO "remains as evidence of its leading role in the world." Meanwhile, the European countries see NATO as an "instrument to restrain the nationalization of German foreign policy and any hegemonic impulses" it might harbor. Moreover, NATO as an organization followed the "law of self-preservation and self-reproduction." Eastern European countries want to join NATO not because Russia was a threat, but because "they want to free themselves from extraordinary military expenditures and create a favorable climate of trust in which they can realize difficult economic and political reforms." Entry into NATO "affirms their European identity" as a way station on the road into the EU. NATO also cemented the U.S. presence in Europe.[117]

THE EMERGENCE OF THE LIBERAL ESSENTIALIST MIDDLE

How should we have expected Russia to have behaved in 1999? It surely had plenty of options. A great deal can be understood by paying attention to Russia's Internal Other, Moscow's relationship to the regions, the Federal Center's desire to reassert authority over its eighty-nine constituents, and Russia's fear that the Chechen secession was only the beginning of the demise of the center more generally. Russia had similar fears internationally. The collapse of the Soviet Union had destroyed its centrality in the socialist world, the world revolutionary alliance, and its coequal status with the other superpower, the United States. Russia had clung to a central position

---

[115] On a U.S. desire for Russian disintegration, see Yakovlev, "Constructive Ambitions and Irrational Interests," 14. For the limitation of U.S. ambitions to the Caucasus, see Vanin and Zhilin, "Results," 6; Defense Minister Igor Sergeev, quoted in Leonoid Gankin, "War and the MIA," *Kommersant*, 16 November 1999, p. 1; Arman Dzhilavyan, "The Caucasian Sky Darkens," *NG*, 10 November 1999, p. 5; Oleg Odnokolenko, "In the Balkans NATO Is Fighting with Russia," *Segodnia*, 10 April 1999, p. 3.

[116] Gadzhiev, *Vvedenie v Geopolitiku*, 338.

[117] Ibid., 315–18. On the nonthreatening character of U.S. BMD deployment, see Georgii Bovt, "The ABM Has Flown," *Segodnia*, 10 September 1999, p. 3.

in the world as a great power in a multipolar world, largely through two identities: nuclear state; and as a legally constituted, authorized, and legitimated member of the UNSC, G-8, OSCE, CE, and international community writ more generally. Russia did not want to lose its great power identity, but it expected to maintain it without balancing against the United States.

With just these identity relationships in mind, it is possible to make a fair degree of sense out of Russia's response to NATO's war against Yugoslavia and NATO expansion. The question is why did Russia feel so much more threatened by NATO's bombing of Yugoslavia over Kosovo than it did over NATO's creeping expansion to the east? The answer is that Russia's identity was being read through Chechnia in 1999. Kosovo was Chechnia; Belgrade was Moscow. The only thing differentiating Russia from Yugoslavia in the minds of NATO was Russia's nuclear status. This also put a limit on the threat from NATO expansion—if push came to shove, Russia possessed the ultimate security guarantee. So, Moscow would not be bombed like Belgrade, but Chechnia might still end up like Kosovo because the West might understand Chechen demands for independence as it understood Kosovar demands.

A second theme in Russian foreign policy that flows out of domestic identity discourse was the differentiation between the United States and Europe. As elaborated in chapter 4, all the Russian discourses, save the NWR, considered genuine Russian identity to be far closer to Europe than to the United States. This was reflected in Russia's foreign policy. Although Europe was not seen as an ally, it most certainly had greater potential to become an ally than did the United States. Because Russia no longer regarded itself as the center of an empire, a revolutionary alliance, a Slavic community, or even a former union, it had far more modest foreign policy ambitions. Russia's understanding of its own decentered identity and of the danger presented by its internal Chechen Other combined to suggest a number of features about how Russia would apprehend the external world and Russia's peripheral place in it.

First, being a great power was a sure way to move closer to the center of world politics. The Soviet Union was lauded in all the discourses for having accomplished not just this task, but still more, becoming the other superpower in a bipolar world. The most consistent proponents of Russia's great power identity were the NSR adherents: communists, agrarians, and assorted national patriots. This great power status was read through the Soviet past and had significant consequences from that perspective. The NSR version of great power status rested on material military power in binary opposition to the unipolar hegemon, the United States. This almost exclusively material view of the competition with the United States ensured that the NSR understood relations from a geopolitical perspective. Establishing or countering balances of power in the world were a common way for the NSR to think about how Russia should position itself in the world.

This conviction that the United States was out to thwart Russia's efforts to retain or achieve great power status, and perhaps even to destroy Russia itself, was linked to the NSR view that the NWR were unpatriotic fifth-columnists in the thrall of the United States. They were responsible not only for destroying the Warsaw Pact, the Soviet Union, and now Russia, but were willing to deliver what was left of Russia to the United States. The perverted market democracy was the cause of Russia's decline, its dramatic decentering, and the NWR was responsible for this outcome. The NSR not only blamed it for this, but assumed its adherents acted as the deliberate henchmen of the hated External Other, the United States.

The NSR understanding of the United States as the unipolar center was accompanied by a failure to differentiate between the United States and its western allies. This inability to apprehend difference, just as the orthodox opponents of Khrushchev and Mikoyan in 1955 could not countenance difference within the Soviet Union and so within the socialist community or among Third World nationalists, made the European countries ineligible as possible allies against the U.S. bid for global domination. But this unavailability of Europe was due to U.S. domination and coercion and Europe's acquiescence in its own subordination, not a voluntary choice by Europe to be a United States ally. In this way, there was some glimmer of hope for the NSR that Europe might eventually distance itself from the U.S. hegemony, but not in the immediate future.

The events in Chechnia were understood as U.S. efforts to cause Russia's disintegration. (There is a parallel between the 1999 Russian view of Washington aiming at Russia's soft southern underbelly and the 1955 Soviet view that the Third World was imperialism's vulnerability.) And Kosovo was Chechnia. That is, the dismantling of Yugoslavia, first Slovenia, then Croatia, then Bosnia, and now Kosovo, was just a dress rehearsal for the dismembering of what was left of Russia, starting with the Caucasus.

The NSR essentialization of Russia's ethnonational identity also had implications for Russian foreign policy. In the case of NATO's bombing of Yugoslavia, the Russian Left much more frequently than any other discursive formation understood the Serbian victims as members of a Slavic family in which Russia was a critical member. Remember, as well, that whereas the other discourses found the Russian Orthodox Church to be a problematic constituent element of Russian identity, the NSR discourse accepted it.

Finally, the NSR was especially sensitive to the issue of peripheralization because it itself was the social periphery of Russia. Its rural constituents were ridiculed; its economic base was in a shambles; and its political base was impotent to counter the urban, modern, post-Soviet, non-Soviet center in Moscow.

The NWR was as eager as anyone else, including the NSR, to see Russia back in the center of world politics. But it would get there only by becoming the West, by making itself a worthy ally of the United States, by becoming part of its universal and universalizing alliance. The NWR shared the consensual position that Russia should be a great power, but it understood the meaning of that identity differently from the NSR. Whereas the NSR concentrated on the material aspects of great power status, the military wherewithal to compete for geopolitical advantage vis-à-vis the primary U.S. threat, the NWR understod being a great power to be a status conferred by other great powers, first and foremost the United States, as a sign of juridical legal sovereign equality and authorization. Russia's permanent position on the UNSC and membership in the G-8, CE, and OSCE was seen as evidence that Russia remained a great power in world affairs.

This legal institutional version of great power status, not unlike the one to which the Soviet Ministry of Foreign Affairs in 1955 adhered, makes NATO's war against Serbia, its operations in Kosovo, and their relationship to Chechnia completely different from the NSR view that Kosovo signified a NATO threat to Russia's very existence. Instead, the NWR argued that the international community, including the United States, supported Russia's sovereign rights in Chechnia. Therefore, there was no U.S. or western threat lurking behind the Chechen rebellion; NATO's war against Kosovo, although deplorable on both humanitarian and international legal grounds, was not a threat to Russian security interests, and whatever harm to Russia's great power status that arose from events in Yugoslavia, it would not be the product of NATO's military exertions but rather of NATO's failure to abide by international legal norms when choosing the mlitary option. In NWR geopolitics, most unlike that of the NSR, balances of power, understood as establishing military alliances to counter the moves of other great powers, were mostly irrelevant to understanding how world affairs worked. It would be more apt to speak of balances of legitimacy or authority, whereby states such as Russia, blatantly weak economically and militarily, were accorded positions in world affairs consonant with their legal, sovereign, and institutional rights, not their capacity to bring force to bear on some putative enemy.

The NWR view of a recentered Russia was one of inclusion in the western club, being in the center, but not being the center, or even a center. This was contrary to both the NSR version of Russia's place and the old Soviet version of 1955. If the NWR center was binarized against any particular Other, it would be against the internal Historical Other of the NSR, insofar as it was the enemy of the United States and the West.

The NWR conceived of the West as an organic modern whole, constituted by commitments to democracy, observance of civil and human rights, and liberal market economics. In this idea there was no meaningful difference between the United States and the rest of the West, to wit, Europe. The NWR understood itself and Russia to be part of this western U.S. civilization. In this light, we can see how easily the NSR understood the United States and its interests to be represented at home, in Russia, by the NWR.

The LE also wished to see Russia recover its central place in world affairs. Unlike the NWR, it did not want Russia to become the West, because the West, despite some important elements, was not equivalent to what was intrinsically Russian. Still less could the LE imagine the United States being Russia's future. Russian must find itself primarily at home, while realizing that some of the achievements of the European West and the east Asian East were fully compatible with that irreducible Russian essence. Of the three discourses, the LE most clearly and comprehensively differentiated between the United States and Europe, the latter being regarded, at least partially, as constitutive of the authentic Russian Self.

The LE was interested in recentering Russia, but this process would not occur either by dissolving Russia's unique identity within a larger more universal western identity or by adopting a binarized relationship with any other identity, as the NSR did with the United States. Instead, the LE expected to achieve great power status primarily through becoming Russia again. This meant remaining true to the elements that constituted a genuine Russian Self. This meant gaining the recognition or tolerance of the rest of the world, especially the totalizing U.S. hegemon, for Russia's uniqueness, its unwillingness to become a carbon copy of the United States.

The LE expected this recognition to be achieved mostly through international institutional legal means. Russia, as a sovereign state, should have the right to order its affairs as it saw fit. It was not expected that material power capabilities would matter in this task of recentering Russia in the world, except in the last instance of nuclear deterrence. Therefore, the LEs did not measure the attractiveness of potential allies through material geopolitical considerations, unlike the NSR. Its treatment of Chechnia, and, derivatively, NATO's war against Serbia largely shared the NWR confidence that these two conflicts were not equivalent. Chechnia threatened Russia's distintegration, but NATO's military actions on behalf of Kosovo did not portend a NATO, western, or U.S. threat to Russia's sovereign authority over its territory. NATO's actions were regrettable, even barbarous, but they were not cause for insecurity. Far more threatening, from the LE point of view, was the U.S. threat to unilaterally violate the international legal norms that helped underpin Russia's position in the center.

Finally, whereas the NSR easily integrated Serbs into the Slavic family headed by the Russians, the LE presumed a single, exclusive Russian identity; it did not travel well to other nations, even Slavic nations. Unlike the NSR, the LE was liberal—it did not see Russians as the apex of some hierarchy of Slavic nations; instead it stood alone with a set of unique characteristics that together constituted the Russian Self. Although being Russian might imply closeness to Slavs in general on some dimensions, it might just as well imply distance and difference on others. Indeed, the LE assumed that there were certain aspects of non-Slavic peoples, in Asia and Europe, that were more compatible with authentic Russians than the qualities of some Slavic brethren.

In sum, the LE discourse benefitted greatly from the twin crises of August 1998 and April 1999. In both cases, the collapse of the ruble and NATO's bombing of Belgrade, the NWR alternative was exposed as bankrupt, both literally and figuratively. But just as important, the NSR discourse was wholly unable to capitalize on the NWR collapse. Its own economic program of the Soviet past was roundly rejected, and its seemingly irresponsible calls for going to war in the Balkans struck most as, well, irresponsible. The LE discourse, with its measured acceptance and rejection of both External and Internal Others, the western future and the Soviet past, captured the broad discursive consensus of Moscow in 1999.

6/

Identity, Foreign Policy, and IR Theory

Although this book was deliberately designed not to test alternative theories of some outcome in the first instance, its findings about Soviet and Russian identity and foreign policy have implications for other theoretical positions. Conclusions are hard because they demand that we come to closure on issues we are only just beginning to grasp. This involves excluding some points of interest in favor of others, even though the excluded points, for many readers, may seem to be much more interesting and important. The two sets of implications I concentrate on in this concluding chapter are how the theoretical apparatus of social cognitive structure, discursive formation, and identity held up to my empirical tests and how the findings about identity and Soviet and Russian foreign policy may contribute to the further development of both an interpretivist methodology for constructivism and constructivist theories of international relations.

IDENTITY AND DISCOURSE:
SOVIET UNION 1955 — RUSSIAN FEDERATION 1999

Competition among discursive formations is evident in both 1955 and 1999, but especially in 1999. In 1955, the predominant Soviet discourse on the New Soviet Man (NSM) was challenged by those who found difference permissible and even a signifier of socialist strength after the war. This insurgent discourse appeared in the foreign policy debates surrounding not only the rapprochement with Tito, but the acceptance of the entire decolonizing world as potential allies. In 1999, the NWR, the predominant discourse from 1987 to 1993, was discredited by economic failure at home and NATO aggression abroad. The beneficiary, however, was not its binarized Other, the NSR, itself saddled with the identity as the Historical Other, the Soviet past, which was unacceptable to most. Instead, it was the LE discourse that was empowered in its competition with the other three by combining a liberal attitude toward Others, toward difference, against binarization, with a commitment to an unspecified but theoretically knowable authentic Russian identity.

The methodological strategy of remaining open to an inductive recovery of identity, which is truer to interpretivism's epistemological position on intersubjectivity and intertextuality, yielded significant evidentiary and theoretical rewards. Had I simply assumed the typical western modern monadic Self, I never would have been alert to the LE Russian identity of a Self whose constituent elements bear far more resemblance to the (still problematically essentialized) Eastern relational Self investigated by cross-cultural experimental psychologists since the 1980s, but still not yet the default Self of mainstream western social science.[1]

Cognitive Findings

The relevance of cognitive models of identity was instantiated every time Khrushchev understood India through central Asia, Molotov apprehended Yugoslavia through deviations from the NSM, the NSR grasped the United States through the Soviet Cold War past, or Yegor Gaidar appreciated Russia through liberal market democracy in the United States.[2] Molotov and Khrushchev each had a list of diagnostic variables derived from his understanding of the NSM, and each had a different level of tolerance for deviation from that identity before it was deemed dangerous. These different Soviet Selves were then used to guide the evaluation of Tito and his fitness as an ally. This process is ubiquitous in the empirical chapters of this book.

But the limits of cognition were on display, too, because without situating these identities in a social context, their meanings remain beyond our reach. Each of these apparently discrete identities articulated itself into a discursive formation and its challengers. These larger intersubjective structures not only provided a more comprehensive, and so comprehensible, meaning for these identities, but also intimated how these discourses could be articulated across a range of seemingly unrelated outcomes. It would be hard to see how research uninformed by a social cognitive model of identity employing constructivist and interpretivist techniques could tell a story that links Ehrenburg's novel to Tito's reception of Khrushchev on Biondi Island in June 1955, or Pelevin's opium-smoking advertising man Tatarsky to the collapse of the NWR discourse in 1998–99. The empirically inductive, yet theoretically informed, approach of this book expects there to be such con-

---

[1] Alan Page Fiske, Shinobu Kitayama, Hazel Rose Markus, Richard E. Nisbett, "The Cultural Matrix of Social Psychology," in *Handbook of Social Psychology*, 4th ed. ed. Daniel T. Gilbert, Susan T. Fiske, Gardner Lindzey (New York, 1998), 915–81.

[2] The desirability of marrying cognitive models to social constructivism has been urged by Jeffrey T. Checkel, "The Constructivist Turn in International Relations Theory," *World Politics* 50, no. 2 (January 1998): 324–48; Paul Kowert, "Agent versus Structure in the Construction of National Identity," in *International Relations in a Constructed World*, ed. Vendulka Kubalkova, Nicholas Onuf, and Paul Kowert (Armonk 1998); Paul Kowert and Jeffrey Legro, "Norms, Identity, and Their Limits: A Theoretical Reprise," in *The Culture of National Security: Norms and Identity in World Politics*, ed. Peter J. Katzenstein (New York, 1996), 451–97.

nections in a common social text in which meanings constitute one another across a cultural field, no matter how seemingly unconnected they may initially appear to be.

The relevance of these domestic social identities was established by showing how they made possible Soviet and Russian understandings of Others in world politics. If I have provided convincing evidence of this relationship, I have shown that the recovery of domestic social identities is one possible way of making constructivism work all the way down, rather than having it stop at the level of interstate interactions.[3]

Inductive Recovery of Identities

I think this work has vindicated the method of inductively finding identities in texts rather than a priori stipulating which identities, say, nation and gender, are likely to matter and going out to find them in the discourse. With the exception of the ethnonational Russian identity in 1955, none of the identities that turned out to matter in the elaboration of the dominant discourses and, ultimately, in the understandings of Others in world politics, would have been discoverable had I been employing other methods. Had I been testing alternative theories of alliances, for example, the variables in the theories would have directed my search for evidence. Had I been a critical theorist looking for exercise of power, I might have focused exclusively on class and gender, missing the critical issue of center and periphery, one of the few identities that appeared in both cases. I did not assume that identities mask power relations, that individuals need a group identity, that the Self is in any particular relationship to an Other, or that identities are merely instrumental. Indeed, all these and more may be true, but that is just the point—they may be. Why privilege that which can be empirically (dis)established?[4]

Similarly speaking, avoiding looking for norms and roles paid off in the inductive recovery of identities that would not have fit neatly into such categories. Although the role of being a great power was important in both cases, the rest of the identity relationships would not have made themselves available to a researcher as roles. Identities do not necessarily come in roles or as associates of norms. Had I wanted to see whether Russia in 1999 accepted the norms of sovereignty or nonintervention in other sovereign states' internal affairs, I would have quickly observed that Russia condemned NATO's attack on Yugoslavia on precisely these grounds and so accepted

---

[3] Another limitation to this cognitive approach is its failure to consider a more performative account of foreign policy. I thank Jim Richter for flagging this possible alternative.

[4] It is a fair criticism of this work, however, that by ignoring underlying power relationships I have missed part of the story. But at least I have provided some raw material on which other, more critical hermeneuticians can elaborate. See, for example, Janice Bially Mattern, "The Power Politics of Identity," *European Journal of International Relations* 7 (2001): 349–98.

these norms. But even if it were true that Russia accepted those norms, the failure to look more deeply, into how these norms were embedded in a more comprehensive discourse about Russia's relations to its own domestic periphery, in Chechnia and beyond, and how this articulated itself differently in the various discourses of Russian identity, would have deprived us of the capacity to understand what Russians meant by this norm and how it could be applied to other issues. In effect, recovering Russia's identity topography at home in 1999, finding out about the overarching significance of recentering Russia at home, both subsumes the recovery of the norm and gives it the social meaning through contextualization and intertextualization that it must have in order to have a broader and deeper signiifcance within a discourse on Russian identity. The simple recovery of a norm cannot promise this kind of socialization of its meaning.

Moreover, because the meaning of an identity and its associated discourse were established independently of the norm, the meaning and importance of the norm can be evaluated nontautologically, that is, without reference to its putative effect on foreign policy. By finding that the Russian understanding of the sovereignty norm was already embedded in a discourse on Russian great power identity, which was itself connected to the issue of center-periphery relations, including with Chechnia, before Russia asserted a normative objection to NATO's actions in Yugoslavia, we can have greater certainty that the meaning of this norm was more deeply rooted in domestic identity politics and was not only an instrumental invocation against NATO's conduct.[5]

The inductive investigation of Russia's identity relations with Chechnia helped avert the reduction of that relationship to one of ethnonational and religious difference. Had I only had an a priori theory about national, ethnic, and religious difference, I would have found it. This discovery could have too easily satisfied a search whose theoretical specification precluded looking any farther. By not looking for some theoretically preidentified set of identity relations, I found that the 1999 relationship between Russia and Chechnia was one of criminalization, illegitimatization, sovereignty, and recentering, and not only one of ethnonational and religious binarization.

---

[5] Although beyond the scope of this book, it might be argued that an additional test would be if Russia ever invoked this same norm in ways that contravened its interests. This would not necessarily be a sensible test because the theory of identity presented here already presumes that identities, norms, and interests are mutually constituted and, hence, are pointed in the same direction. That is, the Russian denial of the applicability of, the nonintervention norm with regard to Baltic states' citizenship policies would not demonstrate a lack of commitment to this norm but rather evidence of its effect because Russians are discursively constrained to make their case with respect to this norm. See Friedrich V. Kratochwil and John G. Ruggie, "International Organization: A State of the Art on an Art of the State," *International Organization* 40, no. 4 (autumn 1986), 753–76.

Self and Other

Theorists of identity have treated the relationship between Self and Other as inherently conflictual.[6] Moreover, they often limit what can count as someone's relevant Other, most specifically stipulating that that Other must be another person, rather than a thing, idea, image, or history. My work, however, shows that both of these tendencies capture only a small part of empirical reality and so should not be treated unproblematically as universally valid a priori assumptions on which to build meaningful theories of identity.

What was the relevant Other for a Soviet in 1955? Well, it was not just one Other, and those many Others can only be understood within the larger discourse of modernity, such that all Others were arrayed on a continuum of modernity vis-à-vis the most modernizing Soviet Self. The Soviet Self was at the top of a syntactic hierarchy produced by its class identity and an ethnonational identity, which itself was constructed by the appropriation of Russia to fill the void for an absent Soviet origin myth.[7] But the identities of modernity, class, and NSM were not meaningful as mere flesh and blood and their emergence as the important identities of 1955 Moscow points to the problem of theorizing a priori only a particular collection of relevant Others, rather than remaining open to what we can find in any particular social space.

In 1999, the NSR identified itself through the past, a Soviet past, the Historical Other. The binarized relationship between it and the NWR is incomprehensible without due attention to this historical axis of identification because the NWR saw the only threat to its own identity as coming through the resurrection of this constitutive past. And the NSR binarized the NWR because the NRW identity was read through the Soviet historical understanding of the United States during the Cold War. The LR Other was not a person, either. It was any modern, totalizing, homogenizing project, such as that of the Soviet Union and of the United States. The LE Others included all other states, plus the Soviet past, plus the domestic periphery. Again, although each of these could become personified in the form of Chechens or Americans or Chinese, to understand these human Self-Other identity relationships requires a social and discursive contextualization and intertextualization of both.

At the very least, there is no justification for assuming that the identity of a state can be constructed only vis-à-vis other states. In 1955, the Soviet state

[6] As I have laid out in chapter 1. For an excellent treatment of the different relationships possible between the Self and Other in the context of IR theory, see Iver B. Neumann, *Uses of the Other: "The East" in European Identity Formation* (Minneapolis, 1999), especially 1–37.

[7] On the available representational strategies within a discourse, see Roxanne Lynn Doty, *Imperial Encounters: The Politics of Representation in North-South Relations* (Minneapolis, 1996), 10.

was constructed within a metanarrative of modernity within which identities of the center and periphery, rural and urban, class, Russia and non-Russians, and the NSM and difference were all involved in the construction of a Soviet Self. This is not to say that interactions with other states did not construct the Soviet Self as well. Clearly they did, as the cases of Yugoslavia, China, and India very clearly demonstrate. But constructivism does not begin or end at the water's edge. There is an identity terrain that does not know juridical sovereign boundaries; as the evidence shows, discourses travel and identities traverse. In 1999, the three main discourses of NSR, LE, and NWR had Historical Others, Internal Others, and External Others, respectively. Only the last falls in the category of state-to-state construction.

The Self and Other need not be human, and the Self and Other need not be theorized to be in fixed relationships to one another. The idea that relationships of binary opposition, suppression, and assimilation must characterize the Self and its Other and that therefore conflict and violence are the inevitable concomitants of identity relations is empirically refuted by the findings of this book.[8] Instead, these three critical a priori relationships are joined by relationships of therapy, accommodation, differentiation, and similarity, each of which appeared in Moscow in 1955 and 1999.

Nihilation was evident in NSR-NWR identity relations—each demanded the public disavowal of the other for redemption. These were also binarized pairs, understood as wholly dangerous and completely antithetical to each other. In 1955 the predominant discourse on class, modernity, and the NSM was characterized by both binarization and nihilation, the latter in the physical sense under Stalin. Suppression was evident in ethnonational Russian identity's understanding of non-Russian peoples of central Asia, whose religious and national identities must be suppressed to preserve the modern Soviet project. Assimilation was the relationship characteristic of the challengers to the predominant Soviet discourse on modernity, who argued that the modernizing power of socialism would render national difference moot. A therapeutic relationship existed between the Soviet identity represented by Khrushchev and the Yugoslav identity of 1955, the expectation being that whatever differences existed between the two would be detoxified by contact and interaction with the older Russian brother, just as Ukraine had come to be a part of the Soviet project. These are the kinds of identity relations presumed to operate most frequently in politics: the Self, which needs to constitute its identity with regard to an Other, feels the danger and vul-

---

[8] Others acknowledge variety in these relationships, too. See Jutta Weldes et al., eds. *Cultures of Insecurity: States, Communities, and the Production of Danger* (Minneapolis, 1999); David L. Blaney and Naeem Inayatullah, "The Problem of Comparison or the Two-Handed Choke: International Relations and Modernization Theory as Mutually Constitutive of the Modern Political Imagination," (paper presented at the International Studies Association Annual Meetings, Los Angeles, March, 2000).

nerability of that interdependence and responds with exercises of discursive power in order to restore the illusory monadic Self.

But there are relationships that, although less commonly theorized, were quite common in the discursive formations of 1955 and 1999 Moscow. The LE accommodated itself to the differences it apprehended in Asian and European Others; it changed its own conceptions of the Russian Self in interaction with these Others without denying the difference, or suppressing, nihilating, or assimilating its carriers. Perhaps the most common strategy is differentiating the Self from the Other such that the latter becomes irrelevant to the Self's identity—it is the least-reported and it is usually treated, even in this book, as a nonevent. But to the extent that it happens, it delineates the boundaries of an identity, a discourse, and a domain of relevance. For example, the NWR saw no difference between itself and Asians or Africans or Europeans or Slavs on an ethnonational basis because ethnonational identity was not part of the discourse that constituted it. It operated instead in a supranational realm, as did their modern Soviet predecessors, identifying with democratic liberal market capitalism, no matter where it flourished.

Similarity is perhaps the most complicated of identity relationships. In the discussion of constructivist IR theory later in the chapter, we see just how problematic an issue it can be for studying world politics. Similarity was reflected in the Soviet relationship with China and the NWR relationship with the United States. But the implications for their ultimate relationships could not be more different because of the different kinds of discourses in which these two relationships were embedded. This observation underscores the value of recovering a social context for any observation of identity and not just assuming relationships that look the same are the same.

For instance, China was the Soviet Union's closest Other. It was the Other most capable of subsituting or replacing the Soviet Self and so was at the same time very threatening and very reassuring; hence, the relationship was one of ambiguity and complexity. China threatened Moscow by being an alternate Self that Others could identify with as the vanguard of the socialist revolution in the world. Moreover, and this amplifies on Molotov's fears about identifying Yugoslavia as socialist, whatever happened in China, a great socialist power equal to Moscow, could be read as an authentic practice to be emulated by other aspiring socialist states, including the Soviet Union! As long as China adhered to the Soviet model, all was well; a powerful revolutionary country only reproduced the power of Soviet identity. But if it were to deviate, all Molotov's fears about Yugoslavia could be multiplied by one thousand. Note that the main difficulty between the Chinese and Soviet identities could be resolved easily if only the Soviets would accommodate Chinese identity, rather than trying to assimilate it to the Soviet model. But Soviet identity could not do this because of the metanarrative of modernity in which the predominant Soviet discourse was embedded. As long as the Soviet Union was the center of the world revolutionary process, vanguard of the working class at home and abroad, it placed China in a necessarily subordinate role. Deviance by China was danger, discursively speaking.

In the case of the NWR and the United States, we see quite a different relationship with a closest Other. Instead of subordination of, there was subordination to; instead of assimilation of, there was assimilation to. The NWR understood Russia as the United States, as much as through the United States. This made them already desirous of being the United States, not merely establishing a relationship with it. Whereas Soviet Moscow reserved the right to redefine China right out of the socialist camp, the NWR gave the United States the power to redefine Russia any way that Washington wished. The danger of China to the Soviet Union was a function of the location of China in the predominant Soviet discourse. The United States was not similarly situated in the NWR discourse. Instead the United States was at the top of a teleological hierarchy of modernity, with Russia a willing acolyte, not a center. But what the U.S. Other did mattered just as much for the security of the NWR identity as what the Chinese Other did mattered to Soviet identity. The U.S. war against Yugoslavia in 1999 was as damaging to the NWR vis-à-vis their discursive competitors as the Great Leap Forward was going to be to the Soviet identity after 1957 vis-à-vis its Chinese competitors in eastern Europe and the decolonizing world.

Logics

Everyday logics were apparent in Soviet and Russian discourses. Khrushchev's continual return to central Asia to understand India, and the decolonizing world more generally, is an excellent example of the logic of thinkability. It was not that he, and many other Soviets, could not think differently. It was simply that the predominant discourse had already excluded all other alternative ways of thinking about premodern societies on the road to socialism. Although it was possible to imagine a different world, the probability of doing so was very low and was manifest in the fact that the texts from the period show precious little evidence of any contemplation of alternatives. The Soviet periphery was heuristically available to Khrushchev because of the predominant discourse on modernity in which it was situated. At every stop in India and Burma, Khrushchev offered his advice on how things could be done better, just as if he were visiting Uzbekistan or Kazakhstan. Before CPSU Presidium member Lazar Kaganovich made an official visit to Czechoslovakia in 1955, he received a memorandum from the Ministry of Foreign Affairs outlining the political scene in that country. Its categories of analysis were consistent with the NSM at home, a checklist of features that together constituted the ideal Soviet Self.

Russia in 1999 had more room for the logics of thinkability and imaginability to operate, but even in this relatively varied discursive space, it was hard for any discourse to imagine Russia as anything other than a great power, even if only a regional one, within the former Soviet space. That Russia could continue to decline, might even distintegrate more, was unthinkable within all the discourses except the LR. Becoming the United States is very thinkable for the NWR; becoming the West, but not the United States was very thinkable for the LE; and becoming either was unimaginable to both the NSR and LR. What explains these differences was the different identity relationships that constituted each of the four discourses.

The logics of consequentiality and appropriateness also operated. At the March 1955 CC plenum, Presidium members repeatedly invoked the normative argument that the Soviet Union must or should behave in a particular way toward Tito because they were both socialist countries or because international law, and its implied sovereign rights, demanded it. When the great power identity of the Soviet Union was present, the discourse shifted to a consequentialist logic: if we lose Yugoslavia, then the United States will be able to threaten us militarily; therefore, we must restore relations with Belgrade.

We can see from these examples how both the logics of consequentiality and appropriateness speak to choices made in fear of incurring some kind of cost, whether material, moral, or affective, by acting contrary to the logic of the situation. But the everyday logics do not work this way at all. They are constitutive logics in the social and cognitive sense. They are not invoked to justify some calculation of interest; they make that interest possible by making thinkable and imaginable particular discursively constructed ways of apprehending reality. And this reality is part and parcel of both Self and Other.

Identities and Interests

Soviet and Russian interest in a particular country was related to the discursive formation and its constitutive identities. The NSR discourse constructed Belarus as an interest to Russia by dint of its geopolitical value in the competition with the United States and as the addition of a republic most similar to the Russian Federation. The NWR, on the other hand, did not apprehend Belarus as a Russian interest because it had no geopolitical value vis-à-vis the United States, which the NWR wished Russia to become, and because its economic condition was the absolute antithesis to the liberal market ideal. In 1955, Molotov argued that an alliance with Yugoslavia was important for the Soviet Union because of Yugoslavia's geopolitical value against NATO, but only if it were concluded between the two states, not the two parties. Molotov contended that an alliance at the party level would threaten Soviet interests in its own socialist identity. At the same time,

Khrushchev and Mikoyan agreed with Molotov's geopolitical arguments, but understood Yugoslavia as a valuable socialist ally, a demonstration that difference need not betoken deviance and enmity.[9]

Being able to explain the absence of interests, the presence of interests, and the kinds of interests is one of the promises of an interpretivist constructivist approach to identity. Because interests are attached to identities that are themselves embedded in discourses, it is possible to endogenize the origins of interests in a theory that is nontautologically specified. There is no backward induction from the choice to the interest in order to make it explicable. Instead, it is possible to infer implied interests from identities and discourse and then see if they in fact are present at the moment of choice. This appears to be a better, or at least an alternative, way to theorize interest and choice than exogenization. Moreover, from the perspective of mainstream social science, being able to explain a range of interests and their absence based on a single variable, in this case a socially constructed discursive formation, is superior to an ad hoc account for each interest or a well-informed exogenous guess.

Claims

In chapter 1 I make several points about interpretivist knowledge production. First, its reliability should not be in any greater doubt than that of mainstream social science. Second, if the theoretical account of identity and foreign policy works here, it should work elsewhere, especially given the demanding conditions of the Soviet case. Third, generalizations beyond the two cases should be quite cautious. And fourth, claims to validity are very modest; any scholar, in principle at least, should be able to reinterpret the move from the intertextualization of sources to discursive formations and be able to collect a different sample of texts that might yield a different set of narratives altogether.

The social cognitive model of identity and foreign policy choice has performed sufficiently well to merit testing in other historical locales. It has survived the hard post-totalitarian case of the Soviet Union, furnished plausible understandings of a wide variety of Soviet and Russian Others, and demonstrated covariance, or a close relationship, between different identities and discursive formations and different understandings of these other states.

I expect the discourse on modernity to provide a compelling account of Soviet relations with the decolonizing world for many years after 1955. I expect the discourse on difference and deviance to experience a real test with reality in eastern Europe in 1956. I predict the same with respect to China, but with even more dramatic consequences for Soviet views of the Self be-

---

[9] The differences between Molotov and Khrushchev may also have been about state and party identities. James C. Richter, *Khrushchev's Double Bind* (Baltimore, 1994).

cause China was not just any Other but the single closest Other and because it offered an alternative model for the same decolonizing world that Soviets believed was comprehensible through their own central Asian experience.

The generalizing claims based on the evidence for 1999 have to be less confident than the ones based on the data from 1955 because no archival sources were used to test the implications of the domestic identities in 1999. Having stipulated that, I predict that, to the extent the LE discourse remains the center of Russian identity politics, Russia's continued aspiration to avoid becoming the United States and concerted effort to draw closer to Europe and form ad hoc tactical relationships with China and Iran. If the United States continues to take unilateral actions in the world that violate Russia's normative geopolitical identity, the NWR discourse and its associated identity will eventually disappear from the scene, simultaneously resuscitating the prospects for the NSR. But recall that the NSR has a clear limit, given its roundly discredited and disliked Historical Soviet Other; because of this, only the most extreme of U.S. foreign policy adventurism can push the center of Russian discourse toward the NSR position, along with its nationalist, neofascist allies. But, of course, such U.S. behavior is not at all excluded.[10]

The LE middle will remain committed to restoring Russia's economic and military material capacity to act like a great power, but with the aim of securing Russia's position as the center of the former Soviet Union, not of Eurasia, as NSR geopoliticians advocate. If the LE efforts to become Europe succeed—its economic and political reforms bear liberal socialist fruit; the outcome in Chechnia begins to look like that recommended by the OSCE and CE; NATO expansion either stalls or continues to appear innocuous; and Europeans do not submit to Washington's will on BMD—Russia could reach the LE promised land. Russia would remain Russia, although in a relationship with Europe, secure against the United States, while not becoming it, the center of a post-Soviet region held together by economic and cultural ties, not insecurities and dangers. By far the most important sources of discursive movement here are the success or failure of economic reform and the denouement in Chechnia. The only external force capable of affecting Russian discourse in the nearest future after 1999 is U.S. unilateralism.

Alternate Routes to Identity

The issue of validity arises because the intepretation of the particular sample of texts I use here is only one possible way of finding identities and re-

---

[10] As I am writing these words, the U.S. government is trying to enlist Russian support in the fight against international terrorism. I predict, based on the discursive analysis of 1999, that the LE will respond to such an offer positively, insofar as it is read through the danger from Chechnia, and the NWR will gain discursively at the expense of the NSR, whose binarized hostility toward the United States will preclude them from supporting such an alliance, despite the advantages for reestablishing the center in Chechnia.

lating them to foreign policy. There are three broad strategies that can be used: broadening, deepening, and quantifying. The most obvious additional approach is to use different samples of texts. In 1955, for example, more plays, poetry, movies, non-Russian publications, regional publications, and scholarly journals in other fields, such as history, philosophy, and economics, can be collected. In 1999, movies, TV broadcasts, radio shows, theater, romance novels, how-to books, regional newspapers, Duma proceedings, official statements and documents from the foreign ministry and CIS, and publications about the oligarchs can be analyzed. This first strategy of broadening involves only adding more and different texts.

The second strategy of deepening involves the practical recovery of discursive practice through ethnography and the linguistic recovery of discourse through textual analysis. Instead of reading Soviet and Russian identities, it is possible to observe and live them through ethnographic participant-observation fieldwork in Russia itself. Instead of reading descriptions of the social relationships that prevail between men and women, Russians and non-Russians, center and periphery, we can observe, experience and record these identities in practice. Ethnography deepens our understanding of identity by experiencing it as practice; linguistic anthropology deepens our understandings of how the language in texts performs within a social context. Instead of expanding our collection of texts, we can concentrate on a far smaller collection and pursue a semiotic analysis of the performative speech contained within the discourse. This approach involves exploring how those in power manipulate discourse and identity to reproduce their own privileged positions, a critical political account of identity rather than the cognitive one offered here.

The third strategy involves building on what has already been demonstrated in this book. If we accept the identities, discourses, and related foreign policy implications as hypotheses to be tested further, the next step is the use of focus groups or large-n surveys to test the validity of these hypotheses. Do people really cluster the way I say they do in the four discourses of 1999? A factor analysis of a survey whose questions have been derived from my findings can provide an answer to that. Do people really understand Chechnia as a criminalized rather than an ethnonationalized Other, and does this issue relate to the broader identity of center-periphery, as I contend? A well-constructed series of focus groups using protocols based on the evidence presented here can help answer this question.

In sum, the research in this book has demonstrated the promise of a social cognitive model of identity, shorn of a range of a priori assumptions and equipped with an interpretivist methodology of deep induction and thick intertextualization. It has shown the full panoply of relationships between Self and Other, the importance of the logics of thinkability and imaginability, the connection between identities and interests, and the capacity to link domestic discourse to foreign policy choice. But, in addition, the research shows that it has the capacity to combine in many ways with other approaches to the same question, thus not rendering itself incommensurable to the scholarly interests of its Others.

SOCIALIZING CONSTRUCTIVISM: IR IS WHAT STATES (AND SOCIETIES) MAKE OF IT

The findings of this book have important implications for three approaches to world politics: neorealism, normative constructivism, and systemic constructivism. I argue that neorealism captures only a fraction of empirical reality with its assumption that different distributions of power tend to produce different propensities toward balancing behavior by great powers; that normative constructivism's focus on norms per se excessively narrows constructivism's theoretical domain, depriving it of its own social ontology; and that systemic constructivism's focus on interaction among states as the site for state identity production is insufficient to account for the range of identities that states in fact possess and needs to domesticize itself and become constructivist all the way down.

Neorealism

As a systemic theory of international relations, neorealism treats as a virtue its inability to explain or predict the foreign policy behavior of any state, including the actions of those great powers that are its only actors.[11] Instead, the theory claims to be able to show why the state system tends more toward balancing behavior by its actors under one distribution of capabilities (bipolarity) than under a second (multipolarity.) Because it is particular states, great powers, that engage in this balancing behavior, it should not be unreasonable to infer some testable hypotheses about great power foreign policy, at least with respect to the balancing behavior, from this structural theory of international relations.[12] According to neorealist theory, the United States and the Soviet Union should have balanced against one another through the accumulation of allies, development of weaponry, and appropriate responses to the other side's moves anywhere on the globe where "it may lead to significant gains or losses for either of them."[13] Kenneth

---

[11] Kenneth A. Waltz, *Theory of International Politics* (Reading, 1979).

[12] Indeed, Waltz himself, in his otherwise structuralist book repeatedly cites foreign policy evidence to support his structural theory. Mastanduno concludes, as well, that neorealism offers falsifiable hypotheses about great power foreign policy. Michael Mastanduno, "Preserving the Unipolar Moment: Realist Theories and U.S. Grand Strategy after the Cold War," *International Security* 21, no. 4 (spring 1997): 52–53.

[13] Waltz, *Theory of International Politics,* 171.

Waltz terms the entire period from the end of World War II to the collapse of the Soviet Union in 1991 a case of of systemic bipolarity.

Apparently neorealists cannot agree on which kind of distribution of power best characterizes the world since 1991. Is it U.S. unipolarity because the United States has the largest share of economic power, and preponderant share of military power in the world?[14] Or is it a kind of rump bipolarity, given Russia's possession of nuclear weapons? Waltz hardly clarifies matters, writing in 1993 that the world remains bipolar but "in an altered state" because Russia can provide for its own security, but then, only seven years later, categorizing the world as unipolar.[15] Nevertheless, only a multipolar distribution of power could predict what actually occurred in 1999, a failure of Russia and other great powers to balance against the United States, and this is the only distribution of power neorealists apparently do not entertain as a valid description of contemporary international politics.[16] Regardless of whether the world is unipolar or bipolar, neorealists agree that other powers should be balancing against the United States and that if they are not now, then they will at some unspecified time in the future—if "not today, then tomorrow."[17]

Waltz himself claims that the creation of the Warsaw Pact by Moscow in 1955 as a response to the Marshall Plan and the creation of NATO, vindicates his

[14] As argued in Mastanduno, "Preserving the Unipolar Moment," 49–88; Christopher Layne, "The Unipolar Illusion: Why New Great Powers Will Rise," *International Security* 17, no. 4 (spring 993): 5–51; William C. Wohlforth, "The Stability of a Unipolar World," *International Security* 24, no. 1 (summer 1999): 5–41.

[15] Kenneth A. Waltz, "The Emerging Structure of International Politics," *International Security* 18, no. 2 (fall 1993): 52; Kenneth A. Waltz, "Structural Realism after the Cold War," *International Security* 25, no. 1 (summer 2000): 27–28.

[16] In the same year that he asserted the world was unipolar, Waltz also wrote in another publication that it was "gradually becoming multipolar." Kenneth N. Waltz, "Intimations of Multipolarity," in *The New World Order. Contrasting Theories*, ed. Birthe Hansen and Bertel Heurlin (Houndmills, 2000). 1. Perhaps out of frustration with the intractability of specifying neorealism's only causal variable, the distribution of power, some notable realists have distanced themselves from association with this structural aspect of neorealist thought altogether, acknowledging it might not explain as much as was previously thought. See, for example, Randall L. Schweller, "Realism and the Present Great Power System: Growth and Positional Conflict Over Scarce Resources," in *Unipolar Politics. Realism and State Strategies after the Cold War*, ed. Ethan B. Kapstein and Michael Mastanduno (New York, 1999), 28–68; Joseph M. Grieco, "Realism and Regionalism: American Power and German and Japanese Institutional Strategies during and after the Cold War," in *Unipolar Politics. Realism and State Strategies after the Cold War*, ed. Ethan B. Kapstein and Michael Mastanduno (New York, 1999), 319–53. For an empirical work that concludes that polarity is not relevant to the explanation of great power conflict, see Ted Hopf, "Polarity, The Offense-Defense Balance and War," *American Political Science Review* 85, no. 2 (June 1991): 475–93.

[17] Waltz, "Structural Realism, after the Cold War," 27, 30–41. In this work, too, Waltz denies neorealism can be falsified by foreign policy outcomes while simultaneously adducing such outcomes to demonstrate the empirical validity of the theory.

account of bipolar balancing.[18] He goes on to claim that Soviet aid to Egypt also confirms his theory, because Moscow was balancing against the United States by reaching out to allies in the decolonizing world.[19] But as we know from the evidence presented in chapters 2 and 3, the Soviet Union had not balanced this way until 1955. In other words, during the Cold War from 1945 to 1955, a period that saw a blockade of Berlin, the creation of NATO, a war in Korea, and anticolonial wars in Indochina and Algeria, neorealist theory mispredicts the same outcomes its adherents cite to validate the theory in 1955. What explains Soviet balancing behavior in 1955, to the extent that Soviet actions can be called that, are the changes in the Soviet understanding of itself and what this understanding implied about the decolonizing world, Yugoslavia, and China to the Soviet leaders who sought alliances there.

Had Molotov's version of Soviet modernity prevailed, with its fear of dangerous difference, an alliance with Yugoslavia would have been effected against the United States, and this would have been consistent with neorealist expectations: a state-to-state collaboration to balance against U.S. power. But alliances in the decolonizing world, in Egypt, India, and elsewhere, would not have been consummated because they would have been inconsistent with Molotov's discourse of deviance; these possible confirmations of neorealist theory would not have happened. Moreover, the Soviet alliance with China would have deepened because in Molotov's discourse the Soviet Union's closest Other was even closer and would have become still more so had the actually predominant Soviet discourse been rejected. In that eventuality, Yugoslavia, shorn of a socialist identity, would not have contradicted China's own view of itself and so would not have posed an obstacle to China and the Soviet Union becoming still more similar.

But what actually happened in 1955 shows that even if there is some structural tendency toward balance, whether it happens depends on the identities of the parties concerned. The Soviet effort to ally with Tito in 1955 was only partly driven by geopolitical concerns, the rationale expected by neorealists. Indeed, the other three parts of the Soviet rationale—identification with a socialist Other, identification with a subordinate Slavic brother, and atonement for past violations of commitments to international norms of sovereignty and nonintervention—have nothing to do with neorealism, and, yet, without them Soviet actions could not have been possible. How do we know this? Because for the previous eight years the Soviet Union had regarded Yugoslavia as an enemy although the structural aspects of international politics were the same.

Moreover, the alliance with Yugoslavia, embedded as it was in a Soviet discourse on permissible difference, sowed the seeds of serious and growing

---

[18] Waltz, *Theory of International Politics,* 171.

[19] Ibid., 172.

differences with China on the issue of socialist identity. Because of the Soviet tolerance of deviance from the ideal in Yugoslavia, the closest Other, China, had its own ontological security violated; what had not been socialist before Khrushchev's trip to Belgrade in May 1955, let alone after the February 1956 Twentieth Party Congress speech, became socialist thereafter, an expansion of the boundaries of a socialist identity that reverberated throughout the bloc. Although that reverberation lost the Soviet Union an ally in China, an ally neorealism predicts Moscow would have made efforts to hold dear given its geopolitical significance, it made allies of dozens of decolonizing states that had heretofore been dichotomously identified as part of the West, the most hostile Other.

Although there was a great deal of geopolitical justification by Soviet leaders for accepting Austria's neutrality (I am not sure whether neorealism predicts ceding positions to the predominant power or not) and some for improving relations with Tito, there was virtually none in discussions about the decolonizing world. Here, alliances were understood through the Soviet periphery in central Asia. These vast parts of the world were to liberate themselves, politically and economically, from the thrall of imperialism by accepting the vanguard role of Moscow in their liberation struggles. Again, even if the rationale had been geopolitical, why did it take until 1955 to balance against the United States in these parts of the world? Is it not because the predominant discourse had shifted with Stalin's death and that Molotov's efforts to claim that all difference was deviance rang hollow in a society going through the Thaw, in which many, many innocuous and even productive differences were emerging? I think this is a more adequate explanation for one of the most consequential foreign policy actions of the Cold War. Without this move toward the toleration of difference, it is hard to imagine that the horrors of Vietnam, Angola, Afghanistan, and Cambodia could have occurred.[20] Prior to this domestic differentiation, Soviets simply had no thinkable or imaginable interests in these places.

Again, it cannot be due merely to structure, which remained unchanged, or to interaction with the United States, because Washington, Paris, and London had been continuously involved in the decolonizing world since the end of the war. The only reasonable explanation appears to be the change in the discursive construction of Soviet identity at home and its articulation in the foreign policy discourse of the time.

The fact that in 1999 Russia had not balanced against the United States by allying with other countries is contrary to neorealist predictions. But instead of merely accepting neorealist assurances that it must eventually occur,

---

[20] It is the cruelest of ironies that toleration of difference at home was connected to so much eventual carnage in the rest of the world.

the research here on the alternative discursive formations that constituted Russia's 1999 identity terrain can suggest when, discursively speaking, neorealist predictions are most likely to come true. If the NSR discourse were to become predominant, there is no doubt that Russia would attempt to balance against the United States.[21] But this only amplifies the fact that international structure, understood as the distribution of capabilities, is indeterminate. If neorealism's predictions must rest on particular identities and discourses predominating in a state, then it is hardly sufficient unto itself to understand, explain, or predict this outcome—and this outcome is the only dependent variable neorealist theory offers.

For the NSR, a Belarussian accession to the Russian Federation and an alliance with Yugoslavia were actions aimed at balancing against the United States. In this respect, the Russian Left most closely accords with the predictions of neorealist theories.[22] There is a close connection between the NSR discourse, which binarizes and dichotomizes political forces at home, and neorealist theory, which posits that bipolarity dichotomizes and binarizes the globe. The NSR, like neorealism, in fact believed the world was bipolar. As Aleksandr Dugin, a member of the Duma from the National-Bolshevik Party and a well-known geopolitician, argued, "any conflict . . . must be connected to those global forces which compete at the planetary level. We are talking about the competition of the Atlanticist pole with the Eurasian pole. . . . "[23] If Dugin's ideas, and those of his NSR colleagues, had won out in the discursive competition in Russia that unfolded in the 1990s in Russia, neorealists would now be citing Russia's balancing behavior as vindication of the theory's predictions under uni/bipolar conditions. But the empirical record is not so supportive.

Earlier, it looked as if the NWR discourse was predominant. The NWR identification with the United States was partially consistent with at least two strands of realism, if not neorealism. Randall Schweller's ideas about "bandwagoning for profit" come to mind. In Schweller's parlance, the NWR was engaged in the "piling on" variety of bandwagoning; it was trying to ally with the side that had already won the Cold War, in hopes of sharing in the spoils.[24] Indeed, this was precisely how the NSR understood the actions of these putative fifth-columnists. But the NWR desires to become the United

[21] But recall that Europe was not an available ally for the NSR, because it assumed Europe's subordination to Washington. This allied unavailability for reductionist ideational reasons is not comprehensible under neorealism.

[22] Just as during the Cold War, it was only a particular kind of Soviet decision maker who understood the world as predicted by deterrence theory. Ted Hopf, *Peripheral Visions: Deterrence Theory and American Foreign Policy in the Third World, 1965–1990* (Ann Arbor, 1994).

[23] Aleksandr Dugin, "Caucasus Footprints of Atlanticism," *KZ,* 10 September 1999, p. 3.

[24] Randall L. Schweller, "Bandwagoning for Profit: Bringing the Revisionist State Back In," *International Security* 19, no. 1 (summer 1994): 72–107.

States, to exist under U.S. hegemony, and to dissolve Russia's identity into the western liberal capitalist Other appear to violate the fundamental realist rule of sovereign autonomy and self-preservation, and so realism's applicability to the Russian case still appears to be limited. Another version of realism, Steven David's "omnibalancing," offers a possible reason for why the NWR were inclined to sacrifice Russia's independent Self for a western identity—it feared its dichotomized Other, the NSR, so much, that it preferred to bandwagon with the United States in order to balance against this domestic threat.[25] The only limitation to David's realist theory of domestic threat, as too with Steven Walt's realist theory of balances of threat, is the absence of an account of threat that is endogenous to either theory.[26] One of the advantages of a social constructivist account of a state's identities and interests in other states is that it endogenizes the origins of threat within the discourses that constitute that state. In this way, for example, we can see how NSR and NWR discourses constituted threats to one another and so predict how they would regard other states beyond Russia's borders, without resorting to post hoc specification of the nature of other states.[27]

But neither the NWR nor the NSR discourse dominated in Russia in 1999. Instead, it was the LE understanding of Russia's need to recenter its authentic Self vis-à-vis its own internal periphery, as well as the modern world, that dominated. Neorealism has a hard time capturing the meaning of this discourse for Russian behavior. It would appear that realism is most relevant in explaining a state's behavior if that state is dominated by a discourse that binarizes and dichotomizes both external and internal Others, in the way that Soviet discourse on Austria did in 1955 or the NSR did with regard to NATO and Yugoslavia in 1999. But the predominant LE discourse of 1999 did not have this kind of binary logic in it. Instead of the binarized bipolarity of the NSR discourse or the homogenized unipolarity of the NWR, the LE understood the world as one of multipolar difference. Each state, or at least each great power, was endowed with the sovereign right to be its authentic Self. Instead of balancing against threats from other states, the LE balanced against the threats emanating from Russia's decentering at home and abroad.

[25] Steven R. David, *Choosing Sides: Alignment and Realignment in the Third World* (Baltimore, 1991). See also Deborah Welch Larson, "Bandwagon Images in American Foreign Policy: Myth or Reality?" in *Dominoes and Bandwagons: Strategic Beliefs and Great Power Competition in the Eurasian Rimland*, ed. Robert Jervis and Jack Snyder (New York, 1991), 85–111.

[26] Stephen Walt, *The Origins of Alliances* (Ithaca, 1987).

[27] This is also a problem in Schweller's post facto identification of revisionist and status quo states. Knowing how international politics has worked because of the existence of states that have engaged in expansion rather than in the protection of the status quo is interesting, but still more interesting is a theory that can demonstrate how these two simplified types of states may be possible, both through domestic and interstate discursive practice. Schweller, "Bandwagoning for Profit."

Again, and not inconsistent with David's notion of omnibalancing, the Russian state was balancing against the weakening of the domestic center and consequent growing estrangement of the periphery from that center. Although Chechnia was the most dangerous manifestation of this domestic Other, the empowerment of the periphery in general was the central threat to the maintenance of both the Russian Self and Russia itself. In this way, any external threat exacerbating this internal danger was to be balanced against. Although this might result in actions that look like balancing against an external threat, they are not comprehensible within the neorealist frame; they must be situated instead within the domestic identity context in which they are constituted.

A comparison of NSR and LE understandings of NATO's war against Yugoslavia demonstrates why this difference is crucial. Both discourses inferred that the United States was threatening Russian interests there, but the NSR inferences were not based on events in Kosovo but rather were already discursively internalized by the very identity of the United States for the NSR and therefore for Russia. The United States was not the LE binarized Other, as it is for the NSR. If it were, a neorealist account of 1999 Russian foreign policy would look quite accurate, but it is not. Instead the LE understood the threat from the United States in Kosovo through the war in Chechnia, through the center-periphery relationship prevailing in Russia, and through the project of recentering Russia more generally in the world and at home. In this very important way, LE interests in U.S. actions in Kosovo were contingent on the state of center-periphery relations at home, not on an a priori discursive understanding of the United States as Other or on a bipolar distribution of power in the world. The LE balanced, but not against other states per se. Instead it balanced against its own internal Others—which we might call balancing without binarization.

Finally, essentialized difference implied that alliances would not be entered into on the basis of common identity because all identities were fundamentally unique. But this did not mean the absence of a rationale for alliances because the LE felt threatened by Others in the world that could undermine Russia's identity at home, and this meant the United States is the single greatest potential threat in the world. This implies an effort to protect Russia from both modernities: the one offered by the NWR in the form of becoming the West and the one offered by the NSR in the form of a return to Soviet modernity. Although protection against both these threats was primarily a domestic matter of reconstructing a genuine Russian daily life, help in the form of tactical alliances with Europe, China, Japan, or Iran were not foreclosed. But they would not be alliances of identity; they would be alliances for identity.

In sum, neorealism cannot account for the failure of the Soviet Union to balance against the United States in Yugoslavia and the decolonizing world before 1955, it cannot explain the Soviet Union's inability to remain allied with China after the 1950s, and it cannot explain Russia's failure to balance against the United States after the collapse of the Soviet Union in 1991. Neo-classical realism, balance of threat, and omnibalancing are each able to offer accounts consistent with at least some of the behavior of Russia since the end of the Cold War, but each of them fails to theorize its most important variable in a way that endogenizes its origin and effects.

Normative and Systemic Constructivism

Although I prefer not to contribute further to the proliferation of constructivisms,[28] I distinguish here three approaches to constructivist IR theory that have significant differences, that is, differences that have very real implications for how world politics can be explained, how research on it might be pursued, and what kinds of arguments about it can be made. I call these normative constructivism, which focuses on states' adherence to international norms; systemic constructivism, which seeks to account for interstate identity structures; and social constructivism, the approach of this book, which relies on domestic socio-cognitive roots of state identity. These varieties are not mutually exclusive; all three should be included in any constructivist account. My own contribution to social constructivism is only an incomplete effort in itself. That said, here I show how the research in this book might render problematic some of the conventions of research associated with both normative and systemic constructivism. I urge strongly that domestic society, its identities, discourses, and relationships to the state, must be brought back into any constructivist account of world politics.

There are two potential problems with normative constructivism's focus on state adherence to norms. First, it pays insufficient attention to the domestic context within which any international norm is embedded, especially the domestic discursive context with its associated social identities and practices. Second, it increasingly accepts consequentialist logic, the conflation of the logic of appropriateness with that of consequentiality, and more or less disregards the logics of thinkability and imaginability.

Perhaps it is the case that a focus on international norms is an artifact of systemic constructivism's claims that state identities are primarily the product of interaction among actors at the international level. Perhaps this explains why some of the most important constructivist scholarship involves identifying an international norm of interest and then investigating how it

---

[28] Ted Hopf, "The Promise of Constructivism in IR Theory," *International Security* 23, no. 1 (summer 1998): 171–200; John Gerard Ruggie, "What Makes the World Hang Together? Neo-utilitarianism and the Social Constructivist Challenge," *International Organization* 52, no. 4 (autumn 1998): 855–85; Dale C. Copeland, "The Constructivist Challenge to Structural Realism," *International Security* 25, no. (fall 2000): 187–212.

came to be adopted or rejected by states.[29] This might be called the "weak cognitivist" approach to investigating the "processes which produce the self-understandings of states, their identities," by looking at the "normative and causal beliefs that decision makers hold."[30] But this is precisely the problem, stopping our assessment of how a state's identity is constructed once we have found the empirical evidence of a decision maker adopting a particular norm. Rather than ending the search, this should begin the process of re-constructing the social discursive context that made possible the particular understanding of that norm so that it could be adopted by the decision maker. John Ruggie, in summarizing what constructivism has heretofore ac-complished, points out that its practitioners are not "beginning with the ac-tual social construction of meanings and significance from the ground up"[31] but rather trying to establish the existence of a particular collective social fact and its impact on behavior. Following Ruggie's advice, we have to bring society back into constructivist accounts of international politics. At best, normative constructivists describe the politics surrounding the contestation of a norm, politics being construed as the struggle among branches of gov-ernment, bureaucracies, and interest groups, but without delving into the social construction of the meanings of the discursive instruments being used in these struggles.[32] Whereas constructivism, or the boundaries of mean-

[29] I have in mind there Martha Finnemore, *National Interests in International Society* (Ithaca, 1996); Kathryn Sikkink, "Human Rights, Principles Issue-Networks, and Sovereignty in Latin America," *International Organization* 47, no. 3 (1993): 411–41; Nina Tannenwald, "The Nuclear Taboo: The US and the Normative Basis of Nuclear Non-Use," *International Organization* 53, no. 3 (summer 1999): 433–68; Richard Price, "Reversing the Gun Sights: Transna-tional Civil Society Targets Land Mines," *International Organization* 52, no. 3 (summer 1998): 613–44; Audie Klotz, "Norms Reconstituting interests: Global Racial Equality and US Sanc-tions Against South Africa," *International Organization* 49, no. 3 (summer 1995): 451–78.

[30] Andreas Hasenclever, Peter Mayer, and Volker Rittberger, *Theories of International Regimes* (Cambridge, U.K. 1998), 136. In referring to normative constructivists, I absolutely do not have in mind the work of Onuf, Kratochwil, or Weber, each of whom Hasanclever, Mayer, and Rittberger term "strong cognitivists" who have integrated the linguistic, as opposed to merely sociological, turn into their work on norms in international politics. Nicholas Greenwood Onuf, *World of Our Making: Rules and Rule in Social Theory and International Relations* (Colum-bia, 1989); Friedrich V. Kratochwil, *Rules, Norms, and Decisions: On the Conditions of Practical and Legal Reasoning in International Relations and Domestic Affairs* (Cambridge, Mass., 1989); Cynthia Weber, *Simulating Sovereignty: Intervention, the State, and Symbolic Exchange* (Cambridge, U.K., 1995).

[31] Ruggie, "What Makes the World Hang Together?" 870–84.

[32] This is also where Milner and Moravcsik stop, perhaps indicating a common boundary for meaningful politics shared by liberals and normative constructivists. Helen V. Milner, *Interests, Institutions, and Information: Domestic Politics and International Relations* (Princeton, 1997); Andrew Moravcsik, "Taking Preferences Seriously: A Liberal Theory of International Politics," *International Organization* 51, no. 4 (autumn 1997): 513–53. This shared account of politics, in part at least, inspired Jennifer Sterling-Folker to lump the two research pro-grams together. Jennifer Sterling-Folker, "Competing Paradigms or Birds of a Feather? Con-

ingful intersubjectivity, stops at the water's edge for systemic constructivists, it appears to stop at society's edge for normative constructivists.

Nina Tannenwald's important work on the "anti-nuclear taboo" in Cold War U.S. foreign policy, had it abided by Ruggie's advice, might have explored how this particular norm was related to other identities of the U.S. Self and domestic social practices. She points out that the nuclear taboo was consistent with a U.S. view of itself as civilized.[33] But how did the United States come to understand itself as civilized and vis-à-vis which external, internal, historical, or imagined Others? Were the discourses associated with a rejection of the nonuse of nuclear weapons also associated with a "civilized" U.S. identity? If so, how were they discursively different? In what kind of relations were they? Without a thick social narrative on war, civilization, and perhaps morality, the constructivist account is quickly reduced to the choice or rejection of the norm by a decision maker rather than a social account of the configurations of intersubjective meanings that made possible the very thinkability or imaginability of these choices.[34]

Richard Price's work on the adoption of the land-mine ban shows movement in this direction. Among many other factors that he lists for how norms may be adopted, he suggests that new international norms succeed because they resonate with domestic norms.[35] This could fruitfully mean an effort to recover the domestic normative context before assessing how a decision maker regards a norm, assuming constructivists believe that a decision maker is part and parcel of her social context and not only driven by the roles and rules of office.

One of the consequences of not having a discursive account for the emer-

---

structivism and Neoliberal Institutionalism Compared," *International Studies Quarterly* 44 (2000): 97–119. Some who are concerned with strategic culture also are constructivists at the elite or bureaucratic level, with no explicit concern with social discourse more deeply or international norms more systemically. For example, Elizabeth Kier, "Culture and French Military Doctrine before World War II," in *The Culture of National Security: Norms and Identity in World Politics*, ed. Peter J. Katzenstein (New York, 1996), 186–215; Alastair I. Johnston, *Cultural Realism: Strategic Culture and Grand Strategy in Chinese History* (Princeton, 1995).

[33] Tannenwald, "Nuclear Taboo," 437.

[34] See Joseph Underhill-Cady, *Death and the Statesman: The Culture and Psychology of U.S. Leaders During Wartime* (New York, 2001).

[35] Price, "Reversing the Gun Sights," 616. Price even sweepingly declares that a "complete account of international norm change and resistance would require the empirical investigation of the domestic politics and culture of all states" (616). At this stage, just one state so investigated would be a big step forward. Indeed, two IR scholars who do not subscribe to constructivism, Chaim Kaufmann and Robert Pape, express some degree of surprise that constructivists pay attention only to the "acceptance of obligations to a universal moral community" rather than realizing that it is the collection of domestic identities in eighteenth-century England that explains British advocacy of a ban on the slave trade from Africa. Chaim D. Kaufmann and Robert A. Pape, "Explaining costly International Moral Action: Britain's Sixty-Year Campaign against the Atlantic Slave Trade," *International Organization* 53, no. 4 (autumn 1999): 644.

gence of a norm's acceptability is the charge that "constructivists do not provide a theoretical basis for understanding why one norm rather than another becomes institutionalized."[36] This criticism can be avoided if we provide the reader with a picture of the discursive terrain of a society, its identities and practices, such that the adoption and rejection of norms are implied by the discursive formations that have been empirically identified independently from the decision maker's choices. This kind of research goes to heart of the problem of the hypothesized fit between international norms and domestic discourse.

Some normative constructivists have made the argument that the more universalistic a norm seems to be internationally, the more likely it is that it will be adopted, because of the logic of appropriateness presumed to prevail among states seeking legitimacy.[37] Although plausible, no doubt often true, and consistent with John Meyer's version of sociological isomorphism, it is confounded by the Russian case here, wherein the LE, NSR, and LR discourses, to varying degrees and in various ways, celebrated the uniqueness of individual states, consciously and deliberately rejected any universalizing assumptions, and desired to find a space in international society where the writ of universalism did not run. Indeed, the only discourse that admitted universalist pretensions was delegitimized on these exact grounds.[38]

The normative constructivist answer to why states adopt or reject norms often seems consequentialist, sometimes conflates the logics of consequentialism and appropriateness, and does not entertain everyday logic at all. Norms are not infrequently presented by these scholars as instrumentalities to be used to advance some interest of an actor; when they are, this is consequentialist logic. Alexander Wendt, in the conclusion to *Social Theory of International Politics*, writes that agents "choose from among available representations of the Self who one will be, and thus what interests one intends to pursue. . . . "[39] What a social constructivist finds theoretically interesting

---

[36] Ann Florini, "The Evolution of International Norms," *International Studies Quarterly* 40, no. 3 (September 1996): 363–89.

[37] John W. Meyer, John Boli, George M. Thomas, and Francisco O. Ramirez, "World Society and the Nation-State," *American Journal of Sociology* 103 (1997): 144–81; Finnemore, *National Interests in International Society*, 29; Martha Finnemore and Kathryn Sikkink, "International Norm Dynamics and Political Change," *International Organization* 52, no. 4 (autumn 1998): 903–7; Price, "Reversing the Gun Sights."

[38] Kaufmann and Pape also find the normative constructivist assumption that an international norm must be "cosmopolitan" to work domestically to be empirically inaccurate. Kaufmann and Pape, "Explaining Costly International Moral Action," 642. Empirically speaking, neorealists are vindicated by the NSR and normative constructivists by the NWR.

[39] Alexander Wendt, *Social Theory of International Politics* (Cambridge, U.K., 1999), 329. He also offers only three reasons for an actor to observe a norm: coercion, self-interest, and recognition of the norm as legitimate (250, 267–68, 288). There is no consideration of Weberian habit or Durkheimian custom and, so, no exploration of everyday logics.

in this statement is the issue of "available" identities because it is the social cognitive structure, and its constituent discourses, that implies which identities the agent might "choose." But the very idea of choice seems excessively consequentialist, as if an actor has some pregiven interest that it can advance through the appropriate choice of an identity or a norm.[40]

An actor who chooses a norm based on who he is (i.e., who finds a norm compatible with his own identity and so accepts it and its behavioral implications) describes a situation located right on the boundary between the logic of appropriateness and the everyday. The difference between the two logics is whether there is any instrumental value to this choice or whether it is simply a constituting act. Norms as "standards of behavior,"[41] or norms chosen in order to legitimize an individual's government[42] are only a short step to the fully consequentialist logic of norms being specified as utilities.[43]

Stating that normative constructivists stop before theorizing society in no way implies that they do not and have not theorized what matters in international politics. In fact, there is significant evidence from the cases in this book that decision makers do in fact use norms according to the logics of consequentiality and appropriateness, leaving behind the kind of "justificatory communication trail" expected by normative constructivists.[44] My only concern is that we do not limit ourselves to that trail alone.

Perhaps the most significant empirical validation of normative constructivism in this book is the Soviet great power identity in 1955. This is an example of an instrumental use of a norm; its reproduction at the interstate level, with apparently no deeper societal construction than the political elite and the foreign policy bureaucracy; and an implicit set of oughts and ought nots for Soviet conduct vis-à-vis other countries, in this case Yugoslavia.[45] Recall that the recognition of the sovereign equality norm both constrained Soviet exercise of its power with respect to Belgrade and at the same time reduced the danger of the Soviet great power identity with respect to weaker states more generally. In the context of Soviet relations with the decolonizing world, for example, the acknowledgment of the normative obligations

[40] Again, this is precisely why Sterling-Folker sees so little difference between constructivism and institutionalism—pregiven interests and an instrumentalist, or neofunctionalist, as she would have it, logic of choice. Sterling-Folker, "Competing Paradigms."

[41] Klotz, "Norms Reconstituting Interests," 451.

[42] Ian Hurd, "Legitimacy and Authority in International Politics," *International Organization* 53, no. 2 (spring 1999): 379–408.

[43] Finnemore and Sikkink, "International Norm Dynamics and Political Change," 910.

[44] Ibid., 892.

[45] On socialization in international institutions, see Alastair Iain Johnston, "Treating International Institutions As Social Environments," *International Studies Quarterly* 45 (2001): 487–516. On constructivist IR scholarship's treatment of sovereignty as an institution, see Christian Reus-Smit, "The Constitutional Structure of International Society and the Nature of Fundamental Institutions," *International Organization* 51 (1997): 555–90, including note 27 on 562.

assumed by all states provided a way of reconciling Soviet great power status with amicable relations with weaker and smaller states. In the joint statement marking the end of Nehru's visit to the Soviet Union, both sides agreed that "smaller and weaker States have a vague and possibly unreasoning fear of bigger Powers."[46] Recognizing this security dilemma, both declared that adhering to the five principles enunciated in Bandung was the best remedy for these irrational concerns. Through the support of and adherence to these international normative practices, the Soviet Union could soften its image as a traditional great power. In 1999, Russia's regard for the international norms of sovereignty, nonintervention, territorial integrity, and antiterrorism worked to enable the strategy of Russia's recentering, both at home and abroad, but also imposed a constraint on Russia's thinkable reactions to other states' treatment of the Russian diaspora, especially in the Baltic states.

Price has pointed out that a society can demand that its government adhere to a normative commitment that it has already made.[47] In this formulation (consequentialism), the government's need to justify a deviation from its own normative holding meets popular discourse—the public's capacity to articulate its interest within the confines of a particular normative language. In 1955, Soviet elites found themselves faced with precisely this issue. Having declared that difference was permissible within socialist reality, citizens continually tried to hold the government to that normative standard, indeed, tried, within that language, to test how far the boundaries of difference could go before the state's conception of its ideal identity was threatened. In this way discourse provided both its own limits and also the practices capable of redefining those limits in interaction between society and the state. We can see the same process occurring with the delegitimization of the NWR discourse in 1999. Having constituted itself according to market and democratic identities at home and the hegemonic order of Washington abroad, the perversions of the former and violent acts of the latter combined to discredit the NWR according to its own discursive practices.

In sum, the normative constructivist research agenda is important, but its social reach is limited and its focus on the instrumentalist logics of consequentialism and appropriateness is narrow. The findings here imply both a need to bring society back into constructivism and a need for greater attention to how discourse, identity, and social practice not only affect the very imaginability and thinkability of interests and choice, but also provide an additional source of empirical evidence for the operation of norms themselves.

In this section I discuss some aspects of Alexander Wendt's work on systemic constructivism in light of the evidence in this book. Given the fact that "to

---

[46] Reprinted in *New Times* no. 27 (July 8, 1955): 2.
[47] Price, "Reversing the Gun Sights," 616.

be sure, *Social Theory of International Politics* does not adduce much empirical evidence to support the claim that these what ifs are in fact the case,"[48] it is reasonable to see what a collection of thick empirical evidence has to say about these "what ifs." I assess here the "what ifs" of collective identity, collective identity and international cooperation, and the idea of systemic culture.

Wendt argues that collective identity occurs if a state understands, at least partially, its interests as involving those of another state. And this understanding results through an identification with that other state, not through instrumental or institutional logics of consequentiality or appropriateness.[49] There were several examples of collective identity in both Soviet and Russian foreign policy. In numerous discussions of their socialist allies in eastern Europe, the appreciation of a common class identity made the Soviets expect that these alliances were natural communities of identical interests; in relations with states with Slavic peoples, Soviets at all levels remarked on the special identity relationship that arose from this commonality. Khrushchev referred to the Soviet Union and China as if they were partly one another. He was explaining to Burma's Prime Minister U Nu that a prime objective should be to become a truly independent country. He then said that "with friends like China, we have even greater possibilities to become more independent."[50] In other words, mutual dependence, or interdependence, between two socialist powers such as China and the Soviet Union would produce independence with respect to the rest of the world. Such a conceptualization of relations between states made possible this seemingly counterintuitive position that dependence was actually the road to independence. Such an achievement was possible only if the Self and Other are understood as being partly one another. Perhaps the implications of collective identity could not be expressed more eloquently: dependence cannot exist among those who understand each as part of the Other.[51]

In the case of Russia in 1999, it would be fair to say that the NWR dis-

---

[48] Alexander Wendt, "On the Via Media: A Response to the Critics," *Review of International Studies* 26, no. 1 (January 2000): 174.

[49] An excellent empirical example of this and reconstruction of how it emerged and what it implies is in Thomas Risse-Kappen, *Cooperation among Democracies: The European Influence on US Foreign Policy* (Princeton, 1995). And, if ever empirically demonstrated, the democratic peace theory as well.

[50] Center for the Preservation of Contemporary Documentation, fond 5, opis 30, delo 116, stranitsa 230.

[51] The Soviet-Chinese relationship, an alliance between two most undemocratic states, should give pause to claims that only democracies can develop mutual sympathy and trust or care about one another's fate. For example, Risse-Kappen, *Cooperation among Democracies*, 30–31, 204. For a counterclaim see Maria Fanis, "Hegemonic Peaces: Why Democracy Is Neither Necessary nor Sufficient to Produce Peace between States" (Ph.D. diss., University of Michigan 2001).

course also operates on an assumption of collective identity with the United States and the West. Russia's restoration presupposed the closest possible relationship with the United States and Europe, a relationship so close it could be regarded not as an alliance but as a fusion of identity horizons, a sublimation of Self into a closest Other. The NWR wanted to become the West, not form a partnership with it.

The transformative logic of Wendt's systemic constructivism works through the move from one international systemic culture to another, from a Lockean world of self-restraint due to a role identity that accepts the norm of sovereignty to the emergent Kantian world of collective identity, where each state is Other-regarding because of its recognition of itself in the Other.[52] I explore here whether this specification of identity underpredicts the amount of cooperation in a world short of the Kantian ideal and does so by failing to recognize that there is a great deal of identification in another state that occurs in the conceptual space between Lockean and Kantian worlds.[53] In other words, there is a continuum of identification, not a dichotomy; states may find themselves in Others and have their understandings of Self and Other fundamentally influenced, long before they become that Other.

Wendt places identity relations on a single axis of meaning, from negative to positive.[54] As the cases in this book show, this move simplifies too much. In 1955, for example, Soviets saw both danger and opportunity in Yugoslavia, a great power and backwardness in China, and periphery and promise in India and the rest of the decolonizing world. How could it be otherwise because Soviet identity also was marked by ambiguity, contested meanings, and complexity? In 1999, whereas the NSR discourse arrayed other states along a binary axis of negative and positive, the predominant LE discourse was most decidedly eclectic. Its understandings of China, Europe, and the United States were all mixed because of the authentic Russian Self that was to be found in each and every Other, along with elements of Others deemed irrelevant, threatening, and uncategorizable.[55]

Moreover, given a state's many identity relationships with other states, it is quite likely, because identities are produced through interaction, that any

---

[52] Wendt, *Social Theory of International Politics,* 229, 300–305.

[53] This is one of the grounds on which Sterling-Folker bases her argument that the only difference between neoliberal institutionalism and constructivism is that the former explains why short-term cooperation develops and the latter explains long-term cooperation. But, in fact, as I argue here, there is a vast terrain between these two accounts, for which constructivism should offer understandings. Sterling-Folker, "Competing Paradigms," 97.

[54] Alexander Wendt, "Collective Identity Formation and the International State," *American Political Science Review* 88, no. 2 (June 1994): 386.

[55] Neumann, *Uses of the Other,* 34–35, also has problems with Wendt's simplification of the identity terrain.

single state has a range of identity relationships with other states, from orthogonal irrelevance and most dangerous Other to levels of identification
with the Other up to the closest Other. None of this is to say that Wendt and
others who focus on collective identity are wrong to argue that it is sufficient,
at least under some conditions, to produce cooperation among states, only
that collective identity is probably not necessary to account for some of the
cooperation we observe, even in Hobbesian and Lockean worlds.

One unintended consequence of this attention to collective identity over
partial identification with the Other is an emphasis on the need for coop-
erating states to have similar or even identical domestic orders.[56] But the LE
discourse of 1999 was empowered to cooperate with others because of its
identity of essentialized difference, not in spite of these differences. Indeed
it was the promise of the homogenizing identification with the United States
that discredited the NWR discourse in the eyes of other Russians and posed
a large obstacle to cooperation between Moscow and Washington. Being secure in difference might, in some cases at least, make identification with
Others abroad, and consequently cooperation, more likely, not less.[57]

Charles Lipson differentiates between the prospects for cooperation between two states in the areas of economics and of security. He does so on
the basis of the assumptions that underlie strategic game theory, including
relative transparency, incentives for exploitation, and costs of being suck-
ered.[58] There is no reason not to think that relations between states cannot
be characterized as well by different levels of identification, such that some
realms of interstate relations are more likely to be characterized by Kantian
collective identity, others by partial identification with Others, still others by
the thin identity terrain of Lockean normative appeals to sovereignty and
international law, and yet still others by binarized identities of hostility, or
Hobbesian realism.

[56] This is how Adler and Barnett seek to apply Deutsch's conception of security community. Emanuel Adler and Michael Barnett, "A Framework for the Study of Security Communities," in *Security Communities*, ed. Emanuel Adler and Michael Barnett (Cambridge, U.K.,
1998), 36. See Karl W. Deutsch, *Political Community at the International Level* (New York, 1954),
26–36. Wendt's belief in the sufficiency of collective identity to produce cooperation is
matched by the assumption that, with the exception of the democratic peace, identities and
interests constructed at home are likely to result in more narrow conceptions of both. Alexander Wendt, "Levels of Analysis vs. Agents and Structures: Part III," *Review of International Studies* 18 (1992): 184. Sterling-Folker, I think rightly, observes that systemic constructivists
implicitly treat national identities as a problem to be transcended, in Wendt's case via collective identities beyond the state. Sterling-Folker, "Competing Paradigms," 110.

[57] Andrew Hurrell, "An Emerging Security Community in South America?" in *Security
Communities*, ed. Emanuel Adler and Michael Barnett (Cambridge, 1998), 256, for example,
reports that, as cooperation and integration have deepened between Argentina and Brazil,
their domestic identities have diverged.

[58] Charles Lipson, "International Cooperation in Economic and Security Affairs," *World
Politics* 37, no. 1 (1984): 1–23.

Finally, it could well be the case that collective identity may not even be sufficient for cooperation. If we look at the evidence about the Soviet identification with China as its closest Other, we see that the very finding of the Soviet Self in the Chinese Other accounts for an exceptionally close relationship. But this very closeness made China's differences with Moscow that much more dangerous to the Soviet Self and perhaps ultimately made possible the collapse of that alliance. Moreover, beyond the identity logic of closest Others, the Soviet-Chinese relationship was situated in Soviet identity discourse more generally, which included the hierarchical class syntax of Soviet modernity and the subordination of the periphery to the center, both of which positioned China as an inferior, not a position likely to be countenanced by China once the Soviet Union itself, after 1956, had shown itself to be a deviant from socialism.

Wendt's three kinds of world-historical ideational structures—Hobbesian, Lockean, and Kantian—are a very powerful heuristic for understanding international politics at the systemic level.[59] The cases in this book vindicate each of them. But this is a problem because a systemic culture, by definition, should account for the system, not be marked by subcultures in which international politics is not carried on according to the master culture at the top. Instead of this systemic effect, we find that cultures are distributed according to historical time, particular pairs of states, and certain issues.

Moreover, these systemic cultures themselves are too uncomplicated, yielding only three identities—enemy, friend, or rival—where dozens would be too few. In 1955, for example, the Soviets understood India, China, Yugoslavia, and its eastern European allies as friends, but the last three were in fact rivals, discursively speaking because any changes or deviations in their identities threatened Soviet socialist identity. India, a friend, was deemed an enemy on the issue of Taiwan, Delhi having supported the British on this issue instead of the Chinese.

These three systemic identities in turn yield only three roles for states— revisionist, status quo, and collectivist—each of which is traced back to the three systemic cultures.[60] But it turns out that empirically these three are not mutually exclusive. It would seem to make sense, for instance to call the Soviet Union and China in 1955 collectivist revisionist states because each

---

[59] These three cultures are attributed by Wendt to Hedley Bull's Hobbesian, Grotian, and Kantian cultures. Hedley Bull, *The Anarchical Society* (London, 1977), 39.

[60] Wendt, *Social Theory of International Politics*, 247–85. There is a long tradition among IR scholars of classifying states in an effort to understand the characteristics of a particular epoch. See Richard Rosecrance, *Action and Reaction in World Politics: International Systems in Perspective* (Boston, 1963); Schweller, "Bandwagoning for Profit," 72–107. Ruggie calls the a priori specification of roles for states a characteristic of "neo-utilitarian" IR theory. Ruggie, "What Makes the World Hang Together?" 867.

was finding itself in the Other while simultaneously being committed to challenging the status quo in Asia.

Wendt's confidence in the systemic quality of these cultures leads to the assertion that because they are constant, the distribution of capabilities might explain a great deal. Suddenly, a variable that was to be intersubjectively understood becomes stipulated as having a single objective, or perhaps interobjective, meaning. His paradigmatic example of this is the "cultural structure of the Cold War."[61] But it would seem that there was far greater variation within the Cold War than any structural account can accommodate. There was a great deal of cooperation on nuclear arms control, an ultimate commitment to the status quo in Europe, and a sanguinary acting out of the enmity in the decolonizing world. How could a single culture account for all this variety? It would be better to understand the U.S.-Soviet relationship both historically, in terms of the identities and discourses that predominate in the given period, and thematically, according to how the relevant issues and regions were understood within these discourses and identities, rather than assuming that some common structural template can be placed on top of these social relationships without destroying meaningful variations.

In sum, what is problematic about systemic constructivism is mostly a function of the fact that it is systemic. As does any systemic theory, it simplifies, categorizing complexity away and making a priori assumptions about the nature of its units and their interactions that may do so much violence to empirical reality as to cast doubt on the utility of the project. I am not willing to support that kind of judgment against systemic constructivism, especially given its vast improvement over the realist structural alternative and the absence of any fully articulated and tested reductionist alternative. It is important, however, to point out the limits to the systemic project.

Social Constructivism: Bringing Societies Back In

There are several problems that can be addressed without necessarily sacrificing the advantages of a systemic IR theory. These include the inclusion of social identities in any understanding of state identity, the inclusion of everyday logics in understanding how identities work, and, not unrelated, the consideration of a noninstrumentalist account of the relationship between identity and interest.

Including the domestic construction of state identity makes an IR theory reductionist only if we stipulate that a state's identity, independent of interaction with external Others, is the cause of a state's foreign policy. But social constructivism assumes that a state's identity in international politics cannot be constructed at home alone—it is only in interaction with a particular

---

[61] Wendt, "Collective Identity Formation"; Wendt, *Social Theory of International Politics,* 109.

Other that the meaning of a state is established.[62] One of the most promising aspects of a discursive conceptualization of identity is that it is seamless; it assumes no boundary between meanings within and outside the state's official borders. The assumption that meaningful Others exist both at home and abroad differentiates a social constructivist account of the domestic from those that assume either the primacy of the internal or the external or that there are different domains for the two.

The failure to include the domestic face of the state has been one of the most frequent criticisms of all systemic theories.[63] But the bracketing of the domestic for constructivists has particular implications. Wendt's revisionist, status quo, and collectivist states are "pre-social" and "exogenously given," the latter a criticism lodged against neorealism by its constructivist critics. The identity of the state is placed "outside analysis."[64] Jennifer Sterling-Folker has suggested that it is the failure to theorize the domestic that has led systemic constructivists to assume pregiven collective interests to make their theories work. Martha Finnemore and Kathryn Sikkink consider domestic politics important only because a government's desire for legitimacy at home might cause the choice of a particular international norm, thus implying that the domestic has no constitutive effect "other than in relation to collective systemic interests."[65] This move effectively elides society as an agent in the construction of a state's identity, except in the very limited realm of normative appropriateness.

It is not likely that either context, domestic or international, will dominate in the construction of state identity. Indeed, social constructivism assumes that all state identities are a product of both.[66] Having said that, I admit that one of the most intriguing findings of this book contradicts this assumption and supports systemic constructivism. The great power identity of 1955 was constructed institutionally and seemingly independently of so-

---

[62] Wendt, *Social Theory of International Politics*, 147.

[63] James G. March and Johan P. Olsen, "The Institutional dynamics of International Political Orders," *International Organization* 52, no. 4 (autumn 1998): 945; Milner, *Interests, Institutions, and Information*, 254; Helen V. Milner, "Rationalizing Politics: The Emerging Synthesis of International, American, and Comparative Politics," *International Organization* 52, no. 4 (autumn 1998): 759; Robert O. Keohane, *International Institutions and State Power* (Boulder, 1989), 60.

[64] Steve Smith, "Wendt's World," *Review of International Studies* 26, no. 1 (January 2000): 161.

[65] Sterling-Folker, "Competing Paradigms," 109; Finnemore and Sikkink, "International Norm Dynamics and Political Change," 903 n. 41.

[66] Wendt intimates as much, writing that "when states interact, they do so with their societies conceptually in tow." Wendt, *Social Theory of International Politics*, 201, 11–13, 21, 28, 141; "Levels of Analysis," 184. On the necessary connection between the inside and the outside of the state in identity construction, see Jutta Weldes, *Constructing National Interests: The US and the Cuban Missile Crisis* (Minneapolis, 1999), 244–45 n. 12.

ciety, although its precise meaning was related to domestic discourses on modernity. In 1999, on the other hand, the discourse on recentering Russia was the site for great power identity, its concern with sovereignty, and participation in global governance. It could turn out that identities that are uniquely dependent on other states for validation, such as being a great power or having sovereign legitimacy, are also uniquely the realm of systemic constructivism.

What constitutes an interaction between states needs to be clarified. From a social constructivist perspective, interaction need not involve the copresence of two actors, such as an international meeting. It is the relationship between the knowledge each has of the other, not physical colocation, that drives the construction of identity. In Russia in 1999, after all, a great deal of the identity terrain was described by discursive relationships with an identity that had nominally and materially disappeared not ten years before: the Soviet Historical Other.

Other scholars have used a constructivist approach to link the identity of states to foreign policy and international relations.[67] Jutta Weldes makes the boundaries of this task clear:

> Meanings . . . for states are necessarily the meanings . . . for . . . individuals who act in the name of the state. . . . And these . . . officials do not approach international politics with a blank slate onto which meanings are written as a result of interactions among states. . . .
> Their appreciation of the world, of international politics, and of the place of their states within the international system, is necessarily rooted in collective meanings already produced, at least in part, in domestic political and cultural contexts."[68]

The job of social constructivists, then, is to find out what is on that slate that decision makers are bringing with them into their interaction with external Others.

Perhaps a fear of reductionism has led systemic constructivism to neglect a constructivist account of identity and interest. Instead of endogenizing the

---

[67] Peter J. Katzenstein, *Cultural Norms and National Security: Police and Military in Postwar Japan* (Ithaca, 1996); Christian Reus-Smit, "The Constitutional Structure of International Society and the Nature of Fundamental Institutions," *International Organization* 51, no. 4 (autumn 1997): 555–89; Thomas U. Berger, *Cultures of Antimilitarism: National Security in Germany and Japan* (Baltimore, 1998); John Gerard Ruggie, "The Past as Prologue? Interests, Identity, and American Foreign Policy," *International Security* 21, no. 4 (spring 1997): 89–125; Rodney Bruce Hall, *National Collective Identity: Social Constructs and International Systems* (New York, 1999); Neumann, *Uses of the Other.*

[68] Weldes, *Constructing National Interests*, 9.

construction of interests within a theory of state identity, as is done in my account of a social cognitive structure and its constituent discourses, the state is assumed to have pregiven interests, not unlike the practice of mainstream neorealist and neoliberal institututionalist IR theories.[69] Wendt stipulates four interests derive from the "corporate identity" of the state, implying that all states have these interests. These interests are security, ontological security (which is assumed by my thin cognitive identity model), mutual recognition as a legitimate actor, and domestic development.[70] These interests as enumerated here are not so much objectionable, as they are unnecessary and theoretically questionable. If constructivism accounts for state identities that are created in interaction with other states, why assume that some identities, and not a multitude of others, are inherent to all states? It seems to be a slippery slope to competing lists of essentializing features of the state and its interests. Again, as in much else, I prefer to avoid preloading my theory, instead relying on the deep inductive recovery of which interests differentiate states from one another and which they share.[71]

Wendt's systemic constructivism also adopts a consequentialist and instrumentalist logic when it comes to explaining the relationship between identity and interest. This could be due to Wendt's desire to reject the poststructuralist position on the autonomy of discourse.[72] He writes, for example, that "actors whose interests are constituted by a structure will have a stake in it."[73] I do not understand why an agent whose identity and interests are constructed by a discourse need ever develop an interest in that discursive structure per se.[74] Nor do I see why the rejection of poststructuralist accounts of language need imply the adoption of instrumental rationality to explain how identities and interests relate. Soviet leaders, in 1955, for example, understood the United States as the imperialist Other, which constituted themselves as the binarized peace-loving progressive Self. But would Soviet interests not have been better served by an understanding of the

---

[69] Milner, *Interests, Institutions, and Information*, 15, 241; Milner, "Rationalizing Politics," 772; Moravcsik, "Taking Preferences Seriously" 513–25; Andrew Moravcsik, *The Choice for Europe: Social Purpose and State Power From Messina to Maastricht* (Ithaca, 1998), 24. Sterling-Folker offers a similar criticism of pregiven interests, in "Competing Paradigms," 101, 109.

[70] Wendt, "Collective Identity Formation." The not unrelated five material human needs are physical and ontological security, sociation, self-esteem, and transcendence. Wendt, *Social Theory of International Politics* 131–32.

[71] Wendt acknowledges that "it is striking how little empirical research has been done investigating what kinds of interests state actors actually have." *Social Theory of International Politics* 133.

[72] Ibid., 175–78.

[73] Ibid., quotation on 248. See also 319.

[74] Sterling-Folker uses Wendt's manner of specifying an interest in an institution as evidence of neofunctionalist, and so neoliberal institutionalist, logic. Sterling-Folker, "Competing Paradigms," 100.

United States as a potential socialist Other, like China, for example? Why would the Soviets have had an interest in constructing a powerful enemy for themselves, as opposed to constructing a powerful friend? I think it more accurate to say that social cognitive structures are stable because of the many everyday social practices that reproduce them, not because agents have an interest in the reproduced product.

Another instrumentalist claim is that actors acquire their identities and interests by imitating "those whom they perceive as successful, and . . . such imitation tends to make people more homogenous."[75] This is a most materialist conceptualization of identity construction that assumes that the power of daily social practice works only so long as an individual cannot compare herself to a more successful identity. I wonder, then, why the NWR did not corner the identity and interest market in Russia in 1999, having identified itself with the richest and most powerful Other in existence, the United States? Somehow, the NSR, having identified with the collapsed and bankrupt Soviet Union held their own, and the LE, the predominant discourse, found its Self in a still-to-be-imagined authentic Russian past and future. It is hard to find an instrumental logic to the operation of these identities and their interests in other states in the world. As for homogeneity being facilitated through identity construction, this is precisely the process that LE, LR, NSRs consciously deplored and fought against. Moreover, even in the Soviet Union of 1955, there were signs of difference and deviation from the homogenizing modern Soviet project. It is unclear what a constructivist theory of international relations gains by making assumptions like these about identity, especially if their absence, as in the work presented in this book, does not appear fatal to theorizing about and empirically demonstrating a less consequentialist account of identity and interest.

Wendt also appears to stipulate in advance which identities are more important for actors. "Identities are arranged hierarchically . . . by an actor's degree of commitment to them; some are fundamental to our self-concept, others are more superficial."[76] But if identities are constructed in relation to Others, how is it possible to specify a priori which ones are more fundamental? It would seem that the importance of an identity should vary according to the Other(s) with which a Self is interacting. So, for example, the NSR, when interacting with Yugoslavia, experienced an enhanced importance for their ethnonational Russian identities, but this was not true when interacting with Americans. It seems Wendt must periodically suspend the operation of constructivist principles in order to keep his units sufficiently homogenous and invariant so as to be able to theorize at the systemic level about them.

The difference between Wendt's understanding of identity and interest and the possibility raised in this book can be seen in his example of the

---

[75] Wendt, *Social Theory of International Politics*, 325.

[76] Ibid., 231.

United States and the Bahamas.[77] He claims the Bahamas knows the United States will restrain itself from invading the Bahamas. I think this is the wrong way to conceptualize the relationship. The Bahamas does not know the United States will restrain itself; instead, a U.S. invasion of the Bahamas is unthinkable or unimaginable to the Bahamas. It is not that they know something about the United States; they are far past the point of deliberating over U.S. intentions—confidence in U.S. inaction is far more deeply embedded in the identities and discourses of the two states, such that the idea of invasion never even comes up as a possibility. This is true stability in a social structure, not periodically entertaining the idea of its disruption and then deciding that it will not occur. Thinking that the United States is restraining itself against what it might want to do is a far thinner reed to lean on than never thinking about the United States having any possible intentions in the first place. If order in the world really works as I suggest, according to logics of unthinkability and unimaginability, relationships are far more stable, institutions are far more durable, and enmities and amities are far more long-lived, even in the absence of a Kantian world.[78]

Consider how former U.S. Secretary of State Henry Kissinger described the workings of the special relationship with Britain, a prime example of everyday logic. This relationship

> involved a pattern of consultation so matter-of-factly intimate that it became psychologically impossible to ignore British views. They evolved a habit of meetings so regular that autonomous American action somehow came to seem to violate club rules . . . The relationship existed on no legal claim; it was formalized by no document; it was carried forward by succeeding British governments as if no alternative was conceivable. British influence was great simply because it never insisted upon it.[79]

[77] Ibid., 360.

[78] On the power of unimaginability, see Reus-Smit, "Constitutional Structure," 569–70. Hedley Bull writes of the social order secured by habit or inertia. Bull, *Anarchical Society*, 46. Deutsch writes of the "habits of compliance." *Political Community at the International Level*, 40. Tannenwald describes the nuclear taboo as making nuclear use "unthinkable." Tannenwald, "Nuclear Taboo," 460. On discursive intelligibility and the land-mine ban, see Price, "Reversing the Gun Sights," 628–29. On discursive (im)possibilities and imaginability, see Roxanne Lynn Doty, "Foreign Policy as Social Construction: A Post-Positivist Analysis of U.S. Counterinsurgency Policy in the Phillipines," *International Studies Quarterly* 37, no. 3 (September 1993), 298–302, 314; Doty, *Imperial Encounters*, 4–6; Weldes, *Constructing National Interests*, 16. For a contrary view, that habit is a thinner intersubjective reed than explicit reference to shared norms, see Bially Mattern, "Power Politics of Identity," 355–58. On a different logic, the logic of arguing inspired by Habermas's theory of communicative rationality, see Thomas Risse, "'Let's Argue!' Communicative Action in World Politics," *International Organization* 54, no. 1 (winter 2000), especially 4.

[79] Quoted in Risse-Kappen, *Cooperation among Democracies*, 212.

The international politics imagined by a social constructivist IR theory is one of segmentation and hybridity. Different issue areas, regions, dyads, and communities are each characterized on a continuum ranging from geopolitics to society; from responses to brute force to adherence to discrete rules to daily practice within a social cognitive structure; from sovereign autonomous identities to relationships between the Self and Others, to the Self as part of the Other and vice versa; and from the logic of consequentiality to appropriateness, to intelligibility, thinkability, imaginability, and possibility. Although any understanding of world politics requires a theorization of the domestic and the systemic, there would be no systemic theory of world politics because world politics has no predominant system; it has subcultures, each of which can be understood only by examining how states constitute themselves in their societies. The answer to the question of who are enemies and friends begins at home.

Finding out precisely how a state's identity affects the construction of its interests vis-à-vis another state demands that the social context in which that state's collection of identities is being discursively constructed be investigated as deeply and broadly as possible. This means exploring not only how that state's identities are produced in interactions with other states, but also how its identities are being produced in interaction with its own society and the many identities and discourses that constitute that society. A discursive ethnography of state identity is called for, one, frankly speaking, that goes far beyond the effort made here in this book.

Finally, there is no necessary contradiction—epistemological, ontological, or methodological—between an interepretivist theoretical account of identity, interest, foreign policy, and world politics and the comparison of the resulting understanding to a potentially competing understanding or explanation offered from a theoretical approach grounded in utterly different foundational assumptions about how we know what we claim we know, how we stipulate what are meaningful entities in the world, as long as we agree that it is possible to evaluate the competing claims that result. But the desire to test competing theories must not eclipse the commitment to the interpretivist techniques that are necessary to reconstruct the intersubjective social structures that constitute meaningful realities in any social space, including world politics.

This book, and especially this chapter, has been long on critique. Let me end the book, then, with a few words of praise for Sovietology—yes, Sovietology. In 1984, I took Marshall Shulman's introductory graduate course on Soviet foreign policy. In that course he described the method by which he wrote *Stalin's Foreign Policy Re-Appraised*, a work that challenged the conventional wisdom that nothing had changed in Soviet foreign policy after World War II until Khrushchev consolidated his power in 1956.[80] Shulman told us that he had worked with blank newsprint and a drafting board. He had three different sheets, one for international events, one for Soviet foreign policy, and one for Soviet domestic politics. He arranged them in chronological rows and categorical columns and he made entries for each day. Every few weeks or months, he sat down with all the sheets and tried to see whether any kind of unobvious coherence emerged that could connect an international event to a Soviet action, at home or abroad. In this way, he came up with connections that were not so apparent when thinking in a more linear fashion.

He also described his friend and colleague, Michel Tatu, *Le Monde's* long-time correspondent in the Soviet Union, in his small Moscow apartment, buried in piles of Soviet journals and newspapers from all over the country, piecing together what was to become a classic analysis of the Khrushchev regime, *Power in the Kremlin*.[81]

Well, was Shulman not the premature interpretivist scholar of foreign policy, searching for meanings across time and space, hoping to find gestalts where only isolated episodes were manifest? Perhaps Shulman's methods are embedded somewhere in my brain, perhaps not. But surely they should be credited with producing a particularly rich and social account of Soviet foreign policy. Although I know little about Brzezinski's methods, I could pay the same tribute to his first book.[82] It, too, exemplifies the capacity to keep all the stories going at once, Soviet domestic politics, the particularities of each of the countries of eastern Europe, including their unique histories, and Soviet relations with each. What emerges in that book is a differentiated story of different relationships, told over time, all the while resisting the temptation to seize on some facile generalization.

I would be thrilled if only a fraction of this Sovietological sophistication and wisdom were faintly evident in my book. And still more so if this book rekindled an interest in the texts, history, society, and politics that constitute the subjects of international relations.

---

[80] Marshall Shulman, *Stalin's Foreign Policy Reappraised* (Cambridge, Mass., 1963).

[81] Michel Tatu, *Power in the Kremlin* (New York, 1969). See also Donald S. Zagoria, *The Sino-Soviet Conflict* (Princeton, 1962).

[82] Zbigniew Brzezinski, *The Soviet Bloc: Unity and Conflict* (Cambridge, Mass., 1960).

Index

CPSIA information can be obtained
at www.ICGtesting.com
Printed in the USA
LVHW090041170619
621277LV00027B/54/P